AMERICAN GIRLS IN RED RUSSIA

AMERICAN GIRLS
IN RED RUSSIA

Chasing the Soviet Dream

JULIA L. MICKENBERG

The University of Chicago Press

Chicago and London

The University of Chicago Press, Chicago 60637
The University of Chicago Press, Ltd., London

Published 2017
Printed in the United States of America

26 25 24 23 22 21 20 19 18 17   1 2 3 4 5

ISBN-13: 978-0-226-25612-2 (cloth)
ISBN-13: 978-0-226-25626-9 (e-book)
DOI: 10.7208/chicago/9780226256269.001.0001

Library of Congress Cataloging-in-Publication Data

Names: Mickenberg, Julia L., author.
Title: American girls in red Russia : chasing the Soviet dream / Julia L. Mickenberg.
Description: Chicago : The University of Chicago Press, 2017. | Includes bibliographical references and index.
Identifiers: LCCN 2016041702 | ISBN 9780226256122 (cloth : alk. paper) | ISBN 9780226256269 (e-book)
Subjects: LCSH: Americans—Soviet Union—History. | Women—United States—History—20th century. | Women—Soviet Union—History. | Women and socialism—Soviet Union. | Feminism—Soviet Union.
Classification: LCC DK34.A45 M54 2017 | DDC 305.420947—dc23 LC record available at https://lccn.loc.gov/2016041702

♾ This paper meets the requirements of ANSI/NISO Z39.48-1992 (Permanence of Paper).

For Edie, who has lived with this book her entire life.

And for Dan, who made everything possible.

CONTENTS

Introduction: "American Girls in Red Russia"   *1*

PART I   Tender Revolutionaries and Child Savers   *35*

1   Dreaming in Red: Reformers, Rebels, and
a Revolutionary Babushka   *39*

2   Child Savers and Child Saviors   *69*

PART II   Living and Working in the New Russia:
From Kuzbas to Moscow   *121*

3   "A New Pennsylvania": Seeking Home in Siberia   *129*

4   "Eyes on Russia": Gal Reporters on the *Moscow
News*   *163*

PART III   Performing Revolution   *201*

5   Dancing Revolution   *207*

6   *Black and White*—and Yellow—in Red: Performing Race
in Russia   *243*

PART IV Trials, Tribulations, and Battles *281*

7 Heroines and Heretics on the Russian Front *291*

Epilogue: Red Spy Queens? *325*

Acknowledgments *337*

Abbreviations *343*

Notes *345*

Index *411*

"American Girls in Red Russia"

By spring 1932, the "American girls in red Russia" had begun to attract notice:

> Armed with lipstick and toothbrush, and with an insatiable lust for the bizarre and exciting, American girls have been invading Moscow. Two hundred strong and more, chic, smart young women have come barging into the Red capital, some lending the boys and girls a hand in building Socialism, others seeking husbands among the lonely American engineers, or romantic young Russians, always ready to pay homage to the glamorous American girl. Stenographers, nurses, dancers, painters, teachers, sculptors and writers—serious maidens, determined to take part in the new life that is growing so swiftly. Pauline Emmett, a tall, robust lass from Illinois, fled from the social whirl and chose instead the Soviet frontier, where she edits a magazine for American workers and swings a pick and shovel when she's called for social work. Fay Gillis, Brooklyn aviatrix, is hoping to fly for the Soviets. Jeanya Marling, barefoot dancer and raw

Fig. 0.1 Milly Bennett, "American Girls in Red Russia," *EveryWeek*, May 28–29, 1932, Milly Bennett papers, Hoover Library, Stanford University.

vegetable faddist from Los Angeles, marched into Moscow to help organize an international theater. These pert, slim-hipped girls, fresh-faced
and eager, wearing bright American clothes, are a delight to the eye tired
of the shapeless drab of Soviet garments.[1]

This breezy description is slightly adapted from a syndicated 1932 news
article by Milly Bennett, a divorced journalist from San Francisco, and
one among the legions of American women drawn to the Soviet Union
in the early 1930s. She'd arrived less than two years earlier to accept a staff
position on the *Moscow News*, the Soviet Union's first English-language
newspaper, which journalist Anna Louise Strong started in 1930. Bennett
and the women she describes were part of a now-forgotten trend.

We don't usually think of Moscow as a popular destination for American women in the early twentieth century. A mythology surrounds the
"lost generation" of Americans who sought out Paris in the 1920s, but
few know about the exodus of thousands of Americans—former Paris
expats among them—to the "red Jerusalem" not long after that.[2] Even
fewer are aware of "red Russia's" particular pull for "American girls," or,
more accurately, independent, educated, and adventurous "new women."
For a significant number of Americans—and Westerners more generally—who rightfully questioned the human costs of a social system structured around industrial capitalism, the mere existence of a society ostensibly dedicated to the public good rather than individual profit was
a source of tremendous hope.[3] And while most Americans greeted the
Bolshevik revolution with skepticism and even fear, a large swath of activists, idealists, and cultural arbiters, many feminists among them, had a
very different reaction.

Well past the end of the Cold War, it has remained difficult to come to
terms with what in the 1920s and 1930s amounted to nearly ubiquitous
attention to the Soviet Union among reformers, intellectuals, and members of the artistic avant-garde. We have forgotten both the daring spirit
of the new woman and the widespread interest in the "Soviet experiment."

Along with legions of "American girls" who are now forgotten, revolutionary Russia attracted many of the country's most distinguished
women, among them fiery orators and free love advocates like Emma

Goldman, who claimed inspiration from brave Russian women who were willing to sacrifice their lives to defeat czarist tyranny and who rejected conventional morality by "discard[ing] marriage and living in total freedom." It attracted progressive reformers and settlement house workers like Lillian Wald, whose Henry Street Settlement House, a fixture on New York's crowded Lower East Side, hosted numerous Russian exiles and proselytizing revolutionaries in the years leading up to the Bolshevik revolution. It drew suffragists like Alice Stone Blackwell and Crystal Eastman, who used Russian models to imagine revolutionary new ways of conceiving women's citizenship. It lured dancers such as Isadora Duncan, who set off for Soviet Russia in 1921, at the twilight of her career, and stayed long enough to start a dance school and marry a famous, drunken Russian poet, and Pauline Koner, who came to Russia fifteen years later, at the dawn of her dance career, "to complete what Duncan began." The African American actress Frances E. Williams came to Moscow in 1934 in search of professional opportunity, adventure, and a chance to experience life in a land that had supposedly eliminated racism. And photographer Margaret Bourke-White went to Russia in 1930 (and again, and again) because "things are happening in Russia, and happening with staggering speed. . . . The effort of 150,000,000 people is so gigantic, so unprecedented in all history."[4] These women and many others traveled to the "new Russia," or devoted years of their lives to it from afar. From even before the Bolshevik revolution, women in the United States looked toward Russia for female role models.

Beginning in the late nineteenth century, the new woman—hair upswept, demeanor purposeful, sights set on paid or creative work, social reforms, or causes like free speech, free expression, or free love—became a familiar figure on the streets of US and European cities and in fiction, art, and advertising. And she came to embody the promise and perils of modernity. Until the end of World War II, Russia and the Soviet Union helped American new women envision themselves, society, and possibilities for the future. Such women, in turn, played an important role in shaping their compatriots' image of Russia.

This chapter in American women's history highlights themes basic to the development of Western feminist thought, ideas about citizenship, motherhood, love, work, creative expression, child-rearing, sex, and friendship, and also about class, justice, and the ideal society. American women who felt drawn to Russia wanted to witness or feel part of the most dramatic set of events on the world's stage. They also hoped for a new era of female possibility, in which women would not be merely politically empowered and economically independent, but also equal partners in love and equal builders of a new world, a classless society, where culture, education, and social welfare counted for more than profit.[5]

The story of American new women and the new Russia has been as much repressed as forgotten. As the horrors of Stalinism became undeniable, both the romance of revolutionary Russia itself and the utopian imagination driving that romance were cast as naïve, irrational, embarrassing, even dangerous. In *Assignment in Utopia*, journalist Eugene Lyons described a range of witless female pilgrims who were easy targets for Soviet propaganda: "Virginal school teachers and sex-starved wives came close to the masses, especially the male classes, and some of them were so impressed with the potency of Bolshevik ideas that they extended their visas again and again. A few of them emerged to write shrill books about the Soviet Union's 'new unshackled attitudes,' the equality of the sexes, abortion clinics."[6] For Lyons, descriptions of Western women in Moscow functioned primarily as a vehicle for dismissing everyone caught up in the romance of red Russia.

During and even before the Cold War, repentant communists' reports cast a dark shadow over what Vivian Gornick has called the "romance of American communism," especially as that romance was tangled up in the Soviet Union. By the late 1940s, most Americans saw the Soviet Union as an "evil empire," and those who once expressed enthusiasm for the Soviet experiment either recanted or kept quiet about it.[7] By the logic of the Cold War that came after, such enthusiasm reflected badly on suffragists, reformers, journalists, and creative workers whom some might otherwise wish to hold up as models. But this narrative of disenchantment clouds our ability to understand the enchantment itself: the real depth of interest, hope, and fascination that the Soviet Union represented for many people, even when those feelings were mixed with a sense of the gap between Soviet realities and ideals.

Although we might admire the idealism of this story's protagonists, we also have to recognize their mistakes and the horrific aspects of the Soviet system that some of them never or only belatedly acknowledged. Though American women's romance with Russia may not represent a usable past for feminists or for the Left in general, like any good love story, the heartbreak and disappointments are just as gripping as the romance, and are, perhaps, even more instructive. The aspirations and foibles of idealists from an earlier generation tell us something about what continue to be women's most pressing concerns.

New Women, Feminism, and Revolutionary Russia

Seeming to threaten all established government authority, the figure of the bomb-toting revolutionary and a series of actual revolutions in Russia were terrifying to many people in the United States. But the failed revolution in 1905, the collapse of the czar's autocracy in March 1917, and then the seizure of control from the Provisional Government by the Bolsheviks in November 1917 were thrilling to others for whom "darkest Russia" had represented both the worst abuses of government power and the toleration of assorted evils from wife-beating to decadent elites sponging off the toiling masses.[8]

And the revolution held a particular thrill for American women under the sway of feminist ideas, among them self-identified feminists as well as others who refused to prioritize gender over economic concerns. Well before the Bolsheviks took power in 1917, the revolutionary Russian woman became an almost mythic figure in the United States. Events in Russia attracted attention from US female activists in all realms: those working to expand women's citizenship and property rights and their role in public life; those looking to improve social welfare, sanitation, hygiene, childcare, and education; and those who saw the psychological, sexual, and economic emancipation of women as but one piece of a "complete social revolution," to use the words of one of feminism's early twentieth-century adherents. This revolution went beyond efforts to get women the vote or to make laws more equitable. It meant professional opportunities for women. It meant psychological emancipation from social expectations. It meant romantic relationships based on mutual attraction and shared values and an end to the sexual double standard. It meant the possibility of women being mothers and also having careers. It represented, as suffrage activist Carrie Chapman Catt put it, a "worldwide revolt against all artificial barriers which laws and customs interpose between women and human freedom."[9]

Indeed, the embrace of feminist ideas in the United States can be traced in significant ways to an earlier generation of Russian radicals, especially Jewish women, who imported socialism into the United States and came to political consciousness through reading and discussing works like Nikolai Chernyshevsky's *What Is to Be Done?* (1863), which saw the liberation of women as fundamental to the creation of "new people." If the Russian Revolution gave conservatives their most enduring bogeyman, it offered others, including many feminists, tremendous hope. As Christine Stansell has noted of the radical, bohemian milieu in New York's Greenwich Village, "events in Russia acquired an immediacy almost unimaginable today," affecting the "collective sense of possibility" in profound ways.[10] This was especially true for women.

The right to vote, which Russian women were granted not long after the February Revolution, continued under the Bolsheviks. But that was just the beginning. Leaders proposed steps toward the emancipation of women, including plans for the "socialization of housework"—in the form of public laundries, kitchens, and childcare—so that women could fully participate in the wider labor force. In contrast to bourgeois societies where women were forced to "exchange their domestic and sexual services for men's financial support," under communism, it was predicted, wage-earning women would encounter men as equals, and "the family itself would wither away and women and men would unite their lives solely for love." Women gained property rights, barriers to women's education and professional advancement were officially eliminated, and women were promised equal pay for equal work. Along with creating public laundries, dining halls, and childcare facilities to free women from what Lenin called "the old household drudgery and dependence on men," a new family code passed in 1918 made divorce easy, abolished the category of illegitimate children, and provided working women paid

Fig. 0.2 Nina Allender, "America First / Russia First," from *The Suffragist*, March 1917. As soon as Russian women gained the vote, shortly after the February Revolution, American suffragists began advertising the fact that "darkest Russia" had granted women the vote before the supposedly more enlightened United States had. Comparisons to Russia continued in American feminist magazines after the Bolshevik revolution.

maternity leave before and after birth, whether or not they were legally married. According to historian Wendy Goldman, "In its insistence on individual rights and gender equality, the Code constituted nothing less than the most progressive family legislation the world had ever seen."[11]

Under the leadership of Bolshevik feminists Alexandra Kollontai and Inessa Armand, the Zhenotdel, a special arm of the Communist Party created in 1919 to communicate policy to women, became an advocate for women's concerns. Such efforts make clear that there was a great deal to be done. And, in fact, the Bolsheviks only reluctantly included women's liberation in their program, rejecting feminism as a distraction from class concerns. Much of the legislation they passed was designed "to neutralize gender differences" rather than to emancipate women. Even so, Lenin himself would insist in 1919 that Soviet Russia was the only place in the world where "there is complete equality between men and women." In the years following the Bolshevik Revolution, feminist journals in the United States not only highlighted the fact that Russian women were granted suffrage before their American sisters. They also avidly followed Soviet efforts to establish communal dining halls, laundries, and nurseries. They noted Soviet marriage laws aimed at equalizing power relations within marriage and fostering unions based on mutual affection rather than economic considerations. They pointed to liberalized abortion regulations; they noted the program of sex education; they highlighted the role of women in Soviet government, professions, and industry; and they praised the "sweeping and unhampered work of social reform" undertaken largely by women.[12] No surprise, then, that American new women were eager to see the new Russia for themselves.

The Call of Revolutionary Russia

It was with great anticipation that American women began heading to the new Russia after 1917. Madeleine Doty, who was exploring the world war's impact on women, embarked on a harrowing two-week journey by train across Siberia from China. On the train, "cigarette butts and ashes covered the floor. The air grew fouler and fouler, but no one opened a window." Thankfully, the train stopped frequently. Most travelers carried tea kettles with them, and at stations they would rush out to fill the kettles from huge samovars of boiling water. "Then from every compartment floated the odor of tea, the smell of cigarettes, and the babble of voices." The journey gave Doty a taste of what she was getting into. At one station, a Siberian woman, "demand[ing] that clothing be sent to her town in exchange for the foodstuff being sent to Petrograd," boarded the train. "She was full of tales of her village. Two deserting soldiers had just visited her town and raped a young girl. The women had risen up in wrath and beaten the men and thrust them out." This was just one more bit of evidence that "it was a crude, elemental world, full of hot passion, into which I was rushing." Petrograd was in the "throes of [the Bolshevik] revolution" when Doty arrived. Despite her trepidation, her first impression was hopeful: "Everywhere there was movement and action but no violence. People stopped to argue. Voices rose high, and arms waved wildly. It was a people intensely alive and intensely intelligent. Everyone had an opinion. . . . My heart leaped up. . . . In spite of suppression they were not servile. They were alive and free. Every Russian I met could talk; even those who could not read or write could talk."[13]

Traveling under very different circumstances but feeling similar excitement and anticipation, Dorothy West headed to Moscow more than a decade later with twenty-one other African American professionals, many of them part of the Harlem Renaissance. They were traveling to the Soviet Union to perform in a film about American race relations, and, off camera, to perform themselves, as Black men and women, in a radically new context. The group's organizer, Louise Thompson, described their destination as "the promised land."[14]

Although nearly every visitor commented on the deprivation and struggles faced by the Russian people, many visitors found even this evidence of obstacles to be overcome as a reason for optimism and hope: At the end of a six-week tour of the Soviet Union in 1935, former suffrage leader Florence Luscomb concluded her travel journal with reflection on the contrasts she had seen, the great poverty and the great promise: "I had seen shabby clothing, ill-conditioned buildings, poorly paved streets. I had seen terrible overcrowding in the cities, swollen by industrialization which developed overnight. I had seen a hardworking people for whom life was still struggling and meager, in terms of material things." Yet her overwhelming impression was that the West had a great deal to learn from the Soviet Union: "I had seen the sure promise that these material deprivations would be overcome. I had seen miracles of achievement not only in engineering and production, not only in education, health, and cultural life, but also in the more intangible things of the spirit." As Luscomb's train headed to the Polish border, she "turned back for one last look of remembrance at the vast, cultivated, fruitful fields stretching as far as [the] eye could see. Arching Russia from horizon to horizon gleamed a rainbow!"[15]

The situation in Russia, as in the United States, changed dramatically between Doty's and Luscomb's visits. Immediately following the Bolshevik revolution, Russian life was shaped not only by the revolution and First World War—from which the Bolsheviks withdrew almost immediately, to their allies' dismay—but also by civil war and famine. During the period of War Communism (1918–1921), banks and industry were nationalized, free trade was almost completely prohibited, and grain was requisitioned from the provinces in order to feed soldiers in the cities. Coinciding with an Allied blockade in response to the Bolsheviks' separate peace with Germany—and Allied support for the Whites in the Russian Civil War—this was a period of great hardship, especially as famine swept large swaths of the country in the summer of 1921. Just months earlier, the Bolshevik government had begun restricting immigration, and it became difficult for foreigners to gain entry. A few American women, among them the former suffrage activist Jessica Smith and the labor journalist Anna Louise Strong, joined famine relief efforts in Russia—less for humanitarian reasons and more to witness and take part in the revolutionary transformations that young Russians, redeemed from hunger, might effect. Other American women made their way to Russia around this time by joining communes organized under the Society for Technical Aid to Soviet Russia.[16] Ruth Epperson Kennell, who was tired of her domestic duties and bored in her marriage, signed on with a commune in the Kuznetsk Basin of Siberia, leaving her young son with her mother-in-law. Kennell's two-year experiment with socialized housework, collective responsibilities, and a very different moral code shaped the rest of her life.

The period of the New Economic Policy (NEP) reinstituted private trade on a limited scale between 1922 and 1927. Along with relaxation of the draconian measures that characterized War Communism came a far more open cultural climate as well. The utopian atmosphere and range of cultural experiments made this a heady time to visit, as improving economic conditions led the Bolsheviks to begin to encourage tourism, despite the challenges of traveling in the Soviet Union. Visitors remarked not only on the sacrifices patiently endured by the Soviet people as the cost for future comforts but also on the bold new educational practices and tremendous array of theatre characterized by kinetic movements and innovative staging. They noted the Russian people's hunger for learning, their "avidity for new ideas and forms," and their infectious hope for the future. And many remarked on the new Soviet woman, active in public life, and, thanks to "new privileges and new obligations," exhibiting a "new spirit."[17]

The First Five-Year Plan (1928–1932), a massive industrialization drive, created labor shortages that led the Bolsheviks to actively recruit foreign workers. With the onset of the Great Depression at almost the same moment, the fact of full employment in the Soviet Union lured thousands of industrial workers from the United States to Russia. Engineers and laborers came to build bridges, dams, and buildings; a large contingent of auto workers came from Detroit.[18] Work permits were usually arranged through Amtorg, the Soviet trade representative in the United States, although many people came on tourist visas hoping to find work once they arrived. By 1932 close to a thousand foreigners—among whom Americans represented the largest number—were coming to the Soviet Union every week. At the height of industrial development in the Soviet Union, approximately thirty-five thousand foreign workers and their families were living in the Soviet Union. A significant proportion of these were American.[19] More men than women came, but the "American girls in red Russia" were a visible presence, and these women looked to their Russian sisters with great interest.

Under the First Five-Year Plan, which created thousands of new jobs in industry, ordinary women could become "heroines of labor": Dusya Vinogradova, the "girl Stakhanovite" (a worker who exceeded quotas), was celebrated in a pamphlet published by the Communist Party of the United States in 1930 as "Miss U.S.S.R.," offering a sharp contrast to the "Miss America" of any era. During this period, the Bolsheviks stepped up efforts to punish workplace discrimination against women and increased funding for childcare. In 1929 the Zhenotdel initiated a campaign for the "cultural reconstruction of daily life," which in effect "set the public agenda for state policies toward women in the 1930s." To increase women's participation in the workforce, families were strongly encouraged to join "living communes and artels" with shared child-rearing and housekeeping. An unwritten social contract emerged in which women workers began to assume that the state would provide social services to lessen their domestic burden.[20]

Revolutionary Tourism, Political Pilgrims, and Soviet Techniques of Hospitality

Although "the Soviets aspired . . . to alter not merely the views but also the world views of visitors," visitors themselves had their own motives for coming to the Soviet Union. A few examples from VOKS, the All-Union Society for Cultural Relations with Foreign Countries—established in 1925 to orchestrate visits with foreign artists, educators, scientists, filmmakers, athletes, and other prominent figures, as well as those connected with Soviet "friendship" societies—make this clear.[21]

In 1926 Lucy L. W. Wilson, principal of the South Philadelphia High School for Girls, requested that she be given the opportunity to visit schools and other educational institutions, to meet with educators, and to see any relevant material that might aid her in writing a study of Soviet education. The American dancer and dance critic Edna Ocko asked for help getting tickets to dance performances. Barbara Sweet, a student at Stanford, met with a VOKS representative at the start of a two-month visit, noting her interest in learning more about national minorities in the Soviet Union. A twenty-nine-year-old psychologist from Philadelphia asked if she could visit hospitals and clinics, mentioning her desire to gather evidence to counter the "lies about Soviet institutions she'd found in American newspapers." F. Blackwell, an African American woman who had worked as a librarian in New York, expressed a desire to do related work in the Soviet Union.[22]

What tourists, Americans on official visits, and foreign residents in the Soviet Union all had in common was an interest in Soviet efforts to change the very meaning of work. In theory Soviet workers, directly benefiting from their labor as participants in the collective, escaped the alienation that characterized wage earning in a capitalist society. For the new woman, who defined herself through work (rather than through her family or romantic partner), travel to the Soviet Union tended to be freighted with a sense of vocation. This sense of vocation could be specific to a woman's profession, whether social work, education, journalism, or something else. The fashion designer Elizabeth Hawes, not wanting to be "just a tourist" during her 1935 trip to the Soviet Union, met beforehand with someone from the Soviet consulate in New York to arrange to show samples of her work to the Soviet dress trust. Cornelia Cannon, who gained the opportunity to go to Russia because her husband, a prominent scientist, received an invitation to deliver an address in Leningrad, made it her business to study Soviet birth control. Catherine Bauer, a New Dealer, an urban planner, and one of America's leading authorities on affordable housing, clearly felt it almost a necessity to research Soviet housing and urban planning as part of her work.[23]

Even for nonprofessional women, a visit to the Soviet Union was often rooted in the idea that "mothering the world" is every woman's work: How can the world be made more humane? How can social services be improved? This idea of improving the world went beyond social welfare to more metaphysical themes: Can love be changed to eliminate the double standard? Can human beings evolve to value cooperation over competition, and generosity over selfishness? What cultural forms facilitate this evolution?

Despite their varying interests, visitors did tend to see many of the same places, or the same kinds of places. In addition to the requisite trips to factories and collective farms, they typically were directed to parks, theatres, museums, art galleries, nurseries, schools, and public health institutions such as hospitals, maternity homes, and "prophylactories," which supposedly reformed former prostitutes. Many female tourists commented on their visits to the Institute for the Protection of Mothers and Children and the Palace of Motherhood, "with its scientific study and clinical work on all questions touching the health and well-being of mother and child; its plans for fighting disease and mortality; its courses for doctors, midwives, pediatrists, nurses; its model institutions," and its exhibits, showing, for instance, "a bright-faced peasant woman with a healthy baby in one arm, a book in the other." The former suffrage activist Rebecca Reyher, on a 1929 trip, visited model schools, a home for former prostitutes, a maternity hospital, and a sanitarium, and also met with representatives of the Zhenotdel. She commented in her diary on the social services to women provided by a factory she visited, noting the "lovely, light, airy rooms" in the nursery and the Zhenotdel representative's comment "We are citizens first, women second."[24]

Because her mother had worked since the age of five as a laundress, Frances E. Williams found Soviet attention to children profoundly moving: "Schools were always available for your children, even nursery schools or pre-primary things were planned so that they were near, if you worked in a factory or wherever you worked. . . . And you didn't have to again hoard your money and know all the right people to get your children into college and be in debt all your life."[25]

The Soviet "techniques of hospitality" designed to steer foreign visitors to the sites that those in power wanted them to see—and away from those they wanted to keep hidden—have become legendary, and have been offered up as proof that the great advancements touted to the rest of the world by the Bolsheviks were designed to dupe unwitting "political pilgrims." However nuanced, studies focusing on these efforts are prone to minimizing genuine efforts toward social transformation in the Soviet Union and flattening out our understanding of the women and men who were drawn there.[26] Sites demonstrating the Soviet Union's work on behalf of women and children became major tourist destinations not just because Soviet leaders wanted to showcase these efforts but also because travelers found these places deeply compelling.

All visitors were naturally drawn to aspects of the Soviet system that resonated with their own interests. The writer Sanora Babb went to Russia in 1936 to attend the Moscow Theatre Festival, but because of her interest in agriculture she visited a collective farm. That experience was clearly one of the highlights of her visit. She took striking photographs of farm women who looked strong, powerful, and proud of their work, and she noted, "The activity on the farm is tremendous, yet the relationship of these people is intimate, neighborly, something possibly requiring a new name, the old ones having been so much abused, for a new and healthy kind of relationship."[27]

Anna Rochester and Grace Hutchins went to the Soviet Union as tourists, but as feminists they made a concerted effort to see how the revolution affected women, a concern one finds in nearly every account by a woman. Indeed, journalist Ruth Gruber's *I Went to the Soviet Arctic* (1939) was conceived of as a study of women's role in the Soviet Arctic, but, as she put it, "their activity would have made any stranger stop and take notice. They presented such a sensational contrast to the women I had found in most of Europe." Gruber discovered women in in leadership positions all over the Arctic and also found them doing physical labor that elsewhere was usually reserved for men: "they paved streets, built houses, sawed wood, hauled lumber and loaded ships, working side by side with men."[28]

Even visitors who liked what they saw usually recognized that the Soviets wanted them to take certain impressions away with them.[29] For the playwright and director Hallie Flanagan, who visited in 1926–1927 and then again in 1930, the Soviet Union occupied a central place in her vision of theatre for the masses, an ideal she subsequently developed as director of the New Deal's Federal Theatre Project. Most of Flanagan's writings describe her excitement about Soviet cultural achievements, especially its theatre. But Flanagan's description of her guide in Moscow, a young Komsomol (Communist youth organization member) named Kori, suggests that Flanagan was well aware that her hosts had their own agenda.

Kori, who wears a "jaunty scarlet beret" and "shabby little shoes which click so rapidly over the Moscow cobbles," radiates "electrical waves of energy." She "is determined that you shall miss nothing: you shall see a Kolhoz and a Rabfac [a collective farm and a workers' training school]. . . .

You shall visit the Palace of Labor, the Kremlin, the Atheistic Museum, and the Park of Culture and Rest; you shall attend a factory meeting, a worker's club, and a performance of the Red Army." Kori can recite statistics off the top of her head. She "is not only omniscient, she is omnipotent. We penetrate the walls of the Kremlin, we interview officials, we attend political meetings, we secure seats in the theatres where there are no seats." Kori repeatedly emphasizes all the advancements women have achieved in the Soviet Union and the official positions they have attained.

> Do I realize that in the Rabfacs, the worker's colleges, girls are working beside men, learning to be engineers, technical experts, mill hands, lathe hands, operators of tractors, day nurseries or factories? Have I heard that the People's Commissar of Finance is a woman, as is the Assistant Educational Secretary? Do I understand that women are organizers and directors not only of nurseries, clubs, reading rooms, diet kitchens, parks, food factories, theatres, schools, but also of brick factories, textile mills, and metal works?[30]

Flanagan was glad to learn this, but, clearly, a little annoyed at having the information shoved down her throat.

Although it was difficult for Americans to travel without a Russian guide or translator, especially if they did not know the language, many visitors "took pains to prove that they saw the 'real Russia' and escaped manipulation at the hands of Soviet guides." Flanagan, for example, knew she was being manipulated and was open about this fact to her readers, perhaps to suggest that her account of all the positive things she saw could be trusted. Other visitors boasted of traveling "hard," of finding little palatable to eat, of soap's unavailability, and of lumpy beds, icy weather, flies, filth, and other challenges. All of this gave credence to claims that their experience was authentic. Lillian Wald, who visited the Soviet Union in 1924 as a guest of the government, later declared, "We saw whatever we wanted to see, and some of the most interesting places were visited without programme or the chaperonage of our hosts. There seemed, indeed, a very general desire to have us see everything—particularly the worst in their institutions, for they were severely troubled."[31]

New Men and New Women

A big attraction of the Soviet Union for visitors from the West was not simply the chance to witness a society in transformation, but, more fundamentally, the chance to be reborn in a radically new context. Trotsky had made an "improved edition of mankind" a goal of the Bolshevik revolution; as historian Jochen Hellbeck has maintained, "To reforge humanity and create an earthly paradise was the raison d'être of the Communist movement."[32]

For Soviet citizens, there was intense pressure to conform, both outwardly and even in one's private thoughts, to the ideal of a self brought into true being through socialism. But conformity had its rewards, to the point that most Soviet citizens truly wanted to believe what they were told to believe. Soviet ideology and experience offered much to outsiders too. Shortly after arriving in Moscow in December of 1934, Pauline Koner wrote in her diary: "Since arriving on Soviet soil I've felt different, the air smelled different and the land looked different. . . . Moscow is the most energizing and invigorating place in the world."[33]

For those who identified with "the movement," the sense of having a role in history "lifted us above ordinary life, made us proud and different and courageous. It made us seem to ourselves better than the man or woman who did not belong to this great movement." Both for Soviet citizens and for visitors, the chance "to escape one's atomized existence and comprehend oneself as a particle of a collective movement" had an almost religious attraction. "Moscow is a miracle city, and the martyrdom submitted by Russia will be for the future that which the crucifixion was," Isadora Duncan declared not long after arriving in 1921. "The human soul will be more beautiful, more generous, and greater than ever dreamed by Christ. . . . The prophesies of Beethoven, of Nietzsche, of Walt Whitman are being realized. All men will be brothers, carried away by the great wave of liberation that has just been born here in Russia."[34]

Rose Pastor Stokes, who'd renounced her Orthodox Jewish upbringing to embrace Communism, described her 1922 visit to Moscow (as a delegate to the Fourth Congress of the Communist International, or Comintern) in similarly religious terms:

If, after years of reaction, when your eyes had strained vainly in the black-ness for sight of a red banner floating on the breeze, you suddenly found yourself in some wide space prophetic of the Spring of the world where, from East, West, and South there converged a dozen streams of humanity no longer ice-bound by the Winter of Oppression, merging, and flowing before your eyes a vast season of scarlet streamers, apparently exhaustless as the sea itself—how would *you* feel? . . . I wept. Not quietly, and briefly and decently, but long and loud and hard: with all the bitter things in me, with all the sweet. I sobbed and laughed through my tears. All the pent-up feeling that had gathered during years of struggle at home, broke through, as my eyes beheld the glory of the coming of the Dawn.[35]

Not a few of those attracted to the Soviet Union had originally come from religious backgrounds but came to believe that humans had the power to change the circumstances of their existence, with rewards here on earth rather than in the hereafter. Anna Rochester and Grace Hutch-ins, a lesbian couple who met and became activists through their involve-ment with progressive Christian organizations, found that "the spirit of the communist who does not seek his own individual glory but who submits his personal life to the interests of communism" resonated with the "rhetoric of the whole person" that the two women derived initially from their Christian faith.[36] Communism became a new kind of faith for the secular age, materially embodied by the living example of the new Russia, in which advancements brought about by science and scientific thinking challenged the ethereal foundations of religious belief.

For many Jews with Russian roots, both Palestine and the Soviet Union were popular sites of "magic pilgrimage," both homelands of a sort with utopian promise, both places where new people were being created along with new civilizations. While Palestine called as a Jewish home-land, the Soviet Union offered Jews with roots in the Russian empire a chance to reformulate, now in terms of "class and political solidarity," their emotional connection to a land once known for its brutal oppres-sion of Jews. The Soviet Union outlawed anti-Semitism, and the creation in 1928 of a Jewish autonomous region known as Birobidjian in the So-viet Far East attracted support and drew settlers from the United States, who hailed the idea of a "a territorial enclave where a secular Jewish culture rooted in Yiddish and socialist principles could serve as an alternative to Palestine." Indeed, for Jews, as for African Americans, part of the Soviet Union's attraction was the possibility of having distinctions like race or ethnicity no longer matter. Louise Thompson was only one of many African Americans who spoke of the Soviet Union as a "promised land" that had supposedly eliminated racism.[37]

It was certainly easier to idealize the Soviet Union if you didn't have to live there—or at least if you didn't have to *stay* there. Visitors experienced difficult conditions, but they were far better than those endured by Soviet citizens. And visitors, if they kept their home citizenship, generally had the security of knowing they could leave. Mary Leder, who was forced by circumstance to give up her American citizenship, regretted doing so for the rest of her life. Leder came to the Soviet Union in 1931 as a sixteen-year-old daughter of idealistic Russian-Jewish parents who decided to leave their home in Los Angeles and immigrate to Birobidjian. Quickly concluding that she couldn't possibly live "in the middle of nowhere, on an island in a sea of mud," Leder went off on her own to Moscow. There she was told that she could not get a job without her passport, which she had left with her parents. Leder wired her father, who sent the passport by registered mail. However, it never arrived. Now the only way she could find work was by taking Soviet citizenship. When her parents decided to leave the country after two years, Mary was forbidden from joining them. She remained in the Soviet Union until 1964. Other Western women who became Soviet citizens were less lucky than Leder, ending up in prison camps, or dead.[38]

Even for visitors who stayed a year or less, the many dark sides to the revolution could be difficult to overlook. *Desire* held greater sway than *belief* for many, if not most, visitors. In other words, rather than having faith that the revolution's promises were being realized, they experienced desire that they might be. This made it possible for people to rationalize things that would otherwise be hard to tolerate. "I am getting redder every hour," Jessie Lloyd wrote to her mother from Moscow in July of 1927. "Really, I have heard such a lot of favorable things from non-communists that I am quite impressed." She admitted that arrests were all too common, but, as a Russian comrade had told her, "in America, the Bourgeoisie arrests many workers. Here, the communists arrest some bourgeois."[39]

"The thing you have to do about Russia is what you do about any other 'faith,'" Milly Bennett wrote to a friend in 1932. "You set your heart to know they are right. . . . And then, when you see things that shudder your bones, you close your eyes and say . . . 'facts are not important.'" Some early supporters of the Bolsheviks—perhaps most famously Emma Goldman and Alexander Berkman—quickly became disenchanted.[40] Others let desire, ideology, and knowledge of the Soviet Union's positive achievements cloud their assessment of what was necessary or acceptable in the name of revolution, usually with less self-knowledge about the process than Bennett expressed.

Red Homecomings

Many immigrants from czarist Russia, disillusioned with their experience in the "golden land" of the United States, sought ways to return to their homeland, and thousands did so immediately following the revolution. Sonia Luben, a Russian immigrant living in the Bronx and working in an orphan asylum, wrote in broken English to American Communist Party (CPUSA) officials in 1926 practically begging to be sent to the Soviet Union: "I dare to ask you . . . to be comradely enough and not add more bitterness to the great portion of which I have had and still have in coming and staing [sic] here." She had pictured an "easy and beautiful life" in the United States but instead found "sorrow" and "hardships" as well as a "convent-like" existence. In light of her wish "to work and strive for the betterment of the world," Luben believed she ought to be able to live where workers with her skills were "so much needed," and where she might "see and enjoy the obtained freedoms for which I have been fighting as almost a child."[41]

Luben's appeal to the CPUSA merits comment. Not only did the Soviet government restrict immigration by individuals between 1921 and 1928, the CPUSA, so as to preserve its own numbers, also limited the number of members it allowed to immigrate to the Soviet Union.

American Communists often did make visits, sometimes for extended periods: to attend Congresses of the Comintern, to train at the Lenin School or KUTV (the Communist University of the Toilers of the East, serving cadres from the colonial world, which included African Americans), or to do specialized work. They tended to live among other Communists (e.g., at the Lux Hotel in Moscow) or, if not physically separated, to associate primarily with one another. Still, although party members had a clear sense of being part of an elect group and could sometimes form an insular community, in many contexts the distinction between Communist and fellow traveler was one of degree rather than kind, and it is a mistake to assume a neat separation between the two. On the other hand, it's also clear that, as Sheila Fitzpatrick has noted, "the mere act of traveling to the Soviet Union did not . . . make a fellow traveller." In some instances, time in the Soviet Union transformed curious tourists into fellow travelers, or fellow travelers into committed Communists. Other times, it had the opposite effect.[42]

New Women and the "New Morality"

For those who, like Luben, experienced conditions in the United States as "convent-like," or who felt confined by its moral standards, the Soviet Union had a special attraction. The Bolshevik revolutionaries, in promising to "remake" human beings and transform everyday life, also promised to transform love, forecasting intimate relations based on a true meeting of minds and bodies, free from economic concerns or unnecessary social strictures.[43] Such rhetoric resonated with longstanding utopian traditions in the United States in which "free love" (defined in various ways ranging from unrestricted polyamory to committed relationships that were not bound by law), sexual equality, and the communal upbringing of children were common ideals.

In reality, the Bolsheviks themselves were divided on the subject of sex. Within the first ten years following the revolution, a series of family codes made abortions legal and free, provided state recognition for de facto marriages, simplified divorce, and decriminalized sodomy. These new codes suggested, as one Soviet jurist wrote in a legal commentary, that consenting adults "were free to express their sexual feeling in any form." But a new openness to sexual questions led to confusion over gender roles and expectations. And, in fact, Soviet moral codes were very much in flux. Freer sexual behavior in the mid-1920s, especially among the young, provoked mixed reactions, with critics claiming that sexual promiscuity threatened the very foundations of the revolution.[44]

Alexandra Kollontai, the most prominent Bolshevik feminist, wrote extensively about sex and morality under communism. She believed bourgeois marriage oppressed women, and she also famously insisted that "the sex act should be recognized as an act neither shameful nor sinful, but natural and legitimate, like every other manifestation of a healthy organism, like the satisfying of hunger and thirst." Many young people in the Soviet Union seized upon Kollontai's effort to make sex a private affair between consenting adults as evidence that sexual license was somehow radical. Some—men especially—"simply assumed that sexual and political revolution went together" and equated sexual constraint with other bourgeois behaviors that should be rejected as antiquated relics of the old way of life. Jessica Smith noted in 1928:

> If smoking had been forbidden in certain places formerly, some young people thought it necessary for every class-conscious worker and Comsomol [sic] to attend meetings with four cigarettes hanging out of his mouth, to be contemptuous of all anti-tobacco and anti-alcohol propaganda. If bourgeois circles had nice manners, they argued, then the proletarian must be rougher than ever, never fail to keep his hat on in the house and spit on the floor. . . . This applied not only to matters of conduct, but to matters of love. Since there had been no time for dalliance in the heat of struggle, the really revolutionary lover in the days that followed could not be bothered with the delicacies of courtship, but came to the point at once, and the girl who objected to coarse language and "pawing" was accused of not having outlived her bourgeois prejudices.[45]

On the other hand, much of the Bolshevik leadership was notoriously puritanical, perhaps most famously Lenin himself. Responding to what became known as the "glass of water" theory (that "the satisfaction of the sex impulse ... will be as simple and as inconsequential as drinking a glass of water"), Lenin reportedly said to the German Communist Clara Zetkin, "Of course, thirst must be satisfied. But will the normal person in normal circumstances lie down in the gutter and drink out of a puddle, or out of a glass with a rim greasy from many lips?" Lenin suggested that unlike drinking water, sexual relations could produce a new life, making intimate matters not just the concern of individuals but a social issue that demanded consideration of one's "duty towards the community."[46]

Although Kollontai's critics condemned her supposedly immoral views, Kollontai herself argued that "wingless eros," or sex without love, "sapped physical energy, blocked the development of 'sensations of sympathy and psychological bonds between human beings,' and was based on female dependence on the male." For her, the socialist ideal was "winged eros," under which "respect for the personality of the other and the ability to consider others' rights" creates "a mutual sincere sympathy." Under winged eros, love is not only absolved of possessiveness; it is both subordinated to and nurtured by the ideals of the collective, or "comradely solidarity." For Kollontai, as for many of the US women who became interested in her ideas, winged eros was only to be realized under socialism.[47]

In the United States, the new Soviet attitude toward morality in general and male-female relationships in particular was seen as part of a larger transformation of human psychology under socialism. "In many fundamental ways human beings behave, think, and feel differently than in other countries," journalist Ella Winter proclaimed in 1932, by which time Soviet "morality" had actually limited the freer sexual practices characteristic of just a few years earlier. "Men do not think about women the way they used to; women do not think about work or marriage, children or cooking, the church or politics, as they did formerly. ... The kind of individual generated by our individualist, *laissez-faire* order is not developing in the Soviet Union. Human beings are constructing the new order, but the new order is also forming human beings."[48]

Under this new order, the false propriety of bourgeois convention was cast aside for social relations that were ostensibly more natural. "Much of what seems almost license to tourists in Russia is only a result of the very simple, frank, and earthy attitude Russians always have taken to-ward sex," Winter noted. American visitors frequently expressed surprise and sometimes discomfort about "an absence of inhibitions, restraints, suspicions, in the customs regulating the relations of the sexes," as they discovered the Soviet practice of nude swimming or found themselves placed in an overnight train compartment with a member of the oppo-site sex.[49]

The left-wing press in the United States almost uniformly hailed a revolution in morals in the Soviet Union, claiming that bourgeois mo-rality not only repressed humans' natural instincts but also oppressed women. In the enormously influential collection *Sex and Civilization* (1929), V. F. Calverton ("the Karl Marx of the sexual revolution") de-clared that in the Soviet Union "woman has at last become a human be-ing with the same rights and privileges as men." He went on to argue that the legal position of women in the Soviet Union augured a new moral economy in both social and sexual relations. Russian-born US journalist Maurice Hindus likewise insisted that the Bolsheviks were "seeking to emancipate sex from legal, metaphysical, religious and certain social pre-judgments, for women as much as for men."[50]

On the Right, tales of Soviet sexual excess were closely tied to fears about radical politics. In American Communist writer Myra Page's novel *Moscow Yankee* (1935), a witless Detroit worker on his way to Moscow declares with anticipation: "And oh baby, there's free love in Russia!" False tales of the "nationalization of women" (that is, women becoming property of the state), a "Bureau of Free Love," and elite young women being given over to "red soldiers, sailors, and marines" were easy fuel for those wishing to condemn the revolution.[51]

But if tales of free love and the nationalization of women were pri-marily manufactured by the Right, even some liberal commentators were troubled by aspects of the Bolsheviks' "new morality." Journalist Dorothy Thompson suggested in 1928 that Russia's "emancipation" of women had come at too high a cost: "One wonders, after living awhile in Russia, whether the process could not better be called 'sterilization' than 'eman-cipation'; whether Russia, by its simplification of Eros to merely the most convenient formula for satisfying the sexual urge and populating the state, is not building a civilization more hostile to everything which is essentially woman than any in the world." Thompson insisted, "Marriage and love have not been 'freed.' Only new bonds have been established, and without the sentimental and emotional associations which helped to make the old system tolerable." As Thompson saw it, the laws punished the virtuous and rewarded the promiscuous. As historian Wendy Goldman has argued, "By facilitating what some considered 'free love,' the new laws promoted what others considered 'depravity,' blurring the line between freedom and chaos."[52]

The family codes passed in 1918 and 1926, in theory enacted to destroy "the old rotten foundations of the family and marriage" (i.e., property and female obedience), in practice diminished a woman's ability to care for her children. A wife's livelihood could be threatened by the law requiring her husband to give up to a third of his earnings toward the support of another woman's child. On the other hand, laws requiring fathers to contribute to their children's support whether or not they were legally married to the child's mother were difficult to enforce. According to *New York Times* correspondent Anne O'Hare McCormick, "If any one imagines that this wide liberty gives satisfaction to the liberated, he need only talk with the older women, of whom many are tragic in their desire for security instead of freedom."[53]

American women in the Soviet Union had mixed experiences when it came to sexual matters, but significant numbers found the relative openness in the sexual realm attractive at a time when even arming women with *information* about birth control was illegal in the United States. While Dorothy West was in Moscow, a friend wrote urging her to "soak up all the Russian birth control rules and share them with your friends." Ruth Kennell, returning to the United States in 1928 after living for six years in Russia, where she shed a Victorian outlook on sex, (temporarily) escaped her marriage, and took a series of lovers, both American and Russian, suggested that the freedom around sex and birth control in the Soviet Union was a higher form of morality than what one finds in the United States: "The main difference I see between Moscow and New York is that in Moscow a woman is free to give her love, and here she is compelled to sell it."[54]

Despite rumors of "free love" in Russia, American visitors were often struck by how oversexed *Western* culture seemed in comparison. "Nowhere in restaurants or theatres are there displays of pictures of voluptuous maidens in a variety of semi-nude poses, such as greet the eyes of the visitor at every step on certain streets in Berlin," Maurice Hindus insisted. "The revolutionaries regard the exploitation of a woman's body for commercial gain as a vicious insult to womanhood. Nowhere in Russia are pornographic pictures peddled around openly or secretly—they are not to be had. The Russian public does not crave and does not demand vicarious forms of sex excitement." Even before the Five-Year Plan put most Russians into a working frenzy, Russians appeared far from sex crazed to American observers. In Jessie Lloyd's unpublished novel "A Flapper in Russia" (based partially on Lloyd's experiences living in Moscow from July 1927 to September 1928), the female narrator complains that Russian men barely look at her body: "If they look at you it is sort of an intense stare at your face, as if they were trying to figure out what your character was like." It makes her wonder, "Doesn't anybody flirt in this town?"[55]

The sexual ethos became increasingly restrained in the early 1930s. Antisodomy legislation was enacted in 1933, after which the young actor Milly Bennett had met and married in Moscow was sent to a prison camp for his "homosexual past."[56] Abortions, a touchstone of the "new morality," were made illegal in 1936 and divorces became more difficult to obtain. By the mid-1930s, although Russians still sunbathed nude, "free love" was a thing of the past.

Feeling Like a New Woman

Both Russians and Americans fetishized the new Soviet woman for her natural beauty, strength, and athleticism, even as they emphasized Russian women's supposed lack of attention to their physical appearance, their focus on *inner* change. "A new mental cast is developing in Russia, and a new woman is the product of this period of evolution," photographer and journalist Margaret Bourke-White wrote in the *New York Times* in 1932. "She is characterized not so much by beauty as by sturdiness, self-reliance."[57] Most American women visiting the Soviet Union recognized that, in fact, their clothes were nicer, and even their skin and teeth were better than those of Soviet women. Nonetheless, these women, in their nicer clothes, with creature comforts awaiting them at home, envied and sought ways to embody the new Soviet woman's "inner revolution," her work ethic, and her social commitment.[58]

While actual conditions for the majority of women workers in the Soviet Union remained almost unimaginably difficult, the liberated, class-conscious woman worker became a dramatic symbol of the revolution's achievements. This was especially true for outside observers who placed significant hopes in the Soviet experiment during a period of retrenchment for American women: the women's movement in the United States has been characterized as experiencing "decades of discontent" between 1920 and 1940 as organized feminism lost momentum following the suffrage victory, as those calling themselves feminists scaled back demands for social welfare, economic opportunity, and sexual emancipation in the face of red baiting, and as the New Deal upheld a male breadwinner ethic (and enforced the idea that women's primary role is in the home) by forbidding wives of employed men to work for the WPA. Thus the Soviet Union's social and economic transformations, though often traumatic for that country's citizens, excited many outsiders. The African American poet Helene Johnson wrote to her cousin Dorothy West in the fall of 1932, "Dot baby, just imagine, you're part of that great new economic laboratory, part of a splendid experiment. . . . I can't help but envy you so much."[59]

Hallie Flanagan experienced Russians in general and Russian women in particular as authentic, purposeful, and uninhibited by outworn social convention: "These shabby workers and peasants, soldiers and Komsonol [sic] girls, surging over the cobbles, carrying in their hands black bread wrapped in newspaper, and sprays of lilac, have a certain free directness of carriage, a release from the tyranny of the proper thing, a lack of make-up, either physical or mental." As in Moscow's stripped-down theatre productions, bespeaking the possibility of not only performing but also inhabiting a more authentic self, Soviet women's "lack of style" seemed to augur "the beginning of a new style."[60]

Suffering, Violence, and the Utopian Imagination

The figure of the emancipated, athletic, smiling worker-heroine became a kind of veneer, a performance, disguising both the limits of the Soviet welfare state and the limited nature of female emancipation under the Bolsheviks. Although new laws enacted in the immediate aftermath of the revolution were designed to emancipate women, few women actually benefited from them. Although thousands of women joined the Communist Party, enrolled in literacy classes, and at least became conscious of their right to demand more equitable treatment, material shortages and deep-seated sexism within Russian society limited women's gains. On top of the chaos created by the world war and the revolution, the civil war and the famine ravaged the Russian people: between 1916 and 1921, sixteen million Russians died from war, starvation, cold, or disease. Under these circumstances, state services were understandably overwhelmed.[61]

Efforts to improve economic output and reduce costs during the NEP led to cuts in funding for day care and other institutions for children and women, inhibiting women's ability to enter the workplace. Men routinely sabotaged women's training in skilled trades, effectively diminishing their earning capacity. And despite regulations forbidding the practice, employers often discriminated against women, especially married women, to avoid the potential costs of granting them paid maternity leave or time off for nursing. They also dismissed pregnant and nursing women, again despite regulations.[62]

And women made only limited advancements in public life: While a small number held visible or important posts (e.g., leading libraries, museums, and social welfare institutions), they could in no way be said to have assumed leadership roles in proportion to their number. According to a 1929 report by Anne O'Hare McCormick, "Women share more manual labor but succeed to no more of the really important offices than are meted out to them in the most conservative political systems." Although working women made gains during the First Five-Year Plan, many women were forced into the workplace by economic need and found state facilities to ease their domestic burdens woefully inadequate.

Conditions in factories remained "appalling." In the agricultural sector, the drive toward collectivization of farms produced modest gains for women, but these material gains barely compensated for "the extensive dislocation and trauma caused by collectivization," as compliance was forced upon millions of peasants. And, in the early 1930s, a terror-famine in the Ukraine disproportionately affected women, as many men had left the countryside for jobs in cities.[63]

The situation worsened. Economic conditions began improving by 1932, but increasingly frequent public trials of alleged saboteurs, culminating in the Moscow show trials of original Bolsheviks, became the public face and ostensible rationale for the Great Terror in which over a million Russians, as well as foreigners (including a number of Americans), were arrested, sent to prison camps, or killed. Moreover, with the new restrictions on sodomy, abortion, and divorce, state surveillance and the repressive political atmosphere increasingly extended into private life. The distinction between illegitimate and legitimate children was restored in the mid-1930s, and women began receiving awards for bearing and raising large numbers of children.[64]

Eventually the violent and repressive aspects of Soviet life became more visible to visitors and less easy to rationalize. Although many things impressed Cornelia Cannon during her 1935 visit, she was deeply troubled by the treatment of the former aristocracy and opponents of the regime: "These are things that burn one's heart and turn the greatest achievements of the Soviet government to dust and ashes," Cannon wrote in the diary she prepared for her family.[65]

A series of show trials in Moscow from 1936 to 1938, encompassing almost the entire leadership of the Communist Party, followed by a purge that led to the arrest, imprisonment, or death of over a million Soviet citizens, brought serious criticism from many people in the United States, including leftist intellectuals frustrated with what they perceived as a Stalinist hijacking of the Left. Even so, the Popular Front against fascism, which coalesced in the mid-1930s and operated in the United States as an informal coalition of Communists, independent radicals, and New Deal Liberals, retained its political and cultural influence until 1939. The Nazi-Soviet nonaggression pact caused many people to leave the Communist Party or to give up their ties to Communists. The US-Soviet alliance during World War II temporarily revived the image of the new Soviet woman, as she battled Nazi hordes with bravery resembling the Russian revolutionaries of an earlier generation.

After the war and the fragile alliance ended, the Cold War fostered an association between dissent and communism, and between communism and spying. The Soviet Union came to be seen as fundamentally geared toward the "subversion or forcible destruction of the machinery of government and structure of society in the countries of the non-Soviet world." By the time a new generation of American radicals and rebels came to consciousness in the 1960s, the Soviet Union's lure to tourists, reformers, job hunters, and feminists was already a dim memory to most. The cohort of activists that grew out of civil rights and antiwar agitation on university campuses specifically identified itself as a "New Left" to distinguish itself from an "Old Left" that had foundered on the shoals of Stalinism and naïve acceptance of the Soviet "line."[66]

Cruel Optimism

Certainly, significant numbers of women who visited the Soviet Union were either very critical or at least had mixed opinions about what they found. Many others became disenchanted, disillusioned. But what especially interests me is the "cruel optimism" that made large numbers hold steadfast to an ideal that not only was forced on a people with unimaginable ruthlessness but was ultimately perverted by obsessive paranoia that justified the arrest, exile, and murder of millions, many of whom were, in fact, loyal to the regime. American women were drawn to the Soviet Union because it embodied a promise of the good life and explicitly included women's emancipation in that promise. The very conditions of modernity—under capitalism or under communism—make the feeling of wholeness, which women (and men) longed for and continue to long for, ever fleeting.[67] But what of that yearning?

To argue that those who became invested in the transformative possibilities of the Russian Revolution were delusional minimizes the complex nature of their motivations, their desires, and their experiences.

Moreover, the same ideal that justified Bolshevik terror fueled radical imaginings at home, internationalized feminist sensibilities, and generated new ways of coping with the conditions of modernity. Revolutionary Russia's appeal corresponds to a longstanding, and continuing, desire among women to "have it all." It held out the promise of women finding companionate and egalitarian relationships, professional satisfaction, reliable and nurturing childcare and schools for their children, and the chance to build a world they could believe in.

Antifeminists' success at tying the leftist feminists' agenda to "un-American" activity (i.e., Bolshevism) suggests why sexual containment and traditional gender norms became so prevalent in the postwar period, as all echoes of Soviet practice became suspect. In the United States, popular constructions of the Soviet woman as unfeminine, unstylish, laboring, and desperate for consumer goods, and of the American female spy as a guileful sex addict, helped shore up what Betty Friedan called the "feminine mystique," or the idea that women could only find real satisfaction in life by becoming wives and mothers.[68]

American feminists' now-forgotten attraction to Russia tells us something about who and where we are now, about embracing other forms of cruel optimism: "leaning in" to careers, finding a "third metric" for success, becoming "tiger mothers," or insisting that motherhood is indeed a profession and full-time job, or perhaps even proclaiming that patriarchy is dead and women should just get over it. These formulations may bring even less meaning and sustenance to women's lives than did the vision of a new society actively working to better the human condition.[69]

This book is structured thematically and semichronologically. From before the failed revolution of 1905 through the Second World War, and gesturing toward what came after, the book follows the experiences of a number of women whose lives often intersected and whose stories are woven throughout. Several women for whom the Russian revolutionary project became a defining aspect of their lives—Anna Louise Strong, Ruth Epperson Kennell, Isadora Duncan, Lillian Wald, Margaret Bourke-White, and others—pop up in multiple chapters, serving as threads between disparate themes. Drawing on diaries, private correspondence, and memoirs alongside published writings, I seek to understand the ways in which Russia and the Soviet Union affected women's very sense of themselves, their relationships, and their vision of an ideal society.

These women were reformers, journalists, performers, and/or creative writers; some were committed Communists. In Russia and the Soviet Union, they found, variously, professional success; shocking poverty, starvation, and disease; open-minded attitudes about race and sex; narrow-minded attitudes about race and sex; striking examples of artistic experimentation; horrifying violence, paranoia, and fear; deeply engaged audiences; sexual satisfaction; and inspiring examples of commitment.

However paradoxically, a significant number of freedom-seeking women from the United States were drawn to and materially aided a regime practicing terror and repression. With all its contradictions, revolutionary Russia fostered core elements of American feminist sensibilities, and women's very sense of themselves and their role in the world, in ways that until now have been unexplored.

TENDER REVOLUTIONARIES
AND CHILD SAVERS

A combination of factors in the late nineteenth and early twentieth century made a certain kind of American woman ripe for
supporting the Russian revolutionary struggle. The explosion of
print media and international reporting brought oppression by
Russia's imperial regime and revolutionary challenges to that regime closer to home at a moment when American women were
collectively declaring their own independence: by graduating
from college in unprecedented numbers, by pursuing careers, by
publicly protesting an array of injustices, and by demanding sexual freedom and equality in marriage. By the 1910s, American
women reformers had also become leading exponents of a new
"progressive internationalism" that challenged American empire
building and aimed toward "cooperation with other peoples in
pursuit of world peace and social justice."[1] Efforts to bring democracy to "darkest Russia" loomed large on the progressive in-
ternationalists' agenda, as pogroms, crackdowns on dissent, and
the martyrdom of women increasingly put Russia at the center
of what appeared to be a worldwide battle of democracy against

tyranny. Of interest to new women in the United States, beyond the very striking fact of women's direct involvement in revolutionary activity in Russia, was that the ideal of female equality—in education, in the professions, and in romantic relationships—was taken for granted by almost every revolutionary organization in Russia, from Populists to Social Democrats.

Widespread empathy in the United States for victims of czarist oppression grew from a sense that there was something universal in the popular Russian yearning for freedom and justice, and from feelings of affinity with the Russian people, based on similar geography (a large frontier region with an indigenous population) and parallel histories of slavery and serfdom. The socialist journalist Anna Strunsky wrote of the Revolution of 1905, "It was not only a war for national freedom but for the creation of a social freedom never yet seen on land or sea. The movement was a creative force carrying everything before it, fixed on the idea of freedom and justice." Settlement house reformer Lillian Wald insisted a decade later that the person "who does not see in the gigantic struggle in Russia a world movement for freedom and progress that is our struggle too, will not comprehend the significance of the sympathy of the many Americans who are friends of Russian freedom."[2]

The collapse of the autocracy and assumption of power by the moderate Kerensky in early 1917 produced jubilation in many quarters in the United States and was celebrated in settlement houses, suffrage parades, and labor unions. Even after the Bolsheviks assumed power, violently suppressed all opposition, confiscated private property, and withdrew Russia from World War I, they enjoyed considerable if somewhat tentative support from most radicals and many progressives in the United States, including significant numbers of the reformers who for years had worked for "Russian freedom." Female progressives were especially interested in Soviet experiments vis-à-vis the "woman question": the suffragist Mary Winsor declared following a visit to the Soviet Union on the tenth anniversary of the revolution, "When the Bolsheviks came into power, Lenin said they must not leave standing one brick of the whole edifice of woman's degradation; civil, legal, and political. So they tore it all down and women now enjoy equal rights with men."[3]

As civil war followed the revolution, and then famine followed the civil war, American women were aroused to action: to convince Congress to end an inhumane blockade so that food and medicine could reach Russian mothers and children, and then to support relief efforts for regions devastated by the 1921 famine that threatened millions of children with starvation and put Soviet Russia's future in doubt.

Historically, American women had entered the public sphere at home and abroad through service work with maternal dimensions that cast a benevolent glow on US imperial projects. Both the dawn of the new woman and the radical thrust of the Social Gospel changed this dynamic considerably. Now women asserted their freedom to travel abroad while opposing militarism and imperialism and "explicitly allying their voice and cause with peace."[4]

The Social Gospel inspired a host of efforts geared toward healing the world, eliminating poverty and injustice, and promoting social harmony—creating a "kingdom of God on earth." Such theology moved many people to embrace not just government reforms but also socialism, as faith in God proved inadequate to the pressing problems of the day. The Bolshevik revolution, despite being partly premised on Marx's belief that "religion is the opiate of the people," quickly attracted the sympathies of many Christians who saw no necessary conflict between the basic values of Communism and those of Christianity. The Jewish tradition of linking messianic thought and *tikkun olam* (healing the world) with internationalism had received its greatest impetus in late nineteenth-century Russia, as the Haskalah, or Jewish Enlightenment, drew thousands of Jews into revolutionary movements. And many Jewish socialists came to believe that the Bolshevik revolution would end the persecution of Russian Jews. But they also feared that the humanitarian crisis following the revolution might well prevent the revolution's promises from being realized.[5]

That crisis created a moral imperative to feed, clothe, and heal Russian children: given the chance to thrive under the new regime, starving, sickly children could be transformed into new people, redeemed not just by American food and medicine but also by socialism. The cumulative effects of war, blockade, and famine created a socially acceptable justification for middle-class women to enter a realm otherwise seen as unfit for them. They came to save the Russian children, but quite a few, consciously or unconsciously, also hoped to gain a kind of redemption themselves.

Dreaming in Red

Reformers, Rebels, and a Revolutionary Babushka

Writing in the summer of 1905, Anna Strunsky, the "girl social-ist of San Francisco" (and an immigrant from Russia), neatly summarized the appeal of Russia's female revolutionaries to young women like herself: "So it was that woman who was without honor resolved on becoming glorious; she who was a chattel vowed in her heart that she would be free; she who had been ignorant and helpless, hardly a mother and wife, hardly a sister and help-meet, insisted on the right to learn, to take on culture, to seek happiness in the happiness of others, to grow in the stature of a human being. . . . She stood in the gray dawn of freedom, a self-conscious individuality, a woman at once war-rior and priestess."[1]

By writing and speaking on "Russian freedom," American new women fed popular expectations in the United States about what a new Russia would look like—what form it would take, what place women would have in its governance and public life, and also how Russia's political transformation would affect work, ed-ucation, motherhood, love, and sexual relations—in ways that predicted a longer-term feminist investment in Russia and the Soviet Union. Moreover, the fact that Russian terrorists and assassins, especially women, were hailed as heroes in the United States in the decades leading up to 1917 predicted a willingness on the part of many Americans to accept violence as a necessary part of Russian justice.

Tender Revolutionaries

Before 1917 Russian revolutionaries were often portrayed in the United States in romantic and heroic terms. Beginning in the 1880s, popular translations of works by Russian novelists such as Alexander Herzen, Leo Tolstoy, and Ivan Turgenev, memoirs by revolutionaries (some of whom had immigrated to the United States or England), and novels by American and British writers helped foster an image of Russian revolutionaries as "selfless and highly cultured individuals who turned reluctantly to violence, and then only to assuage the oppression of the masses."[2]

Films and plays continued this pattern while also linking the United States to Russian struggles for freedom. Israel Zangwill's play *The Melting Pot* (1909) concerns a daughter of Russian nobility who becomes a revolutionary and then, in exile in the United States, turns settlement house worker. She marries a Russian Jewish immigrant whose parents had been killed in the Kishinev pogrom. The United States thus becomes the place where a Christian and a Jew from the Old World, joined in a quest for freedom, can find happiness. In *Beneath the Czar* (1914), one of several films made prior to 1917 that showed sympathy for the Russian revolutionary struggle, Anna Pavlowa agrees to spy on suspected revolutionary Prince Rubetskoi to save her nihilist father from torture at the hands of the police. However, she falls in love with the prince and becomes a revolutionary herself, fleeing to the United States with her lover and father.[3]

Within both fictional and documentary accounts, the Russian revolutionary *woman* elicited unending commentary for her bravery, selflessness, and devotion. In January 1906, after Socialist Revolutionary Maria Spiridonova shot a provincial councilor known for his brutal suppression of peasant unrest, Spiridonova's suffering at the hands of Russian

A TYPE OF THE YOUNG WOMEN UNIVERSITY STUDENTS
WHO TAKE ACTIVE PART IN THE REVOLUTION

Fig. 1.1 From Leroy Scott, "Women of the Russian Revolution," *The Outlook* 90 (1908), 915–28. Scott's article also contains images and discussions of Catherine Breshkovsky, Vera Zasulich, Sophie Perovskaya, and other revolutionaries. (Scott describes Sophie Perovskaya as "the most famous of present-day revolutionists. She was sentenced to death for shooting a brutal vice-governor, but public sentiment was so strong in her favor that the government dared not execute her and she was sent to hard labor in Siberia.")

authorities made her a martyr in both Russia and the United States. The *New York Times* printed the full text of Spiridonova's court testimony, in which she declared: "I undertook the execution . . . because my heart was breaking with sorrow and it was no longer possible to live with the tales of the horror . . . ringing in my ears." American journalist Kellogg Durland described her as "a delicate girl . . . with soft, blue eyes" whose "wavy brown hair" was "draped over her temples in order to hide hideous scars left by the kicks of the Cossacks." Beyond highlighting her suffering and bravery, Durland asserted what would become a refrain: women's role in the Russian struggle was "unique among the revolutionary movements in history."[4]

"The Russian woman has shared like and like with men: in leadership, in the dangerous clandestine education of the masses, in throwing the terrorist's bomb, in prison, in Siberian mines, on the scaffold. So willing have they been to die for the sake of progress that with many death has become an ambition," Leroy Scott wrote in 1908. Emphasizing revolutionary women's nobility and "tenderness," Scott insisted these traits did not stand opposed to the women's violent deeds but, in fact, provided their rationale: "It is this very tenderness, this intense feeling for the victims of tyranny, that has impelled so many gentle-souled women to tyrannicide."[5]

The "Little Grandmother" and the Friends of Russian Freedom

For many Americans, Ekaterina Breshko-Breshkovskaya, known in the United States as Catherine Breshkovsky, Babushka, or the Little Grandmother of the Russian Revolution, came to personify the Russian revolutionary cause.[6] Breshkovsky combined unflagging commitment to justice at great cost to her own comfort with remarkable charisma. Her 1904–1905 tour of the United States, during which she made a personal connection with dozens if not hundreds of women and men and inspired thousands of others, revitalized an American movement for "Russian freedom" that had begun in the 1880s. It also helped convince significant numbers of women, young and old, that the battle against tyranny in Russia was their concern as well.

Born in 1844, Breshkovsky (née Verigo) was a daughter of Russian nobility who renounced her own privilege. As a teenager, Katia Verigo started a school for her family's serfs, and throughout her life she remained committed to educating the masses. As a young woman, she found herself in a train compartment with Prince Peter Kropotkin, a leading revolutionary thinker. Their long conversation made a strong impression. On a visit to Saint Petersburg, she fell in with a group of revolutionaries and yearned to join their activities. Following the practice of many ambitious Russian women who chafed under their parents' control, Katia used marriage as a route to freedom, and at twenty-five she married a liberal student from a nearby landholding family. Although fond of her husband, Catherine made clear to him from the beginning that justice for the Russian people would always be her priority. The couple worked together for several years, educating peasants and advocating for their rights. But when Catherine chose to adopt illegal tactics, she and her husband amicably parted ways. Breshkovsky joined a revolutionary commune in Kiev in 1873. There she gave birth to a son, whom her sister-in-law agreed to raise. Breshkovsky insisted, "I knew I could not be a mother and still be a revolutionist."[7] Later she claimed to be mother and grandmother to thousands.

A year after her son was born, Breshkovsky, like hundreds of others, went "to the people" in order to educate peasants and foment revolution.[8] This led to her arrest and imprisonment, including four years in solitary confinement. When finally brought to trial, Breshkovsky offered no defense and openly declared herself a revolutionist. She was rewarded with five years of hard labor in the Kara mines (the first woman to receive this sentence) followed by Siberian exile.

During one of her Siberian exiles—this time after an attempted escape from prison—Breshkovsky met George Kennan, an American Russia expert who was to dramatically change her fortunes, as well as those of the Russian revolutionary struggle in general. Employed by the Russian American Telegraph Company to survey a proposed telegraph route, Kennan had first ventured to Siberia in 1864. He wound up spending several years in remote areas of Russia. Back in the United States, he lectured extensively and published ethnographic descriptions and travelogues, becoming one of America's most respected authorities on Russia. In 1884, as a staunch defender of the czarist regime, Kennan proposed to study the Siberian exile system in order to answer Russia's critics. Because of his outspoken sympathy for the czarist government, he gained full cooperation and access.[9]

A preliminary expedition did little to change Kennan's views, but on a longer trip, from May 1885 to August 1886, exiles showing almost unfathomable "courage fortitude self-sacrifice and devotion to an ideal" changed Kennan's outlook completely. He wrote to a friend shortly after returning to the United States: "I went to Siberia regarding the political exiles as a lot of mentally unbalanced fanatics bombthrowers and assassins and . . . when I came away from Siberia I kissed these same men good bye with my arms around them and my eyes full of tears."[10]

Kennan encountered Breshkovsky in a remote area of the Transbaikal in 1885. He described her as having "a strong, intelligent, but not handsome face, a frank, unreserved manner, and sympathies that appeared to be warm, impulsive, and generous." Though Kennan noted "traces of . . . suffering" on Breshkovsky's face, he insisted "neither hardship, nor exile, nor penal servitude had been able to break her brave, finely tempered spirit, or to shake her convictions of honor and duty." Leaving their meeting, Kennan could imagine only a grim future for Breshkovsky. However, her last words to him were hopeful: " 'Yes, Mr. Kennan,' she said to me just before I bade her goodbye. 'We may die in exile, and our grand-children may die in exile, but something will come of it at last.' "[11]

Indeed, something did. Kennan's articles in the *Century*, his lecture tours (which reached close to a million people), and, finally, his 1893 book *Siberia and the Exile System*, the *Uncle Tom's Cabin* of the Russian penal system, caused a sensation. During Kennan's over eight hundred lectures around the United States, he often appeared in the rags and shackles of a Siberian prisoner, and he left audiences spellbound. After Kennan's address at the Washington Literary Society, Mark Twain rose to his feet, tears in his eyes, and proclaimed, "If dynamite is the only remedy for such conditions, then thank God for dynamite!"[12]

On the way home from his transformative 1885–1886 Siberian trip, Kennan had met Sergei Kravchinsky (a.k.a. Stepniak), a Russian revolutionary and assassin living in exile in London. Stepniak's 1882 book *Underground Russia* had done much for the cause, but Kennan inspired him to do even more.[13] Building on Kennan's connections, Stepniak undertook a tour of the United States. In 1891 he started the Society of American Friends of Russian Freedom (SAFRF) in Boston with the help of authors William Dean Howells and Mark Twain, along with Boston Brahmins including Unitarian minister and abolitionist Thomas Wentworth Higginson, Quaker poet and abolitionist John Greenleaf Whittier, Julia Ward Howe (composer of the "Battle Hymn of the Republic"), and several children of abolitionists, among them William Lloyd Garrison's two sons and Alice Stone Blackwell, the daughter of abolitionist Henry Blackwell and feminist Lucy Stone.

It is not simply coincidence that former abolitionists and their children launched the "Free Russia" movement in the United States. Like white women who had sympathized with the predicament of enslaved African Americans, new women in the United States came to identify with revolutionary women in Russia, admiring their principled devotion to social justice, their willingness to sacrifice everything for a noble cause, and their commitment not just to equal rights but also to an egalitarian ideal in private life.

In 1903 widespread outrage over the Kishinev pogrom (in which 49 Jews were killed and more than 500 injured, and 1,300 Jewish homes and businesses were looted or destroyed) brought renewed attention among Americans to czarist cruelty. Inspired by Leo Tolstoy's novel *Resurrection* (1899), in which a Russian official refrains from assaulting a group of political prisoners because he fears attention from foreign newspapers, Alice Stone Blackwell decided to revive the dormant SAFRF, believing "it might be useful to spread news about the misdeeds of the Russian government through the American press."[14] The newly reconstituted organization wound up sponsoring Catherine Breshkovsky's visit to the United States in 1904.

Aware of growing public opposition to the czarist regime in the United States, the Socialist Revolutionaries decided to send one of their most articulate and sympathetic members on an American tour to raise money and build support for the revolution. Breshkovsky had personally experienced some of the most harrowing of the government's punishments, from prison to exile. She was also still remembered in the United States from Kennan's sketches.[15] Finally, she was decidedly grandmotherly in her appearance. She thus offered a kinder, gentler image of the Russian revolutionary.

Upon her release from exile in 1896, Breshkovsky had immediately resumed her activities, joining a neo-Populist group organized by chemist Gregori Gershuni, who used his scientific expertise to plan and execute attacks on government officials. In 1901 Breshkovsky and Gershuni helped found the Socialist Revolutionary Party (Partia sotsialistov-revoliutsionerov, sometimes abbreviated as PSR), or Socialist Revolutionaries (SRs). Although the "terrorist" label has uniformly negative connotations today, in the context of the Russian revolutionary cause, the term resonated quite differently. SRs and most of the other Russian terrorist groups did not set out to kill innocents but rather to attack and strike fear in those who had been personally responsible for persecuting opponents of the regime. Their rationale was that because no legal means of protest existed, violence was an unfortunate necessity. Terrorism was seen as an expression of intense sympathy for good people who suffered unjustly. It served as a warning to other potential oppressors. And it brought a kind of awed admiration for those willing to stand up to those in power. As Gershuni was said to have declared at his trial, "History may forgive you all the blood you have shed and all the crimes you have committed . . . but it will not forgive you for forcing the apostles of love and freedom to take up arms." Although Gershuni was arrested for his SR work, Breshkovsky escaped to Romania and from there undertook her US tour.[16]

Two non-English-speaking SRs in New York asked anarchist and orator Emma Goldman to arrange a meeting with the SAFRF to solicit support for Breshkovsky's visit. Goldman was eager to help. Indeed, her very approach to life had been shaped by a desire to embody the Russian revolutionary ideal. Born in 1869 in the Russian province of Kovno, Goldman was raised in an Orthodox Jewish family. When Emma was thirteen, her family moved to Saint Petersburg, where Czar Alexander II had recently been assassinated by members of the People's Will, a Populist group. Goldman became caught up in the maelstrom of new ideas that flooded Russia during this period: the nihilists, among whom women and men fought "shoulder to shoulder," "became to [Goldman] heroes and martyrs, henceforth [her] guiding stars."[17]

By the 1880s "nihilist" was practically synonymous in conservative circles with "bomb-thrower," but for rebellious types it signaled commitment to the "radical remaking of Russian society" and the creation of a "new people," themes at the center of Chernyshevsky's *What Is to Be Done?* (1863), a book that Emma Goldman devoured as a young woman in Saint Petersburg, just as Anna Strunsky would devour it as a young immigrant in the United States. That book's female heroine, Vera Pavlovna, seeks and finds both sexual emancipation and socially useful labor through her involvement in a revolutionary milieu. She initially enters into a platonic marriage to escape a stifling and oppressive family life; later, living her personal life on terms that suit her, Vera organizes a sewing cooperative that produces beautiful, useful things while simultaneously offering other women a road to independence. Vera then studies to become a doctor. Marked by her "black woolen dress of the plainest description," short hair, education, and independent spirit, the female nihilist, or *nigilistka*, was the most striking representative of the new ethos of a generation of activists who rejected convention, adopted characteristic "manners, dress, [and] friendship patterns," and embraced a radical materialism, choosing faith in science over faith in God.[18]

Although many Russian men cited as inspiration a minor character in Chernyshevsky's book, Rakhmetov—a revolutionary who sleeps on wooden planks, subsists on black bread and steak, studies intensively, and performs gymnastics daily—women consistently cited Vera as a role model. Emma Goldman, not long after immigrating to Rochester, New York, left a loveless marriage, embraced anarchism and free love, and moved to Manhattan, where she "hoped to realize [her] dream of a cooperative shop . . . something like Vera's venture in *What's* [*sic*] *to be Done?*" She even set up her living arrangements to echo Chernyshevsky's novel, moving into an apartment with two men who shared her commitment to free love. Events in Russia were never far from Goldman's mind, and more than once she contemplated returning to aid the fight.[19]

So it was that Goldman came to act as the liaison between the Russian exile community in the United States and Breshkovsky. Goldman joined a local branch of the Socialist Revolutionaries, believing that organization offered the best means of supporting a cause that had captivated her since childhood. Suspecting the respectable SAFRF would not want to associate with a known firebrand, Goldman, in secret collusion with Alice Stone Blackwell, invited the SAFRF president William Dudley Foulke, a distinguished lawyer, civic reformer, and art patron, to the home of "Miss E. G. Smith." Under this guise, the notorious anarchist Emma Goldman drank tea with Foulke and Stone Blackwell in her apartment and obtained Foulke's pledge to sponsor and publicize Breshkovsky's visit.[20]

Babushka on Tour

Breshkovsky arrived in New York in the fall of 1904 and was immediately surrounded by adoring fans in New York's radical immigrant community. Goldman hung back, "not wishing to swell the number" of admirers. She approached that first encounter with great anticipation. "The women in the Russian revolutionary struggle, Vera Zassulitch [*sic*], Sophia Perovskaya, Jessie Helfman, Vera Figner, and Catherine Breshkovskaya, had been my inspiration ever since I had first read of their lives, but I had never met one of them face to face," she recalled. She found Breshkovsky staying in a badly lit, poorly heated flat, "dressed in black . . . wrapped in a thick shawl, a black kerchief over her head, leaving the ends of her waving gray hair exposed." She looked like an old peasant woman, except for her eyes, which conveyed youthfulness as well as "wisdom and understanding." Breshkovsky's effect on Goldman was remarkable yet also typical: "Ten minutes in her presence made me feel as if I had known her all my life; her simplicity, the tenderness of her voice, and her gestures, all affected me like the balm of a spring day," Goldman recalled.[21]

Social settlements' outreach to recent immigrants, many of them from Russia, made settlement houses especially welcoming to Breshkovsky. Seeking to ameliorate the negative effects of industrialization, urbanization, and immigration, settlement workers turned out to be some of

Breshkovsky's most important allies, and major promoters of "Russian freedom" more generally. Influenced by the prevalent Christian socialism of the day, settlement workers also took particular inspiration from Russian thinkers such as Leo Tolstoy, whose personal brand of Christian anarchism called for asceticism, communal living, and nonviolent resistance, and Peter Kropotkin, whose philosophy of "mutual aid" revised social Darwinism's creed of "survival of the fittest" to claim an evolutionary advantage to society's best cooperators. For many of these reformers, then, Breshkovsky seemed like a font of wisdom and a model of dedication to a righteous cause. Residents from wealthy backgrounds were impressed by the fact that Breshkovsky had given up her own material comfort to support the betterment of the masses. For women who had found in settlement house work a socially acceptable way to influence the public sphere, Breshkovsky offered an especially compelling model of a meaningful life lived to its fullest.[22]

Just before Breshkovsky left New York to begin a circuit of lectures and meetings, Goldman hosted a gathering for important members of the settlement community, including "gentlemen socialists" from the University Settlement, among them Graham Phelps Stokes, Leroy Scott, Kellogg Durland, Arthur Bullard, and William English Walling. They were joined by Lillian Wald, whose Henry Street Settlement House was a kind of hub for Russian revolutionaries passing through New York.[23] A handful of University Settlement men wound up being so impressed by Breshkovsky that they decided to go to Russia in order serve her cause directly.

Lillian Wald hosted Breshkovsky for several weeks and afterward became one of her most avid supporters. A German Jew from a well-established, liberal Rochester family, Wald felt a sense of duty to her impoverished brethren arriving from Eastern Europe. Although Wald met only a few female revolutionists in person, women nonetheless struck her as the revolutionaries' most significant representatives. As she noted in her 1915 memoir, "The young women, intrepid figures, are significant not only of the long-continued struggle for political deliverance, but of the historical progress of womankind toward intellectual and social freedom." Among all the revolutionaries she met, she called Babushka the "most beloved of all who have suffered for the great cause" and described her as "a symbol of the Russian revolution." Wald recalled evenings around the fire listening to Breshkovsky's tales of prison, exile, hard labor, and her work on behalf of others. Most remarkably, Wald recalled, Breshkovsky had "looked back upon that time as wonderful because of the beautiful and valiant souls who were her fellow-prisoners and companions, young women who had given up more than life itself for the great cause of liberty."[24]

Wald put Breshkovsky in touch with Hull House director Jane Addams in Chicago, who likewise hosted Babushka. Addams's outlook and work had been deeply influenced by Tolstoy, whom she had met in Russia in 1896. Several years before that, Hull House hosted Kropotkin, whose philosophy of mutual aid was a revelation to both Addams and her partner Ellen Gates Starr. Though Breshkovsky suspected that Addams was wary of her radical ties, Starr and Babushka formed a deep connection. Wald may have also connected Breshkovsky with Helena Dudley, who hosted Babushka at Denison House, the Boston settlement she directed. Dudley later insisted that no six years of her life had been as valuable as the six weeks she spent with Babushka.[25]

Without a doubt, Breshkovsky's closest friend and most tireless supporter in the United States was Alice Stone Blackwell. Hailing from a distinguished Massachusetts family of reformers, a "rather tall, very thin" unmarried woman living frugally on an allowance provided by her father and devoted to Russian freedom and woman suffrage, Stone Blackwell was at the center of a network of women who corresponded with Breshkovsky for decades.[26]

Stone Blackwell once claimed that Kropotkin's *Memoirs of a Revolutionist* (serialized in the *Atlantic* between September 1898 and September 1899) drew her into the struggle for Russian freedom, but her family heritage of abolitionism and women's rights predisposed her to feel sympathy for the Russian cause. After almost singlehandedly reviving the SAFRF in 1903, Stone Blackwell began using the suffrage-oriented *Woman's Journal*, founded by her parents but now under her direction, as a forum for the Russian cause. For instance, a 1904 article by Charlotte Perkins Gilman compared Russia's oppression of Jews to the treatment of African Americans in the United States. The *Woman's Journal* was one of the few news outlets run by whites that made this connection.[27]

Stone Blackwell's skills as a publicist contributed enormously to the success of Breshkovsky's US tour. She wrote press releases, editorials, articles, and letters to the editor and sent them out on a regular basis to dozens of newspapers. She also occasionally lectured for Russian freedom, and she sold her own "translations" of Russian poetry. Though constantly working, Stone Blackwell always wished she could do more; as she wrote to Breshkovsky in January 1905, "Like you, I wish that I had four heads and twelve arms."[28]

Shortly after Breshkovsky's arrival in New York City, Stone Blackwell began lining up events in the Boston area and also helped Breshkovsky make important contacts in New York. Most notably, she connected Breshkovsky with Isabel Barrows, a doctor, a linguist, and the wife of the national prison commissioner, Samuel J. Barrows.

Isabel Barrows worked tirelessly for Breshkovsky. She translated Babushka's writings from French into English, gave her English lessons, introduced her at speaking engagements, and took her into her family's influential social circle. "Aunt" Isabel (as Stone Blackwell called her) also began lecturing on the situation facing Russian prisoners and dissidents, parlaying the authority she held on such matters by virtue of her husband's position. One of Barrows's lectures inspired a woman in the audience to donate fifty dollars for a bomb: "Not that it was spent for that. Not yet anyway," Barrows half-joked. Over time, three generations of the Barrows family became involved in the support of Breshkovsky and her work.[29]

Stone Blackwell and Breshkovsky did not actually meet until December 1904, by which time Breshkovsky had been in the United States for several weeks. After their first meeting, Stone Blackwell wrote, "She is a wonderful woman. We discussed Terrorism." Though on the surface more a staid New England spinster than a free love rabble-rouser like Goldman, Stone Blackwell was unapologetic in her support of efforts to unseat the czarist regime by any means necessary. In correspondence with Breshkovsky's protégé, George Lazarev, Stone Blackwell expressed willingness "to render service to the cause of Russian freedom on very short notice, without explanation." Perhaps because of her unquestioned re-spectability, she took special delight in collaborating with Goldman to craft Goldman's E. G. Smith persona, revealing their ruse with evident relish to select friends.[30]

Stone Blackwell received more requests for Breshkovsky to speak in the Boston area than she could possibly handle during a ten-day stay, forcing a return engagement. Breshkovsky spoke almost every day, some-times twice. Her biggest event in the Boston area was a gathering of three thousand people in Faneuil Hall sponsored by the SAFRF. There, after speeches by William Dudley Foulke, Henry Blackwell, Julia Ward Howe, and Abraham Cahan (editor of the Yiddish *Jewish Daily Forward*) and several more addresses in Polish, Yiddish, and German, Breshkovsky stepped up to the podium. She was greeted by such sustained cheering that she could not proceed for several minutes. An article in the *Woman's Journal* described the scene, "Handkerchiefs waved, hats were flung up into the air, words of affection in five languages were rained upon her from all parts of the hall, and the applause was deafening."[31]

In this as in all her lectures, Breshkovsky emphasized the importance of moral and material support from all civilized nations, the readiness of the Russian peasants for self-government, the threat that Russia's rulers posed to freedom everywhere, and the righteousness of all those opposed to the czar. Her speech was met with a standing ovation, and newspapers featured her prominently the following day. An article in the *Boston Her-ald* was headlined "Cradle Rocked for Free Russia!"[32]

From Boston Breshkovsky returned to New York, where she ad-dressed a large audience at Cooper Union. She also spent more time in the settlements, at private homes, at immigrant gatherings, and also at several girls' schools, where she sang the virtues of education and ser-vice. Goldman served as Breshkovsky's interpreter at several events. She also arranged a number of private gatherings with influential acquain-tances. After long, late evenings speaking in public, Breshkovsky would often spend the night at Goldman's flat, bounding up her five flights of stairs. When Goldman asked the older woman how she managed to maintain her youthfulness and energy, despite years of prison and exile, Breshkovsky replied: "I had much to inspire and sustain me. . . . But what have you in a country where idealism is considered a crime, a rebel an outcast, and money the only god?"[33]

Publicly, Breshkovsky offered praises for the United States, whose citizens, she argued, were morally bound to support her cause. To her own comrades, however, she complained of Americans' relative stinginess when it came to offering real material support for the Russian Revolution. As she wrote to Felix Volkhonsky, a Russian émigré and SR living in London, "Damned America finds some nice excuses. Rich and poor ladies fuss over me, take care, but there is still no money. . . . The newspapers write about Russia very well and correct, their reports are very full and detailed; [everybody] sympathizes with the people, and tears down the government and the czar's family; agrees that one cannot avoid violence—and yet doesn't give any money. [They are] greedy like all the rich, and cowards."[34]

Breshkovsky's speeches drew huge crowds of varying political stripes. In Newark, New Jersey, Hugh M. Pentecoast, a radical preacher from New Harmony, Indiana, introduced Breshkovsky as a living monument to freedom. In Philadelphia, Breshkovsky attracted an audience so large that she had to follow her first address with a second one a few blocks away for an overflow crowd of one thousand. Breshkovsky drove the crowd wild by waving a red flag that had been presented by an audience member. She also threw her arms around a surprised Reverend Russell H. Conwell after he introduced her, followed by a welcome from the notorious anarchist Voltairine de Cleyre, speaking "not as an American, but as an anarchist."[35]

Breshkovsky painted images of suffering, indignity, and injustice in gripping detail. She described marching on foot across the frozen steppes, with a gun pointed at her back. She told of meeting peasants in small mud huts, so stirring grown men with reminders of the oppression that they and their loved ones had endured that they cried out, causing cows in the next room to start bellowing. In one speech, she recalled a group of female convicts forced into prostitution by the government, "by which plan every officer, every functionary, and every soldier, along with their friends and acquaintances, might profit according to his desire." Such indignities gave the revolutionaries "a right, nay a duty, to combat with all our strength, and by every means in our power, the despotism which is the supreme cause of the woes of our land." It also proved why liberty-loving Americans must support their efforts.[36]

Breshkovsky was in Chicago on Bloody Sunday, the January day that thousands of peaceful marchers in Saint Petersburg, led by the dissident preacher Father Gapon, were massacred. She was now in greater demand than ever. Women rushed in such droves to hear Breshkovsky speak at one event that several were trampled. And now her fundraising efforts paid off: by the time she left, cutting short her tour to join the growing revolution, she had raised $10,000, which she used to buy weapons; Goldman helped her ship them to Russia through a reliable contact.[37]

Many of Breshkovsky's friends and admirers urged the aging revolutionary to stay in America, citing the danger that surely awaited her in Russia. An acquaintance of Stone Blackwell's in Boston insisted that the "best thing" would be for Breshkovsky to stay in the United States to "raise money to buy arms and ammunition, and arm the peasantry." But Stone Blackwell knew Babushka would go, had to go: "The news from Russia makes me almost wish to go there myself and help," she confessed.[38] Breshkovsky headed back to Russia in March 1905.

Those who met Breshkovsky never forgot the experience. Helena Dudley profusely thanked Babushka for the model of conscious living she offered: "You showed us all how life should be lived—for great ends and not for comfort or personal gains in any way. It's more help to meet one person who *lives* as you do than to read all the books in the world about noble living." Ellen Gates Starr of Chicago's Hull House had a similar experience. "I can hardly tell you without seeming extravagant to your so modest self what was the experience of knowing you. You seem to belong to all souls, all minds, small and great. There are, indeed, no boundaries or limits of family, nation, or race to your wonderful, loving human interest, which entrances us all." And Helen Todd, a factory inspector in Chicago, wrote Breshkovsky, "You brought so much into our lives here in Chicago that the whole city seems less worth living in now that you are gone." Years later, as an outspoken member of the National Woman's Party, Todd was one of many activists for woman suffrage in the United States who explored how the Russian Revolution might offer new models of women's citizenship.[39]

The Romance of Russia

Though often tempted to follow Breshkovsky back to Russia, Goldman stayed in New York and started a business as "E. G. Smith, Vienna Scalp and Face specialist." While she actually did treat clients, her office at 17th Street also served well as a cover for her Russian work. During the summer of 1905 on Hunter Island, Manhattan, Goldman, her niece Stella, and some other friends played host to a Russian theatre troupe led by Paul Orlenev and Alla Nazimova. Goldman spent her days that summer commuting back to the hot city; in the evenings, she would join the Orlenev troupe around a bonfire, singing to Orlenev's guitar accompaniment, "the strains echoing far over the bay as the large *samovar* buzzed, [and] our regrets of the day were forgotten. Russia filled our souls with the plaint of her woe." Goldman helped set up a theatre on the Lower East Side for Orlenev's troupe, whose American premiere coincided with a general strike in Moscow and Saint Petersburg in October. To Goldman, it seemed as though the revolution was coming to its fruition:

> The news of the Russian revolution of 1905 was electrifying and carried us to ecstatic heights. . . . The ferment in the Tsar-ridden land had finally come to a head; the subdued social forces and the pent-up suffering of the people had broken and had at last found expression in the revolutionary tide that swept our *Matushka Rossiya* [Mother Russia]. The radical East Side lived in a delirium, spending almost all of its time at monster meetings and discussing these matters in cafes, forgetting political differences and brought into close comradeship by the glorious events happening in the fatherland.[40]

The dancer Isadora Duncan was touring in Russia at the time of the Bloody Sunday massacre, and later she claimed that the sight of a funeral cortege for the victims was what made her decide to devote her life and work to the "down-trodden." The failed 1905 revolution and a series of pogroms against Russian Jews, both of which sent waves of immigrants into the United States, did much to further turn American sympathies against the czarist regime.[41]

While Goldman worked from the United States, in the fall of 1905 Anna Strunsky, with whom this chapter opened, felt irresistibly drawn to Russia, not just by the revolution, but also by a letter from the gentleman-socialist William English Walling, whose encounter with Breshkovsky had inspired him and several other men from the University Settlement to head to Russia. Their Revolutionary News Bureau became the hub for US news of Russia beginning in 1905. Walling, impressed by Strunsky's work for the California Friends of Russian Freedom, invited the twenty-eight-year-old to join him in Saint Petersburg. Coming off of a failed romance with the author Jack London, Strunsky decided to go, taking her younger sister Rose along as a chaperone. The sisters told their father they were going to Geneva, which was only partly a lie: after Geneva they went to Berlin, where the young women obtained visas from the Russian consulate by misrepresenting themselves as native-born citizens of the United States. They arrived in Saint Petersburg on the Russian Christmas Eve.[42]

Saint Petersburg in 1905 was a "great bazaar of the revolution." Vendors sold pamphlets with portraits of Marx, Bakunin, and Kropotkin. Bookshops featured photographs of revolutionaries such as Sophia Perovksaya, Vera Zasulich, and Vera Figner. A "cartoon portray[ed] the Czar swimming in a sea of blood, mice gnawing away at the foundation of the throne."[43]

Like Goldman, Anna Strunsky had dreamed of returning to Russia for years: "From earliest childhood I felt the spell of that world. I felt the call of its many sorrows, I felt the infatuation of its martyrdom out of which grew the unparalleled heroism of its people. Voices from buried men and women reached me across a distance of an ocean and two continents, hands seemed stretched towards me, hands which in thought and fancy I grasped and covered with tears." Strunsky, "like all Russians," and many Americans as it turned out, "saw in Russia not Russia but the world."[44]

Anna Strunsky's return to the land of her birth had special resonance for another reason: "I found Russia the same hour that I found love," she professed to her father within weeks of her arrival. Anna confessed the truth of the trip but insisted that it was "fated": "Russia had stood for quite other things, but the man I love and who loves me, so tenderly, dear, as tenderly as mother, and as deeply has opened vistas before me and changed the face of things forever."[45]

Walling (known as "English") hailed from a wealthy, distinguished family: his grandfather had been the Democratic candidate for vice president in 1880, and English attended the University of Chicago and Harvard Law School. But Walling's sympathies, like Strunsky's, were with victims of poverty and injustice: he worked as a factory inspector and helped found the Women's Trade Union League in 1903. Walling was one of several wealthy, Anglo-Saxon men from the University Settlement (Graham Phelps Stokes and Leroy Scott were the others) who married immigrant, Jewish women, all of whom became active supporters of the Russian Revolution.[46]

For Strunsky, excitement and anxiety about the revolution became immediately intertwined with her feelings about Walling. During her first two weeks in Saint Petersburg, she and Walling saw a young man get shot at a restaurant for refusing to sing "God Save the Czar." The pair fled in terror, but the dramatic event seemed to awaken their love: "We were basking in the effulgence," Strunsky said of the feelings that arose that night, "the Russian spirit so fixed on freeing itself, and were receiving as from the source of all inspiration a new faith. We were being born again."[47]

The couple married in Paris in June of 1906 (May Day on the Russian calendar). Karl Marx's grandson attended. Strunsky insisted that it was comradely love, and not marriage or any other convention, that held them together: "Our love is as free as the soul," she wrote her parents that summer. "We hold each other and will hold each other forever, by no force in the world except the force of love."[48]

Despite what Strunsky had told her parents, her relationship with Walling was often strained. And as she questioned her husband's love, she also lost confidence in her work. The two lovers had planned to collaborate on a book about the revolution, and they set about visiting peasant villages and interviewing revolutionaries, but Walling's confidence and certitude as a journalist had the effect of freezing Strunsky creatively. She wrote continuously but rarely finished things. She found it difficult to balance the demands of family life, creative work, and activism. She became pregnant within a year of marriage and was devastated when the child died after five days. Four more (surviving) children followed in quick succession. Walling and Strunsky apparently gave up their collaborative writing project: *Russia's Message* (1908), one of the most important contemporary English-language accounts of the 1905 revolution, was published under Walling's name alone, while most of Strunsky's writings on Russia, including her magnum opus, "Revolutionary Lives"—describing "children of the Revolution" of 1905, individuals "created of passion, of grief, of despair, and of hope; of a divine intolerance toward intolerance and oppression; of a divine ecstasy for justice and love"—remained unpublished.[49]

Strunsky and Walling encouraged the writer Maxim Gorky to take a fundraising tour of the United States to build on the excitement Breshkovsky's visit had generated. Gorky's tour began auspiciously in April 1906 but ended in scandal when the *New York World* revealed that Gorky's traveling companion, the actress Madame Andreyeva, was not his wife but his lover. Quite suddenly, many of Gorky's engagements were canceled, hotels refused him and his companion, and his audiences shrank dramatically. Gorky's wife, from whom he had been separated for some time, even wrote a letter in his defense to the American press. It was to no avail. Making matters worse, Gorky sent a telegram of comradely greetings to striking United Mine Workers, led by the notorious William D. Haywood, who also led the recently founded Industrial Workers of the World. Gorky's implicit expression of affinity between Russia's revolutionary struggles and the plight of American workers made him even less popular with the American establishment.[50]

Gorky did find refuge with the A-Club, a group of artists and intellectuals living cooperatively in a mansion at 3 Fifth Avenue in New York City. The "club" included several former University Settlement residents who were outspoken supporters of the Russian Revolution, among them Ernest Poole, Leroy and Miriam Finn Scott, and Mary Heaton Vorse. The A-Club became a kind of unofficial "press bureau for the Russian 1905–1907 revolution" and center for visiting Russian revolutionaries. Mark Twain, a neighbor of the A-Club, had joined the others for dinner with Gorky before the scandal broke, but later he canceled plans to host a literary reception with William Dean Howells in Gorky's honor.[51]

The prudish response by the American press and public, and the failure of Gorky's sponsors and advocates to come to his defense, points to an association in the popular imagination between socialism and sexual license. Indeed, many of the revolution's supporters feared being tarred with the taint of immorality. Certainly Babushka's lack of visual sex appeal had heightened her effectiveness as a public face of the revolutionary movement in the United States.

The association between revolution and unconventional sexuality did not come out of nowhere. As Emma Goldman noted in her autobiography, "All true revolutionaries had discarded marriage and were living in freedom." Chernyshevsky's influential *What Is to Be Done?* has been described as essentially "a novel about free love." In Chernyshevksy-inspired communes in Russia, "communal living was always arranged in such a way that every person was free to live with whomever he or she wished, and to change partners when the impulse arose." Many Russian radicals believed in the liberating power of love, unfettered by social convention. Bakunin, the father of modern anarchism, raised all of his wife's children, despite the fact that they were fathered by his close friend. Lenin himself, though often considered something of a puritan on sexual matters, loved two women, his wife, Nadezhda Krupskaya, and his beautiful, brilliant mistress, Inessa Armand. Although in the United States only a radical fringe embraced "free love," its principles inspired the same cohort of "American moderns" who celebrated the Russian Revolution when it came in 1917.[52]

Strunsky and Walling were lucky to have been out of the country at the time of Gorky's disastrous visit, which highlighted the breach between Greenwich Village's avant-garde and respectable society. However, they were staying at the A-Club in early 1907 when Breshkovsky's comrade Gregory Gershuni came for a visit that, in contrast to Gorky's, attracted very little attention. By Strunsky's accounting, the fact that Gershuni had escaped from Russian prison in a barrel of cabbage seemed to be of greater interest to the American public than the message he carried.[53]

During this time, Anna's sister Rose, who almost singlehandedly ran the Revolutionary News Bureau in Anna and English's absence, became more directly involved with revolutionary activities. She sheltered assassins in her room in Saint Petersburg and then, after moving to Finland for greater safety, hid dynamite in her quarters. Against the warnings of Socialist Revolutionaries, Rose returned to Saint Petersburg in late summer 1907. Ten days after Anna and English joined her there, Rose was arrested. Hours later, English and Anna were arrested as well. All of them were released within twenty-four hours, thanks to intervention by US secretary of state Elihu Root. For both Anna and Rose, the experience of imprisonment with Russian revolutionary women deepened their commitment.[54]

"How Narrow Seems the Round of Ladies' Lives": Babushka and the Revolution'

Breshkovsky, in the meantime, having avoided recapture for nearly two years after returning to Russia, was caught in 1907 and immediately imprisoned, provoking an international outcry. A petition featuring the signatures of fifty prominent New Yorkers was sent to the czar, to no avail. Isabel Barrows, "heartsick to think of that caged eagle," twice traveled to Saint Petersburg to present a petition to the Russian prime minister. Barrows disingenuously claimed to know nothing about Breshkovsky's calls for violence, telling the prime minister she had come as "one old woman pleading for another."[55] The prime minister rejected her arguments.

Breshkovsky's trial became linked to that of Nicholas Tchaikovsky. This was mainly because of the timing of their arrests, although they were, coincidentally, known as the grandmother and father of the Russian Revolution.[56] Breshkovsky's trial in March 1910 lasted only two days. When asked her profession, Breshkovsky declared that she was a revolutionary. Her sentence of lifetime exile in Siberia was actually considered mild by most of her supporters. Even so, the trial and sentencing produced a new wave of outspoken support for Breshkovsky and for the revolution.

Poet Elsa Barker published a tribute to Breshkovsky in the *New York*

Times that was reprinted widely. It begins by comparing Breshkovsky to ladies of leisure in the United States: "How narrow seems the round of ladies' lives / And ladies' duties in their smiling world / The day this Titan woman, gray with years / Goes out across the void to prove her soul!" And it ends with a message of hope and inspiration that Breshkovsky's travails offered those same women: "You are too great for pity. After you / We send not sobs, but songs; and all our days / We shall walk bravelier knowing where you are."[57]

Lillian Wald, visiting Russia in 1910 as part of a world tour, had hoped to see Breshkovsky but quickly concluded her efforts would be fruitless. "In Russia a great movement has just been crushed," Wald told a reporter, "and the situation at present seems hopeless." Wald had discovered that "tales of [Breshkovsky's] heroism, though suppressed in the newspapers by the Government, had leaked out, and that though she is imprisoned she is still through these stories a factor in the revolution and an inspiration." Going on from Russia to England, Wald focused her energies on meeting with exiled revolutionaries: Tchaikovsky (who had secured his release), Kropotkin, "and some of the 'comrades' who had given all and would gladly give more for their cause."[58]

Rose Strunsky, now back in New York, used the publicity surrounding Breshkovsky's trial and sentencing as an occasion to publish several pieces on revolutionary figures she had met. Her August 1910 piece "Siberia and the Russian Woman" begins with Breshkovsky but puts her sentencing in the context of women's ongoing bravery and activism on behalf of the revolution. Likening the young women she met in prison to "beautiful nymphs and dryads," she describes them in admiring and almost eroticized terms: "Their bodies were lithe and supple and showed strongly underneath their little waists and skirts. And such gentleness in the touch of their hands, and such tenderness hanging around the eyes and mouth!" In prison, these women seemed at the height of their loveliness: "The Russian woman revolutionist is not in her element on the streets," Rose insists. "She hurries along in a little black serge skirt—the inevitable pockets bulging with literature—and a short black jacket and fur cap; uncorseted, bent forward, her hair first braided and then pinned low on her neck; with an intense manner, as if she were in great anxiety not to miss the Czar and throw the bomb. She needs a prison to show her off."⁵⁹ Strunsky's descriptions hint at the possibility that the Russian revolutionary ethos provided not only a model for romantic love but, in some cases, a substitute for it.

Breshkovsky herself, though nearly always portrayed in grandmotherly terms, had experienced erotic love, leaving a husband, and then a child, for the revolution. Thus her offhand reference to Helena Dudley, Alice Stone Blackwell, and Ellen Gates Starr as "you three virgins who have devoted yourselves to serving the world without asking anything of it" implies that some women's erotic desires were sublimated to passion for the revolution. Yet all these women had long-term relationships with other women. Nontraditional erotic relations, from heterosexual unions defined in terms of "free love" to homosexual partnerships, often went hand in hand with commitment to social transformation and, by extension, support for the Russian Revolution.⁶⁰

In exile in the Siberian village of Kirensk, on the Arctic Circle, Breshkovsky was sustained, materially and emotionally, by the kindness and generosity of her American friends. Isabel Barrows took it upon herself to collect and send funds each month to the extent that authorities allowed. But following the death of a contributor, an aging Barrows, fearing for Breshkovsky's well-being after her own death, wrote Mary Hilliard, headmistress of Westover, an elite girls school in Connecticut. She told Babushka's story and asked whether the girls might be willing to help her. So it was that the girls of Westover School "adopted" the terrorist Little Grandmother of the Russian Revolution. Barrows was overwhelmed with gratitude. To Hilliard she wrote: "Their unconscious influence will reach from Westover far over the Russian steppes to cold Siberia, bringing light and warmth and gladness, not only to Babushka, but to every exile whom she knows. They place their hands in their pocketbooks and lo; they touch worldwide interests."⁶¹

In return for the generosity of friends (and strangers), Breshkovsky sent long, thoughtful letters full of wisdom and advice for living a rich, full life. To her "young friends and comrades" at Westover she commented, "All my life I strained to serve my fellow human beings—for I understood that nothing in our world is so high spirited, so beautiful—as the human soul. It can be spoiled, can take a fauls [*sic*] course, a bad direction while running through life's difficulties, but when rightly addressed, rightly shown to its very end from its childhood—our mind and feelings are apt to gain the more elevated regions of the divine spirit."[62]

In December 1913, aided by funds from her American friends, Breshkovsky nearly managed to escape. A male political prisoner had dressed himself in Breshkovsky's clothes while the elderly woman, wearing his clothes, traveled for five days across the tundra. Within miles of the border, Breshkovsky was caught, moved to an even more remote location, and placed under greater surveillance.

Americans continued to hold meetings in support of Breshkovsky and to petition Russian authorities on her behalf. They extended sympathy as well as amnesty to other exiles and revolutionaries. Onetime bomb-thrower Marie Sukloff was warmly welcomed at Hull House and Henry Street Settlement. Child welfare pioneer Grace Abbott recalled later, "After one of our long arguments at the Hull House dinner table, the woman from Siberia [Sukloff] laughed and said 'I haven't felt so much at home since I first joined the Terrorists.'" Isabel Barrows's daughter, Mabel Barrows Mussey, eventually set Sukloff up in a comfortable home in Croton-on-the-Hudson, where she stayed until the Bolshevik revolution lured her back to Russia.[63]

The Russian feminist Alexandra Kollontai made a five-month propaganda tour of the United States in 1915 aimed at building support for Lenin and the Bolsheviks and at convincing Americans to stay out of the war that had already consumed much of Europe. "Victory of the warring nations will mean nothing to the common people of the victorious country," she insisted. Like Breshkhovsky, Kollontai was a daughter of the Russian nobility who had cast her lot with revolutionaries. She was part of a rival faction, but the two women shared many admirers. Visiting eighty-one US cities and giving speeches in German, French, and Russian, usually at events sponsored by the Socialist Party, Kollontai not only spoke against war; she also gave speeches on feminism, calling motherhood (in comments reprinted in papers ranging from the *Daily Ardmoreite* in Ardmore, Oklahoma, to the *Bismarck [ND] Daily Tribune*) "not only a private privilege but a social duty, which the state should insure." Like Grace Abbott, Julia Lathrop, and other child welfare reformers, Kollontai supported mother's pensions, day care, child labor laws, and other improvements in maternal and child welfare. Positive statements about Kollontai's work by members of the Children's Bureau would later be used against the American child welfare movement.[64]

Greeting the Revolution

When revolution finally came to Russia in February 1917, American women and men who had followed and supported various revolutionaries for years were ecstatic. Lillian Wald wrote to Alice Stone Blackwell, "Rejoicing with you over news so wonderful it strains the power of realization. News just received from New York that Duma has ordered a committee to escort Babushka to Petrograd."[65]

During the journey by sledge from Minusinsk, Siberia, to the nearest stop on the Trans-Siberian Railway, and, later, on a train, Babushka was repeatedly asked to give speeches. By the time she arrived in Saint Petersburg, her train car had become filled with flowers from admirers. She was greeted by thunderous applause and introduced as "the woman who inspired the Russian Revolution." Installed in an office in the Winter Palace, Breshkovsky was chosen to serve in the Preliminary Parliament of Russia. She joyfully celebrated the revolution's victory, declaring "If we all aspire towards freedom and equality what differences can there be between us? What is there to disagree about?"[66] Plenty, as it turned out.

The Little Grandmother of the Russian Revolution: Reminiscences and Letters of Catherine Breshkovsky, which Alice Stone Blackwell edited and published in November 1917, ended with inspirational words that Breshkovsky had once written to an American friend: "We ought to elevate the people's psychology by our own example, and give them the idea of a purer life by making them acquainted with better morals and higher ideals; to call out their best feelings and strongest principles. We ought to tell the truth, not fearing to displease our hearers; and be always ready to confirm our words by our deeds."[67]

The timing of Stone Blackwell's book implied Breshkovsky's ties to the Russian Revolution as it ultimately played out, but in fact she was an outspoken foe of the Bolsheviks, whose authoritarian structure and repressive methods repelled the more democratic (though still violent) SRs. Not long after the Bolsheviks' victory over the more moderate Provisional Government, Breshkovsky went into hiding and ultimately into exile in Czechoslovakia. At one point in 1918, the American media reported that she'd been shot by the Bolsheviks. Yet many of Breshkovsky's American allies, though sympathizing with her plight and understanding why she condemned the Bolsheviks' dictatorial methods, refrained from criticizing the new regime.[68]

Breshkovsky scheduled a return American tour in 1919 in order to build support for the SRs' efforts to undermine the Bolshevik government and, more practically, to raise money for the legions of children made orphans by the chaos in Russia. Visiting Westover School for the first time, Babushka was delighted to meet some of the idealistic young women who had supported her for years. One student recalled that upon arriving Breshkovsky "caught sight of one of our colored maids . . . [and] fairly flew from one maid to another, throwing her arms about each one in turn, kissing them first on one cheek, then on the other, saying brokenly 'dear children; not long from slavedom—so happy here and so free.'" She listened to a group of girls sing and then offered them renditions of Russian folk songs and even dances (she was seventy-six). And she addressed the girls, switching between English, French, and Russian, about conditions in Russia and her hopes for the future, "always with the simplicity of a child, so naïve while so wise, so outgoing toward all the world, with such a wealth of experience." It was one of the most unforgettable experiences of this young woman's schooling. As she recalled, Breshkovsky "seemed as she moved among us to create a wonderful atmosphere of heroism and eternal hope."[69]

During this tour, however, Breshkovsky also alienated some of her old friends. They feared that in proclaiming the evils of Bolshevism (even testifying to Congress), Babushka would only help reactionary forces in both Russia and the United States. Right-wingers eagerly lapped up and promoted Breshkovsky's tales of Bolshevik treachery. "Wherever she went [Breshkovsky] was feted and acclaimed by all the enemies of socialism, while most of the working people regarded her with grief and

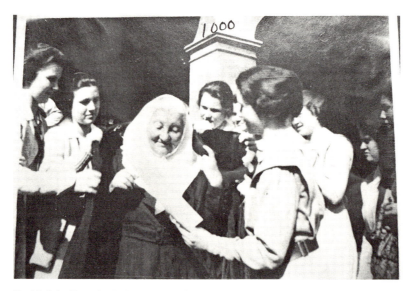

Fig. 1.2 Babushka and girls of Westover in 1919. Image courtesy of Westover School, Middlebury, CT. Though this picture was taken fifteen years after her first visit to the United States in 1904, Breshkovsky's appearance is remarkably similar to that in photographs from her earlier visit.

bitterness," Stone Blackwell recalled. She felt that Babushka had an idealized and naïve view of the United States: "She would not believe us when we told her that our government was just as selfish as the governments of Britain and France; that the great financial interests which largely control our foreign policy would much rather see the monarchy restored in Russia than to see any sort of Socialist government allowed to succeed there." Privately Stone Blackwell admitted that she herself would rather have seen the Provisional Government succeed than the Bolsheviks, but compared the situation to the French Revolution, in which that revolution's "worst excesses" were preferable to "restoration of monarchy and reaction." Wald, likewise, refused to publicly condemn the Bolsheviks, insisting that the new government should be given a chance to succeed or fail on its own terms.[70]

The journalist Louise Bryant, who had met with Babushka in Russia after the February Revolution, speculated on why the "Little Grandmother" refused to support the new government: "There is nothing strange in the fact that Babushka took no part in the November revolution. History almost invariably proves that those who give wholly of themselves in their youth to some large idea cannot in their old age comprehend the very revolutionary spirit which they themselves began; they are not only unsympathetic to it, but usually they offer real opposition. And thus it was that Babushka, who stood so long for political revolution, balked at the logical next step, which is class struggle. It is a matter of age."[71]

Anna Strunsky sought out Breshkovsky immediately after her arrival in New York City in 1919. By this time Strunsky's marriage had fallen apart because of ideological differences: English supported US entry into World War I, while Anna didn't; English was appalled by the Bolsheviks, while Anna thought they deserved a chance to prove themselves. Strunsky asked Breshkovsky "why she attacks the Bolsheviki who, like her, were propagandists of socialist principles and who, in the long history of the revolution, had also gone to Siberia and the scaffold for their ideas." Babushka explained that Lenin and his followers cared more for principles than for people, they inhumanely believed that ends justify means, and they had given all to "the masses" without regard to the "thieves and robbers" who "took advantage of their propaganda." Strunsky was unmoved. Perhaps Breshkovsky had become an elitist, Strunsky mused: "When the idea is taken up by the many, it loses some of its disembodied purity and its glory." Strunsky suggested that Breshkovsky was basically a nationalist rather than an internationalist: "Returning to see the miracle of a free Russia with her own eyes, and to be to the Russian people as well as to the rest of the world, a living symbol of the tragedy and the triumph, and the struggle for freedom, she found herself defeated at the moment when she seemed to reach the pinnacle of happiness. Bolshevik Russia could not have her sanction or her support. If these were indeed her children, she could not follow them."[72]

Emma Goldman was among those who chided her old friend in 1919 for criticizing the Bolsheviks. Only a few years later, however, Goldman, in exile, changed her tune, predicting the disillusionment that many Soviet supporters would eventually face. After being deported to Soviet Russia under the Alien Act, Goldman was horrified by the Bolsheviks' violent suppression of all opposition. Feeling compelled to act on her conscience, she publicized the truth as she knew it, making the distance between her and her former comrades in the United States more than geographical, and predicting the way in which views about the Soviet Union would come to divide not just Left and Right in the United States but also the Left itself.[73]

The tremendous dedication among a range of women to Catherine Breshkovsky, a hero in her time who is now forgotten—like many others featured in Strunsky's still unpublished "Revolutionary Lives"—offers a vivid reminder of what originally attracted idealistic, independent, and liberated American women to the Russian revolutionary struggle. In the years immediately following the Bolshevik revolution, some of these same reformers and rebels would support or even join relief efforts to save Russian children from the ravages of war, famine, and disease, which threatened to destroy the new Russia before its promises—including its promise to transform women's lives—could be realized.

Child Savers and Child Saviors

In an unpublished short story by Louise Bryant, an American woman working for a relief agency in Bolshevik Russia becomes deeply attached to a child, Serge, who lives in a home for refugee children in Petrograd.[1] A happy and well-fed seven-year-old when the story begins, Serge "had all the sun of the south in his eyes and all the music of silver bells in his voice. He was happy and undisturbed and, therefore, restful." During World War I, while fleeing the Germans, Serge became separated from his parents, relatively well-off peasants. He briefly joined a peasant couple on their journey to Petrograd, but in the bustle of the city Serge again found himself alone. Tired and hungry, he threw himself on the ground and began to sob: "A man stopped, then two, then a woman; soon a crowd gathered. They offered him kopecks; he pushed them away; he was lonesome and demanded affection. Russian crowds are peculiar; they are childlike and curious and easily stirred. People walk blocks to give money to beggars. And although Russians weep easily they cannot bear the sight of tears."

A "lady from California" in the crowd, "being truly feminine," took to Serge, and "began at once to love him," bringing him to the children's home where she volunteered. She fretted over him, made plans to take him to the country, and secretly hoped to adopt him. "Anyone with half an eye could tell that the Lady from California was making all her plans to fit Serge. She was teaching him English, remarking wistfully all the while that it would be nice to go home again."

"I used to feel uneasy sometimes when I watched the two together and realized how deeply she loved Serge," the story's narrator notes. "He would ask her every now and then if she thought he would ever see *Momashka* and *Popashka* again and she would always tell him hurriedly that she was *sure* he would. But the lines around her mouth tightened and sometimes she looked almost hard. After all, she was a lonely woman and so we forgave her for whatever was in her mind."

The Lady's plans are not to be realized: Serge's parents eventually and miraculously find him in the refugee home. Watching the boy sitting with his father on a schoolroom bench, happily catching up on the years that have passed, "the Lady from California felt old and forgotten. She waited five minutes, ten minutes, fifteen . . . and they did not notice her. She moved a little closer and coughed. 'Serge,' she said, and there was a high, broken note in her voice, 'what about our trip to the country?'"

Serge's story was based on that of a real boy, Vanya, the centerpiece of Bryant's chapter on Russian children in her book *Six Red Months in Russia* (1918). Vanya had wound up in a refugee home staffed by Americans and was eventually found by his father, who twice a week had walked for miles to scour lists of refugees in various camps. If what was striking about the real story was the fact that the boy and his father were actually reunited, in the fictionalized account this happy reunion is clouded by the obvious sense of loss on the part of the "Lady from California." One wonders whether the Lady from California was, like Serge, based on a real character.

Bryant's depiction of the Lady from California suggests the multiple motivations that drew female relief workers to Russia in the years immediately following the revolution. But this image of the female child saver redeeming the suffering Russian child—and in turn redeemed by the Russian child-as-savior—is complicated by the fact that a number of middle-class women joined Russian relief efforts not only for humanitarian reasons but also to gain entry into revolutionary Russia at a time when essentially all other avenues were closed to them. To varying degrees, they saw relief work as a way to witness and support the revolution.

The apparent contrast in Bryant's story between the proper, spinsterish relief worker and the radical, feminist journalist we know to be the narrator is also somewhat deceiving. The "I" of Bryant's story "used to feel uneasy sometimes" when she saw how much the Lady from California loved Serge. But both "I" and "the Lady" not only yearned to help "Serge" but, in different ways, needed him and were bound to Russia through him. Serge—and by extension Vanya—points to the pivotal role that Russian children played as objects of sympathy, as sources of hope, and as the rationale and essential vehicle for American women to enter Bolshevik Russia.

Humanitarian acts are not just about meeting the needs of others but are always tied to the particular needs and desires of the humanitarian. "Of course, help to the starving is spontaneous philanthropy, but there are few real philanthropists, even among American Quakers," Leon Trotsky is said to have remarked in September 1921 as humanitarian aid to Soviet Russia shifted into high gear with the onset of famine. "Philanthropy is tied to business, to enterprises, to interests—if not to-day, then to-morrow."[2]

A significant number of Western women traveled across the sea and beyond to save Russian children; some, in doing so, believed they were also helping create the dawn of a new world. Russian children—members of the first generation to be shaped by the new, revolutionary ethos— had become central figures in the American Left's fantasies of social regeneration. In 1918, as the radical *Liberator* published accounts of life in Bolshevik Russia by visitors like Louise Bryant, John Reed, and Albert Rhys Williams, it also serially published Floyd Dell's treatise on the "new education," *Were You Ever a Child?*, which linked political revolution in Russia to revolutionary ways of raising children. Critics of American culture would seize on these new child-rearing and educational practices as key to raising a "new generation" who would reject the competitive business ethic of capitalism and create a "new society, more humanistic than any of old, more creative and joyous and inspiring." Announcing plans in 1921 to move to Russia to start a dance school, Isadora Duncan famously declared, "I am eager to see if there is one country in the world that does not worship commercialism more than the mental and physical education of its children."[3]

But hope mixed with horror: as famine swept over a large swath of Russia in the summer of 1921, that country's youngest people became almost unrecognizable as children. When British suffragist and juvenile writer Evelyn Sharp visited Russia in January 1922 to publicize Quaker famine relief, her shock at encountering starvation in the countryside was compounded by the idyllic vision of childhood she had seen in Moscow. "The children are adorable, very merry and inclined to be cheeky if one nearly runs over them with a sleigh because they won't move out of the way," she wrote during one of her first days in Moscow, adding "One rarely sees a child that isn't chubby." A forest school near Moscow seemed to her "a kind of fairyland, avenues and avenues of fir trees stretching away in all directions, with paths of trodden snow, along which boys and girls come skimming on skis, looking delightfully healthy and jolly." A week later, arriving in Samara, Sharp was chastened when she told a Quaker relief worker, Violet Tillard, how charming she found Russian children. "Russian children who are starving have no charm for me," said Tillard, who would herself soon die of typhus.[4]

The suffering Russian child was a double travesty because Soviet childhood was so precious: "I feel more than 'sympathy' with the destitute children of Russia," Helen Keller insisted when asked if the Bolsheviks might name a children's home for the blind in her honor. "I love them because round them clings the sanctity of the ideals and aspirations, the incredible courage and sacrifices of a people who uphold the hope of humanity. . . . The thought is unbearable that they should be sorrowing in a land where there is a passionate desire 'to bring the light of joy into every child's eyes.'"[5] Relief workers had the task of restoring childhood to Russian children. Once this was accomplished, only then could the Bolshevik project of creating new people, new men and new women, truly begin.

The American Friends Service Committee (AFSC) was the only US relief organization to allow women workers on the ground in Russia during the famine. It also refused to apply a political litmus test to its workers (and did not require volunteers to be Quakers). A key player in Russian relief efforts, the AFSC also became a crucial vehicle for women such as Jessica Smith, Anna Louise Strong, and Anna Haines to enter Russia and then launch long-terms efforts on behalf of not just Russian children but also the Bolshevik future. These women, of varied political sensibilities, also had varying levels of success in their endeavors. Anna Louise Strong's intense efforts on behalf of Russian children—and her spectacular failures—are perhaps most instructive.

Suffragists and Soviets

After Louise Bryant left Russia in January 1918, she began a lecture tour, speaking about the revolution and also in support of the radical suffrage organization the National Woman's Party (NWP). Visiting Washington, DC, in the winter of 1919, Bryant spoke at an NWP-sponsored gathering devoted to discussing conditions in revolutionary Russia. Interest in this topic was only to heighten among feminists as their battle for suffrage began to wind down, despite antifeminists' efforts to tar them as "Bolshevists" and un-American.[6]

Just months after the suffrage amendment was passed by Congress in June 1919, a group of women from the NWP (including Harriot Stanton Blatch, Lucy Gwynne Branham, Helen Todd, Helen Keller, Mary Dreier, and Alice Lewisohn) organized the American Women's Emergency Committee (AWEC) to protest an Allied blockade of Russia. Several had referenced revolutionary Russia in their activism to press the supposedly more enlightened US government into likewise granting women suffrage. Both the blockade and the landing of US troops in areas of Russia not controlled by the Bolsheviks were undertaken under the guise of protecting American and Allied interests in the war against Germany; however, the blockade of Soviet Russia continued until July 1920, and unofficially until August 1921, when the American Relief Administration agreed to provide famine relief to a million Russian children.[7]

In the fall of 1919, a peaceful demonstration against the blockade by Russian immigrants was met with violence from police and bystanders alike; in response, the AWEC organized its own series of protests in New York City. On November 2, 150 women marched down Forty-Second Street in Manhattan. At the head of the group, Lucy Branham, "little, young, extremely pretty and a veritable torch of enthusiasm," held an American flag; another woman held a placard reading "We Are American Women." Others carried signs saying "Milk for Russian Babies."[8]

Several weeks later, thirty-five women from the AWEC marched downtown carrying similar banners. Laying a wreath on the tomb of Alexander Hamilton, Mrs. M. Toscan Bennett, a society woman from Hartford, Connecticut, addressed Hamilton's spirit in a speech Louise Bryant had written: "No man better knew than you how hard it is for a new nation to establish itself. . . . It was due to you that trade, which had been cut off from us—was re-opened, it was due to you that American ships were no longer seized by foreign powers. . . . Today, by an inhuman food blockade, . . . America is responsible for the starving of women and children in Russia." Helen Todd then led the women as they marched single file down Wall Street—until Todd was stopped by a policeman and taken in for questioning.[9]

In December, the AWEC published full-page appeals in progressive and radical papers such as the *Nation*, the *Survey*, and the socialist *New York Call*. Echoing campaigns against child labor, one appeal deplored the "bitter cry of the children," highlighting the idea that children's humanity and vulnerability superseded national loyalties: "Hundreds of thousands of children, little children such as ours, are perishing for want of food and medicine in Petrograd, Moscow, and other Russian cities," the appeal declared. Now, with the blockade, "they face the coming Christmas with the world's gates of mercy seemingly shut against them." The AWEC requested one hundred thousand donations for a "Christmas ship," "loaded with goods required by the most needy." Donations were to be sent to the AWEC's treasurer, Jessica Granville Smith.[10]

Over the course of two years, the AWEC raised funds, demonstrated, and lobbied for normalizing relations with Soviet Russia. It also worked closely with the AFSC to coordinate relief efforts. Avowed feminists, women of the AWEC recognized that they could gain greater public sympathy for their work if they emphasized their commitment to helping children. Testifying on behalf of the AWEC in January 1921 before a congressional committee on foreign relations, Harriot Stanton Blatch (daughter of feminist pioneer Elizabeth Cady Stanton) emphasized the threat to civilization posed by Russian children being starved by the blockade: "If our children and the children of Russia and of the near East and the central powers continue to be kept apart by enmities the whole time, continue to have blockades, those children are never going to be normal men and women."[11]

Lucy Branham, who, like Jessica Smith, would shortly travel to Russia and aid AFSC efforts, cited a recent report by Arthur Watts, the British Friends representative in Moscow, describing "the terrible condition among the women and children." Watts's report on "the provision for children in Soviet Russia" did emphasize the dire need for clothing, shoes, soap, food, medicine, school materials, and shelter for millions who had been orphaned. However, although neither Blatch nor Branham mentioned it, Watts also described a range of programs that the Bolsheviks had instituted for the care and education of children, from exhibitions on motherhood to rest homes for working mothers (who were entitled to eight weeks of paid leave before and after giving birth), "milk depots," infant homes (with "very efficient staffs"), children's gardens ("a delightful picture on a warm summer day with little boys and girls at play dressed in single tunics of varied colours just as full of life as one could wish"), children's colonies (with their striking "communal spirit"), and children's theatricals ("everything possible is done to develop their appreciation of the artistic"). Indeed, the report concluded, "if Russia had only the supplies, her children would be thoroughly well cared for and . . . in a short time her institutions would be examples for the rest of the world to follow."[12]

Although foreigners' observations of Soviet Russia were sharply divided (largely along political lines), on the matter of the Bolsheviks' care for children, Watts's conclusions represented something close to a consensus not only among the majority of Quaker volunteers but also among the bulk of liberals and progressives from the West. Margaret

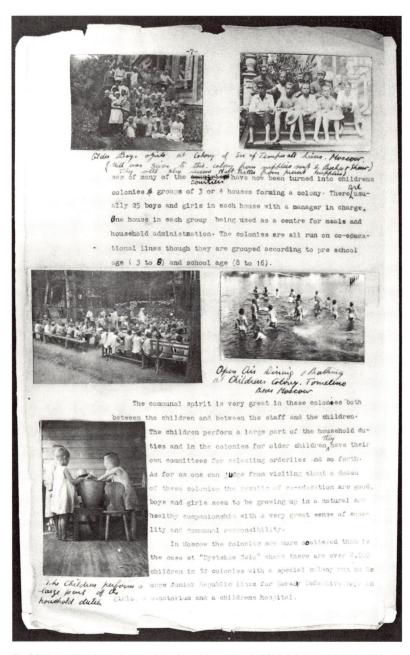

Fig. 2.1 Arthur Watts's report on provision for children in Russia, 1920. © Religious Society of Friends (Quakers) in Britain. Used with permission. The report shows the need for relief but also emphasizes Soviet Russia's positive efforts on behalf of children.

Barber, who'd been part of the original British Friends mission to Russia, devoted significant space in a 1920 report to effusing over Bolshevik programs for children in the form of singing, dancing, and theatricals, and she remarked on the children's self-discipline and their deep desire to learn: "Bolshevik Russia may be the most barbarous country today," she conceded, "but her children are having the best opportunity to prove her the most enlightened country of tomorrow." Jerome Davis, reporting in the *New Republic* on Quaker relief work in Moscow in November 1921, repeated Watts's praise for Bolshevik efforts vis-à-vis children but also added, "The Bolshevik government has publicly stated that in Russia the children come first, that, as long as there is not enough food for all, the children shall have a priority claim. More money is spent on education and food for them than ever before in Russia." Bryant herself echoed these sentiments as a new wave of volunteers began arriving in Soviet Russia in December 1921 and January 1922: "Relief workers will be surprised to find just how much work has been done, for no other war ridden country has so systematically and so earnestly tried to take care of its children as Soviet Russia."[13]

"Children Are the Same to Us the World Over"

Despite the Soviet government's best efforts, by the summer of 1921, the situation confronting the Bolsheviks was more than they could handle. Outdated farming practices and an unreliable climate meant that Russia was long susceptible to periodic famines, but the famine of 1921 was the most extensive and most damaging in modern Russian history. Lowered food prices had induced peasants to dramatically reduce the amount of land under cultivation, as the Allied blockade, which followed on the heels of a blockade by the Central Powers, undercut the market for Russian grain. At the same time, the Bolsheviks instituted "grain requisitioning" to feed the Red Army and to provide for city workers; "requisitioning" was basically a euphemism for forcibly taking peasants' "surpluses." Many peasants responded by refusing to cultivate more than a bare minimum of acreage. By 1920 nearly half the arable land in Russia had gone out of cultivation. When drought in 1920 and 1921 brought repeated crop failure, the results were disastrous. The fledgling Bolshevik government was utterly unprepared to deal with the enormity of the problem it faced. Moreover, the civil war, itself exacerbated by dwindling food supplies, weakened the transportation system, limiting the government's ability to distribute food in areas where it was most needed.[14]

Across thirty-four provinces, twenty-five million people were affected by the famine. In certain provinces, 90 percent of the population was starving, with a significant proportion facing death. In some areas, the famine killed close to 95 percent of all children under three and nearly a third of those who were older. Reports of cannibalism and mass graves, alongside harrowing photographs of children with swollen bellies, wearing rags and listless expressions, shocked the world into action.[15]

In the United States, the Friends of Soviet Russia (FSR), a left-wing group closely tied to the Workers Party (the underground predecessor of the CPUSA), appealed to a broad swath of the labor movement as well as to women of all classes, urging their sympathy both on humanitarian terms and as an act of solidarity with the workers' republic: "Russian women and children must not die because imperialism wants new sacrifices," noted an FSR pamphlet filled with heartrending photographs (several of which were borrowed from the Quakers) of children suffering.[16] The FSR was quick to emphasize the failure of the US government to act promptly and appealed to the sympathies of individuals. The Quakers, by contrast, eschewed political messages and focused on the crisis at hand, which was itself almost unfathomable.

AFSC worker Anna Haines, back in the United States after months in "the heart of the famine country," quickly put things into a chilling perspective: "When one has seen garbage carts full of dead babies, and older children and grown-up people dying from starvation on the streets, and the farm machinery which is almost more important in Russia than human life, scrapped and rusting on the wayside, one loses all desire to follow the fashion of beginning a talk with an epigram or a funny story."[17]

Jessica Smith, writing a year or so later, described a small hut in one of the "richer villages," where four women and two children lived: "On the raised platform where they all sleep one woman is sick with malaria, and

FRIENDS' WORK IN FAMINE STRICKEN RUSSIA.
A GROUP OF FAMINE CHILDREN.
SEND YOUR HELP EARMARKED RUSSIA TO FRIENDS' RELIEF COMMITTEE. 27, CHANCERY LANE, W.C.2.

Fig. 2.2 British Quakers postcard. © Religious Society of Friends (Quakers) in Britain. Used with permission. This same image was used in a booklet published by the Friends of Soviet Russia.

a boy of twelve huddles under a threadbare blanket. His mother lifts the blanket. His face is swollen horribly, his feet are puffed up to twice their size, while the bones in his emaciated body make sharp angles in his thin shirt. When we ask how long he has been suffering like this his distorted face begins to work, and his body shakes with jerky little sobs."[18]

Bryant had concluded her portrait of Russian children in *Six Red Months in Russia* with a plea to help them. Acknowledging that her sympathies toward the Bolshevik revolution might not be shared by many of her readers, Bryant appealed to more basic, human sympathies: "Whatever vast difference of opinion we may hold with the majority of the Russian people, children are the same to us the world over."[19]

That sentiment is at the crux of what historian Thomas Laqueur has called the "humanitarian narrative," in which the accumulation of facts can move readers to feel a personal connection to the suffering of ordinary strangers. That narrative depends, first, on the amassing of detail to create a "reality effect" and, second, on the presence of a "personal body," which exists "as the common bond between those who suffer and those who would help." The onset of photojournalism heightened this humanitarian effect: as Susan Sontag has suggested, "Being a spectator of calamities taking place in another country is a quintessential modern experience."[20] In the case of Russia, this humanitarian discourse was employed on multiple fronts, but especially through verbal descriptions and striking photographs of children, to bind Americans to the future of Russia.

Authors of a radical humanitarian discourse—which contrasted sharply with the humanitarian narrative put forth by relief agencies such as the quasi-governmental American Relief Administration (ARA) and even the ostensibly neutral American Red Cross (ARC)—aimed to build sympathy for the regime by showing that, while the Bolsheviks made children's welfare their top priority and were raising children in such a way as to predict a glorious future, only Americans had the resources to alleviate suffering. This discourse would serve as a key means for enlisting the support of Americans—and American women in particular—for the Bolsheviks.

At a maternity home, where emaciated mothers were giving birth to already-starving babies, journalist Mary Heaton Vorse (one of the few American journalists given permission to enter the famine zone) described "tiny, dying skeletons, jerking their heads from side to side, even in sleep searching with their blue mouths for food." They, like the boy Smith described, are "ghosts of children." And indeed, these children are specters, warning: *This is what they will all look like if you do not help. You may not like the Bolsheviks, but children are the same the world over.* George Bernard Shaw famously declared, in regard to his willingness to help "enemy children" through the Save the Children Fund, "I have no enemies under seven."[21]

World War I proved a key moment for showcasing "the new American internationalism" whereby Americans demonstrated their common commitment to innocent victims of conflicts within and between nation-states. Russia's humanitarian crisis became a rallying cry not just for supporters of the Bolshevik revolution but also for its opponents, an occasion for showcasing democratic and religious values at work. A range of relief organizations, from the Jewish Joint Distribution Committee (JDC), to the American Friends Service Committee (AFSC), to the

Save the Children Fund, were created during or right after World War I. The ARC, though founded earlier, expanded its operations during and immediately after the war. Although usually operating in concert with US foreign policy, the ARC did provide food and medicine to Russian children in Petrograd while American forces battled Bolshevik troops in Siberia. The JDC focused initially on rebuilding communities devastated by war and pogroms. It became an important player in Russia but was hindered in its effort to provide direct relief by ongoing violence there against Jews.[22]

Both British and American Quakers formed international service organizations during the war specifically to create alternatives to military enlistment. Quakers held that "our duty is to move among our fellow-men, kindling their highest nature by the fire in our own souls," with "friendship and whole-hearted generosity." Most fundamentally, Quakers were (and are) dedicated to pacifism and to ending the conditions that produce wars. They believe in "the human capacity for goodness" and stress "person-to-person interaction."[23]

The Social Gospel in general and Quaker theology in particular pointed to ways in which those who work to end human suffering are as much redeemed by their actions as the hungry and the sick are succored by relief.[24] Unlike evangelical Protestants, the majority of Quakers felt less compelled to spread the message of their religion than to enact their faith through deeds. And many were happy to take on non-Quaker volunteers who appeared to share their values. This combination, and the prominence of women in Quaker life, put the AFSC in a unique position when American aid to Russian famine victims shifted into full gear. The Friends also occupied a unique position as intermediaries who were by and large trusted by liberals, American Communists, and Russian Bolsheviks alike.

The ARA, created by congressional appropriation at the end of World War I to distribute relief to war-torn countries, quickly became the largest and most powerful relief agency in the world. It also came to play an outsized role in Russian famine relief efforts, eventually bringing all other relief work by US agencies under its umbrella. Herbert Hoover, whose work feeding starving Belgians during the war earned him a reputation as an outstanding humanitarian, headed the organization. Though it became a private charity in 1919, the ARA remained closely associated with the US government through Hoover, who served as head of the US Food Administration and then as secretary of commerce while directing the ARA.

In the immediate postwar period, the ARA provided aid to thirty-two countries, including parts of White Russia, but withheld aid from Bolshevik-controlled areas. At one point Hoover proposed offering food relief to Soviet Russia if the Bolsheviks would cease military operations within the country, but he did not offer to end American assistance to counterrevolutionary forces or the blockade. Not surprisingly, the Bolsheviks refused Hoover's offer.[25] The famine changed these dynamics considerably: the ARA became the largest supplier of Russian famine relief. Even so, the ARA's association with the US government, and a tacit understanding that both entities opposed the Bolsheviks, framed popular perceptions of the ARA's relief efforts. Moreover, the ARA's reach was limited by the fact that it would only feed children, who by popular consensus were both the neediest and the most deserving of relief.

For American women, the Russian famine highlighted a dynamic tension between, on the one hand, starving Russian children-to-be-saved and, on the other hand, "red-cheeked," "capable, happy, and eager children" who were beneficiaries of a Soviet program to create "self-reliant" builders of "the first socialist commonwealth in the world."[26] This tension between the child-to-be-saved and the child savior of civilization echoed a tension within feminism: namely, women's contradictory desire to be mothers—of their own children, and of the world's children—and to be free from the burdens of motherhood. The Russian child and the Soviet system of child-rearing and education in a sense offered the possibility of having it both ways.

Isadora Duncan, learning that famine was consuming large parts of the country in which she had recently landed with great hopes, had the idea of going to the famine district and "making a film *only* of the children," which could become the basis of a popular appeal aimed at helping "*them*." Her idea was to make the children look both "beautiful" and "pitiable": "I shall teach the children some gestures that would make people forget politics and come to their aid."[27] Her scheme, not surprisingly, went nowhere, but her vision of teaching starving children to dance and then disseminating an image of dancing, starving children to evoke admiration, pity, and support from Americans says it all: children were an unfathomable burden and the only source of hope.

Quakers and Feminists

Because of their focus on helping the most needy rather than on achieving any particular political ends, the British and American Quaker relief units gained nearly unimpeded access to the Russian people as well as the American public, who generously funded their efforts. The AFSC had been in Russia essentially since the organization's founding in 1917, when representatives joined a delegation of the British Friends War Victims Relief Committee (BFWVRC). After the ARA, which ordinarily did not allow women to volunteer in the field, officially took control of American relief operations, it made an exception for the AFSC because it already had women in Russia. Thus, during the famine the only female relief workers in Russia were there under the auspices of the AFSC.[28]

Certainly, Quakers as a group were not of one mind when it came to the Bolshevik regime, and many were actively opposed to it—perhaps most notably Hoover himself. But there were well-placed individuals in the American and British relief organizations who saw no necessary conflict between the Bolshevik promises of a new world of justice and equality and the Quaker call to create a kingdom of God on earth. Among the Quakers, even some active opponents of the Bolshevik regime recognized the utility of appealing to labor and the Left, especially those who wished to avoid directly contributing to the ARA.

Less than a month before Louise Bryant and John Reed first landed in Saint Petersburg to document the course of the revolution, Anna J. Haines and several other women representing the AFSC arrived in Buzuluk in west Central Russia, where the BFWVRC had established an outpost a year earlier to deal with nearly three million people who had been driven from Poland and neighboring areas by advancing Germans. At the time of her application to the AFSC (in June 1917, hardly a month after the organization was founded), Haines was thirty years old, tall, and, by her own accounting, "overweight for my height" but "fairly active" and in "good health." She had graduated from Bryn Mawr in 1907 with degrees in politics and economics, taught in public schools, served with the Children's Bureau, and worked at North House, a settlement in Philadelphia, for three years. Most recently, she'd been an inspector at the Bureau of Health in Philadelphia. Though of Quaker background, Haines was forthright about "not making this application under the auspices of a religious call." Still, she professed to be a pacifist and expressed her willingness to work with others who were more religiously motivated.[29]

In this first expedition, Haines headed the American group, served as liaison to the British Quakers, and acted as the intermediary between the AFSC office in Philadelphia and the Soviets. Over at least three extended visits to Soviet Russia, she spent nearly a decade there, moving from war relief to famine relief to health work; at one point she returned to the United States to train as a nurse so that she might start a nurses' training school in Russia. Haines was no fiery radical, but she believed the Bolshevik regime had the best interests of the Russian people—and children in particular—in mind. Haines's article "Children of Moscow," published in March 1922, encapsulates the attitude toward Soviet children that Haines, Watts, and many other early volunteers shared.[30] Haines recalled attending a military parade and standing next to "a squat peasant with an enthusiastic youngster on his shoulder." At one point the child leaned down to ask his father if he should get down: "The father held the child higher. 'Stay where you are, little one,' said he. 'I can see only the bayonets, but I want you to see more.'"

This anecdote seemed representative to Haines: "Wherever I had gone during the three years that I had been traveling up and down the country engaged in relief work with the Friends, I had seen the older men and women, with the flash of bayonets always in their eyes, holding up the youth of Russia so that they could 'see more.'" Acknowledging that "Soviet Russia is no utopia," she insisted that a "spiritual change" among the people was perhaps best expressed in the educational system: she described teachers in unheated classrooms, with no pencils, papers, or textbooks, producing some of the most exciting educational innovations she had ever seen, and children who delighted in learning. Indeed, the hardship these boys and girls had experienced seemed to have been a source of growth: "Responsibilities and sufferings unknown to children of other and more peaceful times had given these children an air of dignity and wisdom and reserve that set them apart."

Haines got her first impressions of Russia at the railroad station in Vladivostok in 1917, where the refugee crisis created by the war was immediately apparent. Men, women, and children driven from their homes by the advancing German armies had disembarked from the freight cars in which they had traveled, unable to go any further:

> Hundreds of dirty refugees, old men in evil-smelling sheepskin coats, women in trailing skirts, children whose torn rags showed their vermin-scarred little bodies, bony babies sometimes wrapped only in newspapers, lay or crawled around the greasy floors of the big station. . . . With them came typhus, typhoid, cholera, scarlet fever, diphtheria, scurvy, malaria, and all kinds of skin diseases. . . . At every station on the long trans-Siberian railroad carts were filled with the dead, who were thrown out of the freight cars, and it was only in the early days that there was time to make crosses and set them up to mark the graves.[31]

Although Haines was not a journalist, her vivid descriptions of these horrors had special authority by virtue of her direct access to the Russian people and her AFSC credentials. The humanitarian discourse put forth by Quaker workers such as Haines was as essential as that produced by professional journalists in building sympathy for the Russian people as well as appreciation for the work being done by the Bolsheviks, especially vis-à-vis children.

Haines's background (in settlement house work, at the Children's Bureau, etc.) resonated with an older generation of female reformers whose authority rested on maternalist credentials. But other AFSC volunteers had more in common with feminists like Louise Bryant, as connections between the AWEC and the AFSC would suggest. Although the AWEC was an outgrowth of the feminist National Woman's Party, its public appeals utilized a humanitarian, maternalist discourse (laced with Christian sentimentalism) that focused on innocent civilians, especially children. Although its most publicized project, the "Christmas ship," never materialized (mainly because of the continuing blockade), the AWEC's treasurer, Jessica Smith, donated the approximately $3,500 that the group collected to the AFSC. She also volunteered her own services in whatever capacity she might be able to aid the organization's relief efforts in Russia.[32]

A graduate of Swarthmore College and daughter of the landscape painter William Granville Smith, Jessica Granville Smith was born in Madison, New Jersey, in 1895. After college she worked for the National American Woman's Suffrage Association in New York and then for the National Woman's Party in Washington, DC. She was also active in peace and socialist organizations, including the Women's International League for Peace and Freedom, the Birth Control League, and the Intercollegiate Socialist Society, of which she became executive secretary. Sharp-witted and attractive, Smith was later described by a fellow AFSC volunteer as "a beautiful creature with glorious, golden hair." One of Smith's professors characterized her as someone who "does her own thinking without habitually airing the results," and also insisted she was "entirely unaffected by a charming face."[33]

Though she had attended a Quaker college, Smith herself had no religious affiliation. However, she contended on her AFSC application for work in Russia, "If I joined any religious organization it would be the Friends." Her motivation for volunteering, she said, was to "foster the spirit of internationalism." Indeed, as she put it in more urgent terms: "I feel I *must* do something to help—and by helping in another country I can both satisfy my desire to be of service now and perhaps be better fitted to help in my own country later."[34]

Smith acknowledged on her application that she had little training of obvious relevance to relief work; still, as a suffrage activist, she had worked with many different people, had organized, and had written publicity, skills that might come in handy. Moreover, Smith hoped to make up for her lack of experience with her enthusiasm and willingness to take on any job that she might be given, claiming also that she could leave for Russia at any time. She did not hide her political sympathies, writing

"I believe in the Revolution and am in sympathy with most of the aims of the Bolsheviks." But in line with the Quaker commitment to nonviolence, she did claim to "deplore the use of force." She said that "Russia should be allowed to work out her own destiny with whatever help we can give."

Apparently because of its timing, Smith's application was put on hold: in January 1919 both the American and the British Quaker relief units had left Russia due to a combination of difficulties and dangers arising from the civil war, the blockade (which made communication with relief workers in Russia nearly impossible), and the Bolsheviks' increasing hostility to foreigners. Haines, wishing to stay in Russia, had joined up with the ARC in Siberia, although she found the work much less satisfying: Unlike the Quakers, the ARC seemed to focus on "medical and military work" without giving full attention to the refugee problem and the long-term needs of that community, Haines complained. She found "a lack of serious aim in the work, an unwillingness to study the situation and to apply to most needed, although perhaps the least showy kinds of work."[35] By June 1919, Haines had returned to the United States.

In the fall of 1920, Haines returned to Russia to join Arthur Watts, the representative of the BFWVRC in Moscow and a strong supporter of the Bolsheviks. In Moscow the two of them created a small Quaker outpost focused on giving relief to Russian children. Louise Bryant met Haines during this time and admiringly recalled Haines's "work with the children of Moscow" as "a story all by itself."[36]

Haines arrived in Moscow just in time for "Children's Week." She and Watts saw special performances by children and for children, and exhibitions showcasing work that had been done by young people in schools and children's colonies. Posters and even signs in the sky flashed slogans such as "Children are the hope of the future" and "Children are the happiness of mankind." Communists performed special child-related duties, carrying firewood to children's colonies or gathering statistics related to child welfare.[37] Events like this helped convince relief workers that they shared common goals with the Bolsheviks.

Haines and Watts secured a warehouse and began gathering statistics, visiting institutions serving children, and getting to know Soviet officials, as well as members of the small Anglo-American community in Moscow. Louise Bryant remembered Haines as a "tireless worker, always good natured and never discouraged." She was outside every morning at seven, distributing sweaters, canned milk, or other supplies. And she regularly worked late into the night. "We have so far handed out sweaters, stockings, scarfs and or pinafores to 3500 different children and as we have had to do most of the actual handing over ourselves we have had very little time to eat and sleep. . . . This personal distribution is mighty hard but well worth while," Haines and Watts reported to Quaker headquarters in London in February 1921. They began distributing food and other supplies directly to forest schools, children's hospitals, maternity houses, and kitchens for infants. Letters, artwork, and other tokens of gratitude from children made them feel appreciated: two boys from the School for Young Naturalists even walked five miles through the mud to invite Haines and Watts to an entertainment they had prepared for the first day of spring.[38]

Haines was practically fluent in Russian, which made it easier for her to work closely with Russians. She organized a small Christmas celebration that first year for one of the local orphan asylums: as Bryant recalled, Haines "sat up nights and made ornaments out of the tinfoil that comes wrapped around tobacco and so with some new supplies that arrived just in time she managed a very creditable little Christmas tree for one of the orphan asylums." Haines and Watts quickly earned the trust of Soviet officials "because," as Bryant put it, "they have never been known to take part in politics." The Soviet foreign secretary, Santeri Nuorteva, announced at a holiday celebration in December 1920 that the Friends were the "only Social Service organization against which Soviet Russia had no score for misuse of their mission." Reporting this comment, Haines and Watts insisted to the London office, "Such an inheritance of confidence makes us very desirous not to do and not even to be asked to do anything which might seem to admit of a questionable interpretation."[39]

Using this goodwill, the Quakers began distributing supplies on behalf of other relief agencies, including the ARC, which the Soviets regarded as an "official American body." Not all relief workers or agencies were quite as enthusiastic about Bolshevik educational practices as Haines, Watts, and some of the other Quaker volunteers. Indeed, some Quakers worried about appearing to support the Bolshevik regime, and several asked Haines and Watts to issue a statement clarifying that relief of Russian children did not signify support for Bolshevik aims; Watts and Haines, however, refused, Watts arguing that the Quakers were much more likely to be regarded as "bourgeois philanthropists attempting to persuade the people against their government." In February 1921 the Save the Children Fund expressed concern about supporting children who were required to go to schools where they were indoctrinated with Bolshevik propaganda. Apparently, "for the sake of free meals," those children went to school where "they are persecuted and taught doctrines which they abhor." The Save the Children representative even went so far as to suggest that "Friends working in Russia were the tools of the Soviet authorities." Watts pointed out that schooling was compulsory in most countries and that children were not forced to take part in political lessons. However, if members of Save the Children "wish to be certain that their supplies will not be used as an inducement for children to learn Communistic Doctrine," their supplies could be used exclusively for preschoolers.[40]

The arrival of Haines's bicycle in April (six months after Haines herself) saved her from an hour-and-a-half walk, or two dollars' cab fare each way, from her apartment to the warehouse. Several automobiles came the following month, a little worse for the wear. After a short trip in a Ford that had just arrived, Haines noted, "Its brakes don't work and only three cylinders are active and there is no horn, but the wheels go round and the engine makes enough noise to warn people of our coming." And in any case, "we are delighted to have received [the cars] in time to handle the soap and milk distributions." By June 1921 the office was overcrowded with supplies. "The courtyard of our warehouse is a very busy place with motor trucks, Ford vans, peasant carts, phaetons, and often groups of barefoot children who have come several miles on foot with pitchers and cans to carry away the precious oil."[41] When Watts took a much-needed vacation, Haines ably carried on by herself for several months. But it was clear they needed help.

Watts and Haines agreed that the selection process for additional volunteers must be rigorous: "No one of the dreamy parlour socialist type should be considered; sensation hunters equally undesirable—it will be a hard business job, no more exciting and considerably more uncomfortable than life at home but very interesting and entirely satisfying if you like it." As it turned out, the biggest obstacle to filling their ranks with workers came from the Russians. Maxim Litvinov, the commissar for foreign affairs, announced his refusal to grant passports to AFSC workers until the United States was prepared to receive a Russian trade delegation or representative. However, the onset of the famine changed the situation considerably.[42]

Food as a Weapon: The ARA, the Famine, and the Friends

By midsummer 1921 the Bolsheviks, initially wishing to avoid accepting aid from capitalist countries, realized they had no choice. On July 13, 1921, Maxim Gorky made a public appeal "To All Honest People" to help the land of "Tolstoy, Dostoevsky . . . and Pavlov," urging that civilized nations demonstrate "vitality of humanitarianism" by giving "bread and medicine" to the Russian people. Herbert Hoover himself responded, not as secretary of commerce (that is, as a representative of the US government), but as head of the American Relief Administration, offering aid to Russian children and invalids. Beyond what may have been genuine humanitarian motives, as secretary of commerce, Hoover was eager "to speed the economic and political reconstruction of Europe, not least in order to revive the market for U.S. goods," especially agricultural surpluses. These surpluses had been created by increased wartime production under Hoover's direction as head of the US Food Administration. Hoover had more-ideological concerns as well. He believed that hunger made Bolshevism more attractive and that well-fed Russians would reject Communism.[43] Through famine relief, Hoover reasoned, he could showcase Americans' internationalist spirit and accomplish what military intervention had thus far failed to do.

Under Hoover, the ARA navigated a delicate balance between using the famine as a bargaining tool to promote American interests and appearing to act on a truly humanitarian basis, a conflict in aims that contributed to some difficulties between the ARA and the Quakers. In January 1921 Hoover had offered the AFSC $100,000 worth of ARA food on the condition that American citizens being held by the Soviet government be released; Haines and Watts responded, "We do not regard it to be the mission of a Children's Relief Organization to demand or negotiate the relief of political prisoners." Hoover relented after being assured that the prisoners would at least receive special attention. Haines later complained that an imprisoned ARC worker was getting many more rations than Watts or her: "No one is having a Sunday-school picnic here, but he comes as near to it as anyone I know," she remarked. "The ARA is not popular for all its good works," Anna Louise Strong wrote her father in December 1921, noting that the ARA workers got paid too much, were ostentatious in their spending—amid dire poverty—and did not respect the Russian people or their government.[44]

For its part, the ARA suspected that the AFSC was harboring radicals. Hoover complained, "A militant group of red minded people are trying to undermine the American Relief Administration through the Friends Service Committee."[45] In fact, Hoover had a point, as Anna Louise Strong was to demonstrate.

"I Would Tell Another Story": Anna Louise Strong's Publicity Stunt

Anna Louise Strong's tenure with the AFSC was short, but it is notable because of her early access to the famine zone.[46] Moreover, her work there, and subsequent efforts as "shef," or patron, of the John Reed Colony—an effort to turn famine orphans into productive Soviet citizens with the help of American dollars and American know-how—would provide a launching pad for the rest of her long career in Russia.

Born in 1885 in Friend, Nebraska, Strong descended from the earliest settlers of the American colonies. Her father was a minister and reformer; her mother was part of the first generation of college-educated women. Strong could read and write by the age of four, and was writing poetry by the time she was six. Such precociousness would continue: at twenty-three, she became the youngest student to take a PhD from the University of Chicago. As a child and young woman, Strong had been deeply religious: she looked to God for direction in life, for something to worship, obey, and adore. She imagined one day devoting these energies to a husband: "It really was a god I wanted, a boss, a master, a parent who would continue infancy for me."[47] But long before Strong found a husband, she found socialism, which quickly became her new religion.

While supervising a child welfare program in Kansas City in 1911, Strong was required to eliminate a subordinate's job because of funding cuts. Deeply dismayed, she realized that capitalism created conditions by which a person's livelihood could be destroyed because of a whim of the marketplace. So she decided to devote her energies to socialism, which rejected God in favor of "a super-consciousness" here on earth. Though Strong moved relatively easily from faith in God to faith in socialism, she had trouble embracing the idea of class struggle. She was thus refused when she tried to join the Socialist Party in 1911; she would later find Communists similarly skeptical about her fitness to join their ranks.[48]

After obtaining her PhD (and breaking off her engagement to the civil libertarian Roger Baldwin), Strong began working for the *Seattle Daily Call*, a labor paper that supported the Bolsheviks in the years following the October Revolution. Talk of that revolution was nothing short of thrilling: "We heard of women's freedom, of the equality of backward races, of children rationed first when supplies were scant; these things strengthened our enthusiasm." She sought news of the revolution wherever she could. Later she recalled how "Louise Bryant returned from the revolution in Russia to dazzle the smoke-laden air of the close-packed longshoreman's hall with her gorgeous amber beads and the glamor of the forbidden border. She said to me after the meeting: 'You mustn't think they are pacifists over there because they withdrew from the war. They believe in armed uprising.' " Strong felt "a vague discomfort," but quickly answered, "Of course."[49]

Strong arranged a phenomenally successful speaking tour for Bryant to tell "the truth about Russia" ("at one meeting more than a thousand were turned away," Bryant reported). However, Strong did not dream of going to Russia herself until the famed muckraker Lincoln Steffens— perhaps best known for pronouncing of revolutionary Russia, "I have seen the future and it works"—put the idea in her head. Sitting with her in an "ill-lit booth in Blanc's café," Steffens suggested that Strong volunteer with the Quakers: "They are the only civilians legally permitted by any capitalist government to enter Russia and the only bourgeois admitted by the Bolsheviks," he told her. Strong quickly sent off a letter to the AFSC office in Philadelphia suggesting that the organization could benefit from her skills as a writer. "Publicity based on statistics of immense horror—the millions that are starving—has been done till the public mind is paralyzed. These facts are hardly grasped any more, or else they produce the feeling of hopelessness." Strong proposed that she observe the Friends' work in Russia and write a series of "short, human interest stories, of the gripping sort that papers simply can't turn down."[50]

Instead of agreeing to send Strong to Russia for three months, Wilbur Thomas, executive secretary of the AFSC, offered her nine months in Poland. Strong nearly refused, but then wrote to ask if she might get the chance to do publicity work in Russia if the Soviet government decided to allow it. Thomas responded that she might visit Germany or Austria for perhaps three months but would likely *not* be able to visit Russia. Undeterred, Strong formally accepted Thomas's offer but added, "If the Soviet Government should later relax its strictness, and if the way should open for me to visit Russia also, I assume that country would come on the same basis as Germany or Austria, or perhaps even a little more time, as it has no publicity as yet." Strong sent the letter when she knew Thomas would be out of the country and unable to respond before she'd left. On his return, he found not only Strong's letter but also one from a "concerned Friend" warning that Strong was "one of the worst 'Reds' in the Northwest" and wondering if the Philadelphia office had been "deceived as to her real character."[51]

Strong arrived in Poland in 1921 fully intending to make it a gateway to Russia. In this she was not alone: "Most of the members of their [the Quakers'] mission in Warsaw had originally applied to go to Russia," Strong later contended, "which to all us young left-wing idealists was our land of dream." She befriended the Soviet ambassador in Warsaw, but when he offered her a visa into Russia, she told him she could not simply "abandon the Quakers."[52]

As news of the Russian famine reached Poland, Strong saw her opportunity. She approached the head of the Quaker mission in Warsaw,

Florence Barrow, "a gentle Englishwoman" for whom "Bolsheviks were . . .
neither the world's destroyers nor its saviors," and asked if she might take
a leave of absence in order to go to the famine region. Mentioning her
access to a visa, she proposed to make connections with a press agency,
to "send true news from the Russian famine," and to help relief efforts
in whatever way she could. Poland was being inundated with refugees
from the famine, so Barrow agreed that Strong could go, as long as the
Philadelphia office approved. Strong reminded Barrow that the weekly
train to Moscow was leaving the next day, which left no time to get its
approval. Surely she should not wait another week.[53]

In the meantime, the ARA and representatives of the Bolshevik government reached an agreement on the terms of Hoover's relief mission.
Although the agreement made no mention of the AFSC, Hoover made
clear that "the AFSC should continue its work in Russia only *as a part
of and under the same restrictions as* the ARA." Representatives in both
the Philadelphia and London offices expressed concern about cooperating with the ARA. How would it affect Quaker autonomy? And how
would it affect relations between the Quakers and the radical and liberal groups who had generously supported them? Helen Todd, who now
represented the All American Commission for Russian Famine Relief, a
coalition of labor organizations, urged the AFSC not to cooperate with
the ARA, noting that many people had expressly wished to avoid supporting it because of Hoover's anti-Bolshevik views.[54]

As it turned out, the agreement had little effect on the Quaker missions' work (other than giving them access to more funds, and, to a large
extent, causing the American and British relief workers to split into separate units) or even their autonomy. The ARA assigned the Buzuluk district to the Friends and largely stayed out of their way, and the AFSC
continued to attract volunteers whose investment in Russia extended
beyond humanitarianism.[55] Still, for several months the flow of new volunteers into Russia was held up by ongoing negotiations between the
ARA and the Bolshevik government.

Although Strong had promised not to behave "in any underground
manner" while working under Quaker aegis, upon arriving in Moscow
in late August 1921, she visited the Soviet Foreign Office's press depart-

ment and confided that she "hoped to stay in Russia indefinitely." She would also meet with J. Carr (L. E. Katterfield), who represented the US Communist Party in Moscow, requesting arrangements for her to return to Moscow as a correspondent for various labor papers once her term with the Quakers had concluded.[56]

Arthur Watts, though not expecting Strong, was glad to have her help and suggested she accompany several cars of food and other supplies into the Volga region. The food would not go very far, but Watts suggested it could be "psychologically effective to throw it into Samara; it would let the people know that foreign relief is coming."[57]

Strong left for Samara before Watts received a telegram alerting him to the fact that she wasn't supposed to be in Russia at all. There, Strong "lived in a food train in Samara station, and awakened every morning with the murmur of five thousand children in [her] ears." Each day, she went to health and education offices, children's homes, and hospitals to arrange for the distribution of Quaker supplies, including soap, which was needed almost as desperately as food and medicine. Most of the soap was taken to "receiving stations," a term that fails to capture the horror of the various run-down buildings that "handled, quarantined, and distributed to the hundred or more children that were daily picked up in Samara's streets—brought from distant villages and abandoned by parents who could not feed them. . . . Into these went starving children by thousands, sick with cholera, typhus, dysentery; they had no soap nor change of underwear or clothing; they littered the floor with filth."[58]

What struck Strong most forcefully was not the devastation, however, or even people's will to survive. It was efforts to help others, especially to provide for children. Children's homes and schools were organized, "without mattresses, sheets, books, or clothing," and teachers began holding classes. And Strong discovered that almost all the single-minded, self-sacrificing, and self-assured individuals who made things happen—the "creators in chaos"—turned out to be members of the Communist Party. They became her models and her ideal.[59]

In the evenings, when she was not distributing food or supplies, Strong wrote news stories that showed a side of the famine that, she believed, reporters had missed. "Mine must be a greater story—the tale of . . . disciplined control that made men sow the seed they could not live to gather. I must tell of a life that went on though millions perished—of a barefoot boy in Minsk collecting not for himself but for others; of a food train where a crew without shoes or overcoats toiled in winter blizzards to feed five thousand children."[60] Though Strong was cabling her stories directly to the Hearst news services, she also sent them to the Philadelphia and London offices of the Friends. Only after several of Strong's stories had been published in US newspapers did Watts receive word from Wilbur Thomas that all publicity must go through the Philadelphia office.[61]

Under pressure from Philadelphia, Watts ordered Strong back to Moscow. Strong, however, went on to Buzuluk with several other relief workers, promising to stay only briefly. Despite this insubordination, Watts sent several of Strong's news stories to London, noting she had "cancelled her agreement with the Hurst [sic] press" and "hoped to soon travel to London to speak on behalf of the Quakers," something the London office found highly desirable as they worked to communicate the dire need.[62]

Strong had antagonized the US government as well as Quaker leadership, for in her daily cables to the Hearst syndicate, she "made it quite plain that the Friends had done relief work in Moscow long before Hoover, and that the food I personally took to the Volga reached Samara two weeks before the Hoover shipments arrived. I made it equally plain that the Soviets themselves were contributing, by heroic sacrifice, far more relief to the famine than they got from abroad. I showed an orderly world of health departments, school departments, local authorities fighting a natural catastrophe, instead of anarchy brought into order by Americans." Strong was also later open about the fact that she had "made use of the Friends' Service to reach in the end a purpose alien to their will." Watts later acknowledged that Strong had done an excellent job distributing the rations in Samara, efficiently setting up an operation that "enabled the immediate feeding of numbers of children many of whom might have starved to death pending the arrival of the Hoover trains."[63]

Still, Strong's failure to follow instructions tested even her strongest advocates and had dire consequences, not just for her own health but also for that of another volunteer. Before going back to Moscow, Strong returned to Samara where she volunteered to distribute supplies for the ARA. Strong recalled arranging a meeting between a starving representative of a village famine council and an ARA representative in his richly appointed hotel room. While Strong arranged for the distribution of provisions that would feed only a fraction of the villager's community, the ARA man consumed a giant meal, surrounded by baskets of imported foods and bottles of wine. Not long after this encounter, Strong became severely ill with typhus; the nurse assigned to tend her, another Quaker volunteer, also contracted the disease and died.[64]

In the meantime, the first AFSC volunteers recruited to provide famine relief entered Russia in December 1921. They witnessed unimaginable horrors. Miriam West saw a dog running down the street holding a dead child in its mouth. Beulah Hurley, walking to the Quaker warehouse in the early hours of morning, stumbled over the bodies of a family of four that had starved during the night. Death was so ubiquitous that workers began to greet the sight of it with relief, for it indicated an end to suffering.[65]

Evelyn Sharp, greeting relief workers in the famine zone after a short stay in Moscow, heard about cemeteries where frozen bodies were piled up, waiting for burial, and about a boy so hungry that he had eaten his own hand. At a children's hospital, she found a few beds but no sheets, no soap, and no medicines. Each bed held "two or three famine children, huddled under some old covering, sometimes they lay about on the floor. . . . Some were crying and moaning, some lay motionless and starving as if already more in the next world than in this one; but the majority, with the awful patience of childhood, did not complain, and responded to every sign of a greeting from any of us."[66]

For her part, as soon as Strong could sit up and think clearly, she began typing vivid news stories from her bed and sending them to Philadelphia and London. While London was enthusiastic about these pieces, Philadelphia did not even acknowledge them. Perhaps even more frustrating to Strong was the fact that the AFSC finally hired a full-time publicity worker, and it wasn't her. "Guess they fear my radical tendencies and my independence," Strong speculated. Yet Wilbur Thomas recognized that connections to Labor and the Left could be helpful in fundraising and was relatively sympathetic to radical causes.[67] In fact, the person Thomas chose, Robert Dunn, was open about his socialist inclinations, as was Dunn's friend and eventual replacement as director of publicity in Russia, Jessica Smith.

"There Is Real Unity of Purpose": Jessica Smith and the AFSC

Although Strong made it into Russia before Smith—despite Smith's earlier application—Smith had a longer and more successful career with the AFSC, a less ambivalent relationship with the Soviet Union and Communism, and even better luck with a man both women met in Soviet Russia and eyed as possible husband material.[68] And although she separated from the AFSC mission before her two-year term had expired, Smith maintained good relations with the Quaker leadership in Philadelphia, who continued to print the publicity pieces she periodically sent them.

Smith's departure for Russia in the winter of 1922 was held up when she was denied a passport. She'd heard rumors that all women were being denied passports to Russia, but then began to suspect she was being targeted because of her politics. Indignant, Smith assured Wilbur Thomas that she was a "perfectly safe person." Although admittedly "in general agreement with socialist principles," she was "certainly not a Communist, and not even a member of the Socialist party." Smith pointed out that the Intercollegiate Socialist Society, of which she'd been a leader, was strictly an "educational organization" that "required no political affiliation from its members." Likewise, the American Women's Emergency Committee, of which she'd been treasurer, was "organized solely for the purpose of sending milk and medicine to starving Russians." Moreover, she was "not interested in 'propaganda' work," did not "classify myself under any particular 'ism,'" and believed deeply in what the Friends were doing to foster brotherhood among different peoples.[69] There is no reason to believe that Smith was being disingenuous, but it is clear that going to Soviet Russia was a key step in her full conversion to Communism and a career in what could fairly be described as "propaganda work" back in the United States: she spent close to fifty years editing Communist publications including *Soviet Russia Today* and *New World Review*.

Thanks to intervention from the AFSC office in Philadelphia, Smith's passport application was finally approved on the condition that she promise not to take part in any political activities. Smith found this stipulation "perfectly absurd and unjustifiable," but concluded that since she had "no intention or wish to take part in any political activities," she might as well promise. Smith also revised her application to the AFSC, clarifying that although she had originally been in sympathy with the Bolsheviks, because of their violent methods, she no longer was. But she still contended that Russians ought to be able to "work out their own destiny without interference" and ought to be given aid in order to recover from the famine.[70]

Arriving in Russia in March 1922, Smith was stationed in Sorochin-skoye, on the eastern edge of Buzuluk, as a district supervisor in the food distribution program. She remained for about seven months before moving to Gamaleyevka, a small village about 115 miles east of Kiev. The entire crop of millet had been destroyed by drought, along with most of the wheat, barley, and rye. There were reports of cannibalism the winter she arrived, and Smith was told that none of the villages in the region would survive the following winter without significant aid.[71]

Amid the death and suffering, relief workers bonded quickly and cherished their small community. On a free day in May, Smith, Miriam West, and Cornelia Young "strolled over hill and dale and gathered wild flowers. Armfuls of yellow and purple blossoms repaid them for their efforts." Besides beautiful views from the hilltop, the women saw "soosliks, butterflies, a lizard, bees, and birds. The birds seemed to be observing Sunday in the proper manner by singing in a chorus."[72]

Smith was apparently beloved by both coworkers and Russians. Robert Dunn described her as the "general belle of the ball" for whom "everyone has a pet name." A Russian peasant who was diligently studying English with the help of a tattered dictionary provided by Quaker workers expressed particular gratitude for "gentlewoman Jessica Smith" among the "inappreciables and preciouses Bienfactores Gentlemen Cvakeres [sic]."[73]

By January 1923 Smith had eagerly assumed Dunn's job as director of publicity in Russia, a position she had requested based on her writing

Fig. 2.3 AFSC workers in a Quaker hut in Buzuluk, Christmas Eve, 1922. *Bottom left*, Robert Dunn and Dorothy North "reading an Irish play." *Bottom right*, Ann Herkner. The other two men are Karl Borders and a Russian coworker. The photograph is in the Andree A. Brooks Research Files on Bluet Rabinoff, box 2, Robert Dunn photographs, Tamiment Library, New York University.

skills, her growing proficiency in Russian, and the fact that she felt she was better fit for this work than for administering relief.[74] She published dozens of reports in this capacity and continued writing in the same vein for the popular press, wherein her radical humanitarian narrative gained credence through association with the respectable Quakers. She made clear that the situation was dire: children were ravaged by disease and starvation, many had been orphaned and were homeless, and many would die—they needed Americans' help. But she also asserted that those creative, cooperative, and hopeful children who survived were testaments to the educational achievements of the new regime.

Two of Smith's publicity pieces, "In the Monastery at Shar" and "In the Children's City," both written in February 1923, illustrate these two poles quite vividly.[75] Describing a visit to a home for famine orphans, "In the Monastery at Shar" chronicles a journey through "a long string of devastated villages" that took Smith and a colleague "up a long and gently sloping hill towards the sunset, which was turning all the sky and steppe into one vast pageant of lovely color." Their horse-drawn sleigh traced narrow ruts through the snow, into which poured blue shadows from the sun's reflection. Above, "the sky was a miracle of saffron and pink." Climbing the last hill before sloping down into the valley to enter the village, Smith marveled at the sight before her. The village "lay there like some bit of elfland, wrapped in a rosy glow, the little houses nestling in the cup of the valley, with feathery clumps of trees around them, the church rising like a fairy palace from the side of the farther hill, the great monastery gate looming up before it." Smith and her companion pronounced the village "a heavenly spot for the children!" and told themselves, "Surely they must be happy in a place like this!"

The idyllic setting made the reality of the monastery-cum-children's home more shocking. In a dark room with an "evil smell," a lamp's "smoky flare" revealed the "hard, unpleasant face" of the home's director. But it was the children's faces that were the most shocking: "The pallid faces of the children loom out of the darkness. The kind of faces that grew so familiar to us in those early awful days of last winter [when famine conditions were at their worst], but which we have not seen for a long time. Faces pinched and set in grotesque little grimaces of pain. Wide eyes peering from them, dark with hunger." Taken into the director's office, Smith and her colleague learned that children have begun to die in large numbers, as they had in the worst days of the famine. Once a colony of 250 children, now there were 100.

In the next room, the "somber, mongolian faced little creatures in their black clothes, most of them sick and sore covered," were lined up "in two straight, stiff lines." As though acting out a twisted version of Isadora Duncan's ill-conceived famine film, the children "began to sing with dry, raucous voices, swaying from side to side in disconsolate rhythm, as if they were under some dreadful spell." Smith was horrified: "I have never heard anything more distressing than that weird Bashkir song, filling the low dark room with child sorrow that wrung your heart." A teacher suggested that the children dance as well, but the visitors begged them not to: "We could not bear to see those painwracked little bodies making such a travesty of joy." In another barely furnished room, four children were sick with dysentery; two huddled together on a bench, clutching a blanket, and the other two lay on the floor. "In a few days they would all be dead," Smith predicted. At this home, there was no money to hire a better director, and it was simply impossible to feed or care for all the children.

Smith's report "In the Children's City" offers a striking contrast. Conditions are objectively not much better in the "children's city," but the director and the workers are committed, dynamic, and hopeful about the future. The thermometer reads −30°F as Smith and a Russian comrade start off in a sleigh drawn by a white horse for this place "over beyond Barabonovka," a tiny village on the eastern edge of Siberia. "It is very early in the morning and the smoke is going up in billowing columns from all the little *isbas*, as the peasant women fill their ovens with great armfuls of straw or twigs or wood or kisiki, and put in the kascha for breakfast. . . . The sky is clear, soft blue, and the little low hills beyond Gamaleyevka are iridescent in the morning light." No one is expecting them. The school director and its government representative, or "politikom," are summoned; the former greets the visitors enthusiastically, sharing his visions for the colony's future, and proudly describing the work of the politikom, who is in charge of "the political education of the children." He also keeps up "the spirit of the place." Among the bravest soldiers on the side of the Reds during the civil war, "he would stand up to his full height right in front of everyone when the bullets were flying all around, and the rest of us were all lying flat on the ground," Smith is told. "And now," she reflects, "this intrepid soldier is living among the children, playing with them, picking the little ones up in his arms, teaching them about world brotherhood and peace."

Smith sees several "husky boys" with "sturdy bodies" and "full red cheeks" outside, but she is told that these children are exceptional: they work outside and have warm clothes and enough to eat. Once inside, she sees "a room full of the younger children, all sitting on their beds, with little thin dresses and shirts and at least half of them without shoes or stockings." As in the monastery at Shar, these children also perform for their guests, but this time their performance inspires hope rather than pity: "At a word from their bright looking teacher the little barefoot crew are on their feet, and the room is full of music and motion as they play their little singing games for us and dance through the lovely figures of their folk dances with a verve and a fling you would not have thought possible from looking at their pale faces."

Later she observes the "Children's Soviet" in action, as a group of children reprimand their peers for leaving garbage near the door of one of the houses. She sees some "amazingly clever little crayon drawings the children had made" using crayons given on an earlier visit. She left the "children's city" feeling optimistic about its future, despite all the problems: the "hastily built" stoves were falling apart, there was not enough wood, the sanitation was poor, and the children lacked school supplies, clothing, and shoes. But conditions were markedly improved over what Smith saw on an earlier visit.

> We saw here that same thing at work which is noticeable all over Russia, even in the very worst villages of the famine district . . . "that creative will which by some miracle of buoyancy and optimism insists on building and constructing among hunger and nakedness."[76] We found it among the teachers, who were teaching the children without books, in the Politikom, who was seeing that somehow the fires got built even though there was no wood, and in the resilient souls and bodies of the children themselves, who were creating life out of death and destruction.

Smith's reports were meant not only to show a continuing need for relief but also to demonstrate that Quaker relief was making a difference. Clearly, Smith also aimed to show that the Bolshevik government had the best interests of its citizens in mind. She concluded a piece on the Bashkir Republic: "If the Quakers can keep them alive until the next harvest by that time the government will be able to give them the assistance that will put them on their feet again and make possible the expression of the rich and beautiful elements in the Bashkir nature developed through their long contact with the space and freedom of the plains, in a more settled, but none the less free and fine communistic life."[77]

By early September 1923, Smith told Thomas that she wanted to spend some time developing her own interests: living and studying in

Moscow and doing her own writing. Her concern for famine victims was genuine, but she was clearly yearning to immerse herself in the more cosmopolitan life of Moscow. She also had fallen in love with Harold ("Hal") Ware, a founding member of the American Workers Party, who, under the auspices of the Friends of Soviet Russia, had initially come to Russia in May 1922 to set up a demonstration farm, bringing with him nine North Dakota farmers, twenty-two tractors, and two tons of food, as well as, for the moment, a wife (his mother, Ella Reeve Bloor, a towering figure in the fledgling party, was also in Moscow, rooming with Anna Louise Strong). Strong fell for Ware as well, but it was Smith who won his heart; they would marry back in the United States, in a service performed by Socialist Party leader Norman Thomas.[78]

Wilbur Thomas was supportive of Smith's decision to cut short her service with the AFSC, noting how much he had appreciated her work. "I feel there is a real unity of purpose in the things that we both are trying to do," he wrote in response to Smith's resignation. He also invited her to continue sending publicity. She did, even while acknowledging her increasing sympathy for the Soviet government. Thomas did not see this as a problem: as he wrote her that December, "Your connection with the Soviet authorities and your sympathy with some of the things that are going on in Russia are not a hindrance to us in our work here in this country. That is, up to the present time you have done nothing or written nothing that has given us offence. I do not anticipate that it will because I know that you are very careful in what you write." He conceded that, because she was now independent and submitting stories directly to American news outlets, this could change—"you may get a reputation that would make it rather undesirable for you to be our representative"— but he contended that if she sent stories to them and they were allowed to censor or not use them, "then certainly we can protect ourselves and that ought to be left to our judgment."[79]

This exchange occurred after Smith had published an article in the *New York World* that used her authority as a "Quaker mission worker" to dispute a negative portrait of Soviet schooling, and a piece the *Nation*, "In the House of the Sugar King," about the children of the Musical Art School of Pushkin.[80] This yellow-and-white mansion had been the dacha (or summer cottage) of a sugar magnate until it was gradually taken over by children from the music school, who decided they could make better use of this grand estate. By Smith's accounting, the school's interior seems an expression of childhood itself. The children have made elaborate scenery, and they are building a stage and sewing costumes and curtains. Sounds of music are everywhere. The school's teachers are famous musicians from the Bolshoi, gladly devoting their talents to a new generation of musicians, who treat their guests to a concert that includes singing, dancing, and string solos. "The light is very bad, and two flickering lamps have to be carried here and there, but they do not seem to be in the least daunted by material difficulties. Every child has something to contribute to the program, they are beautifully trained, and some of them are very gifted." After the concert, Smith and her companion perform folk dances with the children, "swinging and whirling around with them to their great delight," and then join the children and their teachers for dinner. Later they hear about how the school had come to reside in the Sugar King's mansion.

As Smith relates it, the school had started in a smaller house, but as it outgrew the space, a deputation of children went to the Sugar King, armed with a letter from the Department of Education, and informed him, "You are one and we are many. You use your house only for pleasure, and we must use it for work." Though the Sugar King refused the children, they persisted, climbing in through windows, moving beds into his living room, taking over the kitchen, and holding classes. "From one room to another the Sugar King retreated before the advancing hordes of children. At last he could stand it no more. He gathered together as much of his furniture and precious possessions as he could in a nearby cottage, and fled to a hospitable border state." Apparently the Sugar King had visited his dacha the summer prior to Smith's writing and was pleased to find it intact. Smith concludes, "He is probably banking on happier days when the old order will return to Russia, and his *dacha* will be returned to him in good condition. But I bank on this vigorous young generation of proletarian musicians and artists and scientists who have come into their own because power has been wrested from the Sugar Kings—and who will not lightly give up what they have won."

Smith at this point was not a member of the Communist Party, although by some accounts she seems to have assumed its values and affect, despite what she told Wilbur Thomas. Alice Hamilton, a pioneering physician and former Hull House resident who visited the Soviet Union in 1924, met both Strong and Smith during her visit. The latter "made a rather dreadful impression" as a woman "ready to go to any lengths for the sake of 'the Cause,'" They discussed espionage and police violence. Hamilton was critical, saying "the cruelty, the midnight arrests, the shooting without real trials, of hundreds" diminished trust in the regime as well as its credibility. Smith allegedly called Hamilton's criticisms "petty bourgeois ideology," adding "The one question I ask is, 'Does that help the Party?' If it does, it is right; if not, it is wrong." Hamilton said, "She was a beautiful creature, with gold-red hair and a profile like [actress Eleonora] Duse's, but I found her a horror."[81]

By the fall of 1924, Smith had returned to the United States and was writing Wilbur Thomas about an agricultural colony in the Caucasus that she and Ware were planning; several other former AFSC volunteers would join what became Russian Reconstruction Farms. While in the United States, Smith did some public speaking both for the AFSC and in other capacities; in January 1925 she addressed a National Woman's Party audience in Washington, DC, on the topic of women in Soviet Russia ("the principle of absolute equality is a part of the Soviet system"), a topic that became the subject of a book that Smith published three years later.[82]

Strong's Children of the Volga

Like Smith, Anna Louise Strong attempted to build on her experiences with the Quakers in order to gain a foothold in Soviet Russia. After recovering from typhus and finishing her service to the AFSC in Poland, Strong spent several months in London and then returned to Moscow as a correspondent for Hearst. Perhaps her greatest coup was landing an interview with Leon Trotsky, who was so taken with Strong that he asked her to give him English lessons, which she did for several months; they may even have been lovers.[83] Although delighted to be so close to this man in power, Strong longed for a more direct role in the Soviet state. She spent several months trying to arrange a Russian-American club in Moscow, but the plan was rejected by the Soviet government: as long as the United States refused to recognize the Soviet Union, no special organization should exist for the comfort of its businessmen and politicians, she was told. Then, in the fall of 1923, Strong was finally asked to play a real role in the Soviet enterprise.

Ruth Fischer of the Soviet Children's Commission invited Strong to help her organize an agricultural commune on the Volga for famine orphans fourteen to eighteen years old: too old for regular children's homes but not prepared to live on their own. Thanks to the world war, civil war, and famine, gangs of homeless children (or *bezprizorni*) had become a common feature in Russian cities, and the existing system of children's homes was strained to its limits. The idea was to create something that could become self-sustaining and a model for other children's colonies. Strong was told that the government would pay teachers and feed the children; as "shef" Strong would be responsible only for bringing "American technique" to the colony and using her connections to help sustain it.[84] Although the John Reed Colony (JRC) was two days' journey from Moscow and Strong knew she would only be able to visit sporadically, she wanted to do it.

Strong visited the makeshift colony in Khvalinsk in the fall of 1923 and was rather appalled at its condition. She then went to the United States for a planned lecture tour, soliciting donations of money, machines, and volunteers that she could send back to help the colony.[85]

She had high hopes: "I knew there were hundreds of Americans who wanted 'a share in Russia's future.' Teachers, farmers, nurses, carpenters were begging to pay their own way over and live on anything to help Russia's children." By May 1924, she was back in Moscow and excited about her newfound work—and the recognition that came with it. The Children's Commission of the All-Russian Central Executive Committee, or VTsIK, had asked her to form an auxiliary committee of Americans in Moscow "to act as sort of patrons for all their children's colonies." Such work, Strong speculated, would offer "contact with industry and agriculture" and "I would have a semi-official sort of standing." She'd also get "lots of extra rights," including the chance to stay at a special resort and even, perhaps, the right to "have my room declared the central headquarters of this committee, and keep it forever!" Representatives of the Quakers agreed to join and allow her to raise funds for the colony through them, although some members of the American group were leery of backing Bolshevik-sponsored colonies.[86]

Looking ahead, Strong speculated, "Shouldn't wonder if this organization, 'Friends of Russian Children' or whatever it gets called, might develop into a big thing." She began writing on letterhead from "Friends of Russian Children (Anglo-American Section) for Helping the Children's Agricultural and Industrial Colonies"; it lists her as director and Jessica Smith as in charge of "work in America." Strong had hoped Smith would recruit and fundraise in the United States; Smith, however, quickly became caught up in plans for Russian Reconstruction Farms. Perhaps not surprisingly, Strong's friendship with Smith began to sour around this time.[87]

Strong had plenty of other connections. She began sending out appeals to influential Americans who had either shown an interest in Soviet Russia or seemed likely to. Among them were Lillian Wald (who would become an important supporter of the JRC); the left-wing socialite and former lover of John Reed, Mabel Dodge Luhan; the iconoclastic economist Thorstein Veblen; the pacifist minister John Haynes Holmes; Lucy L. W. Wilson, principal of the Philadelphia High School for Girls, who would shortly make her own trip to study Soviet schooling; and Ellen Hayes, a math professor at Wellesley College and outspoken feminist who would become the colony's biggest patron.[88]

Strong also promoted the JRC in the popular press. Writing in *Soviet Russia Pictorial*, she described the colony as an example of the Bolsheviks' latest effort to deal with the problem of homeless children in a way that gives older children skills and experience living communally. The Friends Council for International Service in London published Strong's pamphlet *A Children's Colony on the Volga* in the fall of 1924; here Strong described the colony as an outpost for famine orphans not being served by the existing, overcrowded system. Young people were being moved into "colonies in the country, where conditions are healthier and the children themselves cultivate the land and produce their own food." These children, Strong insisted, "respond to the trust imposed in them and are shouldering the responsibilities of communal life," nowhere more than at the JRC, which, she said, has been "constructed in large part" (an exaggeration) by gifts from the Society of Friends.[89]

The picture Strong painted of the colony in the pamphlet is ripe with hope and possibility even as it emphasizes dire need: Spread about the beautiful hills and ravines of Cherumshan are a series of buildings, including "an ancient monastery, repaired by the labour of the children themselves." In "one fine brick building" live the "carpenters," a dozen boys who have made "sixty-five wooden beds, many tables and chairs and benches, many wooden frames." They have even made "two ploughs and four harrows," because they could not afford to buy them, and are eager to begin cultivating their land. Another group of twelve lives over the hill and fashions shoes for members of the colony—when they can get the leather to do it. Their house is large, so the young carpenters have built a theatre there, for "a stage for dramatics is almost the first thing any Russian children's colony installs." Nearby, twenty-nine girls, supervised by "one hard-worked matron," live in three houses. The girls are taught to cook for the entire colony of one hundred children, taking turns while "the rest are milking, or cleaning, or sewing, or working in the garden." They share one sewing machine, using it to "make all the clothes of the establishment." And they garden, sowing and harvesting "potatoes, cabbages, tomatoes, all sorts of vegetables."

According to Strong's pamphlet, the colony's harvest was better than others in the district because the children planted during the Easter holidays, while everyone else was celebrating (superstition held that the spring crop must not be sown before Easter), and the colony was able to take advantage of "the one best rain of the spring." Strong acknowledged, "It is a bit sad to think of children who choose to plough rather than take holidays, but these children were trained in the grim school of the great famine. Their parents died of hunger. They themselves are given a home and land and organization and a little help, but they know that their future depends on their own labours." Besides, they'd taught an important lesson to peasants in the neighboring villages, who, seeing the children's harvest, commented, "God loves work."

Fig. 2.4 John Reed Colony. Anna Louise Strong papers, University of Washington Libraries, Special Collections, UW37340. Used with permission from Tracy Strong.

Strong suggested that the JRC children—who had no choice but to work rather than play—were learning life lessons essential to the new people revolutionaries hoped to create. Not only were these children hardworking and cooperative; they were also generous, according to Strong. As word got out about the colony's successes, more and more children were sent from surrounding villages; the children who had worked so hard to organize, repair, plow, and plant let the newcomers live and eat with them. "They are far more communistic in spirit than one has a right to ask of youngsters," Strong wrote her father in September 1924.[90] They were also playful, according to her portrait in *A Children's Colony on the Volga*. Strong described rest days, during which children played in the woods and swam in a nearby pond. And they were learning: children who could read had begun giving lessons to those who could not; others taught "proper Russian" to those who knew only their "tribal dialects." However, Strong acknowledged, "Of other 'book learning' there has been little; there has been time only to learn sewing and carpentry, and ploughing and blacksmithing, and shoemaking." The children's first priority was to learn to make a living. Besides, "all of them much prefer the workshops to the books." Yet "every evening under the trees" they held a story hour, with "reading from Russian classics" and storytelling. And there were plans to beef up the traditional schooling for these children.

There were also plans to take over a great estate of 1,500 acres about twenty miles down the river. Complete with a meadow, an orchard, a brick kiln, a mill, and living space for three hundred children, a property in Alexievka had been abandoned by its rich landowner after the revolution, and Strong was told the colony could have it all if they proved they could productively use and maintain it. "I imagine that for several years to come the great farm will fill up with children, and when in the end it grows too full, it will organize from its midst new communes of the older ones, sending them forth with horses and implements and food to take up new land and form new communities wherever they are needed in Russia," Strong speculated. "So that we shall not be merely a commune but a Mother of Communes, with connections in many counties and many states."[91] She encouraged Americans to take a role in this process by sending money and equipment, or even by volunteering their labor.

By September the colony had begun taking over the land and buildings in Alexievka, and Strong was corresponding with Americans interested in coming over to work at the colony, mostly through the Society for Technical Aid to Soviet Russia. "Comrade Lipp" had plans to come start a shoe factory. Two farmers from Detroit offered to come with their life savings of $2,500–$3,000, each "prepared to blow it in improving the colony." And they would donate their services as well, asking "merely to be 'members of the commune.'" Strong marveled at her situation: "Never thought I'd be the organizer of a cooperative commonwealth!"[92]

A young Komsomol, Vanya, also donated his services to the commune. At the children's request, Strong sent Vanya to Moscow where "he gathered up about two hundred books for the library by bearding [Gregory] Zinoviev and [Karl] Radek in their dens, and getting all the free copies sent to them by admiring authors, but which they haven't time to read." Anna Graves, a Quaker, was successfully recruited to serve as colony teacher. If Graves could teach the children English, Strong speculated, she could staff the colony with the ready supply of "wandering Americans" eager to help Russian children. Strong asked her father in Seattle to recruit someone from Yakima or Wenatchee with apple-growing experience (someone "who is reliable and with pep") to get the Alexievka orchard going, and had several other volunteers lined up.[93]

Despite Strong's hopeful rhetoric in her publications, her private correspondence reveals that significant problems were evident from early on. "It sounds beautiful when I wrote that the children fired the cook because they could do it alone," she wrote to her father, "but a nearer view of this situation is not so lovely." Although the older girls were skilled bakers, "when the younger ones were on the job there was war in the camp, and much unpleasant comment from the boys." Strong sympathized with the boys' plight: "When all you get to eat is rye bread, and soup made of cabbages and potatoes and a little fat, you want those things to be decently cooked." What Strong referred to as a "boy-girl problem," or even "an armed neutrality between the sexes," extended beyond this. There was, for instance, an ongoing battle over underwear: fabric was scarce and each boy would wear a pair of underwear "so long before he gives it up for fear he won't get another one, and the girls complain that the clothes are so dirty and the supply of soap so scant that they can't get them clean." Indeed, after the washing "there is often nothing left . . . but rags." Strong bought one thousand meters of linen that she expected would "go far to restore the peace," although with only one sewing machine for twenty-nine girls, increasing the clothing supply would take time.[94]

Strong herself was also chafing under the limitations of her role as "shef," which left her with no authority or control and little recourse for dealing with the corrupt manager, Yermeyev, who she felt cared little about the children and their well-being. "I am a bit tired of being merely a 'patron' of a colony; I want to be more of a boss or president," she confided to her father. "Maybe build a Tuskegee, who knows? Or a series of them." (Strong did later briefly establish an American vocational school closer to Moscow, where she paired skilled American workers with young Russian peasants in need of industrial training.)[95]

The fact is that Strong did not actually have time to run the colony herself. And although she was good at raising money and even recruiting volunteers, each time she visited the JRC she discovered more problems and became more frustrated. Returning in the summer of 1925 from what was to become her annual winter lecture tour in the United States, she found the colony "an awful mess" and Anna Graves overwhelmed. Many children were ill with malaria. Food and supplies were inadequate. Strong blamed the manager and wrote to both the Children's Commission and the Communist Party, asking for an investigation and saying that she would "not remain 'shef' unless they removed the manager."[96]

Later, as it became clear that Yermeyev had the support of the local community and the Party—and that nobody better was willing to do the job—Strong grudgingly acknowledged his "energy and resourcefulness" and his eagerness to set productivity records. But she contended, "The plain fact is that there has been no one here who has cared a bit about the children as human beings."[97] Strong complained to her Moscow superiors that the children were "working too hard on too little food," which created obvious problems, as did the lack of heating fuel. Poor sanitation and simple negligence were major factors in explaining why so many children had become ill. One girl with "an advanced case of trachoma" had been "living in the colony for more than a year, mixing freely with the other children, under conditions where towels do not exist and sanitation is frightful." This girl had been given almost no medical attention and had infected several other children.[98]

The girls working in the kitchen had sore, swollen legs from having to carry water in buckets from the Volga. Perhaps they could not be blamed for getting the water from the closest point, a "slough below Alexeivka, filthy with oil and refuse of the village." The kitchen and dining room "were in a condition of chaos." Children had taken most of the dishes and spoons to their own rooms or had sold them. "I saw the children eating, using their hands only to dish potatoes or kasha. They drank the soup direct from the bowl and then used their hands to take the solid part of the soup to their mouths." The toilets, she reported, "are in such frightful condition that no one can use them; everyone uses the field." Children who did use the toilets compounded the problem by standing instead of sitting on the seats, either because of ignorance or because sitting would be too disgusting. School had been "practically non-existent" the past winter: the children had to read and write while sitting under blankets because it was so cold.[99]

Yet despite these conditions, many children told Strong that the JRC was better than any place they'd lived, a fact that convinced her to continue her work. There was also the fact "that these children are infinitely better to organize than any American children—that they behave better, are more tractable, etc."[100]

She recruited Ada Flomenbaum, "an energetic girl of the pioneering type, who speaks Russian better than English." A graduate pharmacist and student of playground work at Berkeley (and a master tailor to boot), Flomenbaum, Strong speculated, would not only teach and work with the girls on sewing but also set up a model playground. Indeed, with the "John Reed Colony as an example," Strong proposed "establishing rural playgrounds along the Volga." A Mrs. Sutta of New York had already promised to donate a playground library; "if you could see these children on Saturday nights sitting stupidly around their social hall, not knowing a single game or folk-dance, and if you knew some of the problems in social life we are facing in the long winter months you would agree that some pioneer playground work of the very simplest type is much needed," Strong wrote in a letter to supporters of the colony.[101]

Strong designated an upstairs room as the colony "living room": "No one this side of Moscow knows what a 'living-room' is for, or ever saw or heard of one," Strong reported to her father. She suspected it might immediately be destroyed or that children would steal all the furniture out of it, but she held periodic "open houses" with tea from Miss Graves's samovar, cocoa, and even candies. At first, only the boldest boys came (lured by the candy, which they grabbed and ran off with), but by the second or third time, the open houses were "real social functions." Some boys actually talked to Strong, and a few girls made it to the threshold. She also taught them to dance the Virginia reel and some simple American games.[102]

Ellen Hayes, who donated $1,000 to the colony for "cultural purposes," urged Strong to start a science program and even talked of coming to teach herself, although Strong confided to her father in August 1925 that "Miss Hayes' dream of teaching science or anything orderly seems so infinitely remote." Strong admitted to Hayes that conditions remained pretty dire in the colony. Still, she talked hopefully of getting the school fixed up and naming it after Hayes, or perhaps Anita Whitney, a colony supporter, former suffrage leader, and Communist from California whose imprisonment for criminal syndicalism made her something of a cause celebre. "I want a woman's name, because here . . . we still have to fight to make folks realize that women are people, and that girls, as well as boys, have a right to knowledge. In this we are also fighting for the new Russia against the old."[103]

Strong's talk of Ada Flomenbaum establishing a "playground" seemed a bit of a joke once she was actually back at the colony (her "job will be much more primitive than that," Strong admitted to Hayes), but Strong did have high hopes of Flomenbaum getting a proper school going, with help from Yavorskaia, a Russian Communist who had directed several children's homes and had tentatively agreed to be a kind of "mother superior" during the summers.[104]

Strong especially hoped that Flomenbaum or another American woman would be able to give some attention to the girls: "They are still in back-woods territory where women are only rather poor cooks for men; their cultural needs, even their desire to learn sewing, is neglected for the needs of the boys. . . . Yet they are of a surprisingly higher type than the boys in the colony, on the whole, very affectionate, hard-working and devoted, with no one of intelligence who takes the slightest interest in them."[105]

Strong's account of the colony in her 1943 novel *Wild River* has one girl actually protesting the gendered division of labor: "The girls were not asked to state a preference. Yermeyev took it for granted that the task of girls was fixed by nature. It was to clean, to cook, to sew. He had asked the Children's Home for a proportion of one girl to four boys since he figured that one girl could clean and cook for four." Strong's character, Stesha, asks if the girls would get "to learn any interesting trades," adding "The Revolution gives us equal rights."[106] In her correspondence from the time, Strong repeatedly expressed concern for the girls but actually never suggested that they, like the boys, ought to learn industrial skills.

Denouement

If in the summer of 1925 Strong could still write optimistically about the children of the JRC and the prospects for their social development ("they are charming, affectionate, intelligent children . . . we have managed to make a living for the youngsters; now we want to make their life worthwhile"), six months later she had no such optimism left. The investigations she had requested the prior summer resulted in Strong herself being blamed for the colony's condition. In January 1926, while in the United States, Strong received a cable saying that if she wanted to save her own reputation ("rendering it definitely constructive not sporadically philanthropic"), she needed to raise $3,000—in less than a month—to finance repairs.[107]

After fuming for a week or so, Strong went to the offices of the Workers Party in Chicago, "for they are especially concerned politically in any failure or scandal which may arise from John Reed colony." Officials in the Workers Party agreed to help Strong raise funds, but then Strong thought better of it: "All of those agreements were conditioned on knowing that our money went through responsible and business-like management." She did not feel she could trust the Russian authorities. Therefore she cabled that she could not send money but would send ten Russian-American "farmers mechanics brickmakers mostly communists." Yavorskaia cabled back, "Must know definitely whether stated amount can be raised to secure brick factory and save colony otherwise chefstvo [Strong] discredited." She felt backed into a corner.

"I consider Yavorskaia is asking me to commit a crime," Strong wrote. "And it makes me very angry. She is asking me to waste money given by workers of this country for Russian children—to waste it in order to save myself from discredit." She went on: "If my reputation in Moscow, Saratov or Wolsk must be saved by such means, let it be discredited." She had raised quite a bit more than $3,000 for Russian children and had "fulfilled every promise I ever made, and very much more." Meanwhile, "not one government department has fulfilled the promises it made to the colony, or has ever been more than spasmodically philanthropic [her perhaps accidental play on the 'sporadically philanthropic' comment] in dealing with the lives of those children." Apparently, the bulk of the money she'd raised for special equipment had actually been spent on food and wages (which the Soviets were supposed to cover), if it had gone to the colony at all. "I am interested in the children of John Reed, and in the educational experiment of making a self-supporting farm; I am not interested in financing more local politicians or giving money without control to people who have wasted it before," Strong insisted. "The children themselves are hungry and cold."

"Every inefficient person from the center down, will keep on making me the goat for their own lacks," Strong concluded. "They have the power; they have the language and the party connections I haven't. I cannot fight them." She threw in the towel: "Let them save their own reputations then by throwing it on me; in the end they would do it anyway, and the children would still be hungry with a badly managed brick factory."

Every step of the way, Strong had found herself fighting an intransigent and often corrupt bureaucracy, and her idealism (and that of some of the children) was repeatedly challenged by circumstances, from a lack of government funds to the infusion of far too many new children, some of them not only unable or unwilling to contribute to the colony but actually more suited to a life of crime ("they stole our blankets and shoes and made our struggling children hopeless," Strong complained).

She'd struggled valiantly to raise money, but even more importantly she'd recruited Americans willing to donate time and labor. Yet many of the people she'd recruited had never even gotten an answer from Soviet officials to their requests to come. Arguably this more than anything had already "discredited" Strong in the eyes of the Americans who had answered her call.

By the following summer, Strong had finally given up on the JRC; what is remarkable is that she held out as long as she did. Looking back on the experience nearly ten years later, Strong wrote in her memoir *I Change Worlds*, "I saw that under socialism, as under capitalism, the varied wills of men survive; that the wish to take part in Soviet life does not of itself bring wisdom; that not even in building socialism—Oh, least of all in building socialism—should one be a credulous fool. I saw with a stab of pain that a brain is needed, even in dealing with comrades."[108]

As all of this unfolded for Strong, Haines returned to Moscow in 1925, taught in a nurse's training school, and studied the Soviet health system; her *Health Work in Soviet Russia* (1926) praised the Soviet system and earned praise from American critics. The AFSC's relief program had been scaled back in June 1924 to focus exclusively on health work due to unspecified circumstances of which "Friends could no longer approve." Haines had been planning an American-run nurse's training school in Moscow, and she received plenty of support for it from the physician and representative of the Russian Red Cross, Marc Cheftel, who turned out to be seeking Haines's goodwill so that she would help him secure a visa into the United States (which she did), where he spied for the Soviet secret police. The school never materialized, and Haines returned to the United States. She remained active in the AFSC and also remained a supporter of various Soviet causes.[109]

Jessica Smith also returned to the Soviet Union, around the same time as Haines, to focus on building Russian Reconstruction Farms with Hal Ware. Smith wrote a book, *Woman in Soviet Russia* (1928), that highlighted not just the advantages afforded women in the new Soviet system but also the great benefits to children: Smith quoted the basic assumption undergirding the preschool curriculum: "Joyous and free should be the labor of an adult under normal conditions as will exist in time, . . . and joyous and free should be the labor of the child." She described "the beginnings of self-government" even in kindergartens, and added, "Self expression in drawing and modeling and all kinds of play is given every encouragement, and music is considered important to 'create a rhythm for the child with his surroundings.'" The children get plenty of exercise and fresh air, and "teachers are instructed to make the life of children an active part of society by having them participate in general holidays, taking them on excursions to factories and social institutions, and by making contacts with other children."[110] A far cry from hungry children with sores on their bodies working twelve-hour days in the fields.

The Quaker house in Moscow lost its lease in 1931 and was down to just two volunteers in the end. However, until it closed, the house remained a center for the American community. The Russian child remained a centerpiece of American progressive, liberal, and radical

Americans'—and especially American women's—investment in Soviet Russia. Indeed, in 1931 a Soviet schoolbook about the Five-Year Plan— *New Russia's Primer,* by the Soviet engineer M. Ilin—became a best seller in the United States, not only because Americans were fascinated by the idea of a planned economy, but also because the subject was considered appropriate reading for children.[111]

LIVING AND WORKING IN THE NEW RUSSIA

From Kuzbas to Moscow

Between 1929 and 1932 Ruth Epperson Kennell published a series of articles—two of them with her friend, Milly Bennett—in H. L. Mencken's irreverent magazine, the *American Mercury*. The articles poke fun at the Americans who began pouring into Soviet Russia beginning in the early 1920s with plans to live, work, and take part in the building of a socialist utopia, as well as the Russians who both needed and resented this influx of foreign workers. Of the seventy to eighty thousand foreigners who came to the USSR in the 1920s and 1930s for work, a large proportion was American. Some were deeply committed to the Soviet experiment. Others were native-born Russians returning home and reuniting with families, hopeful that their lives would be better under a new regime. Still more, especially in the 1930s, came simply for steady work at a decent wage, as the Great Depression and mass unemployment coincided with the First Five-Year Plan and worker shortages in the Soviet Union.

"The New Innocents Abroad," which Kennell published in May 1929, focuses on the Autonomous Industrial Colony of

Kuzbas (AIK), an undertaking that might well be described as an American utopian colony that took root in the wilds of Siberia. "Many and various rebels against American society—budding communists, veteran socialists, I.W.W.'s, labor agitators, dreamers, failures, neurotics and plain adventurers—flocked to Russia after the war," Kennell wrote, maintaining that the AIK "was the most pretentious of the colonization projects." "Pretentious" is perhaps Kennell's way of mocking herself, as one among the five hundred or so Americans who signed a two-year contract pledging "to work at his or her highest capacity in order to create the highest form of productivity, so that they will prove by deeds that the workers are more capable of operating industry than the capitalists," or, put more idealistically, to "build a new REPUBLIC OF LABOR, sword in one hand and mason's trowel in the other, like the builders of Jerusalem in the days of old," to quote a pioneer writing in the *Kuzbas Bulletin*.[1]

As soon as a Bolshevik victory in the Russian Civil War seemed assured, Americans, most of them Russian immigrants eager to return home, began flocking to Soviet Russia. Although the majority in this wave entered without official dispensation, immigration policy in the first few years of the Bolshevik regime was relatively open. As early as 1919, Lenin issued a call to foreign workers to support their Soviet comrades in building socialism. That same year—which is also the year that the CPUSA was founded—Soviet sympathizers in the United States and Canada founded the Society for Technical Aid to Soviet Russia (STASR) to expedite and coordinate immigration to Soviet Russia by skilled workers.[2]

While the civil war and blockade limited the flow from North America, in late 1920 and early 1921, around sixteen thousand Americans entered Russia through ports at Libau and Riga. In April 1921 Soviet officials essentially put a stop to immigration by instituting a more complicated entry process for individuals. Now would-be Soviets had to come as part of an official foreign commune, the vast majority of which were organized by the STASR. And all comers had to be able to offer skills that were demonstrably in demand. Between 1923 and 1926 foreigners organized nine agricultural and twenty-six industrial collectives, with 4,400 and 1,223 members, respectively; at least twenty-four of those communes were primarily made up of Americans.[3]

The Kuzbas colony was the largest of these and was certainly the one that received the most attention in the United States. This had to do, on the one hand, with the idealistic rhetoric used by its promoters, who appealed less to returning Russians and more to those wanting to "demonstrate their capabilities once freed from the yoke of capitalism." It also had to do with the huge amount of press generated by several colonists who defected amid sensationalist claims that they had been misled by colony organizers and, even worse, that the whole place was a den of sin where American women were subject to harassment by "bewhiskered Slavs" whose practice of "free love" was "enforced everywhere under Lenin's rule." Ruth Kennell's reports on the colony's doings were largely sympathetic; indeed, she was among those who personally benefited from the Soviets' "new morality." As she put it, "In the spring of 1925 more than one matrimonial partnership melted, usually on the wife's initiative. The colony women found in Siberia the freedom their souls craved."[4]

Ruth Kennell's experiences as a worker and as a woman in the Kuzbas colony are the subject of chapter 3; through a focus on women at the *Moscow News*, chapter 4 addresses the second major wave of American immigration to Soviet Russia during the early 1930s.

"They All Come to Moscow,"[5] a December 1931 *Mercury* piece, opens with a section titled "The Red Jerusalem": Joseph and Mary arrived in Moscow with fifty dollars and no place to stay. And Mary was heavy with child. "Americans looking for jobs in Moscow usually come to the office of the *Moscow News*, the only English newspaper in all Russia," explained Bennett and Kennell (both of whom, they failed to note, wrote for the paper). "Joseph duly appeared."

Joseph appealed to the "Oldest American Resident": easily recognizable as Anna Louise Strong, who started and edited the *Moscow News*. She contacted the newspaper's print shop, asking "Don't you need a proofreader? You must need a proofreader! Comrade Gordon worked for six months on the *Scott County Chronicle* in Missouri."

The "Oldest Resident" then set out to find the couple a place to live. "This, in fact, is one of her chief occupations in Moscow. She keeps on the trail of rooms like a reporter looking for news. Her head is full of schemes for putting this American comrade out and this one in, or for holding down a room for someone else." She found them a room, which was small and sparse but seemed adequate until a stranger let himself in, arms full of baggage, and proceeded to take off his shoes, get undressed, and make himself a bed on the floor. Unaccustomed to the communal living arrangements both encouraged by Communism and necessitated by the Moscow housing shortage, Joseph and Mary rejected this arrangement.

A new room was found for the couple, but they were still scrambling to prepare for their child's birth: "Hadn't Mary read in the *Nation* how the Soviet Union takes care of young mothers and babies?" They managed to obtain blankets and various other supplies from Americans living in Moscow, they managed to find a hospital with room for Mary, and they managed to get there in time: the latter truly a miracle in a city with few taxis. But after the baby was born, the couple could not afford milk, and they had no warm clothes for the winter. Then they were turned out of their second apartment.

> Reluctantly the two who wanted to stay, who loved to sit on the edge of Communism and hold hands, cabled home for money.
>
> "We love it here," Mary sighed. "The life—the hope in the people! America's stupid. Nothing's happening there. We don't want to go home. If it weren't for the baby . . ." (ellipsis in original)

Most American immigrants to the Soviet Union did not, in fact, display Joseph and Mary's quasi-religious devotion to Communism: thousands simply came for jobs and a guarantee of the most basic living standard. Still, nearly every foreign visitor, from tourists to those seeking work, was curious about the attempt to create an alternative to capitalism on a grand scale. As Kennell and Bennett noted in another *Mercury* article in April 1932, the wave of immigration from the United States that began around 1930 was quite different from the earlier one. "The Bolsheviki no longer asked, Are you in sympathy with the Soviet power? and then as an afterthought, What are your technical qualifications? Instead they put qualifications first, and set about making the newcomers contented with fat salaries in foreign *valuta* and living conditions superior to those of the rulers themselves" (in theory, anyway).[6]

In 1930 the Sixteenth Party Congress agreed to recruit up to forty thousand "foreign engineers, foremen and skilled workers" to aid in the completion of the First Five-Year Plan. In the first eight months of 1931, Amtorg, the Soviet-American trading agency, received applications from over one hundred thousand Americans wishing to emigrate; of these, ten thousand were offered jobs and issued work visas, but thousands more job seekers came on tourist visas. Word was that almost anyone who stayed in Moscow for a week could land a job.[7]

Although most of the industrial workers and engineers who came to the Soviet Union in the early 1930s were men, hundreds of women also came often without men. In a section of "They All Come to Moscow" called "Martyr from the South," Kennell and Bennett described Laura, "a tall, hipless blond with a soft, yearning face and pale blue, expectant eyes." Laura was discovered at a Bolshevik picnic: "She wore a sapphire blue jersey that gave warmth to her eyes, a tricky, little, off-the-face hat and very sheer, very expensive chiffon stockings." Ignoring warnings that her stockings would get ruined, and that she would never find another pair, not in Moscow, she followed the bare-legged, sandaled reporter into a field of cornflowers.

> She lifted gently reproving eyes.
> "Ah'm happy to sacrifice. You-all don't understand. Ah love Moscow. Ah want to make it mah home. Ah'll do anything—sew, scrub—ah can sew real well. Ah make all mah own clothes."

Hearing that Laura can sew, the "Oldest Resident" jumped into the conversation, offering to solve Laura's financial woes with a large pile of clothes that need mending. But several weeks later, the "Oldest Resident" angrily reported that the girl had returned the clothes unmended. The seemingly hapless thing had found a job teaching English.

Bennett and Kennell's article was a satire, but it was based on real incidents and "truths" that emerged from their experiences and perspectives. The *Moscow News* was indeed a center for the American community before the US embassy opened in 1933. Seema Rynin Allan, who arrived in the Soviet Union in 1932 as a recent college graduate, recalled going to the *Moscow News* when she decided to stay longer than the tourist visa she had would allow; Strong took her on as a reporter. Allan also recalled spending a week hunting for a place to live: she settled on a room that doubled as a dentist's office, where she slept on the couch in exchange for giving English lessons to the dentist's daughter.[8]

Laura was a fitting representative of the American new woman, marked by her stylish clothing and easily mocked for her motivations. When photographer Margaret Bourke-White visited the recently established Institute for Research on Women's Styles in Moscow in 1932, she was told that the Russian woman was interested only in sensible clothes that would facilitate her work. Bourke-White felt "ashamed for the bourgeois culture I represented" but was accosted on her way out by an institute designer wielding a tape measure, hoping to copy Bourke-White's "simplest sort of tweed suit," purchased in Paris.[9]

American women in Moscow quite visibly sported fashions that Soviet women could never obtain, even as these same American women hungered to be the sort of people who did not care about clothes.[10] Allan, riding a streetcar in Moscow, rebuffed "a buxom, red-cheeked girl" sitting next to her when the girl began admiring her raincoat. "There are so many raincoats to choose from in America, you get tired of looking for them. . . . I was beginning to feel like a clothes-hanger." She claimed to have come to Moscow because "there isn't much else to do in America except look for clothes."[11]

Like Bennett and Kennell, Eugene Lyons, a correspondent for United Press International who shared his living quarters with the *Moscow News* office, later mocked many of the people who made their way there. "British and American ladies with triple chins and overwhelming bosoms, having tried and discarded other spiritual diversions, now 'found' Bolshevism," he noted, describing one "high strung New York liberal," Jane, who reputedly argued that the elimination of the sexual double standard justified every horror enacted by the Soviet regime: " 'Starvation, forced labor, the extermination of the intelligentsia,' she said, 'bah, it's worth it, it's worth it, I tell you, because Russia has liquidated sex bugaboos. Equality of men and women, the single standard . . . it's worth it!' "[12]

Somewhere between Lyons's chilling and misogynist descriptions and the more endearing but still dismissive portraits crafted by Bennett and Kennell resides a complicated set of truths about American women living and working in Soviet Russia in the 1920s and 1930s, about the stories they told themselves, and about the stories they told others.

"A New Pennsylvania"

Seeking Home in Siberia

In the spring of 1922, Ruth Epperson Kennell and her husband, Frank, answering Lenin's call for technical volunteers, moved from their home in San Francisco to the town of Kemerovo, in the Kuznetsk Basin in Siberia, to join the Autonomous Industrial Colony of Kuzbas. They were to be pioneers of an American colony in the new Russia, the brainchild of the renegade Wobbly (IWW) William "Big Bill" Haywood and several revolutionaries he'd met in Moscow. Ruth became the colony's primary chronicler and publicist, writing magazine articles, a children's book, a memoir, a diary, and scores of letters about her experiences there. In an article that Ruth published in the *Nation*, she described Kuzbas in terms of American industrial and political development: "We are building here," she insisted, "not a new Atlantis, but a new Pennsylvania."[1] Despite the great hopes it represented, the Kuzbas colony is now forgotten (and Kennell too).

Ruth Kennell and other American women fell hard for the utopian appeal of the Soviet experiment, which promised to redefine the terms of domesticity, work, motherhood, and intimate relationships. This "practical" experiment was fueled by hope and desire as much as by machines and engineering. Fleeing the United States, American women in Russia sought a new home that would release them from materialism, individualism, ossified gender roles, and bourgeois morality. For a moment, Ruth thought she'd found what she was seeking in Siberia.

After the death of her father, the young Ruth Epperson joined her mother, Ella, a feminist and free spirit, and older brother and sister in leaving Oklahoma to seek a better life in California. Despite sometimes desperate poverty, Ruth dreamed of becoming an actress, writer, or "leader of her downtrodden sex." As a young woman in San Francisco, Ruth turned her ambitions toward practical ends and became a children's librarian. Hungry for a life of the mind, she married the first intellectual man who paid attention to her, a seminary student named Frank Kennell.[2]

Ruth endured rather than enjoyed their marital relations, but at first it was political differences, not sexual incompatibility, that threatened their marriage. During the First World War, Frank tried to enlist, over his wife's objections, but was rejected because of his poor eyesight. Subsequently, in deference to Ruth's wishes, he became a pacifist and socialist. But they differed on religion as well. He dreamed of becoming a minister, despite Ruth's "bewildering unbelief" in God, and her conviction that she "was in no sense capable of fulfilling the position of a minister's wife." She regularly committed faux pas such as abruptly getting up at a church ladies' sewing circle, "where the ladies were making pyjamas for the Belgians while the minister read aloud a book on German atrocities," and storming out the door in disgust. Even more problematically, Ruth found it almost physically painful to see and hear her husband at the pulpit, finding him "weak and insincere at such times." Here, too, Ruth eventually got her way, as Frank could not find a congregation that wanted a pacifist minister. He got a job in a religious publishing house in San Francisco, and things settled into something of a routine. Ruth's mother, Ella, meanwhile, bought a lot in a cooperative poultry colony in Palo Alto called Runnymede, "an agricultural utopia that drew over a thousand settlers." They called her chicken farm "The Retreat."[3]

Ruth and Frank allied themselves with the Industrial Workers of the

World (IWW), deciding the Socialist Party, which had failed to condemn the First World War, was too tame for their tastes. They devoted their free time to the People's Institute, a center of radical politics and political theatre. Although they and their comrades were thrilled by the Russian Revolution and took an interest in all things Russian, Ruth and Frank did not consider joining the American Communist Party (CPUSA) when it was founded in 1919. Still illegal and underground, the CPUSA "seemed impotent" to Ruth, while the idealistic IWW appeared to be "the vanguard of the revolution in America." Admittedly, she at that time "had a rather vague idea of what revolution meant, having reached only the second chapter of Marx's 'Capital.'"[4]

Despite police surveillance and periodic raids at the institute, things were going well enough until Ruth found herself pregnant, for a second time. Now doctors told her it was too risky to have another abortion. Ruth feared that motherhood would turn her into a "household drudge" and shut her off from the world, but Frank wanted the baby. Almost to her own surprise, when Jimmie (named after James Price, an imprisoned Wobbly) was born, Ruth felt genuine affection for him, love even, and devoted herself to mothering. Frank joined the Society for Technical Aid to Soviet Russia (STASR) and signed Ruth up as well, his enthusiastic activism "proving . . . that parenthood need not cut people off from social endeavors." But Ruth was keenly conscious of history passing her by while she attended to domestic duties.[5] At least those duties were shared, as Frank and Ruth had begun living communally with another couple from the institute. One day a housemate brought home a *Liberator* featuring a paean to Kuzbas: "Wanted, Pioneers for Siberia," by the proletarian bard Mike Gold. Ruth was skeptical but intrigued. Frank, with typical fervor, was ready to pack his bags.

The *Liberator* article presented a call to arms for Americans who rejected a bankrupt civilization devoted to business and consumption and who wanted to do more than stew in nihilistic denunciation of modern society: "Those of the Young Intellectuals who have not fled to the boulevard cafés of Paris, there to sit and sip cocktails in a sort of noble protest against American Puritanism, should try to arrange to meet Herbert Stanley Calvert, who has just returned from Russia with a grand message."

A "wandering 'Wobbly'" who'd worked at Ford's Highland Park plant specifically to gain skills he could take to Russia, Calvert planned to subdue the Siberian wilderness with American machines and men: "He sees the race of man, with these mighty tools in his hands, throwing itself like a disciplined, singing army upon Nature, and conquering her at last; building at last the free society of peace and plenty and brotherhood and creation in the midst of the primeval, unmoral Chaos. He is a poet of power, of real things, materials, of forces and control." According to Gold, "machinery is to be the true Christ of our civilization. It will yet set men free."[6] In Soviet Russia, machines would produce unheard-of freedoms, and social engineering would enable a new kind of human perfection. As in classic utopian literature, it would also enable new roles for women, thanks to socialized childcare, communal dining halls, and companionate relationships not shaped by economic incentives.

Conceived of in 1921 by Calvert, William Haywood, and Dutch Communist and engineer Sebald Rutgers, all of whom had been in Moscow for the Third Congress of the Communist International, the Kuzbas colony was to be a "complete industrial unit," organized in American style yet serving as "a hub around which the communist economy" could be organized. Blessed cautiously by Lenin himself, the colony would release American workers from "wage slavery," and give Soviets the benefit of American technology, know-how, and efficiency, without the poison of capitalism. Advertised as "an opportunity so large and amazing that it takes the breath away," Kuzbas was also framed as specifically American: "It is as if one were being asked to be the founder of a New America," the colony prospectus noted. But this dream was also, founders insisted, "a practical project." However, as much as organizers talked about scientific planning and engineering feats made possible by the elimination of a profit motive, desire, hope, and imagination played a major role in Kuzbas's development. One document spends several pages describing an imagined dinner "at the Dining Rooms of the Central Kuzbas Cooperative" with "white-tiled walls," "comfortable arm chairs," a "feeling of health and intelligence," and exquisite foods.[7]

Benefiting from the region's rich iron and coal deposits, fertile soil, and railroad and river access, the Kuzbas colony was signed into being on

October 21, 1921. Calvert, Rutgers, and Haywood imagined Kuzbas as a site where "international solidarity" could be "practically demonstrated" and as a crucial laboratory for convincing Americans of the Soviet experiment's viability. Success would bring much-needed support; failure would make Kuzbas "the laughing stock of the whole world."[8]

Women were an afterthought for the founders. An apparent excess of "Siberian beauties" and plans for primarily industrial work made it seem unnecessary to recruit more than a few "strong, healthy women who are accustomed to outdoor life, pioneer women" whose presence would "maintain the proper home life and atmosphere."[9] Even so, the colony attracted women who hoped that egalitarian communal living would free them from the burdens of domesticity.

The colony offered women, under the guise of a revolutionary new society, satisfying and worthwhile work, edifying and fulfilling leisure, changes in the very nature of homemaking, and a domestic sphere that encompassed the community. Although Lenin had bragged, as early as 1919, that the Soviet Union had done more for women than any other civilized nation, he also acknowledged that without the full achievement of socialism, "woman continues to be a *domestic slave*, because *petty housework* strangles, stultifies and degrades her, chains her to the kitchen and to the nursery, and wastes her labor on barbarously unproductive, petty, nerve-racking, stultifying, and crushing drudgery." Socialism was still to be fully realized, but Kuzbas would institute it immediately—and with it the gains it promised women. Perhaps most strikingly, beyond release from the "petty domestic economy," Kuzbas also offered the prospect of freedom from bourgeois morality—something Ruth Kennell, for one, did not initially know she craved.[10]

Four weeks after the Kennells saw Gold's piece in the *Liberator*, the New York office of Kuzbas, upon reviewing credentials Frank had previously sent to the STASR, invited Frank and Ruth to Kuzbas. They decided to go. Jimmie, now eighteen months old, would say with Frank's mother.

Like all volunteers, Ruth and Frank took the "Workers' Pledge" that Lenin had drawn up in sanctioning the colony: all volunteers must be able and willing to endure hardship and privation, must agree to "work at his or her highest form of productivity," must establish friendly relations with the Russians, and must "subordinate him or herself to the discipline of the Colony," accepting final authority from the Soviets. Colonists paid their own traveling expenses and had to contribute at least $300 (about $4,000 today) "for necessary tools and machinery." They had to commit to a two-year contract, get their teeth checked, and obtain smallpox vaccinations before leaving. And they were told to bring various supplies: sheets, pillows, and blankets; a teakettle, stewpot, drinking cup, and dishes; and clothes suitable for Siberian winters (average Kemerovo temperature in January is −4°F). They were discouraged from bringing bulky furniture, but sewing machines, kitchen utensils, electrical appliances, and extra dishes were welcomed. They were guaranteed insurance, vacation, sanitation, and education typical of the rest of Soviet Russia (at least on the matter of sanitation, this wasn't promising very much).[11]

Ruth began having nightmares about leaving her young son, nightmares that would continue to haunt her in Russia: "I dreamed I came downstairs and reached up to a platform to lift Jimmie down, when he slipped out of my arms and struck his head on the side of the steps," she wrote in a letter to her brother. "When I picked him up he was unconscious, and I was frantic to know what I should do to revive him. I was afraid he was dead. I do not remember beyond this. I recall looking down at his white face and thinking that if only he came to life, I would never leave him again."[12]

Yet going seemed like the right thing to do. As "Ernita" (the stand-in for Ruth in Theodore Dreiser's thinly veiled sketch of her Kuzbas years) is said to have insisted, "And whether it was motherly of me or not, in this crisis it seemed to me that this was my opportunity, not only to escape from an unsatisfactory existence as a housewife, but to satisfy my passion for service—to prove that a mother could do the world's work and still be a mother."[13]

En route to Kuzbas, Ruth and Frank passed through New York, which represented everything they were trying to get away from, "a big, merciless machine, grinding out profits for the few and making drudgery for the many." Ruth put gnawing thoughts of her son behind her as the SS *Rotterdam* left the harbor on July 22, 1922. All 135 members of the

Kuzbas group stood on the upper deck, singing "The Internationale" and waving a red flag. At the dock, workers waved another red flag, and Ruth and her comrades went wild with excitement before realizing that it was only a signal flag.[14]

Frank and Ruth were part of the fourth group of "pioneers" traveling to Kuzbas from the United States. Though all ostensibly Americans, most were foreign born: from Finland, Russia, Lithuania, Germany, Croatia, Austria, Yugoslavia, Switzerland, Sweden, Cuba, Poland, and Hungary. They had come from every part of the United States: there were miners from Pennsylvania, Illinois, and West Virginia; an engineer and a farmer from Alaska; and a Seattle chicken farmer with a dozen Rhode Island Reds. Aboard the ship, Ruth and Frank quickly became the social center of the group, organizing evening entertainments, including dancing and singing. One night they directed a pantomime about their reasons for going to Siberia. Comrade Svingle played the czar, wearing a huge tin can on his head, and sitting on his "golden throne," a packing case. A towering Finn, representing the Russian workers, came forward singing the "Marseillaise" and knocked the czar off his throne. Allied soldiers and counterrevolutionists arrived to challenge the worker, and were barely defeated before Ruth, "dressed in black, with a haggard face," arrived as famine, circling the worker and his child to the tune of a funeral march. Finally, "KUZBAS" came to the rescue, dressed in white. Driving Ruth/ famine away, Kuzbas raised a red flag and then, arm in arm with the worker, offered a rousing rendition of "The Internationale."[15]

Days passed quickly, and Ruth spent evenings out on the deck, watching the stars and contemplating the future. The steamer stopped in England, and then in Rotterdam, where colonists changed to a smaller ship. At one point, Communists in the group held a private meeting and Ruth felt resentful and left out. Communists, Ruth quickly discovered, held a privileged position, in Kuzbas as in the rest of the Soviet Union.

Despite various ideological and ethnic differences, the group was united in their excitement when their ship passed the fortress of Kronstadt and a golden dome in the distance told them they had reached Petrograd. But they had arrived in "the promised land" two days early, and no one was there to greet them. Far from being feted as heroes, the Kuzbas pioneers were instead treated like "common immigrants." After their baggage was searched and the ship's captain worked through enough red tape to dispose of his charges, the colonists were left to their own devices. That night they slept on the floor in an old mansion that housed the immigration office. Ill from eating some bad sausage, Ruth got only a small glimpse of Petrograd. But she described it as a "stricken city, one of extreme privation, ruin and chaos, misery and desolation." She was glad to be moving on when the group's special train left.[16]

They traveled through the heart of the famine. Devastation was everywhere, highlighting the group's relative comforts and making it hard to guard their own precious provisions, as well as their physical health. The train included a kitchen car, and meals were served during long stops. Colonists would line up in front of it, receive their plates, and then eat, "sitting on the rails surrounded by the omnipresent beggars and homeless children." Ruth complained about several "sentimentalists" in the group who offered bits of food or other goods to particularly pathetic-looking children among the hungry hordes swarming around the train. The Kuzbas colonists had come not as relief workers but as technical workers, Ruth frequently reminded her comrades. The pitiful cries of emaciated children made it, "indeed, hard not to give them all one had," but Ruth was no "sentimentalist."[17]

At one point the train was held up for several days beside a temporary morgue housing cholera victims. The smell was overpowering. Ruth wandered into the nearest town, a "desolate place" with a deserted garden on the grounds of a crumbling mansion that had been taken by the Bolsheviks. At the garden's center was a red wooden monument to the revolution. Making her way back to the station, Ruth found more children begging and scavenging for food. Finally, the train began moving again. Ruth watched the changing landscape from her window. Birch trees and wildflowers alternated with fields being harvested by hand. Close to the Urals, "the rolling meadows and golden fields gave way to hilly country covered with pine and fir forests." But on the way into Siberia, "the country became monotonously flat and we were harassed by mosquitoes; it rained frequently and the dreary stations were mud holes." Ruth imagined the two years ahead with a heavy heart.[18]

It took twenty-four hours to travel the last thirty miles. When the group finally arrived on a hot August day, they were unprepared for the lovely landscape they found, with the Tom River running through town, "flanked by a beautiful wood where maple and birch trees amid tall pines were just turning to flaming colors."[19]

They were greeted by a tall, thin, "distinguished looking man with a Van Dyke beard." This was S. J. Rutgers, who had arrived just a few weeks earlier to assume leadership of the colony, after Lenin deemed Bill Haywood's direction ineffectual. Beside him stood his assistant and interpreter, Bronca Kornblitt, a Polish-Jewish Communist, ill with tuberculosis, and temperamental but iron-willed. Bronca served as a kind of conscience of the colony, and she was fiercely devoted to Rutgers. Haywood, large and imposing with one eye sealed shut from a childhood accident, also stood beside Rutgers; he wore a Russian peasant blouse and a grim expression.[20]

Work at the colony had begun under the nominal leadership of Jack Beyer, a Seminole Indian, sign painter, and Wobbly who, like Haywood, had been arrested on criminal syndicalism charges in the United States but fled to the Soviet Union. Experience thus far suggested that Wobblies made for fiery radicals and good recruiters, but poor managers. To make matters worse, early recruiting had failed to follow an oft-repeated dictum that the colony needed skilled workers rather than political agitators. Colony affairs had been managed via mass meetings during which members argued into the night about how things should be done; afterward they returned to work, exhausted and each doing pretty much as he or she saw fit.[21]

As a result, not much had been accomplished. Frequent mistakes were exacerbated by conflicts with local Russians and probable sabotage by them as well. By the time the fourth group of colonists arrived, many of the once starry-eyed enthusiasts were disillusioned. Early issues of the *Kuzbas Bulletin* had been full of letters and articles celebrating the "pleasure" of working there, where "the effort of *Proletarian Energy*" would "create the *New Industry*."[22] No longer.

Under Rutgers's new administration, worker control had been effectively abolished, and about twenty disgruntled colonists were making preparations to leave. An acute housing shortage left people living six or seven to a room or, worse, in boxcars, railroad coaches, and worn-out tents. Every new wave of pioneers vied for space with Russians, ten thousand of whom were living in Kemerovo before Americans came to settle this supposedly wild (industrial) frontier. Many of these Russians were hostile to both the Bolsheviks and the immigrants threatening their homes and jobs.[23]

Sanitation was even more of a problem than housing. Haywood reported "spots around the town that are little more than an immense dunghill," noting also that "every kind of vermin invade the houses in abundance." Joining the ubiquitous mosquitoes were the flies and cockroaches that swarmed through every kitchen. There was an outbreak of typhus, and a four-year-old American girl had recently died from dysentery.[24]

Even so, Ruth felt thrilled. She and Frank piled their baggage, blankets, and mattress onto a horse-drawn cart and rode to their temporary home, which they shared with the new chief engineer Alfred Pearson and his family. For nearly three weeks the Pearsons and the Kennells would share not just rooms but also a bed as they waited for the Pearsons' bedding to arrive. Rutgers joked that they "were the kind of communists one reads about in the American press!"[25]

While the cart bounced over a rutted dirt road, "native girls, barefoot, smiled at us as we clattered past log cottages with latticed windows, where geese strutted in the dooryard and pigs scurried before the wagon." Their destination was the Stone House, or Dom Prezich, the grandest and most modern building in town, with stenciled walls, high ceilings, and electricity. Once home to the Russian superintendent of the mines, it was now run-down, dirty, and inhabited by "a bewildering number of Russians," whom Haywood had been loath to expel. With the arrival of Rutgers, Russians were gradually being evicted to make room for the American technical staff, adding to the tensions plaguing the struggling community. Perched atop a bluff and housing most of the specialists and managers, the Stone House became known as Parasite Hill.[26]

Ruth temporarily put off her dream of starting a colony library and began working in the office, assisting Alfred Pearson, and teaching children in the colony school, while Frank served as school superintendent as well as colony accountant. Although expecting "complete social equality" in the colony, Ruth quickly discovered popular resentment against office workers and especially residents of the Stone House. Industrial workers soon voted that "white collar stiffs" should work nine hours a day rather than eight. General contempt for office staff was barely disguised.[27]

Petty conflicts *within* the Stone House, most of them revolving around Mrs. Pearson's attempts to convert the Siberian mining town into a Gopher Prairie, highlighted the gender, class, ethnic, and ideological divisions throughout the colony. Mrs. Pearson clashed bitterly with the wife of the office manager, Simon Hahn, barring her from the Stone House dining room and then even from the kitchen, forcing her to prepare family meals on a small stove in the Hahns' room. Ruth was annoyed by the constant squabbling between the Waspy Mrs. Pearson and the Jewish Mrs. Hahn, but even more infuriating was the fact that Mrs. Pearson expected Ruth to "perform those household tasks which tradition had imposed upon my sex." It was one thing to expect unemployed wives to do their share of the domestic work, an issue that would itself become a source of intense conflict in the colony. But Ruth had come as a worker, not as a wife. "Had I left my comfortable home and baby for such a medieval situation as this? No, indeed!—I had hoped above all things to be relieved of household duties and to realize complete equality with men." Although a significant proportion of the colony's women had come as wives or "dependents," quite a few, like Kennell, came as workers: the colony's dentist and doctor were women, as were the school's teachers and the commissary manager. Others worked full-time in the dining hall, hospital, or offices.[28]

By the end of that summer, carpenters had completed a spare if functional Community House. Its "rows of rooms, rough pine partitions, long desolate corridors and a big bare dining-room with oil-cloth covered tables and wooden benches" helped alleviate the housing crisis, but squabbling over living space continued.[29] Ruth and Frank began eating in the community dining room, as Mrs. Pearson had become unbearable, even after they stopped sharing rooms—and a bed—with her and her husband.

Kuzbas Members at home in Kemerovo.

Fig. 3.1 Kuzbas members at home in Kemerovo (postcard). Courtesy of Red Hill Museum, Kemerovo, Russia (with help from Marina Potoplyak).

In this time, Ruth experienced something of true communism. Describing the colony's arrangements, Ruth suggested that although cockroaches crawled on the whitewashed walls of the dining room, and were "likely to drop down on the food at any time," the system of communal living was basically working:

> The food is plentiful and well cooked, though the diet is too starchy; you even grow to like the black bread, sour, soggy, and inclined to mold. . . . Fresh vegetables and meat, eggs, milk, and honey are fairly plentiful, but sugar, white flour, fruit, and soap cannot be obtained outside the imported colony supplies. Those who prefer to do their own cooking are given payocks (rations) for ten days. Soap and tobacco are rationed monthly. All colony members except children and mothers of infants must do useful work. In return the workers receive food, shelter, and certain winter clothing such as fur caps and gloves and felt boots. A community laundry launders ten pieces weekly for each worker. A shoe

shop repairs shoes. We get along very nicely without money in Kuzbas Colony.[30]

"Very nicely" was an exaggeration. Even before control was turned over to the Americans, just the "business of feeding, housing, and managing the lives of four hundred men, women, and children, who lived a purely communal life, entirely without money, proved complicated."[31] Ruth was put in charge of all clerical work related to the daily life of the colony, making her acutely aware of the various conflicts, not just between Wobblies and Communists, or Russians and Americans, but also between different nationalities, and, finally, between men and women.

Ruth helped Pearson with a report that outlined plans to improve and transform the colony under American leadership and solicited funds from Moscow to go forward. She also set about livening up the social side of colony life and "energetically planned parties and entertainments." With Frank's help, she organized a production of the Susan Glaspell play *Suppressed Desires*, a Freudian comedy of manners. Ruth herself was barely suppressing what would soon become all-consuming desires, as the utopian, social desire to be part of a new society expressed itself in a personal, sexual awakening.[32]

As Ruth found herself making a meaningful contribution to the colony, she began to experience feelings she'd never known. Her first day in the office, Ruth met Sam Shipman, a Jewish, Cornell-trained engineer who explained her office duties. "I looked at him with immediate interest; he seemed to stand out from the rest," she wrote later. "He had a tall, well-built figure which appeared graceful even in the khaki shirt and soiled corduroys, thoughtful dark eyes behind horn-rimmed glasses, olive skin and a sweet, sensitive mouth. Altogether he seemed to combine youth and sophistication in the most charming way."[33]

They became fast friends, taking long walks in the woods, whose beauty provided respite from the colony's petty conflicts, conflicts that seemed to exacerbate existing tensions between Ruth and Frank. Ruth and Sam began to see even more of each other after Sam and his roommate Irwin took a room in the attic of the Stone House. The two men would often come down to visit, and while Frank dozed on the bed, the others read out loud, played charades, talked, and laughed. Ruth recalled, "with [Sam] near, life seemed no longer drab or grim; it was colored and softened by a romantic glow." One day when Frank was ill in bed, Ruth and Sam trudged through the snow to retrieve a Russian grammar that Frank had dropped. Spying the grammar, Ruth fell into a snowdrift as she tried to reach for it. Sam helped her up and then the two "stood to our waists in the snow, holding on to one another."[34]

Sam offered a welcome distraction to Ruth. The approaching winter brought cold and darkness, and tempers flared easily. The mines were at that point under Russian control, and when the Russian director ousted three American families from a cottage to make room for a labor union headquarters, several Wobblies strenuously objected, complaining that "American workers were being exploited in a foreign country by local bureaucrats, backed by the Communist party." They (illegally) organized an IWW local and, to Ruth's surprise, elected her as chair. Later the supervisor of the mines stopped by the Stone House to choose rooms for a new mining engineer, also a Russian. There was much speculation about who would have to go to make space for him. Alfred Pearson tried to evict the Hahn family. When Simon Hahn cited a rule that no one could be evicted in the winter, Pearson backed down, but proclaimed that since Mrs. Hahn did not work, the colony laundry should be off-limits to her family. Simon, indignant, declared he could no longer work under Pearson. Rutgers ordered Hahn back to work.[35]

Amid all the conflict and darkness of winter, a bright spot of hope appeared on the horizon: Moscow bureaucrats approved plans to turn the colony over to American control as of February 1, 1923. However, Kuzbas would have to adopt a wage system to conform to the Soviets' New Economic Policy. Under this system, workers were divided into seventeen categories, ostensibly to raise productivity. Colonists feared that the wage system would exacerbate differences between white-collar and industrial workers, increase competition, and all but extinguish dreams of a workers' cooperative. Moreover, colonists would lose all voice in the administration of Kuzbas affairs. Thus, while the colony would officially be "American" controlled, the "autonomous" in its title was effectively rendered meaningless.[36]

Not surprisingly, the Wobblies were unhappy with this new state of affairs, and a large contingent of them resigned. Pending their release, several refused to work, but then were served notice that if they did not work, they would no longer receive *payocks*. A colony meeting was called. The striking Wobblies argued that they had already given more than their share of labor and capital to the colony, with little in return. A Finnish Communist shouted down a Wobbly, who then drew a dagger. Someone else pulled out a gun. Several comrades held back the men and confiscated their weapons. The Wobblies agreed to return to work after a majority of colonists voted that they should do so. But the former strikers sewed the letter "P" (for prisoner) on the back of their work shirts to signal they were working under duress.[37]

Ruth and Frank had been aligned from the beginning with the Wobblies, and although he hadn't joined the strike, Frank continued to support those who had. He claimed the whole undertaking had been misrepresented as "a chance to participate in industrial democracy," making the strikers justified in refusing "wage slavery in a capitalist enterprise, controlled from above." Frank declared that he and Ruth should leave with the others. Ruth, refusing, said she wanted to fulfill her two-year contract. Privately, she had other reasons for wanting to stay; as she wrote in her diary, "I want to stay here—to be free, free!"[38]

But even Ruth was anxious about what the change would mean for the communal living arrangements. As the shift approached, she became nostalgic, musing "I think always the most beautiful and wonderful experience of my life will remain these brief months of utter freedom from the curse of money and private property, when I did my work faithfully side by side with the men, ate my meals in the community dining room, sent my washing to the community laundry, had my shoes repaired by the community shoe shop, . . . and received my monthly bar of soap—all my wants satisfied without spending one ruble of money!"[39]

Sam, as head of the Planning Department, was in charge of assigning the workers into categories. Ruth argued that the simple fact of divisions was wrong. When colony members met to discuss implementation of the categories, Frank proposed that colonists pretend to implement them but in practice share wages collectively. Ruth supported her husband, claiming that communal living was more efficient, and insisting that while perhaps the Russians weren't ready for real communism, Americans were.

Ruth and Frank were outvoted by a large margin: one colonist shouted that if the wage system was good enough for the Russians, it ought to be good enough for them. Another woman, a Communist, sneered, "She [Ruth] wants to teach the Russians how to eat ice cream!" Ruth retorted that if the Americans had nothing to teach the Russians, they had no business being there. Harry Sussman, the colony satirist, had the last word: "Workers of the World Unite . . . And then be divided into seventeen categories!" Rutgers asked Ruth and Frank if they could accept the new system. Frank grumbled, but Ruth said she could manage as long as the communal living arrangements remained: "They mean emancipation for me as a woman worker."[40]

Thirty-seven colonists, including five women and seven children, left on February 3. Several disgruntled colonists aired their grievances to the American press. Ruth and Thomas Doyle, from Baton Rouge, Louisiana, went a step further, accusing the Kuzbas organizers of misleading them and stealing their money. Their experience in Russia, they said, was marked by "months of danger, disappointment, and disillusionment." Worst of all, according to Thomas Doyle, was "the constant insult to his wife by Soviet officials and others who sought continually to convert the colonists to the principle of free love." Adding to the sensational tales of deception, peril, graft, and lust, the Doyles also claimed that another colonist, Noah Lerner, had confessed to orchestrating the deadly Wall Street bombing of 1920. Lerner was arrested and held without bail, but he was released after two weeks on account of lack of evidence. It was another four months before charges against the Kuzbas organizing committee were dropped as well.[41]

As Ruth Kennell saw it, the Doyles had been troublemakers from the beginning, unable to get along with other colonists. Mrs. Doyle had attacked Amy Schecter, the colony teacher, after she sent the Doyle boys home for disrupting class. Kennell suspected Thomas Doyle of stealing supplies from the warehouse he ran. The Doyles' accusations, though specious, cast a pall over the colony, leaving its future in doubt.[42]

The Doyles' complaints about Soviet "free love," while exaggerated, spoke to a growing divide in American society, one that propelled significant numbers of people to seek freedom elsewhere, as suggested by Tom Barker's "Hell in Siberia," a *New Masses* sketch describing the colonists' practice of nude swimming in the Tom River:

> Sundays it is like Rockaway there. The whole crowd is splashing up the water, mom, pop and the kids, the coal digger and the white-collar manager; and—would you believe it—there are few bathing suits.
>
> . . . So many nude swimmers. What a chance for the Watch and Ward Society of America!
>
> The grandest opportunity ever offered an American Puritan, and not a single one around![43]

Ruth finished her "New Pennsylvania" article for the *Nation* just after the Americans assumed control of the mines and the disgruntled Wobblies departed.[44] The article suggested that while some changes ran counter to the colony's ideals, all were necessary for achieving the industrial goals most essential to the Soviets. The new system, she said, with its categories and differential wages, would offer incentives toward productivity. The one mine already under American control had seen a 300 percent increase in productivity in its first few months, and there was good evidence to suggest that the Kuzbas venture was succeeding in its goal of aiding efforts to rebuild the Russian economy, if not in implementing industrial democracy. Moreover, since workers donated 60 percent of their wages toward the dining, laundry, housing, baths, hospital, and other shared services, at least the "rudiments of communistic life" would be preserved. Ruth apparently had made peace with the new arrangements, and she encouraged others to do so as well: "Those who stay and those who come over must expect to accept this program, as they must accept the dictatorship of the Communist Party, without question. It is only upon such a substantial foundation of practical reality that Russia can hope to erect the new social order."

Ruth's assessment of the colony's real successes may have been accurate. By this time it could claim "two sawmills, two theatres, five mines, a chemical plant, three bath houses besides those at the mines, two machine shops, a carpenter shop, a tin shop, a tailor shop, a shoemaker shop, a bakery, and two electrical stations." And at least some of the houses had electricity. But skepticism was rising in the United States. In late March, the *New York World* ran on its front page a series of articles based on reports by two members of the first disaffected group to leave Kuzbas. Even more sensational stories were printed based on the Doyle testimony, though the *Nation* published a letter signed by Ruth and several other colonists that refuted the Doyles' charges. Sussman would later joke that he had been lured to Russia on false promises of free love and nationalized women.[45]

Ruth, for her part, was undeterred by a critical response in the *New York Times* to her "New Pennsylvania" article. Headlined "The Promised Land," the article pointed out that colonists had left Pennsylvania to build a new Jerusalem but were now trying again to build Pennsylvania. The *Times* placed the venture squarely in the tradition of utopian follies, concluding that "Kuzbas may or may not be instructive to the student of industrial organization, but it furnishes useful data to the religious psycho-pathologist." Ruth was secretly pleased to have her work get so much attention.[46]

For several months Ruth had housed a makeshift library in the trade union club, operating it in the evenings, but now she convinced Rutgers to provide space for a library on the top floor of the office building, which she could also use for her secretarial work and for storing colony records and files. She also began collecting and posting mail in the new space. Describing it as "the cultural center of Kemerovo," Ruth claimed the library had "a very wholesome effect on the morale of the colonists." Indeed, other former colonists later recalled the library with fondness.[47]

By spring, Ruth was feeling happier than ever. She found work satisfying and she felt appreciated. Moreover, a blossoming romance with Sam provided an ongoing, pleasant diversion. The snows finally melted, green began to sprout from the earth, and the Tom River began once again to move, swiftly carrying jagged blocks of ice. One evening in early

Fig. 3.2 Ruth Kennell in Siberia, wearing a Russian blouse. Courtesy of Red Hill Museum, Kemerovo, Russia (with help from Marina Potoplyak).

May, Ruth and Sam took a walk in the woods behind the Stone House: "It was like the scene from a Russian play," she wrote in her diary. "The birds sang, and so did the Russian girls lying under the trees. There is a real carpet of violets, and every day there is a new flower."[48]

As Ruth grew happier, she and Frank became more distant. By mid-May Frank decided to return to the United States, without her, though he did leave the door open to returning, possibly with his mother and Jimmie. Frank's decision to leave changed everything. Ruth's time with Sam was now infused with heady anticipation. Quotidian events took on extra meaning for Ruth. On walks in the forest with Sam, Ruth discovered flowers she had never seen before, and the Russian locals who "poured into the woods" apparently appeared for their benefit: "They seemed costumed for parts on this woodland stage—a primitive people living simple, natural lives," she wrote in her diary. The two months of waiting for Frank's actual departure were agonizing. As that date approached, Ruth told her mother, "I think we both need a vacation from one another." A limited sphere of existence, with work in the same building and one room as their living space, had exaggerated their problems, she believed. And yet, Ruth conceded, "I think it is I who have become more weary of our life together. Frank is just one of those loyal, monogamous men who are perfectly satisfied to see their cherished wives 365 days a year, 24 hours a day for fifty years."[49]

Frank's departure, delayed by a train that was twelve hours late, was a tremendous relief for Ruth. After a long day of waiting at the station with him, Ruth returned to their quiet room. Looking out the window at the river below, she heard Sam enter: "I turned and quite frankly and shamelessly went into his arms. From the adjoining room Mrs. [Pearson's] voice, raised to a high pitch, was suddenly quite distinct: 'She'll have to git out and stay out!' We fell apart with a feeling of guilt."[50]

But Mrs. Pearson couldn't keep them apart. So began a new chapter for Ruth: "I seemed to move in a dream world, constructed of desires I had never hoped could be realized. All the bonds which conventional society imposed and which I had struggled so long to break—the home, family, household duties, women's inferior position—had been severed one by one; I stood entirely free, alone in the Newer World, economically independent and a useful member of a social group with whose aims I was in accord."[51]

In truth, Ruth did not feel entirely free. She was keenly aware of Mrs. Pearson's disapproval and felt compelled to keep her relationship with Sam secret from the other colonists, who knew her as Frank's wife. Moreover, Ruth's own sense of moral duty kept her, at least for a time, from giving herself entirely to Sam. To complicate matters, just a few weeks after Frank left, Ruth was told that as a single woman she would have to give up the room she and Frank had shared and move to the Community House.

Sam and his friend Irwin helped Ruth move into a comfortable room, which was occupied in the winter months by Kevah "Kitty" Ortt. Kitty, a Topeka housewife who had left her husband to come to Kuzbas, supervised the colony's food rations, earning her the nickname the "pay-ock queen." She and a male companion had built a summer cottage in the woods, and Kitty agreed to let Ruth live in her room until it became too cold in the cottage. Ruth made the best of her new situation, using kerosene to kill the bedbugs she found, and setting up the room as nicely as she could.

She enjoyed long summer days with Sam, finally giving in to the urges she had so long been resisting, noting in her diary, "there are some experiences too intimate and precious to record." Frank, unaware of Ruth's activities, had arrived in San Francisco and almost immediately penned a short article for the *Kuzbas Bulletin*, giving no hint of his own dissatisfaction other than suggesting that pilgrims "must by all means thoroughly understand the way the enterprise is organized and the nature of their places in it as misunderstanding in this matter has led in the past to no end of disappointment and hard feelings." The tragedy of Frank's situation is brought home by a full-page, smiling picture of Ruth in the same issue of the bulletin. She stands in an opening in the woods, and the caption reads, "After all the tales of woe there are still smiles in Kemerovo." During this period, Ruth sent cheerful, gossipy letters to Frank and the family, including one signed "your Free and Independent Little Girl."[52]

Ruth's idyll as a free, single woman living on her own was interrupted by the arrival of a new group of colonists in early September, including a trio who came to be known as the "ladies from Berkeley": Dr. Elsie Reed Mitchell, Helen Calista Wilson, and Elsa Mehlman. "I think their coming has caused more stir than all the other groups put together," Ruth wrote to Frank. "You see, the men are desperate for American girls, and they heard three single women were coming, and in spite of my gentle hints, they *would* have hopes! So there were many expressions of disappointment when the three travel-worn, middle aged, short-haired women appeared in their trousers and boots."[53]

Mitchell and Wilson were a couple. Ruth wasn't sure what to make of Mehlman, a Los Angeles teacher who was to run the school. "She was attired in brown corduroy breeches and Norfolk jacket and had a stately dignity which appalled me," Ruth wrote. Elsa had straight, dark hair with visible gray, brown eyes, and an air of cheerful warmth. Yet Ruth initially disliked her, claiming "This dignified maiden lady reminded me of that sheltered conventional environment I had been trying so boldly to forget."[54]

Part of Ruth's initial dislike of Elsa came from the fact that she was ordered to share a room with her. Ruth objected, saying that Frank might return soon, but to no avail. Elsa moved her things into the room and then blithely climbed into bed, confessing that she'd come, not for love of Russia, but because she was bored and looking for adventure. This was Ruth's first clue that her new roommate was no moralizing old maid. Quickly coming to enjoy each other's companionship, intelligence, and sense of humor, the two women began a routine of pretending to be a married couple, Elsa "as the masterful, doting husband, and [Ruth] as the little, clinging wife. Sometimes it was so funny that we wished for an audience."[55]

After a few weeks, Kitty returned from her summer dwelling, forcing Ruth and Elsa to move to a room at the bottom of the stairs, where every footstep taken by the building's two hundred inhabitants seemed amplified. The space was small, but they set it up comfortably with the help of Walter Popp, an eccentric, brilliant engineer from a wealthy family who showed an immediate interest in Elsa.[56]

The mine workers, upstairs neighbors, seemed to deliberately make as much noise as possible when they got up at 4:00 a.m. Once, late at night, they decided to scrub their floors, creating a tremendous racket and sending water into the room below. Ruth stood on her bed and pounded on the ceiling with a broomstick. This led to a brief pause and then pounding from above in reply, after which the loud scrubbing and dripping resumed.[57]

Like other American women who came to the Soviet Union in subsequent years, Ruth seemed to find that suffering made her experience more authentic. She told her mother that "this Proletarian Hotel" is "no place for members of the intelligentsia like Elsa and me," but explained with evident pride, "I have been having my first taste of real pioneer life since I moved into the Community House—building fires, rustling coal and wood, cleaning the dirty floor constantly—my private life takes much more time now than when I lived on Parasite Hill."[58]

Ruth was aware of a blossoming romance between Popp and Elsa, but she was surprised and somewhat offended when Popp sauntered into the library one morning and presented her with a diagram, outlining a plan for secretly switching roommates. His roommate Toby apparently had feelings for Ruth, and Popp was hoping for some private time with Elsa. Not keen on the switch, Ruth was at least glad to know that Popp had no inkling of her romance with Sam. And as she told her mother, "I can sympathize with lovers, I assure you." So she agreed to do what she could. When Popp came by the next evening, Ruth dutifully went up to his room, whereupon Toby, assuming her presence indicated agreement with Popp's scheme, confessed his love for her.[59] Despite the awkwardness, Ruth enjoyed being an object of admiration, and she spent a number of evenings sitting on Popp's bed reading or writing letters while Toby unhappily watched her from across the room. Once Elsa became aware of Ruth's relationship with Sam, she and Popp began to invite Irwin, Sam's constant (and oblivious) companion, along on their frequent outings.

As she spent more time with Sam, gradually shedding her inhibitions, a new world began to open itself to Ruth: "If only I had not been so ignorant of sex matters when I married!" she wrote to her brother. "You know how cold and prudish I have always been. I thought all that was written about the 'grand passion' was sentimental unrealities. But it is all true."[60] Ruth and Sam took long walks, read books out loud to each other (Sherwood Anderson's *Winesburg Ohio*, Gorky's *Twenty-Six Men and a Woman*, Anatole France's *The Red Lily*), discussed politics, and made love.

By October Ruth began hinting that Frank should not return with Jimmie and his mother. "I am at last satisfying my craving to be an individual, and enjoying it very much," she told him. Noting that it was

Frank who had brought her to Kuzbas, she joked, "I am like the Golem that the Rabbi made of clay that turned against his creator and started on his path of destruction. Having developed with you to an extent where I have become a capable, useful, and rational individual, I want to dash off on my own hook."[61]

Against Frank's suggestion that the family be reunited in Russia, Ruth countered, "How foolish to take a child away from a high state of civilization into a far-away, backward country, for the sake of his education, when that country is trying as hard as it can to build up the very same industrial system we are running away from!" Ruth, in fact, hardly thought about her son these days: "I feel quite happy without him," she told her mother, "and cannot look forward without a feeling of aversion to settling down to family life in Kemerovo, where the secret of my happiness has been my freedom from household responsibilities and my opportunity to be economically independent, the same as any man."[62]

But as Ruth began trying to cut the ties that still bound her, she met pressure to return to old ways. First there was a letter from her mother telling Ruth that she must not abandon her son, that she must come home, and that she must give up her career for the sake of her family. Frank and his mother regularly sent letters describing Jimmie's various problems (illness, knock knees, temper tantrums). The guilt and sadness these letters produced was overwhelming. One afternoon, after reading a letter, Ruth hid in the library stacks and cried.[63]

She was feeling ill and irritable, unable to enjoy her new freedoms. Moreover, by mid-December Ruth knew she was pregnant. She immediately went to the hospital for "treatments" (an abortion) but was still having pains a month later. When Ruth complained to Dr. Nikitina, a brusque Russian woman who was "not interested in women or their diseases," the doctor told Ruth she should have checked back sooner and would now have to be hospitalized. Ruth stumbled home, barely able to walk, and was hospitalized the next day, staying for a week. As she recovered and read Edward Carpenter's *Drama of Love and Death*, Ruth thought about Lenin, who had just died. She was in bed at the start of the twenty-one-gun salute in Lenin's honor but made herself stand up along with thousands of others all over the Soviet Union.[64]

Ruth had not given up the search for what Carpenter hailed as a "new order of existence." Indeed, as soon as she returned from the hospital, she felt the "need to accomplish something." However, she found her views out of step with most of the other women. At a "Women's Meeting," which Ruth only grudgingly attended, she made, by her own accounting, "the only logical and constructive speech" defending a new colony policy that all women (including mothers of young children) would have to work to receive a *payock*. Ruth argued that the old system made dependent wives a privileged class, which served only to degrade them. Her speech did not go over well.[65]

Not surprisingly, the report by the committee on women's work, released a few days later, "disgusted" her. The dependent women objected to working in the kitchen "without pay," and several wives suggested that office workers also give up their pay, which prompted Ruth to complain to her diary, "Why try to practice communism with a lot of cattle?" Mitchell and Wilson, themselves workers (a doctor and secretary, respectively), were more sympathetic to the dependent wives' criticisms, mocking the logic of a system Ruth found reasonable: "Why should women be paid for doing housework? Had not they been doing housework for untold generations as a matter of course? And does not every man whose wife toils uncounted hours being cook, seamstress, housemaid and nurse to a family 'tell the world' that his wife does not work, he 'guesses' he can support her?"[66]

Wilson and several other women suggested to Rutgers that beyond the 60 percent system, all living arrangements could be organized communally. They proposed a "'cooperative commissary' to run the dining rooms, laundry, food *sklad* or warehouse, and store." Rutgers was skeptical, but agreed to the cooperative commissary so that the people running it could figure out what to do with the angry wives. According to Wilson and Mitchell, "Almost the first act of the newly and democratically elected committee was to vote that the women should be paid union rates and work union hours. Thus, eating turned out to be the one department which was salvaged for democracy after the dictatorship [of Rutgers] was established." To some degree this remained true even after the 60 percent system was abolished in the spring of 1924, eliminating, in Ruth's words, the "last remnant of our experiment in pure communism."[67] Workers now simply paid a flat fee to eat in the dining room, which the cooperative commissary continued to run.

Ruth told readers of the *Nation* that the 60 percent system had worked well, and that the "colonists on higher categories voiced no objection to paying more for their food than those on lower wages." But this wasn't really true: Sussman had had more than one outburst against colony wives getting more than their due, and Ruth herself complained privately that she was glad to have the change, arguing that the higher-category workers shouldn't have to support the lower-category workers and their dependent wives. She also insisted that some women would only work if forced to do so: "We had to consider that the women, Russian wives included, were being very noble to be willing to work a little in the kitchen when they could just as well stay home and draw payocks. . . . . The only way to make people work is to lay down the inexorable law: no work, no eats."[68]

Ruth had a fraught relationship with feminism: she was annoyed at the notion that women should receive any special consideration. But she also resented roadblocks to her own ambition and hated the ways that popular expectations of women limited her freedom and opportunities. And if Ruth expressed scorn for women in the colony who had made different choices than she had, her comments about Siberian women were even more distancing. She mocked the colony men who took Russian wives and suggested that the women were in it for economic gain. And she alternately described the local inhabitants as "simple, primitive people," as incompetent, lazy bureaucrats, and as grotesques. In the bathhouse, for instance, "misshapen females with withered breasts, hanging, shapeless breasts, wrinkled, fat stomachs, and knotted legs" were impossible to avoid. Her baths were thus, quite often, "not refreshing."[69]

In her diary Ruth mentioned International Women's Day on each March 8; in 1923 she discussed Russian women carrying banners, and in 1924 she mentioned that she got two hours off from work but noted that she "scorned to celebrate, as Women's Organizations are against my principles." In the 1970s—that is, in a new era of feminism—she remembered things differently, claiming to have hand-lettered a large red banner celebrating women workers, alongside artist Helen Lindley's "heroic figure of the woman mine worker," and then to have marched with other women in frigid weather. Lindley, like Ruth, had come to Kuzbas with her husband, and her marriage, like Ruth's, also dissolved in Siberia. The two women were to have another important connection later.[70]

Ruth's criticisms were undoubtedly tied to her ambivalence about being a mother, wife, and housekeeper, roles that threatened her professional aspirations and her freedom. Frank's letters were a constant reminder of the roles she couldn't quite shed, especially as Frank became increasingly aware that she was trying to extricate herself from family responsibilities. In January 1924 Frank declared that he was giving up on Kuzbas and that Ruth should come home. They were pointlessly burdening Frank's mother and depriving Jimmie of a real family. Ruth, meanwhile, insisted that she was not trying to evade responsibility for Jimmie's care, but she did not want to rush home: "Yours and my family relations have never been so ideal that you can smugly expect me to be, like the conventional wife, eager to resume them again," she wrote.[71]

Frank began to get angry. "I am now convinced that some day, probably not far distant, when the glamor of your present irresponsible life wears off a bit, you will realize too late that you have made a terrible mistake," he wrote in May. "You will face a dreary, lonely future with a sense of irreparable loss and then you will know what a broken heart means." Less than two weeks later, Frank said he wanted a divorce. He was giving up on her and on their shared political commitments: "I shall abandon altogether the things which we worked and suffered for together and shall find entirely new interests. If I should ever marry again, which is not improbable since Jimmie must have a mother, I shall marry a woman who thinks the class struggle is the annual Freshman-Sophomore rush at the university. I expect I shall be quite useful in other fields."[72]

He wrote a few days later to say that he had been too rash and would resume relations for Jimmie's sake. They went back and forth for another six months, with Frank saying he would come back to Russia if Ruth would give their marriage a chance, and Ruth insisting that Frank should make plans independently of her.[73]

Although Ruth's feelings about her sexual relations with Frank were relatively consistent, she did waver on the question of her son, and part of her seemed to want both of them near her. She also had fantasies of domesticity that simply replaced Frank with Sam. She confessed to her mother that although she had made plans to work in Moscow after the end of her two-year contract, her real desire was to fetch Jimmie from San Francisco, then live in Kemerovo with him and Sam: "It means a useful, free life, full of beauty in nature and high purpose."[74]

Such fantasies were fleeting. By the end of August, Ruth was preparing to leave for Moscow, where she had secured a temporary position as a Comintern typist. Ruth and Sam would spend a month together in Moscow before Sam's return to the United States. She still had not told Frank about Sam, nor had she definitively said whether he should return to Russia. Aside from her personal feelings, she did not know whether there was a job for him. However, just as Ruth was leaving Kemerovo, Rutgers told her that Frank could have a job, if she wanted him to come.[75]

In a rare show of decisiveness, Ruth wrote Frank that he should come back, not as her husband, but so they could both be near Jimmie, working for goals that they believed in. Rutgers had perceptively picked up on Ruth's hints that the situation between her and Frank was complicated, but he also advised her that Russia's "new morality" made it "the very best place in the world to solve such a difficult problem because Russia . . . is a 'free country,'" where people had gained "a freedom from conventionalities such as human beings have never known before." Besides, Ruth told Frank, in contrast to America, whose "social system we despise," in Russia "it is permissible and even necessary that we strive inside and outside our working hours to improve it along the lines we believe in." As for Jimmie, if Ruth had earlier worried that he was too weak physically to survive, or that he would be disadvantaged growing up in Russia, she now changed her tune: "When he reaches the school age, whatever facilities he may be given for education, we know they will be preferable to the better equipped but spiritually dead American school system."[76]

Frank, in reply, reiterated his insistence that he would come only if their marriage had a chance. He acknowledged their sexual problems but claimed to be reading Havelock Ellis (the leading sexologist of the day) and others. Ruth was undeterred by his entreaties and annoyed that he kept coming back to sex. "I wanted you to come back to Russia as an indi-

Fig. 3.3 Kemerovo picnic. Courtesy of Red Hill Museum, Kemerovo, Russia (with help from Marina Potoplyak).

vidual believing in Soviet Russia as the best place to work for himself and his family, and not as a husband seeking reconciliation with his wife," she wrote. "Your sex life seems to be of paramount importance to you, superseding all other interests and duties," she complained, adding that Frank apparently thought a man's needs were more pressing than a woman's.[77]

In late August, several colonists held a picnic with cakes, wine, and tea by the river for Ruth and Sam in preparation for their departure for Moscow. A few days later they left. The weeks with Sam in Moscow were bittersweet. Their future was uncertain, and both waited anxiously for a letter from Frank clarifying his intentions. Frank's letters only made Ruth more confused. Sam left in late October. Two months later, Frank finally cabled and said he would come on whatever terms Ruth wanted.[78]

Bereft from Sam's departure and anxious about Frank's arrival, Ruth threw herself into life in Moscow, which, after two years in Siberia, was dazzling with energy, culture, and activity. She wrote long, heartfelt letters to Sam, but assured him that he owed her nothing, that she wanted his love only if he gave it freely. Even so, she complained that she wrote to him more often than he to her. In December she returned to Kemerovo for two months to help with a new project, but she welcomed the chance to return to Moscow when summoned in February 1925 for the Comintern plenum.

Frank arrived in Moscow the day after Ruth. It was not a happy reunion. Ruth confessed her love for Sam, and Frank, hurt deeply, chided her, not for loving someone else, but for allowing him to come all the way to Moscow in hopes that they might reconcile. He was heartbroken, but kind and understanding. Echoing an arrangement from Chernyshevsky's *What Is to Be Done?*, Frank even suggested that all of them live together "in one community, in harmony with the new spirit." Ruth told him the idea was absurd and insisted that "never, never, never could I or would I" live with him, words she would live to regret. Quietly she wondered whether maybe it could work. In the meantime, Frank went to Kuzbas, leaving Ruth second-guessing: Was she right to send him away? Sam, for his part, was writing less and less often, but when they came, his letters were tender enough to keep Ruth hungry for more. Sam promised that he would join her in Russia "just as soon as circumstances permit." Ruth made an extended visit to Jessica Smith and Harold Ware's Russian Reconstruction Farms, exploring the possibility of getting jobs there for both her and Sam, but that, apparently, did not pan out. Frank's mother and Jimmie arrived in Moscow several months after Frank had. Ruth hardly recognized her own child; he had been a toddler, barely walking when she left, and now he was a gangly four-year-old with wispy blond hair. But he took to her right away, calling her "Mama" and accepting her authority. In queues and on streetcars Ruth found herself moved up to the front, given the special privileges that are bestowed on mothers of young children. At the end of a long day of sightseeing in Moscow, Jimmie fell asleep in her arms. "I looked down at his flushed face, framed in the soft, fair hair, and something long forgotten stirred in my heart," she wrote.[79]

Returning to Kemerovo with Jimmie and Frank's mother, Ruth found Frank looking better than ever, and the cottage he was living in was cozy with all their old things. Frank was warm and friendly, but something was different. A few days into Ruth's visit, Helen Lindley, the artist, returned from vacation to the home she now shared with Frank. That evening Ruth caught a glimpse of Helen in Frank's arms.[80]

When confronted, Frank said he was just in it for the sex. Ruth, deeply distraught, sought counsel from Elsa, now married to Popp and living with him in a cabin in the woods. Elsa was entirely unsympathetic. Ruth had left Frank, he and Helen were in love, and Ruth should get out of the picture. When Ruth repeated Frank's story that it was just about sex, Elsa said that Helen, who inconveniently arrived in the midst of their conversation, ought to know this, and proceeded to tell her. Helen ran off in tears, and Frank was furious.

Frank's mother condemned her as well. Ruth had ruined her son's life and was now trying to deny him happiness. With Jimmie beside her, Frank's mother told Ruth that she was selfish and an unfit mother and that she should leave as soon as possible. Jimmie then stood up and struck Ruth in the face, yelling "Bad girl—go away!"[81]

Ruth was reeling. To redeem herself, she joined Frank in an effort to convince Helen that Frank really loved her, not Ruth. To prove that she was not trying to get Frank back, Ruth agreed to a divorce. The next morning, Ruth and Frank rode together by horse-drawn wagon to a village twenty miles away; they each paid half the eight-ruble fee, while a crowd of locals gathered to see the spectacle of an American couple ending their marriage.

Ruth prepared to return to Moscow. But Simon Hahn, just back from New York, told her Sam was planning to rejoin the colony "just as soon as he can get away." Ruth had not heard from Sam in months and had nearly given up on him. But "now, all at once, everything had come to a climax—I was free, Sam was coming, I had a good position offered me in Kemerovo! It was almost too good to be true." If Helen would stay with Frank, they might all live together happily. She asked for time to decide about the job, saying she needed to return to Moscow for a month.[82]

But the future of Kuzbas was looking more and more uncertain. Bronca, Rutgers's loyal assistant, died. Lost without her, he became depressed and physically ill. The new office assistant, a Communist mining engineer named Korobkin, insisted on bringing in forty men of his own, and when Rutgers went off to a sanitarium in Holland to recover his health, Korobkin took control and rearranged the management. Upon his return, Rutgers found many of the Americans gone and himself out of a job. The "new Pennsylvania" had become something else entirely.

Ruth, too, was different. After two years in cosmopolitan Moscow, she felt hesitant about going back to Kemerovo, even before it became clear that the Americans were losing control. "It was once a place of lovely memories, a place I looked forward to returning to with Sam, free at last openly to be together—now it is a desolate little village on the steppes inhabited by abnormal people who know all my innermost secrets," she complained to her mother in May 1926. She was not even sure anymore if she would want to be with Sam.[83]

Late in the fall of 1926, Ruth received a letter from Sam telling her that he had fallen in love with someone else. Ruth graciously offered him his freedom, as she had always said she would. Writing him on New Year's Eve, she remarked on all that was ending: the year, the American colony (which was changing to Russian hands on January 1), their love.[84]

Just before stepping down as director, Rutgers had given Ruth a voucher for money owed to her by the colony, money she thought she would use to go home. But the new Russian head of the Moscow office, an overweight, balding Georgian named Gaft, told her that Rutgers's orders no longer held any weight. If she really wanted the money, he could help her, but she would need to do something for him. When the nature of that something became clear, she refused, but he physically forced himself on her. Small comfort that she was able to bring him up on charges for conduct unbefitting a Communist, or even that subsequently the whole new Kuzbas management was tried and sentenced for mismanagement and other crimes. Ruth was still violated.[85]

Ruth published "The End of Kuzbas," her last installment in the *Nation* on life in the colony, in 1929. She felt increasingly distanced from her experience there. While the Americans' role in the colony was being erased, Ruth insisted that Soviet boasting about Kuzbas as a "model community" proved its success: "Taken as a colonization scheme or a social experiment Kuzbas was a failure. But as an industrial undertaking it succeeded, and its work lives on," she maintained. When Ruth left in 1925, the colony was running at a profit. A chemical plant had opened and housing had improved. The Russians had gotten what they needed from the Americans. But Ruth did feel jaded and could not hide her feelings: "The Kuzbas program, like the whole Soviet program, was inclined to sacrifice individuals to its big, abstract social ideals," she wrote.[86]

After leaving Frank in Siberia, Ruth stayed on in Moscow for two more years, working for most of that time as an English-language librarian in the Comintern. She had affairs with several men, both Russian and American, among them a prominent Russian literary critic, identified only as "Ossip" (possibly Osip Brik), and the *Chicago Daily News* correspondent Junius Wood.[87] She also stayed in touch with Frank, with whom she shared custody of Jimmie. Elsa and Popp, as well as Helen Wilson and Elsie Reed Mitchell, had found work in Moscow, and Ruth visited with them frequently, though she spent most of her time with an Irish coworker from the Comintern, May O'Callaghan, who became a lifelong friend. Ruth went back to the United States in 1928 after acting as Theodore Dreiser's secretary during his Russian tour (and almost certainly becoming his lover as well).[88]

Dreiser's sketch of Kennell would turn her into something of a feminist icon in Russia, even inspiring a journalist to write a book about her in the 1970s. In the United States, Dreiser's sketch does not seem to have attracted as much attention, which was probably a good thing for Ruth, who agonized over whether to allow him to use it. Part of her, certainly, was attracted to the idea that a "great man" like Dreiser thought her story worth telling, and that, by implication, it had significance beyond her own life.[89]

Dreiser concluded his portrait of Ernita somewhat ambiguously:

> While still strong in the Communist faith and all that it meant in the way of freedom for women, she was no longer one who was convinced that it was without faults or that it would not need modification and strengthening in various ways. Besides, her old sureness as to her own virtues and worth had been greatly shaken. . . . Yet in Russia, as I saw it, one may do much. And despite various ills then and afterward, Ernita had decided to stay, because, as she explained it to me, she had learned that life is a dangerous, changeful, beautiful and yet deceiving thing, good or worth while or not as chances aid one, yet always fairly endurable even at its

worst. Besides, as she once said to me, and with a courageous smile: "In my youth and zealotry I had imagined that Communism could and would change the nature of man—make him better, kinder, a real brother to his fellows. Now I am not so sure Communism can do that. But at any rate it can improve the social organization of man some and for that I am still willing to work."[90]

Unique in its particulars but similar in kind to those of American women in other Soviet communes, Ruth Kennell's Kuzbas experience illustrates a way in which modern women attempted to reconcile a universal longing for homeness, or *heimweh*, with a competing desire to flee (*fernweh*) from a homeland that stultified their professional ambitions, condemned their sexual desires, and confined them to "domestic drudgery." Through conscious action to realize a world of hopeful possibility, "utopia" need not be *no place*, but could instead be its alternate meaning, a *better place*. As much as Kuzbas organizers touted the "scientific spirit" underlying the plan for Kuzbas industry, it was the undeniably utopian prospect of a better way of living that made the colony deeply appealing.[91]

It's not clear whether Ruth knew that twenty-nine former colonists who stayed on wound up in the gulag as part of the Great Terror of the late 1930s. Twenty-two of them died there.[92] Throughout her life, Ruth recognized that there could be no perfect community, and no perfect love, an attitude that allowed her to remain, for the most part, optimistic. In 1928 Wilson and Mitchell described the Kuzbas colony scheme as a "lovely, iridescent bubble that burst," giving way to "bitterness and disillusion."[93] Ruth did not necessarily see it that way, though she certainly left Soviet Russia far less hopeful than she was when she arrived.

In coming years, more women would come to Russia from the United States, similarly looking for a fresher, newer version of an American dream that had seemed to fail them. Many would consciously describe what they saw in the best possible light, thinking, perhaps, that their portraits, self-censored as much as they were government-censored, might do something to bring a better reality into being.

"Eyes on Russia"

Gal Reporters on the Moscow News

Reflecting on a 1927 visit, Walter Benjamin suggested that the Soviet Union fostered a new way of seeing—for those predisposed to look in the proper way: "Admittedly, the only guarantee of a correct understanding is to have chosen your position before you came. In Russia, above all, you can see only if you have already decided."[1] The American women who wrote for the *Moscow News* in the 1930s became especially aware of this tension, as the contrast between their published work and private writings reveals. When American women turned their own and the American public's "eyes on Russia," they grappled not only with journalists' usual responsibilities but with their own desires as idealistic, politically engaged women.

Anna Louise Strong started the *Moscow News* in the fall of 1930 at the request of Communist officials who sought a forum and a source of information for English-speaking technical specialists. These people, the Bolsheviks well knew, had varying degrees of investment in the Soviet experiment: only a small fraction came as dedicated pilgrims to the Communist mecca.[2]

Although Strong, a loyal supporter but not a member of the Communist Party, had envisioned a critical, witty, and independent newspaper that Americans both inside and outside the Soviet Union would want to read, she quickly learned that there was no such thing as independent journalism in the Soviet Union, especially not in any forum blessed by those in power. While the paper was never independent per se, the presence of Strong on the masthead and several staffers with a genuine commitment to journalism made the *Moscow News* an odd hybrid of information and propaganda.

Propaganda has been called "the true remedy for loneliness," and this is as true for its audiences as it is for its authors. Propaganda sets up expectations and norms of belief and behavior to which individuals can conform, not just because they are supposed to but because they *want* to, because it makes them feel part of a larger whole. Americans in Moscow who wrote about the Soviet Union for American readers did so not just to influence their compatriots' feelings about the Soviet Union, but also to influence America itself, to make it more like a place they would want to live. And, like diaries from the Stalin era that reveal Russians struggling to live up to a Soviet ideal, Americans' reflections on life in the Soviet Union were exercises in *self*-transformation.[3]

Anna Louise Strong wrote in her autobiography, *I Change Worlds* (1935), "The way out of human loneliness—this was the search that began for me a lifetime ago." This drive was fundamental to the Soviet Union's attraction for many Westerners. To those seeking "wholeness and coherence, the end of alienation associated with the acquisition of individual selfhood," the Soviet Union's lure was existential, even as it represented an unfulfillable fantasy.[4]

Strong's original high hopes for the paper, the paper itself, and the experiences of several female correspondents, all hired by Strong (and none of them Party members), raise an intriguing set of questions: To what extent were the paper's writers merely vehicles for Bolshevik propaganda? Did they believe what they were writing? What did their work mean to them? Desiring fulfilling work, fulfilling lives, and the realization of a new kind of society, these *Moscow News* writers balanced truth and desire in various ways. Strong's intense desire to be a "creator in chaos"[5]—that is, to create something meaningful and positive, to become part of something larger than herself, and, finally, to show herself worthy—influenced the forum she created and its editorial policies, even as publishing in the Soviet Union limited the newspaper's possibilities. In the end, Strong's efforts yielded more frustration than satisfaction, but some of the staffers found ways to make the work serve their own needs. Others ended up facing trials that surpassed anything Strong, even at her worst moments, experienced.

For female journalists in the Soviet Union, writing and publishing offered entry into a male-dominated, international public sphere as well as the possibility of self-realization. The chance to witness, to help create, and then to tell the world about new social arrangements, which included attempts to put women on equal footing with men, had understandable appeal. As "lady" journalists writing in the United States, they had become known for "participatory reporting" and as muckrakers in their own right. Now these women were consciously crafting public personas for themselves as they created a picture of life in the Soviet Union. This inevitably affected not just the way they wrote but also their own self-perceptions. These women had varied and complicated relationships with the work they did as they attempted to reconcile their desire to tell "the truth" with their desire to bring a new set of truths into being.[6]

Anna Louise Strong and the Tradition of Female Journalists in Soviet Russia

The author of over two dozen books and innumerable articles about the Soviet Union, Anna Louise Strong was the most prolific chronicler of Soviet life for American audiences. Strong's amazing productivity made her the most visible among the female journalists who reported on Soviet Russia. Whitman Bassow's claim that "women journalists were rarely seen in Russia in the early years" notwithstanding, female journalists, many of them stringers and freelancers, were key shapers of views of the Soviet Union, especially in the early years.[7]

Louise Bryant, Bessie Beatty, Rheta Childe Dorr, and Madeline Doty offered some of the most vivid accounts of the Russian Revolution.

Other female journalists and photojournalists maintained a presence in male-dominated Moscow press circles at least through the mid-1930s. At the major dailies, in national and international periodicals, and in dozens of books, women offered important insights into the quotidian details of daily living that often escaped comment in the reports of better-known male journalists such as Louis Fischer, Walter Duranty, and Eugene Lyons. Female journalists' choice of subject matter, particularly their attention to cultural life and "women's issues" like childcare, education, social welfare, women's opportunities in the workplace and in civic life, and laws relating to marriage, divorce, birth control, and maternity, also shaped Western perceptions of the new Russia in important ways.[8] The *Moscow News*, as a Soviet-sponsored publication, stands apart from the journalistic oeuvre pioneered by Bryant, Beatty, Dorr, Doty, and others, but many of its reporters also wrote for American newspapers and magazines from the *New York Times* to the *Ladies Home Journal*. The *Moscow News* also offered a steady paycheck for women wishing to live in Moscow.

Louise Bryant provided direct inspiration to Strong. Bryant's *Six Red Months in Russia* (1918) originally appeared as a serial in over a dozen US and Canadian newspapers, ranging from the Hearst-owned *New York American* and the *Toronto Star* (the highest-circulation newspaper in Canada) to the *Waterloo (IA) Evening Courier*. Her pieces are a mix of personal experience, political portraits, and commentary, with special emphasis on women and "women's issues." Bryant, Beatty, and several other correspondents made it their business to counter what they saw as sensationalist stories designed to sell newspapers and to feed an American frenzy for sordid images of the Bolsheviks.[9] Strong later took up this mantle.

Bryant had ties to people Strong very much hoped to get to know, including "the Liberator crowd . . . the Civil Liberties people . . . the Nation." For her part, Strong, not yet imagining her own future as a chronicler of Soviet life, arranged to publish articles by Bryant in the *Seattle Union Record*, the *Daily Call's* successor, which prided itself on giving readers a truthful picture of world events. Strong wrote to Bryant in December 1918, "You can get the idealism and make it glow, without making it seem as transcendentally impossible or as much a part of the spirit world as [Lincoln] Steffens does. You get the human background—the things happening to plain folks as they go along the streets. . . . Your kind of convincing picture is the thing most needed."[10]

Over the course of her initial visit to Soviet Russia in 1921 and 1922—most of which she spent in a hospital bed recovering from typhus—Strong had become obsessed with the idea of painting Soviet life in a positive light for readers in the United States. Although she had seen nothing but devastation, "not for a moment did it occur to me that I could permanently leave this country, this chaos in which a world was being born," she reflected. "It was the chaos that drew me, and the sight of creators of chaos. I intended to have a share in this creation. . . . America was no longer the world's pioneer. The World War had degraded her to be chief of imperial nations." Recalling her first impressions of the new Russia, in 1935 Strong maintained, "It seemed to me—it still seems to me—that Russia was the advancing battlefront of man."[11]

After her recovery from typhus, Strong went back to Poland in January of 1922 to fulfill her AFSC contract but returned to Russia several months later as a correspondent for *Hearst's International* magazine. When she had time, she published in the left-wing press for no pay. She had originally hoped to work full-time for the Federated Press, a left-wing news syndicate, but editors there never made proper arrangements for Strong to live and work in Moscow, and in the end they were happy to have the capitalist press support her. Strong rationalized that she could reach more readers this way, but she felt rebuffed.[12]

Strong was dizzyingly productive as a journalist and a lecturer, living primarily in Moscow but visiting the United States for several months each year to offer testimonials about life in the Soviet Union. However, she could not shake the feeling of being an outsider in Soviet society, and her experience at the John Reed Colony made her question her ability to effect real change. For perspective she traveled to China in the mid-1920s, where Communists had become an influential element in Sun Yat Sen's government. There she would meet several chroniclers of the 1925–1927 Chinese Revolution (which ended with the expulsion of Communists from China) including Milly Bennett, Jack Chen, William

Prohme, and Agnes Smedley, all of whom later contributed in some way to the *Moscow News*. Strong also traveled to Mexico, where the United States and the Soviet Union were competing for influence as Mexico's government sought to stabilize following the revolution of 1910–1920. There she met Russian feminist Alexandra Kollontai, the Soviet ambassador.[13] Strong began to conceive of a unique role for herself as an interpreter of revolutions for the bourgeois press:

> My job became a game between editors and myself; it amused me to see how much I could "put over" of what I wanted to say. I knew the "high paying magazines" would not accept me; they paid high for subtle defense of capitalism in a vaudeville of tales and articles. But scores of other publications were accessible: I had learned the technique of my trade. . . . Some editors cursed my stuff as propaganda, but took it because it was so vivid; then they would follow it by other articles which attacked the Soviets. . . . Some editors liked my stuff and helped me "put it over" on the owners of the papers; they didn't always last. But if one disappeared, others arose.[14]

Strong believed her perspective was not just unique but necessary. She was consciously appealing to the sensibilities of "men of the great plains and cities in the American West"; she used "simple words" and avoided talk of "Bolsheviks" or "Communists," not to trick readers but to bring out the deep empathy and feeling of camaraderie toward Russians that she herself felt. Strong believed that she could simultaneously serve the Communists and speak as a down-to-earth American, and also that she could truly *be* this at her very core, communicating a democratic spirit that she felt her motherland had lost. She saw the *Moscow News* as a way to extend this project.[15]

Starting the *Moscow News*

In 1930 S. J. Rutgers, former director of the Kuzbas colony, suggested the need for a Moscow-based English-language organ as a forum for foreigners' concerns and complaints. Mikhail Borodin, a longtime Bolshevik with whom Strong had become close during his post as chief Comintern agent in China (from 1923 to 1927), knew Strong had wanted to start an English-language newspaper in Moscow and told her the time was now ripe. (Borodin probably also hoped the paper might improve his own standing: after the Bolsheviks failed to take power in China, he was demoted to the post of deputy director of the paper and lumber trust, and then demoted even further, to a factory inspector position, before being given a job at the People's Commissariat of Labor in charge of "dealing with specialists and immigrants from America.") Many Westerners saw Borodin, who had lived in the United States for several years, as intelligent, reasonable, and sensitive to their interests; Strong, certainly, was more than happy to work with him.[16]

Strong had already experienced disappointments and frustrating run-ins with Soviet bureaucracy, but she agreed to get a staff and issue the paper if Borodin would handle the bureaucracy. Strong speculated, in a letter to her father, that the new job "will put me for the first time in actual constant contact with the folks who are creating the new Russia. . . . With a task like this, it seems to me I would have both a greatly increased usefulness and a greatly increased personal acquaintance." She knew there would be challenges: "The chief one would be to write stuff that would really suit the Americans, without making the Russians who read it too mad . . . . but on such technical jobs I am an expert, if anyone." She wanted to create a board of directors representing all the agencies employing Americans—in industry, trade, transportation, and agriculture—and a scheme for financing the paper through subscriptions paid for by these employers in order to keep the paper "independent."[17]

Strong imagined a lively, accessible but intelligent paper with a mix of news, feature articles, letters from readers, and humor, as well as "announcements of excursions, sights of interest, theatres, and whatever else seems wanted in the interest of enabling the English speaking persons here to be well informed and efficient in relation to the life about them." The paper would be pro-Soviet, certainly, but Strong did not want to publish a Communist organ full of heavy-handed Bolshevik jargon.[18]

Despite having asked Borodin to handle the bureaucracy, Strong went ahead and took her plan to Valery Meshlauk, the vice-chair of all

Soviet industry who in the past had praised her books. She reminded him that she was not a Party member and asked if that would be a problem. Meshlauk, endorsing her plan, assured Strong that her non-Party status would actually give the paper greater credibility with foreign specialists, the bulk of whom were themselves not in the Party. Strong, who had been fishing for an invitation to join, was disappointed but decided she would rather work for the Soviets than for the capitalists, whether they wanted her as a "comrade-creator" or merely as a "skilled employee." As she noted later, "From the dark past of my youth sprang up the old defiance: 'They don't want me; then let them see how I can work.'"[19]

Word spread quickly about the new paper. Prominent correspondents including Eugene Lyons, Louis Fischer, and Walter Duranty pledged to consider contributing.[20] Strong wrote to prominent authors she knew, including Sinclair Lewis, Upton Sinclair, Theodore Dreiser, and Lewis Gannett, asking them for articles. And she put together a staff from English speakers in Moscow.

After things seemed in order, Strong left town for a few days; while she was gone, Meshlauk appointed the head of planning for Soviet industries and a loyal party apparatchik, B. S. Vasutin, to serve as editor, and announced that Strong was to be the managing editor. The subordinate position was insulting, but Strong was told Vasutin wouldn't be around much and would not interfere. And so they proceeded.

"A spirit of energetic devotion pervaded our early staff," Strong noted. Though offered a salary of 600 rubles (equivalent to over $9,000 today) a month with extra pay for each article, Strong refused to get more than the Party maximum, and she convinced the entire staff to take the same "shock brigade pledge." "We were sick of the way Russians thought Americans only wanted dollars; we were going to be a noble bunch. We would show these communists who treated us as bought-and-paid-for outsiders that we were as good as they!"[21]

Despite Strong's best-laid plans, it is unlikely that the paper ever covered its expenses through subscriptions; surely it was never "independent," and it almost certainly received funding from the Soviet government. Still, for the first few issues, Strong largely set policy, and things seemed to go as she had hoped, aside from a few run-ins with the censor who had trouble understanding the American sense of humor. Strong gave everything she had to the paper. "We all worked in one small room, writing, typing, interviewing under the feet of a throng of eager visitors." Strong wrote, proofread, and even typed much of the first issue. "I worked flushed with fever or shaking with exhaustion, but my brain was clear, doing everything that nobody else had time for. At last, at long last, I was efficient in this country."[22]

Announcing the newspaper's launch in the *New York Times*, Walter Duranty hailed the "first American paper" to appear in the Soviet Union, and noted that while the paper "not unnaturally presents Russian news in an optimistic form," it "seems creditably free from 'propaganda.'" In retrospect it is ironic to have this assertion from a man who was later faulted for his own uncritical reporting on the 1932 famine and other aspects of Soviet life.[23] But Duranty's awareness of the propaganda question—even as he struggled to maintain his own objectivity—suggests the issue was never far removed for any journalist working in the Soviet Union.

The *Moscow News'* first issue featured on its front page a bold modernist image by Jack Chen showing factories, skyscrapers, a bridge, and a crane, with crowds of people waving flags, surrounding a document labeled "5 Year Plan," which itself rests under a drafting compass and hammer. At the top and bottom of the image are words riffing on Lenin's famous comment that Soviet power plus American efficiency would create communism: "Soviet Power Plus American Technique Will Build Socialism." Under Strong's leadership, the newspaper heralded this theme, pointing to the importance of the American specialists while celebrating Soviet achievements and emphasizing the growing economic crisis in the United States. The first issues told of American workers who pledged to consistently surpass quotas, noted important American and English visitors, and reported on the "unemployment crisis in America." They also reported on sabotage: forty-eight shot for "ruining food," a reminder that there were enemies in the midst, that vigilance was required.[24]

Issues were eight pages long and typically included theatre reviews, book reviews, sports, and news about English-language happenings in Moscow, in addition to unadorned reporting on current events, from a pro-Soviet stance. Nearly every issue featured a photo spread on the last

Fig. 4.1 "Equality an Actuality," *Moscow News*, October 15, 1930. Image © The British Library Board.

page, suggesting a debt to the documentary aesthetic that was becoming pervasive in the United States.[25]

Notably, attention to "women's issues" also marked the paper from the beginning: an early photo spread features women in various professions under the heading "Equality an Actuality." Another article describes how birth control was "scientifically handled by the Soviet State." "Approached from a 'child welfare' standpoint without religious taboos," the Soviet Union's birth control policy and its general attitude toward sex and women's rights set it apart from the rest of the world. (The article does mention that "the state feels that it is the duty of each able bodied woman to bear three to four children".)[26]

The paper would not retain Strong's style or remain "creditably free from propaganda" for long. After three months, Strong went back to the United States for her annual lecture tour, and while she was away, the paper's tenor changed significantly. Tovi L. Axelrod, "a party politician of small caliber," replaced Vasutin, and "articles grew dull and full of revolutionary theory."[27] A trial of industrial saboteurs was covered in such extensive and tedious detail that it was far easier to skip the text and simply concede the men had to be guilty.[28] There were long discussions of the Five-Year Plan and translations of speeches by various Soviet politicians. Nearly all the pieces were unsigned.

When Strong returned to Moscow, the newspaper's office was an entirely different place: Much of her staff had left, and a large new staff of translators and typists had been hired. Strong no longer even had a desk and was forced to write from home, periodically coming in to hold editorial meetings while standing in the middle of the room. The remaining American writers were now mostly just polishing articles from Russian papers handed over by translators who were making twice their salary. So much for the "shock brigade pledge."[29]

Skeptical Propagandists

While Strong was in the United States, she invited Milly Bennett of the *San Francisco Daily News* to join the *Moscow News* staff. Of German-Jewish background, Bennett (née Bremler, in 1900) was known for her quick wit, acerbic writing style, and powerful presence. She had thick, often tousled dark hair and wore heavy, coke-bottle glasses. Friends recalled her "rich laugh" and deep, husky voice, her ability to hold her liquor, and her "extraordinary figure": she radiated an unmistakable sexual energy, despite her "almost ugly" face.[30]

Hired as a cub reporter for the *Daily News* after just two years of college, Bremler took on the pen name "Milly Bennett," which sounded catchier, and less Jewish. As a young woman, she thought the newspaperwoman's life seemed glamorous. But for the first few years of her career, Bennett wound up being more of a "sob sister" or stunt reporter: she spent several months, for instance, posing as a maid and writing accounts of her adventures (e.g., " 'Milly' Quits after Day of Housework," " 'Milly' on New Job Overturns Bowl of Soup," and "Beaus Are Bars to Job, 'Milly' Finds").[31]

Bennett met her first husband, Mike Mitchell, while working for the *Daily News* and followed him to Hawaii when he took a job with the *Honolulu Advertiser*, where she began working as well. She left Hawaii after splitting up with Mitchell in 1926, getting an assignment with the *Advertiser* that brought her to China, where she became managing editor of the pro-Communist Chung Mei news service. She later became assistant editor of the *People's Tribune* in Hankow, where she met Strong. In 1927, when many of her colleagues left for Moscow, Bennett returned to San Francisco.[32]

By the winter of 1931, Bennett, though lucky to have steady employment, was tired of her job, involved with a married man, and hungry for a change. Just over a week after getting a letter from Strong, Bennett was aboard the February 24 sailing of the *Bremen* in New York.[33] Not only did Bennett manage to pack up all her possessions and cross the continent in a matter of days. She also found time while in New York to visit her old friend Ruth Kennell, who was also leaving soon for Moscow but without definite prospects; Bennett told her about the *Moscow News*. Kennell already had some acquaintance with Strong: they'd marched together in a 1924 demonstration in Moscow and knew many people in common. Kennell claimed to "admire" Strong but did "not care for her style" as a writer. Nor did she particularly like Strong as a person.[34] Appealing to her for a job would be one of many concessions Kennell made on her second Soviet sojourn.

Shortly after getting in touch with Bennett, Strong wrote Jessie Lloyd O'Connor and her husband, Harvey (a former colleague of Strong's from the *Seattle Union Record*), to join the paper's staff. Granddaughter of the great muckraker Henry Demarest Lloyd and heir to the *Chicago Tribune's* fortune, Jessie Lloyd, as a single woman in her early twenties, had rented a room from Leo Tolstoy's granddaughter and lived in Moscow from July 1927 to October 1928. While there, she worked as a correspondent for several newspapers, including the *London Daily Herald* and the *New York Times*, the latter in a stint filling in for Walter Duranty. Lloyd had also met Strong during that time, at least initially finding her to be a "dynamo of energy" but "absolutely cold." Rubbing elbows with members of the avant-garde and finding marvelous energy and optimism in the Russian people, Lloyd had been so taken with life in the Soviet Union that she bought an apartment in Moscow, mostly as a way to financially support the country but also perhaps thinking she might one day return.[35]

The O'Connors, now both writing for the Federated Press, greeted Strong's invitation as an exciting opportunity, although unlike Bennett, they did not immediately pack their bags. It's unclear whether the O'Connors' experience or Lloyd's apartment—which Strong asked if *Moscow News* staffers might occupy, at least until the O'Connors' arrival—was the principal motivation for Strong's invitation. In any case, the complicated political situation at the paper made Strong write a few months later to suggest they might wait a bit before coming. For Bennett and Kennell, however, it was already too late.[36]

Kennell would have gone to Moscow regardless. She was feeling rootless and disenchanted despite the fact that her first book, *Vanya of the Streets*, a juvenile about Russia's homeless youth, was about to be published by Harper, in part thanks to editorial advice and connections provided by Theodore Dreiser. Dreiser probably also helped her land her first *American Mercury* assignment. Though a publishing coup, the article had not endeared Kennell to American radicals, and her (then estranged) husband, Frank, insisted it had "closed the door to Russia upon you forever."[37] He turned out to be wrong.

Kennell had secured a contract for a second juvenile, this one about the Kuzbas colony, and thought she might return to Siberia to do some more research. She'd also secured work as a stringer for the Newspaper Enterprise Association. But the real reason for Ruth's trip to Moscow was that she had to get away—from Frank. And she wanted to see Junius B. Wood, a correspondent for the *Chicago Daily News* with whom she had become romantically involved at the end of her first Soviet sojourn.[38]

When Kennell and Bennett met in New York, Kennell seems to have been pregnant with Frank's child, suggesting they had reconciled, but she still couldn't commit to spending the rest of her life with him. The circumstances had left Ruth a wreck: she told her mother, "Without saying too much in print, I might tell you that I am very anxious to get away!" She had some difficulty convincing a doctor to let her go but was able to leave for Moscow on March 5: "Feeling I must see W [Wood], as if it would help, but probably it won't, unless possibly I might see him differently and break that tie, at any rate. Or will it only grow stronger? Or might I decide to keep it, and renew the other?"[39]

Bennett arrived in Moscow not long before Kennell; both women seemed sorry to have come. Bennett wrote a friend within days: "How I wish I were home." In addition to terrible crowding, there were major food shortages. Although foreign workers had access to extra rations, suffering among the masses was unmistakable. And there was no escape from the Moscow winter even though she'd arrived in April: Bennett complained that she "had to smash milk in the pail to pour it for coffee this morning."[40]

Bennett and Kennell must have expected living conditions to be difficult, but unflagging faith in the system—which neither had—would have made these conditions easier to bear. Moreover, the general atmosphere was much more oppressive than it had been just four or five years earlier. Stringent residential rules were in effect. According to Bennett, "If you keep anybody in your room after 12 without registering them, you are not only liable to arrest under city ordinance, but liable to investigation by the GPU [secret police]." Bennett actually seemed more concerned about Soviet prudery and their obsession with productivity than with the Soviet security state: "This 12 o'clock business is probably another goddam plot on the part of the soviet government to make girls go home early so that the boys can get in eight hours of sleep and put in a good day for the soviet union."[41]

Bennett had apparently burned her bridges in San Francisco by leaving her job without notice; her boss warned news agencies around the United States that Bennett had set off to be a "Soviet propagandist." Even so, she did not plan to stay in Moscow for more than a year. "One year is my limit . . . one year," she repeated in nearly all her early letters to friends. Yet she tried to convince herself that the challenges were a small price to pay for the great material she was getting: what a book this could make! The manuscript of her unfinished novel/memoir and her letters to friends offer a striking context for (and, often, contrast to) the perspective in the *Moscow News*. But what is particularly remarkable is that, in keeping with Strong's vision, Bennett did carve out space in the *Moscow News* for capturing the "ordinary affects" of life in Moscow in the early 1930s.[42]

Because apartments were scarce, Bennett stayed with Strong. Only after a few weeks did Bennett fully comprehend the conflicts that had riven the paper; before this point she knew only that Strong was driving her crazy: "There are parts of life that it's just as well not to live . . . and one of them is being forced to live in two rooms with a 46-year-old wench who has driven herself frantic with zeal for Soviet Russia."[43] In her unpublished manuscript, Bennett described Strong (Sophia Amanda Britten) as

> a huge woman, a woman who dominated any scene she marched upon as does the elephant the circus, the bull the arena. A lively, unfading kind of pink and white and blue-eyed American prettiness imprinted on her bigness and even a deceptive kind of gentleness. When she opened her mouth the illusion was smashed. Egocentric as a man, insensitive, high-powered, a screaming, fierce cyclone of a female who carried all before her by the very force of her tonnage. She had an enormous capacity for work and used up everybody she could lay hands on while using herself.[44]

Although Strong was hard to tolerate, her apartment was relatively luxurious: two rooms and a bathroom in a former mansion. Bennett only realized what a good gig she had with Strong when she was forced to find her own place.

Bennett did have a basic commitment to socialism and the Soviet project, or she would never have come. Clearly, though, she was more cynical and less willing to devote her existence to serving a cause that was obviously not as pure as Strong made it out to be. Bennett believed the ideal government was one "that serves the greatest number of people . . . as socialism aims to do," but insisted, "I don't give a damn about devoting my life to thrashing it out."[45]

Within a week of starting work, she had already had a piece thrown out by the censor, whom she called "the little boy Friday of the Secret Police."[46] Yet Bennett did, almost immediately, manage to publish pieces that displayed her distinctive writing style, bringing a new energy to the paper: the vignettes signed by "M.M." (Mildred Mitchell, her otherwise unused married name) practically jump off the page, offering a sense of the sights, smells, and feelings of daily life in Moscow.

One of her earliest signed pieces was a series of anecdotes collected under the heading "The Sidewalks of Moscow." It offers little commentary but instead gives glimpses of women workers going about their jobs with quiet dignity. One woman is an ice breaker on a street brigade: "Black breeches on her sturdy legs. . . . A thick coat over her shoulders. Only her lively face, blooming like a peony from the dark wrap of her woolen shawl, marked her from the men workers. . . . She'd sing out to the men who worked at her side. She seemed to be section boss." Another woman gets her meal in a factory kitchen, singing while she carries a glass of milk in each hand. "Milk is to sing about," Bennett notes. And a woman is described walking down the street with a bucket, brush, and paper, plastering signs after a recent snowstorm. She pastes a flier on the "ornate iron fence of a deserted chapel garden." It reads: "Exhibition of forced labor abroad, free labor in the USSR, at Central House of the Scientific Workers." The scene is completed by the mention of a "lock, big as a man's fist, [which] hangs from the double door of the chapel."[47] The woman plastering propaganda signs must have stirred Bennett for a reason, as she tried to make peace with her own position as a professional journalist who had turned her talents to what was arguably a propaganda vehicle.

Ruth Kennell also brought a mix of hope and skepticism to the *Moscow News*, but found the job's confines harder to stomach and did not last long. Upon her arrival (in late March or early April of 1930), Kennell had sought out Bennett, finding her living and working with Strong. Ever generous, Strong offered Kennell a job and even invited her to share their already-tight quarters. Though unenthused, Kennell thought it wise to accept both. Her perspective was clouded by her troubles and by how different the city felt: a "gray, dirty, strange world, which seem[ed] to have changed so terribly for the worse" in just three years. Kennell's love interest, Junius Wood, also seemed to have changed, greeting her with his secretary beside him, apparently less than eager to resume their relations.[48]

Like Bennett, Kennell found Strong moody and hard to live with, but she had more pressing worries. She wrote her mother, "I've had so many experiences these two weeks, surpassing any in my former Moscow days, incredible, impossible to write. Suffice to say, everything is changed, I must learn all over again, life is terribly hard, food and everything is very scarce, but foreigners, being the most privileged class here, have enough. And the further you get from Moscow, the harder it is, they say." Her former idealism was impossible to sustain now. "My outlook has changed," she told her mother. "I don't mean I think it's hopeless, and isn't going ahead, but at what a cost, and where will such a complete iron dictatorship of a handful end, once they've accomplished what they set out for?" She at least managed to conclude on an optimistic note, "I still think this country acts as a powerful leaven on the world, even if it should fail in its original aim."[49]

Kennell either had an abortion or miscarried shortly after arriving in Moscow and was preoccupied by physical discomfort for some time afterward. She acknowledged that conditions might seem "interesting and amusing" if approached objectively. But in in her current state it was hard to separate her own condition from the misery all around.[50]

Bennett, on the other hand, found it easier to joke about life. She did feel bad for Strong, telling friends how her boss's plan for "a subtle, witty, sophisticated story of Russian life, edited in a manner to win friends for Soviet Russia" had instead turned into "a horrible, bland chunk of typical heavy Rooshian [*sic*] propaganda." But sympathy for Strong's predicament didn't make it any easier to be around her. "For three weeks, for 24 hours a day, I worked, ate, and slept in the same room with a woman who cried and moaned all night in her sleep, . . . who banged typewriters or screamed over the phone all day. . . . She resigned twice a day . . . she beat up on the maid . . . and toward the end . . . she ran screaming into the kitchen one morning and threw dishes crashing into the sink."[51]

Bennett claimed to have gotten "harder and harder berled [*sic*]," even as people complimented her on being so "cheerful" and "easy going." In fact, she had resorted to spending long periods of time in the "can" to get away from Strong, who, by Bennett's telling, finally fell apart. Bennett made arrangements to have her checked into a place for "nervous disorders" and temporarily took over her job, though without credit: "I'm buckling on the old sword," Bennett wrote to a friend, "vowing each morn that nothing will shake me loose from today's self-assurance and diffidence, and finding myself, each frosty noon . . . in a welter of sweat, aggravation." She concluded wistfully: "I hate Russia. . . . It's hard and embattled. . . . Yes, I know the business of loving and hating things, is the business of being alive."[52]

Bennett got into battles with the censor, the printer, and, presumably, the "responsible editor." But she managed to keep her job, and her sense of humor. She marched in a May Day Parade, noting of it, "There were signs—'Down with the gypsy music, jazz, and drink! Sing revolutionary songs!' This was not the kind of banner I carried." Sarcastic though she was in private, Bennett's article on that parade conveys delight and wonder, if not in the parade itself then in the ritual of waiting "six hours" with the workers of Ogonyok (or "Little Flame") Publishing company: "I sit on the kerb and watch Tanya dance. Her feet click on the cobbles of Strasnoi Boulevard. Slender little ankles moving to the tambourin, the plaint of the guitar, the wheezy sweet of the accordion. Tanya's hair burns about her face, golden red as the little clouds that land over the sun, just before it drops behind Lenin Hills. 'Dance my girl, dance,' runs the cry along the kerb. . . . She is our little flame." In Bennett's sketch, the group finally falls into line and begins marching. But the parade is almost an anticlimax. At the end, Bennett writes, "I drop, hot and tired, in the grass

Fig. 4.2 Milly Bennett in a parade with *Moscow News* staffers. Milly Bennett is the woman, second from the right, wearing glasses. Milly Bennett papers, Hoover Library, Stanford University.

of a tiny park. Thousands of other workers sit here. I lean against a giant effigy abandoned by a tired marcher, wiping the dust of Red Square out of my eyes."[53]

Bennett began studying Russian. And she even found herself starting to defend the Soviet system, especially to tourists who were looking for its faults. She and Kennell had shepherded the heavyweight boxing champion Gene Tunney through a May Day celebration in the hopes of getting an interview with him. Tunney complained that people were marching only because of social pressure, to which Bennett countered, "Isn't everything in the world done under social pressure?" Tunney insisted, "Your communism is only a new religion." To which Kennell responded, "Well, it's the only religion, if it is one, that promises the poor and downtrodden comfort on this earth and not in Heaven!"[54] Tunney, of course, was right, but so was Kennell. Communism's promises were never realized (indeed, they came to justify untold horrors), but it is too easy to dismiss communism's attractions, even to those priding themselves on being immune to the foibles of pilgrims who arrived in Moscow expecting to find paradise.

By May 1931 Kennell had moved out of Strong's apartment and was sharing a room with Helen Wilson, a friend from her Kuzbas days now on the paper's staff. Bennett was still living with Strong, who was back after her "female fit." She still found Strong unbearable and still had fantasies about leaving Russia. She'd dream she was "home and glad to be home. Yet in the dream there was always something unpleasant. Her teeth would be dropping out or she'd be running down Market Street without a stitch on." Such dreams suggest fear she might feel powerless and purposeless amid all those bourgeois comforts she now missed. And, indeed, Moscow began to have its own attractions. "M.M." signed a sketch describing a May evening in a park filled with the fragrance of flowers, where gypsies danced and sang, a couple spoke in hushed tones, old men played chess, and a woman in a dark shawl slept on a bench while the Moscow river flowed "smoothly, darkly, crowded with the long, yellow lights of the city."[55]

With only a touch of sarcasm, Bennett described in her novel spring days when Strong's "group" would ride out to the countryside in her new Ford car: "Everybody jabbered at once, hashing over office problems, chewing over Russia—would there be a new loan—were the peasants going into the kolkhozes [collective farms] fast enough?—and sometimes they would meet a band of shabby peasants trudging along the road. Britten [Strong] trembling as if a first lover were caressing her check, would cry, 'How wonderful! Coming from the kolkhoz!' "[56]

Bennett found herself struggling, sometimes almost desperately, to understand how Strong reconciled the constant contradictions with which they had to live as journalists, trying to keep their integrity but also attempting to counter what they perceived as a distorted image of the Soviet Union in the capitalist press. Valery (Bennett's alter ego in her novel) "found herself caught between the propagandizing of the Moscow News and the so-called objective reporting of the bourgeois correspondents. None of it was objective, she knew." One day, after a battle with the censor, Valery tried to turn her aggravation into contemplation: "And why is a Soviet censor worse than the business office censorship on any American newspaper? Isn't he indeed far better? He has an objective, after all, a philosophy that is not concerned with making one man rich at the expense of another." Bennett described Valery "sitting on the floor in front of the rough stone fireplace in Sophia Amanda's room, it was the only open fireplace in Moscow, and fanning the smoke out of her eyes, it drew badly." From this murky perspective, "Valery tried to get the answers to all the problems that beset her. She seemed to believe in those early days that there was a keypath, a way, and if only she could put her troubled feet upon it—that all this Alice in Wonderland would be made clear to her in a blinding flash."[57]

Bennett recognized the hollowness of the *Moscow News'* rhetoric, and the fact that she herself was writing propaganda, even though her signed work often avoided politics. She seemed most disgusted by the gap between Soviet rhetoric of women's equality and the reality of women's lives: As she wrote a friend, "Ha, what a big, fat joke. This feminism . . . this new woman business, if I don't write a book about the half hundred starved, repressed, inhibited. . . . Yeh. I know that lone women were goofy 50 years ago too. . . . But anyhow they weren't befuddled with delusions of freedom."[58]

Strong had written a number of articles that reiterated the theme of "equality an actuality" for Soviet women. She penned a four-part series about women, including the "textile worker Dunia," "flamelike Shadiva" in "golden Samarkand," and "Ustina, the chicken woman" in a commune near Stalingrad. Indeed, the paper contained an almost constant stream of articles—some original, some translated from *Pravda*—remarking on women's gains in the Soviet Union and the improved relations between the sexes. Women's subordination was presented as a structural result of capitalism destined to wither away under socialism: "Apart from professional liars nobody will deny that what in the capitalist countries is a rule in the Soviet Union is an exception," one article insisted.[59] These stories seem to imply that Russians might have forgotten about women's gains without regular reminders.

One of Kennell's first pieces, "Soviets Run Factory Kitchens to Relieve Women of Drudgery," offers a largely positive portrait of a factory kitchen. Kennell noted the abundance of natural light, the large portions, the cleanliness, the impressive mechanization, the comfortable social hall upstairs, and even the slogan on every plate, along with a hammer and sickle: "Communal Eating Is the Road to the New Life." But at the end of the article Kennell admitted: "Tastiness appears to be a factor of secondary consideration in the pressing task of the moment—to provide workers with nourishing food at minimum cost."[60]

Bennett, in contrast, had actually praised factory dining hall food in the paper, describing "good, hot tasty food at bargain prices." In private, however, she complained that this food was awful. Strong argued that freeing women was more important than feeding them delicious food. But Bennett didn't buy it. "This female crusader never discriminated in her own food, gobbled up everything that was set before her, eating was a mere stuffing process to her." Still, Bennett "came to think that it didn't matter what happened to food when she saw that all the Russians got on their ration cards anyhow was black bread, herring, cabbage, with a minimum of sunflower seed oil."[61]

Yet the problems ran much deeper. Just as women were supposed to be liberated by factory kitchens, which neglected the fact that people eat for reasons other than refueling, women were supposed to be freed from the sexual double standard. But reliable birth control, which could save women from the trauma of having an abortion, was almost impossible to come by.[62]

In her journalism, not just in the *Moscow News*, Bennett managed to suppress the frustration she felt about a situation that continued to worsen: writing for the *New York Times* in 1935 about the new emphasis on home, motherhood, and family life in the Soviet Union, she spun these developments as benefiting women: "By no means is woman to be relegated solely to the kitchen or the household, as in Nazi Germany," she wrote. "Instead, her right to share all professions and opportunities with men is recognized more and more. The State, however, realizes that woman, as child-bearer, has a function apart, and that function is now respected."[63]

In drafts of an article that Kennell significantly toned down for publication in *EveryWeek* magazine, she admitted that the Soviet system remained ill equipped to truly liberate women from their domestic duties:

"Women are not deserting their firesides to do labor on an equal basis with men—they simply handle two jobs instead of one." But this was pretty much the situation for American women with career aspirations too, as she noted. "For this reason, American women have been attracted to the Soviet experiment. They still try to find in it the realization of their own dreams." Her published article mostly eliminated discussion of Soviet problems and was called "Where Women Are Really Equal."[64]

Soviet laws vis-à-vis sex—which were hailed in early issues of the *Moscow News* (and elsewhere) as the most enlightened in the world—changed dramatically in the early 1930s, along with social mores more generally.[65] The impact of such legal changes on Bennett's and Kennell's personal lives made it harder for them to shed their doubts about the Soviet system. In October 1931 Bennett met Evgeni Konstantinov, an attractive, talented Russian actor, ten years her junior, whose father had been a wealthy merchant prior to the revolution. She initially described their relationship as a "mild flirtation" with no future, yet they became more involved. "Zhenya" was not only handsome and talented but funny, sweet, and devoted. Less than a year after they met, the two were married, although Bennett was somewhat casual about their involvement, perhaps owing to the ease of marriage in the Soviet Union (she sometimes still referred to Evgeni as "the boyfriend" even after they were married, and neglected to mention her marriage to several friends back home).[66]

Bennett and Konstantinov's happiness was short-lived: in February 1934 Konstantinov was arrested for his alleged "homosexual past" and sent to a prison camp, where he headed an agit-prop theatre troupe, or, as Bennett flippantly put it, he was "doing dances and performing little skits which agitate slothful peasants into planting grain." Sodomy was criminalized in the Soviet Union in December 1933, punishable by up to five years of hard labor; Konstantinov's former privilege made him already suspect in the eyes of the state, and he was part of an early wave of arrests.[67]

Kennell dramatized the impact of Soviet policy on her life in a play she cowrote with an old friend from San Francisco, John Washburne, which ran briefly on Broadway in May of 1933. In *They All Come to Moscow*, Kennell's alter ego, Betty, is desperately trying to get an abortion, at this point still legal in the Soviet Union but becoming difficult to obtain. Mitya (the fictionalized version of Milly's Zhenya) valiantly tries to help Betty, contributing to suspicions surrounding him as a bourgeoisie. She resolves, finally, to have the baby, and the play ends with an effort by the Communist maid, Dasha, to convince Betty to have her baby in the Soviet Union so the child might grow up to be a Communist and not a "boorzhooie—capitalist blood sucker." In reality, Kennell, who had become pregnant with Junius Wood's baby (not long after her earlier pregnancy was interrupted), would go back to the United States and give birth in May 1932 in Syracuse, New York.[68]

Love, Work, and Will . . . and Uncle Joe

Although the new sexual climate would present serious challenges for Bennett and Kennell, Strong, for the first time in her life, found genuine happiness in love, through a relationship she believed could have developed only in the Soviet Union. Speaking from experience in "We Soviet Wives" (1934), Strong wrote, "We ourselves feel that marriage with us has entered a new stage of development, foreshadowed by some of the friendlier companionships of America, but not widely attainable under capitalism," thanks to "the complete removal of property and religious encumbrances and of sexual inequality from marriage."[69] Ironically, it was continuing frustrations with the *Moscow News* that helped bring Strong closer to the man she'd later marry.

Strong's frustration with editor Axelrod ended when he left to edit the *Workers' News*, a new English-language newspaper aimed at laborers. The *Workers' News* was low on quality but grew increasingly popular as the *Moscow News* gained a reputation for being "bourgeois" in orientation. Strong was glad to be rid of Axelrod, but she felt confused about why a second paper was necessary and angry at the idea of a new paper competing with hers.[70] It is hard to believe she was unaware of the class differences between foreign specialists and laborers, which in some ways were more pronounced in the Soviet Union than in the United States. Specialists were in high demand and thus were paid more, had access to greater privileges, and rarely mixed socially with common laborers, American or

Russian. Then again, there was great pride in being a "worker" and a certain shame in seeming to stand apart from them.[71]

At the *Moscow News*, style improved under the smooth-talking new editor, Victor Vascov, but politics didn't. Vascov (whom Bennett called a "big fathead") recruited good writers but gave his handpicked staff special treatment: hotel rooms, first-class travel arrangements, and foreign-food books, which other writers waited months to obtain. Strong felt increasingly powerless and frustrated. She complained to Jessie Lloyd O'Connor about the direction the paper had taken: "Everyone says this change was inevitable; as soon as anything really starts here it gets taken over by good communists. . . . Even my obvious desire to run things in their direction is apparently not sufficient; I was never admitted to the discussions where the paper's fate was being determined, and merely saw my new boss when he summoned me to his office and said he had taken charge." Although tempted to simply quit, Strong feared "resignation would give [her] a black eye among the Russian communists." Strong also feared that people might think she only wanted to work where she could be in charge. She knew she'd been used, but partially blamed herself: that she "could have been naïve enough to believe that I, a foreigner and non-communist, could ever run anything here" would have been "incomprehensible to any Russian."[72] Increasingly, Joel Shubin, formerly the press officer at the Foreign Office and now editor of the *Peasant's Gazette*, became her go-to person for advice, and soon enough the two were a couple. Shubin, a widower, was five years younger, a loyal Communist, Jewish, and the father of a teenaged daughter. Their relationship offered welcome respite.

She finally did try to resign, but Vascov said he did not have the authority to accept her resignation—or even to remove her name from the masthead. "It was clear they hadn't really 'wanted me,' neither my energy nor my efficiency; they had only wanted my 'bourgeois reputation' to take—and throw away," she speculated in her memoir. Strong recognized both her own foibles and those of the Party, which did, in fact use her—though never as much as she wanted them to.[73]

She was encouraged to take a trip around the Soviet Union to report on Americans working in Soviet industries. She recalled, "I saw the trip as a bribe, but I would take it." Her articles on industries in Stalingrad, Kharkov, and elsewhere suggest an effort to keep faith in the Soviet project, even if she was losing faith in her own newspaper.[74]

While she was gone, there were more shake-ups. Kennell was fired in August after refusing to change a film review. She seemed relieved, writing her family that, had she not gotten fired, she might have never broken away from the paper, where her talents had been wasted. Kennell's contempt for the *Moscow News* (and, for the moment, the whole Soviet system) was tinged with a jarring anti-Semitism: "Since my successor is of the Chosen Race the staff is now with the exception of the bouncing ALS who'll probably be bounced one of these days 100% kosher."[75]

Kennell began doing work for the *Chicago Daily News*, where Wood was chief correspondent. She did write one more story as a "correspondent" for the *Moscow News*, an upbeat article describing her visit with former Kuzbas colonists still living in Kemerovo. "Old Kuzbassers" had a kind of iconic status in the *Moscow News*; their venture was held up as the origin point for ongoing contributions by American workers to the Soviet state. Privately, Kennell painted a much darker picture of industrial "progress" under the Five-Year Plan. She wrote to her family: "There was something terribly depressing to me in the sight of that giant modern construction rising out of a weltering mudhole and human beings so like bedraggled ants running in and out of the frameworks and trenches, so busy, so miserable looking. Aside from this hectic new construction, great power plants, coke ovens, blast furnaces, and new houses, nothing is changed, life is getting much harder for the people the more they build."[76] Kennell's own state must have influenced her outlook: she was about eight weeks pregnant at the time of her visit. But what she saw was real enough.

Bennett, "kosher" though she was, figured that she would soon be fired from the paper as well. She claimed to have heard Vascov complaining that there were "too goddam many bourgeois women on Moscow News. He, he said, was going to get rid of them. . . . . Well, Ruth got bounced, sure enough." It seemed only a matter of time, she speculated, before he'd come up with "some way to get rid of me without causing a scandal."[77] Strong returned from her travels that fall, planning to resign, but Vascov still refused to accept her resignation, and Meshlauk ignored her letters and phone calls.

Just as Kennell was making plans to leave Moscow, this time for good, and in the midst of Strong's growing frustration, Bennett and Kennell's satire, which mocked the American "pilgrims" pouring into "the red Jerusalem" and knocking on the doors of the *Moscow News*, was published in the *American Mercury*. It created a minor scandal. In the United States, rumors circulated that Kennell had been deported and Bennett fired as a result. Kennell insisted she had returned home voluntarily and noted that while Bennett was, indeed, nearly dismissed for "literary opportunism," the chief censor had "chuckled over it, [and] said he saw no harm in it." These facts, she claimed, were evidence that "Russia does not fear criticism or jokes at her expense." Safely out of the country, Kennell suddenly found it easier to be pro-Soviet—and, indeed, she remained so for the rest of her life, joining the Communist Party in the mid-1930s and ultimately expressing deep regret about having published her mocking *American Mercury* pieces at all.[78]

Bennett was able, temporarily, to keep her job, thanks to Strong's efforts on her behalf. Strong turned out to be pleased by the attention the *Mercury* piece "They All Come to Moscow" brought her, even later calling herself the "oldest resident" of Moscow, as the article had mockingly referred to her. At least one other *Moscow News* reporter thought the article was "swell" and "pro-Soviet," but Bennett and Kennell were chastised in a *Moscow News* editorial that was printed alongside a letter of apology by Bennett.[79]

Surviving this storm and falling into a comfortable relationship with Konstantinov for a little over a year, Bennett seemed happier than she'd ever been. To a friend, she explained what living in Moscow had taught her about love and work, and why she had started to dread returning to the United States: "It seems to me . . . that the psychologists, whilst concentrating on 'sex in life' in the past 20 years have completely overlooked the importance of 'work in life.' The image of America, flowing with the distressed . . . the horrid anxiety . . . I don't have the guts to come back and look at it." She felt her own faith in the Soviet system growing, even as she recognized its hollow foundations: "You would like it here, I think.

It can be bitter, dark, past understanding. But the thing you have to do about Russia is what you do about any other 'faith.' You set your heart to know they are right. . . . And then, when you see things that shudder your bones, you close your eyes and say . . . 'facts are not important.' "[80]

In March of 1932, two months after the infamous *Mercury* article was published, Bennett was fired, possibly because word got out that she and Kennell had yet another *Mercury* piece coming out.[81] Whatever the reason, like Kennell, she didn't seem sorry about it. But for Strong, losing Bennett must have felt like the final straw. Strong shared her frustrations with a "Russian communist" (probably Borodin, possibly Shubin) whom she knew had been forthright about not having his name used on certain pamphlets. "He was properly indignant," insisting that Russians are especially "serious with names." They had no right, he said, to advertise Strong as associate editor if she did not approve of every article in the paper. He suggested that she write to Stalin himself. Strong was shocked. She had considered writing to Stalin to complain about "the poor style of everything the communists publish for Americans," but it hadn't occurred to her to bother him with "a personal injustice." He told her to "do both."[82]

In any case, Strong followed the advice. Just three days after writing to Stalin, Strong received a call from his secretary notifying her that her complaint was being investigated. The following day, Vascov told Strong that her request to have her name removed from the masthead was granted, but he expressed hope that she would continue to write for the *Moscow News*. Relieved, Strong promised not just to write for the paper but to come to staff meetings and offer advice "as long as at last we are honest." She claimed to have considered the matter settled, but the next evening she received another phone call from Stalin's secretary saying his office staff was ready to have a conference with Strong, Vascov, and "some responsible comrades." Strong said there was no need to bother anyone; the matter had been settled. "Completely settled?" she was asked. She agreed to go to the meeting.[83]

Strong then received a call from Vascov announcing that he was taking her to see Stalin. Her description of the scene that followed is the pivotal moment in Strong's memoir.[84] She assumed Vascov was bluffing and still felt incredulous when he drove to the Kremlin and announced their entry to the guard. They parked near a group of government buildings and went through "an unimposing entrance" and into an elevator. Strong found herself in a large office with several secretaries at desks; one of them waved her toward Meshlauk and Sergei Ivanovich Gusev, another official she had dealt with. Strong assumed that these were the "responsible comrades." But then a door opened to a conference room in which sat Stalin himself along with two of his closest associates, Lazar Kagonovich and Kliment Voroshilov. Strong shook hands with each of the men.

She described Stalin as "stocky and strong, with bronzed face and graying hair about his khaki-colored 'party tunic'; he seemed like a man who is neither tired nor rested but who has worked very long and can go on working much longer, because he knows how to use strength—quiet, with no wasted motion." Stalin asked Strong whether she could follow discussion in Russian. Presumably she answered yes. "His eyes were kind yet grave, giving rest and assurance." They all sat down.

Stalin asked Vascov why he had refused to remove Strong's name from the paper. Vascov answered that he had referred the matter to the Central Committee and had been waiting for their reply. Stalin next turned to Gusev to ask why there had been such a delay, at which point Strong interrupted to note that the matter had been taken care of. Vascov produced a letter showing that Strong's name was going to be taken off the paper but that she had agreed to continue writing. Voroshilov and Kaganovich were indignant, pointing out that her name had been removed only after they began to investigate. But then Stalin turned to Strong and asked if she had agreed to continue writing for the paper under her own free will. She told him she had. He asked her if she planned to sign her articles. She said she supposed she did. Vascov interjected that the only difference would be that her name would no longer be on the paper's masthead. At which point Stalin asked, "Isn't that something of a demotion for her?"

Strong was elated. "He saw that if a useful worker was willing to keep on working yet fought to avoid all credit there was something twisted and wrong. That mutual agreement hadn't deceived him; he saw I had given up hope. He wanted to know what my hope had been before it died; I could tell it from his tone." He looked at Strong, probingly, and asked, "There is nothing more that you want then? Nothing more?" Strong was in awe. "Here was a man to whom you could say anything; he knew almost before you spoke; he wished to know more clearly and to help. Never had I found anyone so utterly easy to talk to." This was Strong's transformative moment, not just on the paper, not even just in the Soviet Union, but in her life:

> Suddenly the will that had been dead within me was alive, flaming and free. I knew now what I wanted; I had known these two years long. Two years? Oh, longer, longer! It came from a deep past. It had been buried under distorted routine; it had been twisted beyond hope. Now again I wanted to bring American efficiency to Russia; I wanted a newspaper to help our Soviet-Americans in their difficult fight. Had there ever been a time when I hadn't wanted it?

Strong found the courage to assert that she did not think there should be two English-language papers. Gusev explained that engineers and audiences abroad would need a "more or less liberal paper" while the growing number of American industrial workers would need "more of a party organ." But Kaganovich suggested that workers would also prefer facts to theory, and Stalin pointed out that if they stayed long enough, workers would pick up the language and get plenty of theory in the Russian papers. Strong, in the meantime, was only just then realizing that the *Moscow News* had from the start functioned more as a paper for engineers and other specialists—she had, she told them, assumed from the beginning that the *Moscow News* was for all English speakers. And now, suddenly, everyone seemed to agree that there *could* be "only one paper": not a "party paper" but a "Soviet paper" (or, at the very least, they all concluded, chuckling, "not an anti-Soviet paper").

Suddenly everything was different. Strong was going to continue on the paper. The two newspapers were going to combine as the *Moscow Daily News*, with Borodin as chief editor. Strong now understood why things had been as they were, and she no longer felt angry. "I have tried to make clear the essence of that small meeting, but I do not think that any words can give it. Everything was so unemphatic; it dealt with such prosaic things. The effect of personality and tone went far beyond the words." Stalin had certainly not seemed to her like a dictator. He was more like a grand facilitator of a collective decision: "It seemed we had all done it," she recalled. And the meeting itself would effect a kind of inner transformation for Strong: "It seemed that work might be forever clear and joyous, if only sometimes one might go to him with questions, and watch one's tangled skein of thought untangle through knowledge deeper than one's own." In Strong's mind, Stalin had not given those in the room a line to follow but had allowed them to create a line that all could agree to follow. He had uncovered the "will to create" that resided in each of them.

Strong was a new person after this meeting. Unofficially she and Shubin already considered themselves married, but they seem to have made it official as Strong finally felt she perhaps could make a place for herself inside the Soviet Union. She described Shubin as a "comrade through whose presence one becomes steadily the person one desires to be." In "We Soviet Wives," Strong positioned herself as part of the Soviet "we," and it is clear that while marriage helped her attain this sense of herself, her words echo something Bennett had expressed about marriage (and love, and sex) being just one part of life, something that many American women, pressured to make a profession out of being housewives, had failed to learn. Strong wrote, "Our husbands go down to the Polar Seas or dare the plateau of earth's highest ranges; they bring up new metals, create new plants, win new empires. But we do not wait at home; we go with them or on similar expeditions of our own. The adventure of revolution, the organized conquest by man of his world, is a flaming excitement before which personal love affairs grow rather pale."[85]

Strong's new sense of at last being part of "the adventure of revolution" helped her accept Borodin's (and her husband's) explanation for why no one was telling the "whole story" about collectivization or the famine, hunger, violence, and deaths that accompanied it. Historians estimate that as many as 14.5 million people died from forced collectivization and a resulting famine between 1929 and 1934. Borodin had said that people knew about shortages from their own food books, and from reports of massive efforts to improve the harvest: "Whom would it help

Fig. 4.3 Anna Louise Strong and Joel Shubin in Moscow, from a group photo taken on a landing field, circa 1934. Anna Louise Strong papers, University of Washington Libraries, Special Collections, UW37339. Used with permission from Tracy Strong.

to know sensational stories of hunger, or the details of our own difficulties? Would it get additional food for anybody? Aren't we doing all that we can?" Strong's book, *The Soviets Conquer Wheat: The Drama of Collective Farming* (1931), published prior to her marriage and meeting with Stalin, certainly gives little hint of the violence accompanying collectivization. Her failure to report on the famine became easier to rationalize as she imagined her work promoting a "collective will" that ultimately served justice.[86]

Bennett reported news of Strong's big meeting to Kennell, who was now back in the United States: "Uncle joe . . . THE UNCLE JOE (and I mean the uncle joe that you think I mean) . . . called ALS into a conference, with himself and two other practically equally important uncles . . . and discussed 'what's the matter with soviet propaganda for Americans!' Imagine! ALS can't breathe." Strong wrote Jessie Lloyd O'Connnor with new enthusiasm for her imminent arrival, explaining how consolidation of the two papers had come as a result of her appeal to Stalin: "He's just the swellest big boss I ever thought to meet. . . . He has a technique of making things decide themselves without apparently imposing his personality, which is the last word in collective direction."[87]

Bennett got her job back, with the new title of copy desk chief, and formed strong friendships with several non-Communist women who joined the staff, including Lloyd O'Connor, who arrived in the summer of 1932, and Seema Rynin Allan, who came about six months later. Lloyd O'Connor found work on the *Moscow News* dissatisfying (she was mostly translating), and, like Kennell, she found Moscow to be a very different, and less pleasant, city than she had known in the late 1920s. She left after less than a year. Allan, a recent graduate of UCLA and a Jew of Russian descent who had lost her job during the Great Depression, stayed a full two years, however, finding a sense of shared purpose that she had missed back home, and meeting the man she'd marry.[88]

And Bennett found a way to survive, to thrive even, amid all the challenges of life, or perhaps *because* of the challenges, which seemed to give life greater meaning. Indeed, in October 1934, after returning from an exhausting six-day train trip in a third-class car to visit her husband in a labor camp, she still found herself wanting to stay in Russia. She wrote to a friend: "Oh—I can go home. . . . My friends tell me that I could even get a job. But I measure picture chasing and sob-story romping, or even the dignity of a beat against my nerve wracking, health shattering, yet entirely stimulating life in Moscow—and I stay on." She tried to explain: "My belief in the workability of socialism comes near to being . . . the only thing I have ever taken seriously—and here— . . . even though you yourself get lost, although you yourself despair—you are always surrounded with those who do not get lost, those who do not falter, those who are so sure they are right. After all, they are fighting for, struggling and striving toward the only hope for the world—the thing that I want to, and do believe in."[89]

Strong, despite her desire to support and rationalize Stalinist policy, backed Bennett's efforts to free her husband, arguing that imprisonment of an American woman's lawful husband for behavior that was legal when it occurred could create an international scandal. Furthermore, she reasoned, it made no sense to take an allegedly homosexual man away from his wife and lock him up in a remote location with thousands of other men.[90]

Efforts to obtain Konstantinov's release—or even to switch his sentence to "free exile," so that Bennett might live with him in Siberia (his idea, not hers)—were to no avail, and, in any case, the strain caused by his arrest and imprisonment became too much for Bennett to bear. By November 1936 they were divorced. Bennett by this time had left the *Moscow News* for good and was mainly writing reports for the International News Service. After a few months, she moved on to Spain, where the civil war in progress seemed like a nobler cause. She also joined the Communist Party, or tried to, maybe because it provided better access in Spain, or maybe because she thought it would affirm the faith she wished she had.[91]

Strong, in contrast, suffered new disappointments. Her memoir did not provide entrée into the Communist Party, as she'd hoped, despite the fact that she had edited the manuscript not only to conform with Borodin's suggestions but Stalin's as well; pages of her manuscript describing her encounter with Stalin were marked up by Stalin himself.[92]

Autobiography, Self-Criticism, and Communism

I Change Worlds tells of Strong's life experiences and her process of self-discovery in the Soviet Union; as Strong explained to Communist Party officials in Moscow, it "uncovers the class character of my past hesitation, anxiety, and emotions." She also hoped it would serve as her unofficial "application form to become a member of the Communist Party."[93]

Strong was aware of the importance of autobiography to Communists. In order to become and remain a member of the Party, one had to regularly submit an autobiography, usually one to five pages long, in addition to a form whose questions also covered background and influences. This was not just for Party officials' information: "Composing their own life stories, each comrade had to understand where he came from, what had brought him to the Party, and what his duties were to the movement." Indeed, Strong wrote in the preface to *I Change Worlds*, "It has done more for me, this book, than it will do for any of my readers." Myra Page, a Moscow correspondent for the *Daily Worker* in the early 1930s, described in a typical statement submitted to the Comintern her family's class origins, her upbringing, her earliest inklings of class divisions and social injustice, her activity on behalf of women's rights and rights for African Americans, her involvement with labor organizing, the Marxist works she had read, and the ways she had served the Party. As part of the expected "self-criticism," Page said she had not fought with "that relentlessness that was necessary" for changes at the *Daily Worker* while she was on staff in New York; her origins in the "southern petty bourgeoisie" might be to blame.[94]

The Communist Party's practice of public self-examination and self-criticism has been compared to Christian rituals of confession and penance thought necessary for spiritual enlightenment. But Communist autobiographies were also used to distinguish "true revolutionaries from imposters." From the Communists' perspective, Strong's 422-page memoir did more to reveal her "individualism" than her fitness for the Party. But from our perspective, the fact that Strong was both attempting to be honest with herself and her readers *and* trying to gain admission to the Communist Party must inform the way we interpret her journalism. Moreover, we can see this dynamic between public pressure and personal desire in the work of other female journalists on the *Moscow News*, from the sarcastic but ultimately credulous Milly Bennett and Ruth Kennell to Rose Cohen, a British Communist who died in Stalin's purges.[95]

In November 1934 Strong formally applied to the Foreign Section of the Communist Party, describing her thirteen years in the Soviet Union as preparation for this moment. She claimed to have delayed applying in part because of "my own emotional instability, due to my petty bourgeois past." She said in her statement that writing her memoir "has caused me to analyze very thoroughly the class sources of this instability and has, I consider, conquered it." She called the memoir her most important piece of writing, one that "gives not only outer events of historic importance, but also the inner changes which brought me at last to the Party."[96]

Two copies of Strong's statement, one in English and one in Russian, are in her personal file in the Comintern's collections in Moscow. In the Russian version, the comments about her emotional instability are underlined in red pencil. Strong was told informally that her application was "premature" and, again, that she would be more useful from "outside." Eager to follow orders but still eager to join, Strong suggested she might become a secret member, thus maintaining the access that her outsider status brought. A representative from the Soviet party wrote an American comrade, asking for advice about Strong's application: "Our friends want your opinion of it. They are not very anxious to accept her." A note placed in her file a few years later describes Strong as a woman with "a great deal of energy, knowledge, and enthusiasm," who "writes well and is prolific," but whose "political and theoretical level are not very high." She is "individualistic" and "thinks highly of herself." She is said to have complained that "the USSR doesn't always treat her well, and doesn't always trust her. She's offended that she's still not a member of the Communist Party."[97]

Although Strong was not able to announce her Party membership in the published version of *I Change Worlds*, she forged ahead, leaving in January 1935 for a lecture tour in the United States to publicize the book, which was well received by reviewers and even made the best-seller list. During this trip, she approached the General Secretary of the American Communist Party, Earl Browder, about joining the CPUSA. He too told her that she would be more useful outside the party. She was insistent, and he finally accepted a check from her as membership "dues," which she continued to send through a neutral contact. She was never sent a membership card or assigned to a party unit. According to Strong's biographer, "What ambiguity remained served all concerned."[98]

Back in the USSR in March 1935, Strong tried to plunge into the work of the newspaper, but it was becoming pointless. The *Moscow Daily News* was printing fewer signed articles, more translations of lengthy speeches by officials, more notices of sabotage trials, and large, smiling pictures of Stalin. Meanwhile, aside from the paper, life in the Soviet Union was becoming harder to handle, as the seeds of the Great Terror—which became full-blown by late 1936—were planted with the assassination of Sergei Kirov in December 1934. Strong did not know what to make of it all, but she did, finally, recognize that she should get out of Moscow. She resigned from the paper in late 1936 and left for Spain.[99]

Strong wound up isolated from the community she had helped build in Moscow, but Kennell and Bennett, and Bennett, Lloyd O'Connor, and Allan, remained close friends for the rest of their lives. "What I really want to convey is how happy they were—when I think about Moscow I think about the people around my parents' dinner table, really enjoying those conversations—it was the great adventure of their lives, despite all they found out later," Allan's daughter explained. "They weren't bitter. . . . They were sardonic about what they didn't know, and about Stalinism, but the excitement of ordinary people changing their lives really stayed with them." All of these women, like Strong, had looked to Moscow and the Soviet experiment for the opportunity to witness, report on, and take part in the development of a new kind of society, "a great drama being unrolled before the eyes of the world," where, in theory, human development was to count for more than profit, and where women, in theory, could combine professional lives with romantic relationships and families unimpaired by economic pressures, a sexual double standard, and unevenly distributed domestic duties.[100]

Exaggerating the successes of this program while minimizing its failures and human costs was apparently the price one paid to succeed as a reporter on the *Moscow News*, or, indeed, in any news bureau in Moscow, where stories putting the Soviets in a negative light could lead to expulsion and the loss of a job. If "a new optics" was "the most undoubted gain from a stay in Russia," as Walter Benjamin said, these American women found that believing was no guarantee of seeing, that desire and hope are both fleeting, and that news, truth, and propaganda are all points on a continuum whose parameters continually fluctuate.[101]

If some women found it hard to balance professionalism, truth, and desire in their role as reporters, others attempted to get a foothold in the "great drama" of Soviet Russia by consciously joining the performances.

PERFORMING REVOLUTION

Performances both create and reveal communities. They link spectators, authors, and performers. And they were essential to the Soviet project of building unity in a war-torn, ravaged, and divided land. Theatre—in the broadest sense—was thus given high priority in the Soviet Union, even in the most difficult times. "No matter what happens in Russia, the theatres go on," Louise Bryant insisted while reporting on the revolution. "There can be war and blockade and counter-revolution and cholera and famine but the theatres are as steady and as brilliant as the stars."[1]

"No other country has developed a theatre so new and strong, so life-centered and so unified, yet so varied in human interest as that of Soviet Russia," British theatre critic Huntley Carter proclaimed in 1924. "This theatre expresses more clearly and more forcibly than any other popular institution in Russia the Russian state of mind and its present amazing revolutionary exaltation, as we might say, and its efforts to create a new culture, new human relations, new conditions of life, new crystallization of labour and thought."[2]

Beyond scripted events presented on stage, the Soviet Union itself was a living theatre, showcasing the drama of everyday life in a new society. Noting the nearly constant stream of "demonstrations, parades, pageants, [and] festivals," filling the air with "banners and festoons and cries," Carter suggested that "in such unending excitement and uplift the new population have expressed themselves in that dramatic form which is innate in human beings, and is unique in the history of the human race."[3]

Performances are *acts*, "the many practices and events—dance, theatre, ritual, political rallies, funerals—that involve theatrical, rehearsed, or conventional/event appropriate behaviors," but *lives* are also performances. The concept of performance allows us to look at individuals as "social actors" who both respond to and shape social expectations and norms in specific ways. One example of this is gender, which is something performed, an identity "instituted through a *stylized repetition of acts*."[4] Women act in accordance with—or in opposition to—popular expectations, in varying social contexts, of what women are *supposed* to be like. For women unsatisfied with their lives in the United States, the Soviet Union, ostensibly a new society, forging new men and new women, offered an ideal context for trying on, embodying, expressing, and creating new behaviors and identities.

In the first half of the twentieth century, understandings of the relationship between expressive movement and the self were especially clear in dance. Two theorists in particular, François Delsarte and Émile Jacques Dalcroze, influenced modern dance pioneers in the United States, including Isadora Duncan, as well as the major directors and actors in Russia and the Soviet Union. Delsarte helped popularize the idea that humans communicate otherwise inexpressible elements of the self and the emotions through bodily movement and gesture. He created a complex lexicon of gestures, each of which corresponded to a particular psychological state. By this logic, dancers, actors, and other performers could use bodily movements to express their true inner selves. Audiences, in turn, could be transformed simply by intently watching these powerful movements. In Russia, Prince Sergei Volkonsky, former director of the Imperial Theatre, adapted elements of Delsarte's work along with Dalcroze's rhythmic gymnastics (known as eurhythmics) to create a synthetic system that influenced physical culture as well as acting, dance, and film theory.[5]

Russia had a reputation for excellence in the performing arts prior to 1917, a reputation that continued into the Bolshevik era. The acting troupe of Paul Orlenev and Alla Nazimova toured the United States in 1905 (with the assistance of Emma Goldman). Despite the fact that most Americans could not understand the dialogue, critics praised the actors' "fervor and realism." One commentator noted "a supple intense effect which wholly lacks the more exaggerated methods of our theatre." Nazimova offered American audiences their first taste of Konstantin Stanislavsky's technique of "method" acting, "a type of psychologized acting that was more nuanced and more based on inner life than was customary in the west." The troupe also appealed to American cultural rebels who appreciated Orlenev's condemnations of American theatre's commercialism. The Moscow Art Theatre's 1923 tour of the United States elicited praises from nearly all quarters, without regard to politics; indeed, Stanislavsky had a singular impact on American theatre, directly inspiring the radical Group Theatre and its offshoot, the Actors Studio, which became the most influential acting school in America.[6]

Similarly, American ballet had been a coarse and trivial affair compared to the high art of Russian ballet. Three major Russian influences changed that: Anna Pavlova, who toured the United States in 1910, Serge Diaghilev's Ballet Russes, who toured the United States in 1916–1917, and Michel Fokine, who immigrated to the United States after the Bolshevik revolution.[7]

The revolution only strengthened American admiration for Russian theatre and, increasingly, film, which was hailed as groundbreaking, innovative, and revolutionary, both aesthetically and politically. Russian films were regularly shown in US art-house cinemas between the mid-1920s and the mid-1930s, and they influenced audiences and experimental filmmakers alike. Sergei Eisenstein's *Battleship Potemkin*, released in the United States in 1926, stunned audiences with its innovative use of montage; and the Russian practice of factography in documentary, which aims to produce not simply an aura of realism but social action, deeply affected US documentarians.[8]

Because Soviet films were being shown in the United States but Soviet theatrical productions, for the most part, were not, many visitors to the Soviet Union spent a lot of time attending live performances. Supporters of the revolution extrapolated from Russia's varied, rich, and often innovative theatre—from nonprofessional workers' theatre to Vsevolod Meyerhold's "biomechanical" technique and unconventional staging—to infuse the entire revolutionary program with possibility. "Biomechanics," which had implications for all forms of performance, involved a complex system of exercises designed to allow the actor "to communicate with the audience by the most dynamic and visually powerful means." Within a Marxist-Leninist framework, the logical conclusion from the belief that particular physical movements could generate desired emotional states was that performance could, and should, serve as a key tool for social advancement, not simply entertainment. The "new person" could be imagined, enacted, and modeled through performance.[9]

US theatre director Hallie Flanagan, who visited the Soviet Union in 1927 and 1930, wound up adapting Russian forms when she later developed the signature genre of the Federal Theatre Project, the "Living Newspaper." But Flanagan was almost as excited about Soviet audiences as she was about Soviet theatre techniques. Of one crowd she noted, "It is full blooded, vigorous, coarse, rough, careless in dress and manner, laughing, jostling, talking, shouting approval or disapproval. . . . It is impossible to tell where audience leaves off and drama begins." Photographer Margaret Bourke-White, five years later, was struck by the attentiveness of Soviet audiences as well as their working-class character. At the opera she sat among "a press operator, her head in a red kerchief; a plasterer, his clothes dusted with lime; a loom tender in a yellow blouse, her only ornament a red rose at her waist; tow-headed machinists in work-worn garments . . . all are absorbed in the opera."[10] While the Soviet government had created a context for both professional and amateur theatre to thrive, the mass of Soviet citizens collectively represented an ideal audience, more eager to authentically experience rather than to put on airs, more deeply invested in the drama of life unfolding around them than in the selfish task of pursuing individual gain at the expense of one's peers.

Whether as journalists, or as dancers or actors onstage or on-screen, or as participants amid the rush of new life on streets, in factories, and elsewhere, American women eagerly traveled to Russia to explore new identities and possibilities through performance and to witness the drama of revolution.

Dancing Revolution

In the spring of 1921, the American dance pioneer Isadora Duncan accepted an invitation from A. V. Lunacharsky, Soviet commissar for the enlightenment, to open a children's dance school in Moscow. She was "sick of bourgeois, commercial art . . . sick of the modern theater, which resembles a house of prostitution more than a temple of art." She wanted "to dance for the masses," for those "who need my art and have never had the money to come and see me." And she wanted "to dance for them for nothing, knowing that they have not been brought to me by clever publicity, but because they really want to have what I can give them." If the Bolsheviks could give her this opportunity, then, she promised, "I will come and work for the future of the Russian Republic and its children."[1]

Although Russia was renowned throughout the world for its dance, after the revolution American dancers were drawn to Russia less to see innovative dance forms than to experience life under socialism and to dance for a revolutionary audience. Despite striking innovations like Nikolai Foregger's dancers, whose mechanical movements mimicked those of machines, for the most part Russian dance was still dominated by ballet in the 1920s and 1930s, even as modern dance took other parts of the world by storm. Indeed, some of the most radical innovators in Russian ballet, most notably Serge Diaghilev's Ballet Russes, performed only outside of Russia: Russian ballet traditions were so entrenched that this effort by primarily Russian-born choreographers, dancers, and composers to "extend the expressive possibilities of ballet" defined itself in terms of "secession" from Russia proper.[2] Thus although the revolutionary dance movement in the United States was directly inspired by events in the Soviet Union, it was American dancers, most of them directly or indirectly influenced by Isadora Duncan, who brought revolutionary forms of dance there.

François Delsarte's popularity in the United States and in Europe helped elevate dance as an expressive art in the early twentieth century. Indeed, Havelock Ellis, a sexologist, Fabian socialist, and freethinker, described dance as the most elemental and essential form of art. The theory of metakinesis, developed by John Martin, the most influential American dance critic of his day, suggested dance's uniquely expressive properties: "Because of the inherent contagion of bodily movement, which makes the onlooker feel sympathetically in his own musculature the exertions he sees in somebody else's musculature, the dancer is able to convey through movement the most intangible emotional experience." Such understandings of kinesthesia, and its relationship to empathy, suggest that the "qualitative dimensions" of bodily movement—"the kind of flow, tension, and timing of any given action as well as the ways in which any person's movement interacts and interrelates with objects, events, and other people"—are elemental components for the expression and comprehension of revolutionary desire.[3]

Modern dance is often described as a feminist form, "pioneered by women" in the early twentieth century. While ballet typically featured women performing dances created by men, modern dance most often featured female choreographers and dancers. Moreover, the reliance in modern dance on improvisation and the loose, flowing costumes challenged older models of spectatorship that made the dancer more an object of spectacle rather than a powerful subject. Isadora Duncan had predicted "the dancer of the future" as early as 1903: "The free spirit, who will inhabit the body of new women; more glorious than any woman that has yet been; more beautiful than . . . all women in past centuries: The highest intelligence in the freest body." This dancer of the future—implicitly Isadora herself—dancing a self of her own creation, unashamed of her body or her sexual urges, revealing, as lyrical leftist Floyd Dell put it, "the goodness of the whole body," powerfully embodied the promise of the new Soviet woman for cultural rebels in the United States.[4] To physically move in ways that expressed a revolutionary ethos could be tremendously liberating; for this reason alone dancers from the United States felt drawn to the Soviet Union where they could experience and attempt to embody that ethos. They also had the precedent of Isadora Duncan's Russian days to follow.

Duncan had been influential in Russia as well as the United States before the revolution; her work and her very persona represented the utopian "Dionysian ecstasy" that fit especially well with Russian "pre-war aesthetic ideals." In the years following the revolution, "dance schools and studios grew like mushrooms after a warm rain," many of them run by dancers trained in Duncan technique. Duncan, it is said, "danced [her] personality into the soul of Russia."[5] Still, although Duncan never renounced her years in Bolshevik Russia, they were marked by disappointments. She charted a rocky path in the Soviet Union that several modern dancers would follow, unconsciously or consciously.

Isadora Duncan and the Revolutionary Soul

"She was our symbol," one of Duncan's contemporaries declared, "the symbol of a new art, a new literature, a new national polity, a new life." Duncan popularized the idea of dance as a gateway to the soul. Inspired equally by ideas of ancient Greek dance and rhythms of nature, Duncan "sought a liberated way of moving that would express a range of emotions. Although her choreography was simple, based on walking, skipping, and running, those steps, combined with pantomimic gestures, a highly expressive face, eloquent stillness, and personal charisma made an extraordinary impact on the audiences of her day."[6] She used plain sets (usually

Fig. 5.1 Isadora Duncan dancing the "Marseillaise," 1917. In *My Life* Duncan writes: "On the day of the announcement of the Russian Revolution all lovers of freedom were filled with hopeful joy, and that night I danced the 'Marseillaise' in the real original revolutionary spirit in which it was composed." Jerome Robbins Dance Division, The New York Public Library for the Performing Arts, Astor, Lennox and Tilden Foundations.

nothing more than a blue curtain) and most often danced to symphonic music solo (but never alone, she would say, for she claimed to embody the collective).

Though born in San Francisco in 1877 or 1878, Duncan lived for extended periods in Germany, Greece, France, England, and Soviet Russia. She was at once an American in the spirit of Walt Whitman and a citizen of the world. She embraced free expression and pioneered a worldwide revolution in dance. Duncan had little interest in politics per se, but she thought of herself as a revolutionary. "I have constantly danced the Revolution and the call to arms of the oppressed," she insisted, linking "dancing revolution" to performing the essence of the liberated self. She claimed that her sympathies had turned toward the "down-trodden" when, on her first visit to Saint Petersburg, she witnessed a nighttime funeral cortege for victims of the January 1905 Bloody Sunday massacre, which sparked the failed 1905 revolution. Twelve years later, "on the night of the Russian Revolution I danced with a terrible fierce joy," she recalled. "My heart was bursting within me at the release of all those who had suffered, been tortured, died in the cause of Humanity."[7]

After dancing "the 'Marseillaise' in the real revolutionary spirit in which it was composed," she performed what has been called the first "revolutionary dance," to Tchaikovsky's *Marche Slave*, enacting the Russian people's movement from oppression to liberation. She hailed the Bolshevik revolution several months later as "the birth of the future international community of love. A new world, a newly created mankind; the destruction of the old world of class injustice, and the creation of a new world of equal opportunity." Duncan aimed to bring her dance, "a high religious art," to this new mecca, where her "dancer of the future" could help fulfill "the ideals of the new world."[8]

Isadora, *Plyaska*, and Silver Age Russia

On her tours through prerevolutionary Russia, Duncan tapped into and came to embody the popular spirit of rebellion during Russia's Silver Age (late 1890s–late 1910s), a period marked by an outpouring of creativity in the visual arts, literature, and performing arts comparable to the

Golden Age of Russian literature (1810s–1830s). Her ideas and work drew on influences that likewise fed the Russian revolutionary spirit, most notably Nietzsche's philosophy, but she herself had a tremendous impact on Russia's intellectual and artistic avant-garde. In Silver Age Russia, "Duncan's ideas appealed to all who went against obsolete traditions, old standards. The free movements of a body liberated from restraint, her constant reaching upwards, represented a chance to form emancipated individuals."[9]

Sergei Diaghilev said Duncan's first performances in Saint Petersburg and Moscow "gave an irreparable jolt to the classic ballet of Imperial Russia." And Michel Fokine felt Isadora embodied the idea of a dance that was expressive, "the poetry of motion." Vsevolod Meyerhold was "moved to tears" the first time he saw Duncan perform. And Konstantin Stanislavsky said Isadora had found the "creative motor" he had so long been seeking.[10] Other Russian critics emphasized the "revolution in choreographic art" she had initiated, in part by exposing her feet and legs, thus revealing the false conceits of the contemporary ballet. The few negative comments about her "coarse sensuality" seem only to confirm the idea that failure to appreciate Duncan's dancing was a marker of decadence.[11]

Duncan's popularity in Russia in the decades leading up to the Bolshevik revolution was tied to Silver Age Russians' attraction to *plyaska*, or movement that "celebrates freedom from the prohibitions imposed by the repressive authorities of the official culture," in contrast to *tanets*, which usually refers to ballet, ballroom, and other more scripted forms. Indeed, "one cannot 'perform' *plyaska*, one can only give oneself to it as one gives oneself to passion or ecstasy." *Plyaska* connotes wholeness, nature, collectivity, and freedom from repressive authority, which "found its embodiment in Duncan and her dance."[12] Isadora's expressiveness filled a popular yearning for authentic experience to counter a morally bankrupt society.

Duncan made much of the notion that her introduction to Russia coincided with the events of Bloody Sunday, though her initial performances in Saint Petersburg actually came *before* that day. In her autobiography she marvels:

How strange it must have been to those dilettantes of the gorgeous ballet, with its lavish decorations and scenery, to watch a young girl, clothed in a tunic of cobweb, appear and dance before a simple blue curtain to the music of Chopin; dance her soul as she understood the soul of Chopin! Yet even for the first dance there was a storm of applause. My soul that yearned and suffered the tragic notes of the Preludes; my soul that aspired and revolted to the thunder of the Polonaises; my soul that wept with righteous anger, thinking of the martyrs of that funeral procession of the dawn; this soul awakened in that wealthy, spoilt, and aristocratic audience, a response of stirring applause. How curious![13]

During her 1904–1905 tours, she met the ballet dancer Anna Pavlova, the great costume designer and artist Leon Baskt, Diaghilev, and other prominent cultural figures. On her second tour, in 1908, she met Stanislavsky, with whom she formed a deep connection. Duncan began visiting Stanislavsky's Moscow Art Theatre any evening that she was not dancing herself. One night, she went up to Stanislavlsky, placed her "hands on his shoulders and entwine[d] them about his strong neck," and proceeded to kiss him on the lips. Stanislavsky returned Duncan's kiss, but then drew back and, looking at her with "consternation, exclaimed, 'But what should we do with the child?' 'What child?'" she asked. "Why, our child, of course."[14]

Isadora's union with Russia's artistic and intellectual avant-garde would in fact produce many children. In addition to the dance studios she inspired, Duncan also had a transformative effect on flesh-and-blood children, both those she taught and those she influenced through her example. Young Stefanida Rudneva (1890–1989) and several teenaged friends, for instance, moved by Duncan's early performances, formed the dance group, school, and commune Heptachor ("Dance of Seven" in Greek).[15]

Seeing Duncan dance convinced Rudneva—who had no dance training—that she "could no longer be the same person." It was her mission in life to dance. She and her friends began having "'white gatherings,' where, dressed in tunics, they improvised to piano accompaniment, to their own singing or to 'inner music.' It gave them 'the feeling of catharsis' and . . . 'protected them from flirtatiousness': from a superficial, petty relationship with life." In halting English the seventeen-year-old Rud-neva wrote to Duncan in 1907, "I have seen you 3 times and from the first moment I saw you I thought: 'this is what I looked for, this is what I dreamt about!' When you first came out a new world appeared before me. . . . I was like one in a dream. I could not speak, I only longed to look at you and to feel in my heart all of your genial beauty." Duncan repre-sented the possibility of another life: "For see—our land is so miserable, our life is full of such dreadful reality, that every moment of forgetfulness for us is much more than you may think it is. That is why every one of us, who are tired and suffering, love you and thank you for your art, for your beauty."[16]

Duncan remained Heptachor's principal inspiration. In 1934, when Soviet authorities shut down nearly all avenues of expression not seen to be properly embodying the ideal of socialist realism, Heptachor none-theless helped perpetuate the legacy of Duncan's work, through published writings and through Rudneva's students, and their students, whose work continues to this day (an Isadora Duncan Museum is Saint Petersburg is perhaps the most visible manifestation of Duncan's legacy).

Duncan in Bolshevik Russia

If Duncan once promised to revitalize the decadence of imperial Rus-sian life, in 1921 it was she who hoped that revolutionary Russia would offer *her* new life after a number of setbacks, most notably the death of her two young children in a tragic accident in 1913. "This coming to Rus-sia is a tremendous experience, and I would not have missed it for any-thing," she wrote not long after moving to Soviet Russia. "Here at last is a frame mighty enough to work in, and for the first time in my life I feel that I can stretch out my arms and breathe." She was thrilled to be creating "a great school of new beings who will be worthy of the ideals of the new world."[17]

Although Duncan projected optimism and excitement, in fact much of her stay in Soviet Russia was marked by frustration and disappoint-ment. When Isadora, her student, protégé, and adopted daughter Irma, and her French maid, Jeanne, arrived in Moscow, they found no one at the station to meet them. They were even more surprised to learn that no arrangements had been made for their lodging. After spending the night in a small hotel room infested with flies, rats, and bedbugs, the three women were temporarily settled in a vacant apartment, while Duncan impatiently waited for news about where her school would be located and when it could open.[18]

In the meantime she attended her first Soviet soirée, at a mansion once owned by a member of the Russian aristocracy. The garish, Louis XV–style furnishings struck Duncan as ugly and inappropriate, and she was shocked and outraged to find a group of well-dressed Bolsheviks in the drawing room contentedly eating hors d'oeuvres, sipping wine, and listening to a young woman playing piano and singing in French. Duncan had dressed in what she thought would be an appropriate outfit for the occasion: her best red tunic, worn with a red cashmere shawl and a red tulle scarf wrapped around her head like a turban. Someone greeted her as "Mademoiselle Duncan," but Duncan interrupted, insisting she be called "*Comrade* Duncan." Then she stood up, glass in hand, to address a roomful of astonished guests: "Comrades, you have made a revolution. You are building a new, beautiful world, which means that you are breaking up all that is old, unwanted, and decayed. The break-up must be in everything—in education, in art, in morals, in everyday life, in dress. . . . I hoped to see something new here, but it seems all you want are frock coats and top hats to be indistinguishable from other diplomats."[19]

Duncan was especially keen on showing the Russians how to properly train their children. She was taken to see a children's colony in a suburb of Moscow, and she offered to give the children a lesson. After watching the boys and girls perform a series of their own peasant dances, Duncan explained, through an interpreter, that they were dancing incorrectly: "These are the dances of slaves you have danced. All the movements go down to the earth. You must learn to dance the dance of free people. You must hold your heads high and throw out wide your arms as though you would embrace the whole universe in a large fraternal gesture!"[20] As with her plan to teach famine orphans to dance in order to foster Westerners' sympathies, Duncan's comments suggest both a dismissive attitude toward Russians' culture and naïveté about the enormous obstacles to be overcome in Soviet society. On the other hand, Duncan's idealism is part of what made it possible for her to have the impact she did.

Duncan did find kindred spirits and even had her share of revolutionary epiphanies. Nikolai Podvoysky, people's commissar for physical education, immediately appreciated Duncan's mission in Russia. Duncan did not wish to train professional dancers; instead, she wished to liberate young people through dance, to give them tools for physical and psychological regeneration, which they could then pass on to others. Podvoysky told her of his own plans to train "strong and splendid athletes," to build "a great stadium for fifty thousand people," and to raise young Soviets "according to the ideals of the new world."[21]

Duncan was thrilled by Podvoysky's vision. But she was not entirely uncritical of him, noting especially his lack of a feminist consciousness. Observing a youth camp under his supervision, she watched a group of girls follow an entourage of boys wearing swimming trunks and tramping down the hillside singing. "I was sorry to see the girls wear bloomers and shirt-waists," she said. "They didn't look as fine and free as the boys." She told Podvoysky that "the bloomers were all wrong and the swimming drawers too. I told him they ought all to wear short tunics like Achilles, and the girls should not follow after the boys, but that they should dance down the hill together, hand in hand."[22]

Duncan's vocal admiration for Podvoysky paid off in the form of his support and patronage. He was instrumental in helping her secure a building for her school in September 1921—a remarkable feat at the height of the famine, when the state clearly had other priorities. The large house on the once-fashionable Prechistenka Street had been reclaimed from the wealthy head of a tea plantation whose wife had danced in the Moscow Opera ballet. Isadora, Irma, and Jeanne moved into the couple's bedroom and boudoir and waited for the rest of the house to be cleared of occupants to make way for the school.[23]

Preparations to create a functioning school moved slowly. Porters, maids, secretaries, chefs, and other personnel came on board, but there was no stove, nor were there pots or pans. There was not enough fuel either. Nonetheless, 150 children were brought to the school. Preference was given to children of industrial workers. The students had little to no dance experience, so Duncan focused on the basics, teaching them to walk "naturally, but beautifully, to a slow march; then to stand, swaying their bodies rhythmically, 'as if blown by the breeze.'"[24]

Although the children's training had barely commenced, Duncan decided to have all of them participate in her first concert in Moscow at the Bolshoi Theatre. It was a gala celebrating the fourth anniversary of the Bolshevik revolution. All seats were to be free. But the workers for whom Isadora had wanted to dance were left outside on the snowy street, held back by a police cordon, as Communist Party elites, government officials, Red Army officers, trade union leaders, foreign correspondents and theatrical people filled the seats. Word had gotten out that she planned to perform to Tchaikovsky's *Marche Slave*, an imperial hymn that contained several bars of "God Save the Czar." Hard-line Communists were scandalized, but Lunacharsky, granted a preview of the performance, found it a "shattering" expression of Isadora's solidarity with the revolutionaries and their victory.[25]

The program ended with "Duncan . . . walk[ing] to the music of the *Internationale* in an energetic, rhythmic step as if summoning masses to struggle, while her hand with two pointed fingers conducted the singing of an imaginary crowd. To the last strains of the music the artist ran upstage, and exposed her left breast, symbolizing a nursing mother giving strength to the popular elements." For an encore, the entire audience stood and sang "The Internationale" as they watched Irma lead 150 children in red tunics onto the stage. Holding hands, the children circled their teacher as they raised their linked arms toward the sky.[26]

At the end of the performance, Lenin himself stood up and cried, "Bravo, bravo Miss Duncan!" Ivy Litvinov, the British-born wife of the Soviet diplomat Maxim Litvinov, was dazzled by the performance: "I have never even dreamed of such a human, living relation between artist and audience," she wrote Duncan, enclosing sketches she'd made of the children dancing ("for you to see how you have made my imagination work so I can't sleep"). "Now you have really given the Moscow proletariat something for their very own." Despite this enthusiastic reception, many people actually "were shocked by [Duncan's] appearance" (for she was older and heavier than they remembered) and, as Litvinov's sketches would suggest, may have been most moved by the sight of the children.[27]

Of the 150 children at the Bolshoi, only 40 were allowed to enroll in the school when it officially opened on December 3, 1921—a far cry from the "thousand boys and girls from the poorest families" that Duncan had requested. But at least for a time, the Soviet government supported the school to the extent that it could, with help, perhaps inadvertently, from the United States, as the children's blankets and much of their food came from the American Relief Administration. Walls were hung with blue curtains to hide the garish taste of the previous owners; a pink scarf covered the chandelier in the main room, diffusing the light. Girls and boys were placed in separate rooms and outfitted with slightly different tunics, but otherwise there was little attention to the particular needs of boys, who one-by-one dropped out until the school served only girls. But these girls adored Duncan, as she did them. Irma would demonstrate the dances while Isadora focused on the "spiritual side of dance."[28]

After less than a year, the Soviet government stopped funding Duncan's school, and she was forced to create a parallel track of paying students, as well as to perform, alone and with her students, to support the school. This was a mixed blessing, for although she had rejected the idea of charging for her performances, tickets were purchased for workers in blocks by labor unions. So she did, in fact, get to perform for the masses.[29]

At a performance for sailors in Leningrad, a near-disaster became one of the highlights of her initial fundraising tour: After her first piece, the lights went out. In the dark, there were sounds of feet shuffling and laughter. Someone whistled; others shouted. Finally, a lantern with a candle in it was found and brought to Duncan, who had been anxiously waiting on the stage. Instead of dancing, she held the lantern over her head and asked the sailors if they would sing for her. The request, translated into Russian, was greeted with silence. But after a few moments, there could be heard a single voice, "rich, vibrant, sure, singing the opening lines of the old revolutionary song, the Varshavianka." And then many voices joined in:

The volume of deep warm tones welled up out of the darkness and poured over the stage where Isadora stood silent and alone. She who loved music more than all else in the world, was thrilled to her heart's core: more thrilled even than she had been on first hearing the Aria of Bach or the Berlin Philharmonic under Nikisch playing the Seventh Symphony of Beethoven. For this mass music welling up from these unseen, simple men was more movingly human, more gloriously elemental than any instrument music had ever seen.[30]

The men continued singing, song after song, and Duncan stood perfectly still, holding the lantern over her head, while tears streamed down her cheeks.

This was one of many times that Duncan would find herself deeply moved by the spirit of the revolution. She described her first May Day in Moscow as a "wonderful sight," the streets like "crimson roses," as "thousands of men, women, and children, with red handkerchiefs about their heads and red flags in their hands, swept by singing the *Internationale*."[31] Later, Duncan was similarly moved by Lenin's funeral procession, as she shivered and waited with thousands of others, hoping to glimpse his coffin. She composed two funeral marches in Lenin's honor, one to the music of Lenin's favorite revolutionary hymn and the other to the "Varshavianka." These dances were well received, but they can be seen to mark the end not just of Lenin but of Duncan's era as well. The next tour, a fundraiser for the school, was a disaster. Her tour of the United States in 1923, with Russian husband in tow, had been even more of a debacle, with Duncan—vocally praising the Soviet Union and condemning the land of her birth—now tagged as a Bolshevik hussy.[32]

Duncan had met the Imaginist poet Sergei Esenin, eighteen years her junior, while preparing for the school's official opening.[33] Witnesses to their meeting attest that there was an immediate, mutual attraction, but their relationship did little to foster Duncan's work. The couple married in order to be able to travel together without causing a scandal, and Duncan claimed the marriage—a legal procedure so different in meaning under communism—did nothing to change her feeling that marriage was "an absurd and enslaving institution."[34] Esenin clearly felt threatened by

Duncan's fame and competitive with her. He was content to share in her glory, buying beautiful clothes with her money, drinking alcohol she provided, and relaxing in her home. He would get drunk and destroy things and she would clean up after him. In tears, she would forgive him and welcome him when he returned after leaving in a drunken rage.

As the "peasant poet"—adored in Russia for his earthy verse and deep devotion to the motherland—descended into alcoholism and violence, many of his devotees blamed Duncan. Maxim Gorky claimed Duncan could never understand her husband's poetry, so superior to Isadora's dancing, which, he said, looked like an older, overweight woman trying to keep warm. It was little solace to Duncan that American audiences were equally unappreciative of her husband, whose foreign status stripped Duncan of her US citizenship.[35] The two split up in the fall of 1923, as Esenin's drunken rampages and infidelity became more frequent. Two years later Esenin committed suicide.

On her final Soviet tour, the sets were all wrong, the transportation was poorly coordinated, the hotels were dirty, and audiences were so unenthusiastic that she could barely raise enough money to pay the orchestra. From a hotel room in Siberia with mice, bedbugs, stained sheets, and pistol shots in the mirror, Isadora wrote to Irma, "I feel extremely *kaput*."[36]

Despite official appreciation for Duncan's embrace of the workers' republic, many perceived her to be out of step with the new era. As one Russian dance scholar has noted of Duncan's Russian early acolytes, "Neither the Heptachorists nor their pupils studied with Isadora. They probably dreamed of it, but—thank God!—it did not happen. I believe that, were they to have studied in one of her schools, they would not have found there what they were looking for, and they would have left."[37]

Natalia Roslavleva, who, like the girls from Heptachor, was also profoundly influenced in her early years by Duncan, "suffered a disillusionment" when she saw Duncan perform in 1923. In her teens Roslavleva had founded a "Society of Young Duncanists" as well as a journal devoted to Duncan's work. However, in the flesh and in a new era, "Even from high up in the gallery, the heavily prancing woman with her exaggerated miming failed to impress me," Roslavleva wrote. "And when her tunic fell off the shoulder intentionally in the '*Internationale,*' exposing flesh that should have better remained unseen, a real crisis ensued" in her mind. Indeed, Rudneva and the girls from Heptachor were similarly disappointed when they saw Duncan perform in the 1920s: "Her previous dance-*plyaska*, free, natural, and joyful, had disappeared, to be replaced by theatrical pantomime."[38]

While Soviet officials were publicly deferential, critics in the 1920s were mostly dismissive. Reflecting on Duncan's significance for revolutionary Russia, Victor Iving, the most prominent Soviet dance critic at the time, could hardly contain his contempt:

> This matriarch of "plastic dancers" is sometimes herself not at all plastic: her legs are widely spread, her feet are placed in a row, flat and heavy, reminiscent of rough wooden sculptures of the Middle Ages. . . . She is heavy getting up from the floor, her back clumsily coming up earlier than her head. She lies, stands, bends, walks, rarely jumps, and stretches her hands. Oh, those constantly pleading hands! What does their supplicatory gesture have in common with the heroic spirit of the motherland of a new humankind, to upbringing which Duncan wants to devote herself?"

Duncan now was "an old, flabby woman" who "tries to disguise her choreographic weakness as a new revelation in art." Other critics complained that she looked too old, that her breasts were hanging, that her chin and neck were flabby, and that she was no longer quick and light.[39]

Duncan actually recognized that her own Soviet star was passing, but the children she and Irma taught suggested that she had, in fact, left her mark. While Isadora was away on her final tour of the Soviet Union, Irma and the school's students decided to offer free classes to Moscow's children. Hundreds of young people showed up at the red stadium in Sparrow Hills for lessons. Dressed in short red tunics, they were led through a series of exercises and taught simple dances; as Irma recalled: "They romped about in the sun singing their revolutionary songs, and from pale sallow children of the city streets they grew during the summer months to happy, sunburnt, and healthy dancing humans." These children, five hundred strong, were there to greet Isadora when she returned from her disastrous

Fig. 5.2 Students of the Isadora Duncan School in Moscow at Sparrow Hills, 1924. Sign text, in part, translates: "A Free Spirit Can Exist Only in a Freed Body. Duncan School." Jerome Robbins Dance Division, The New York Public Library for the Performing Arts, Astor, Lennox and Tilden Foundations.

tour: they marched in formation behind a brass band that played "The Internationale," and carried a banner with the school's slogan: "A Free Spirit Can Exist Only in a Freed Body." Isadora was thrilled to see what the children had achieved in a few short months: "Seeing them rushing forward together, one perceived that they were a band of young warriors and amazons ready to do battle for the ideals of the New World," she wrote.[40]

She spent the next few days teaching the children, whose songs inspired Duncan's final compositions. These dances, to songs such as "With Courage Comrades March in Step" and "The Blacksmith (or Forging the Keys of Freedom)," were different in style, more like the revolutionary dance that was beginning to take hold in the United States:

Unlike the airy, free-flowing style usually associated with Duncan, these dances have a blunt, bound, rooted look to them. There are few of those swelling waves of energy that Duncan usually sent out into space with her lilting arms, tempering the strength of the deep plush steps she took into the earth. The body image emphasizes tension, especially through lunging thighs, laboring arms, and clenched fists. The body is self-contained, a twisting sculptural mass displacing empty space as it goes, rather than a porous entity gliding through its airy surrounds. The group formations are muscularly sculptural in feeling. Even the garments are different—the short squarish tunics frame the materiality of the body, rather than flowing with the body as the gauzy, shapeless chitons did.[41]

Although Irma later claimed these dances were among Isadora's best, they were omitted from a memorial for Duncan held in Paris by her family in 1928. In the Soviet Union, although Duncan herself was mourned as a great supporter of the revolution, "Duncanism"—understood as something qualitatively different from these kinds of dances—was something to be scorned and avoided by dancers. Inspired as they were by the Russian children, Duncan's final compositions marked her recognition that she had little more to offer: as she told Irma, "These red tunicked kids are the future."[42] In September 1924 Isadora Duncan left the Soviet Union, returning to her other adopted homeland, France. Almost exactly three years later, she was dead: while she was riding in a convertible, her flowing red scarf wrapped itself around the car's front axle and strangled her. Duncan's three years in Russia were very much a coda to her career.

While her school continued to operate until 1949 and her legacy was treated with at least an official attitude of respect, by the end of the 1920s, "the new aesthetic ideal was biomechanical exercises for healthy-looking workers and athletes, and not wave-like movements for girls in tunics." Explaining in language that plainly referenced Duncan, Meyerhold said of dance, "We don't need *ecstasy*, we need *arousal*, based upon a firm physical foundation." Meyerhold's own theory of biomechanics not only revolutionized Soviet theatre but also demonstrated the dramatic possibilities of dance. However, this was dance of a certain kind: as Meyerhold wrote, "The actor of the future must first of all be well-formed, rhythmical, able to organize his body in space."[43]

Soviet Dimensions of the Revolutionary Dance Movement in America

Isadora Duncan is generally seen as a precursor to rather than a participant in the radical dance movement that swept New York City and other parts of the country in the 1930s, but her influence on the movement was indelible, and her pilgrimage to Russia likewise set a precedent for left-wing dancers in the 1930s. The US movement is usually said to have begun with Edith Segal's 1924 performance at the Lenin Memorial Pageant in Chicago, sponsored by the Workers' (or Communist) Party. Draped in black, the twenty-two-year-old performed to Chopin's funeral march and then removed her black outer garments to expose a red tunic, as "sadness and mourning gave way to a vision of energy and hope."[44]

Segal, like most of the revolutionary dancers, was a child of Jewish immigrants who had been introduced to Duncan-style dance through settlement houses. Studying at Lillian Wald's Henry Street Settlement and then at the Neighborhood Playhouse with Alice and Irene Lewisohn, Segal became a leading proponent of the radical dance movement. She taught children on New York's Lower East Side and at left-wing summer camps; organized a group of working-class New York women into the Red Dancers, who performed in union halls and various left-wing clubs; and became a regular performer at Communist Party functions, often performing dances on Soviet themes. Her *Dance in Four Parts*, for instance, based on the Lenin Memorial Pageant and created for the children she taught for twenty-five cents a month at the Ukrainian Hall, showed the Russian Revolution, the "building of socialism," and Lenin's death (and a memorial). At the end, the dancers formed a hammer and sickle.[45]

Among the revolutionary dances, Segal's were probably the most baldly ideological, but her employment of Soviet themes was quite common in the 1930s. Sophie Maslow composed *Themes from a Slavic People* in 1934 and *Two Songs about Lenin* (inspired by the 1934 Dziga Vertov film *Three Songs about Lenin*) in 1935. Lillian Shapero, the director of Artef Dance Group, choreographed a program called *One Sixth of the Earth* (the population of the Soviet Union), which included a ballet set to Marc Blitzstein's "Moscow Metro," a song about electrification. The program was performed at a twentieth-anniversary celebration of the Bolshevik revolution in a packed Madison Square Garden in November 1937, just after Shapero had returned from performing at the Moscow Theatre Festival. And the Workers' Dance League, an umbrella organization for various left-wing dance groups, in 1932 sponsored contests called "Spartakiades" derived from the Soviet alternative to the Olympics.[46]

Publications associated with the US Left such as *Workers Theatre* and *New Theatre* regularly discussed dance in the Soviet Union. "The training of a vast army of dancers among the great mass of the population is as important to the government as the training of any army of soldiers for defense. The bodies of the youth of the Soviet Union must be developed and disciplined, and dancing plays an important role in that training, aside from its cultural benefits," noted one 1934 article.[47]

American critics admired the attention devoted to dance in the Soviet Union, and left-wing dancers in the United States clearly took inspiration from Soviet life and culture: from events such as the revolution, Lenin's death (and life), and the collectivization of agriculture, to theatrical techniques such as Stanislavsky's "method," to the Soviet practice of mass dance. But it's also clear that even US Communists were critical of trends in Soviet dance. "It is startling that people who have the finest and most advanced theatre in the world should have practically no new dance," noted an article in *New Theatre*. Still, in Moscow "everywhere you feel the spirit of dance. . . . If we are ahead of them in dance form they are ahead of us in dance spirit."[48]

Edna Ocko, Anna Sokolow, Edith Segal, Mary "Mignon" Garlin, Dhimah Meadman, Lillian Shapero, and Pauline Koner, all of them Jewish, followed the trail Duncan had blazed to Moscow. Each of them relished many elements of the Soviet "new life" but offered few praises for Soviet dance. Segal, who visited the Soviet Union in 1931, said the dance she saw there was "awful. . . . They hadn't learned anything. . . . They had no background of modern dance." Sokolow, who spent three months in Russia in 1934, felt Russian audiences didn't understand her work ("they said I was not revolutionary") and was herself unimpressed by Russian dance: "I said, 'You get on the point and wave a red flag, I don't call that being revolutionary.'"[49]

Mary Garlin (or Garland), who wrote and danced under the name Mignon Verne (or just Mignon), is unique in that what most impressed her in the Soviet Union was Duncan's marked influence. Mignon had studied under Anna Duncan, one of Isadora Duncan's adopted daughters and protégés. When students from Duncan's Moscow school visited the United States in 1930 with Irma Duncan, Mignon was asked to show them around the city. Instead, she "took the Russian girls to her own studio and danced for them," prompting an invitation to come to Moscow and study with them. When the girls were ordered back to Moscow before Irma could fulfill her contract, Irma asked Anna to loan her best students, and so Mignon began touring with Irma in the United States and Cuba.[50]

A year later, with a seventy-two-hour visa, Mignon showed up in Moscow, made contact with one of the Duncan students she had met in New York, and managed to get a six-month visa, which she renewed twice, allowing her to study and dance with the Duncan School in Moscow. After returning to New York, she participated in a mass recital and rally in Madison Square Garden demanding diplomatic recognition of the Soviet Union. There, she met Edith Segal, Anna Sokolow, and other participants in the radical dance movement, whose spirit she appreciated, but whose dances she often criticized as lacking in artistic value.[51]

In the United States, Mignon started the New Duncan Dancers, which she consciously aligned philosophically if not formally with other radical dance companies: "These groups stand for dance art that is socially conscious," she wrote in *New Theatre*, where she was dance editor. Reviewing trends in revolutionary dance in 1934, Mignon asserted, "The thinking dancer realizes that dance art to be significant must express the force of living reality, and that only by allying dance with revolutionary ideology can that reality be optimistic." Mignon believed that "the [Duncan-style] Dance that expressed the love, the joy, the freedom and the profound emotions of all humanity" was revolutionary without needing ideological content per se. The New Duncan Dancers performed Soviet variations on Russian folk dances, a "Soviet cycle," as well as a dance "celebrating the success of collectivization in the Soviet Union" called "The Kolkhozniki," and they performed at a Recognition Rally for the Soviet Union at Bronx Coliseum.[52]

But like Duncan herself, the New Duncan Dancers were controversial. Some critics complained that the dancers were "not quite militant enough," or, worse, that they were "appallingly ungifted, untrained, and inert." "What do the Duncans with their flowing lines have to offer in a world of sharp conflict?" asked a May 1933 review.[53]

The *New* Dancer of the Future

Pauline Koner was of the same generation as Segal, Sokolow, and other leading figures in the revolutionary dance movement, but she was only tangentially connected to it. She grew up in a generally socialist milieu of immigrant Jews in New York City. Though not specifically trained in Duncan-style dance, Koner recognized Duncan as an early influence. In addition to ballet training with the Russian émigré Michel Fokine, a great admirer of Duncan's, Koner studied Spanish dance with Angel Casino, a well-known teacher. At seventeen she had toured with Michio Ito, a dancer from Japan who had himself had been influenced by Duncan and the Ballet Russes and by Dalcroze's eurhythmics.[54]

Koner's eclectic training, exotic looks (long, dark hair, olive skin, and high cheekbones), and tremendous adaptability launched her reputation as an "ethnographic" or "neoethnic" dancer who performed dances based on a variety of traditions; many of her performances had a Far Eastern flavor, such as her roles as an Indian priestess in *Nalamani* (1930) and a Javanese temple dancer in *Altar Piece* (1930). Koner performed such dances in order to demonstrate her own universality, "or her ability to represent a variety of Others."[55]

In 1932 and 1933, Koner spent nine months studying and dancing in Egypt and Palestine; a year later she went to the Soviet Union. Koner's itinerary thus encompassed two of the most popular sites of pilgrimage for Jews in the 1930s, the former a place to be proudly Jewish, the latter a place to shed the burdens associated with Jewishness, as anti-Semitism was now officially outlawed (though still prevalent). While in Tel Aviv, Koner saw "young settlers from the kibbutzim, energetic, sunburned, work-steeled bodies, and minds honed by the difficulties of survival—a look of life in their eyes and a warmth in their heart. . . . The atmosphere breathed enthusiasm, hope, and progress." Koner "felt vibrantly free, as if I had shed an invisible layer of skin, and proud of my Jewishness."[56]

Koner was invited to the USSR after her parents had gone there and presented her press book to the Soviet concert bureau, Gometz. Possibly because of Koner's training with Fokine, officials were enthusiastic and almost immediately offered a round-trip ticket and two-month contract with excellent pay. In the midst of the Depression, it sounded too good to be true.[57] Moreover, both the ethnic variety encompassed by the Soviet Union and the ostensible universality of Communist international-ism promised to take Koner's work in exciting new directions.

She was thrilled by the very idea of being in Russia ("I have to pinch myself to really believe I'm here," she wrote shortly after her arrival). In her diary, Koner's enthusiasm for Moscow is palpable: "I'm mad about Moscow has become a normal phrase for me.... It is the place for work for creative thought and *for happiness*. Its beauty at times is unbelievable."[58]

She arrived in Moscow in December of 1934, just in time for Sergei Kirov's funeral, which she watched from her hotel window. Koner's ar-rival in Moscow at the moment of Kirov's funeral offers a chilling coun-terpoint to the funeral cortege that Duncan claimed to have witnessed in Saint Petersburg, for Kirov's assassination would become the main pretext for Stalin's launch of the Great Terror. If Duncan witnessed the dawn of the Russian Revolution, Koner, without realizing it, was there for the beginning of its demise. Catching glimpses of the "sad but beauti-ful spectacle" that was Kirov's funeral, a five-hour procession in which thousands of people participated, she could only note, "Russia has lost a great person."[59]

Of course, Koner had many other things to be excited about. Within the first few weeks of her visit, she had already been to the Meyerhold theatre: "He has the facility of making anything, no matter how simple, into good theatre," she wrote afterward. "His sense of movement is un-canny and his synchronization is perfect." At the Masters of Art Club, she met and performed for Meyerhold, the film director Vsevolod Pudovkin, and other luminaries. She was a great success.[60]

At her public premiere in Leningrad on January 1, 1935, Koner had another experience that echoed Duncan's. The lights did not arrive, and she became hysterical, refusing to dance. After a half-hour delay, Koner was forced to begin. "I almost went insane," she noted in her diary. "The only way I forced myself to go through with it is by telling myself it would be a new experiment. If I could be successful with all these difficulties it would mean that my dancing even without all the theatrical necessities was what was necessary and successful." The experiment proved a worthy undertaking. "People yelled bravo and this till I was deaf. Encore after encore. Finally at the end I improvised and that too went marvelously." She did not weep tears of joy as Duncan had on the night the lights went out ("I was too tired and aggravated to be happy about it"), but the experience quickly taught her to appreciate Soviet audiences.[61]

For her official Moscow premiere on January 17, Koner had everything she needed, and now she danced with confidence. That concert was also a great success: "I have become famous all Moscow has begun to talk," she wrote in her diary. In Leningrad, she gave several more performances, all well received. At the Theatre Club, which was open by special invitation to artists only, half the would-be audience could not even get in, and "at the end there was such enthusiastic and insistent applause that I almost cried with joy," Koner recalled. "When artists acclaim another artist the victory is indeed great."[62]

She was attending theatre and dance performances whenever she could but was largely unimpressed by Soviet dance—fueling her sense that she had something unique and important to offer. She saw non-Russian minorities dance in their native styles and found dances such as "the hunter's dance, the duck dance, and the shaman" to be "primitive but interesting." In contrast, she saw Russian attempts at modern dance as "banal" and without "nuance."[63]

In Leningrad, Koner saw *The Flame of Paris*, supposedly a revolutionary ballet, but was disappointed. One "cannot create a new emotional reaction when presented with an old decadent style," she noted. By late January, she was thinking about a long-term future in Russia. Although she'd never experienced "such serious active interest in forwarding the dance art," she nonetheless believed "Russia needs a new form in its dancing." After a long conversation with Valia, the interpreter and tour manager who had been assigned to her, Koner reflected that Soviet dance "knows what it wants as far as theme is concerned but its form is outdated. It's up to me to get those together and I shall. All the plans that I vaguely had have materialized of themselves and I hope they shall continue to. My life is taking a completely new turn."[64]

She was invited to a party at the Astoria hotel and found herself seated with the director Vsevolod Pudovkin and the poet, playwright, and scenarist Natan Zarchi. Pudovkin spoke English, which offered a welcome respite from constant efforts to speak in Russian, and he and Koner danced together "all evening." "Could hardly believe he is close to 50," she noted. She was up until 6:00 a.m. "The days are simply too short," she complained. Koner and Pudovkin would begin spending many evenings together, dancing, talking endlessly.[65]

The late-night talking, the dances, the cultural activities, and the teaching seemed to fill Koner with energy. She gave a class to about twenty-five dance teachers in "oriental style," "Spanish style," "Fokine style," and her own style. "People were thrilled," Koner remarked. "This is what I came to Russia to do. Before I leave I shall be creating ballet and having a school of my own. I'm determined to and this is the chance of my life." At a ballet performance, the director of the theatre said he'd like her to give a course at the Marinsky Ballet School, where Pavlova had trained. She had not expected the opportunity to come so quickly.[66]

While she found Soviet dance less than inspiring, Koner was deeply affected by other aspects of life in Russia. She was entranced by her visit to a factory: by the immensity of the machines and the workers' interest and enthusiasm. Her diary contains a long, excited description of blast furnaces: "This when completed is forming the new world of Soviet Russia." The visit "was a thrilling experience." Like Duncan, she was deeply moved by the spectacle of a May Day parade, by the "electric currents vibrat[ing] in the air" as Stalin passed and by the rhythmic movements of marchers through the square. She described Red Square as "awe inspiring," and the parades, red flags, and bands as "a Utopia."[67]

Her conversations with Pudovkin were also deeply inspiring. "He is a strange, hysterical, but brilliant person and I may be able to get much inspiration from him." Two days later, she noted the "tremendous impression" she made on Pudovkin during a concert that evening, and with excitement, she recounted a discussion with him and Zarchi about "how to attack thematic material." The conversation was electric. "I am inspired and thrilled with new impetus to work. I am beginning to orient myself to this mode and have a strong notion that I shall spend a much longer period in Russia than I originally planned perhaps I shall even make my headquarters here," she noted. Pudovkin, who emerged as one of the leading filmmakers of the Stalin era, and whom scholars have since accused of "devot[ing] his great talent wholly to the service of the Party," helped convince Koner that her work should forward the goals of the revolution.[68]

As her two months were nearing their end, Koner decided she wanted to stay in Russia long term: "I am being convinced slowly but surely that Russia is the place for me," she wrote. "The place where I can mold my future. It has the inspiration I need the possibilities I need." Yet she felt something was missing in her life: "One thing I must find here . . . is a companion. It is unnatural for me to go on much longer without anyone to focus my affections upon and without anyone to stimulate me."[69]

In fact, by this time she had already fallen for Pudovkin, who was not only twice her age but also married. "He seems to be quite interested in me," she reported cautiously to her diary after a day filled with "pure fun," and "snow, country hills crisp air and gay spirits," followed by dinner. "But how can one judge the sincerity of men? They are immediately attracted by a pliable body and just as quickly find another." She promised herself she would "be wary and not play the fool as I have so long done." She was kidding herself.[70]

If she was only tentatively wading into the waters of romance, professionally Koner was moving forward full force. A performance on February 19 was part of a program to consider dance trends in relation to "the training of mass dance in the USSR." Koner's *Dance of Longing*, "a modern dance work to percussion accompaniment using my Chinese gongs and bells," was discussed and critiqued: "That I was a real artist and fine musician as well as excellently technically equipped was agreed by all." The filmmaker Sergei Eisenstein, a member of the committee, praised her privately. "I have all intentions of getting down to serious work and creating a group here," Koner noted after this workshop. "I am beginning to see clearly my plan and procedure and etc."[71]

It took weeks to negotiate a contract, but in the meantime Koner continued to perform, finally securing a deal that guaranteed her the highest possible salary. The work was exhausting, and working conditions were far from ideal. Still, she was performing regularly before enthusiastic audiences, maturing as an artist, and eager to see more of the Soviet Union and study its varied cultures.[72]

And she was in love, against her "better judgment." However, there was much to recommend Pudovkin: "He is a person whom I can admire, respect, and learn from. I do not feel as though I am only a body only something to give sensation. I am a person am respected as such and an artist. To talk! To lose oneself in a wild enthusiasm! In the hot surging flame of creation! To exchange thoughts and inspiration." She vowed that if she got hurt she could always "drown [the hurt] in the sweat of my work." Indeed, a poor performance a week later reminded her that she needed to prioritize that work: "Love pleasure happiness all must be secondary and only an alternative never the main issue. . . . I have to work, work, work! And I want to work. I'm aching to create new things better things great things."[73]

She began a month-long tour that took her to the outskirts of Siberia, with Sverdlovsk (now Yekaterinburg) as her base. She visited cities "where Russian dancers rarely went," at one point performing in a circus arena in Chlyabinsk, where she worried that a lion in one of the cages backstage might roar during the performance. After a few weeks, Koner became weary. She complained about the inefficiency and stupidity of the people around her. "I'm going crazy, losing all control of my nerves," she reflected. "I'm just a bundle of shivering quaking nerves. Oh! I can't go on like this. It is impossible." Even a long-awaited letter from Pudovkin did little to settle her. She was having trouble finding decent food, and she felt tired and weak. She had developed a carbuncle under her arm, making it hard to move. She felt lonely, lost, exhausted, and eager to return to Moscow.[74]

But once back, Koner felt a new clarity. Her feelings for Pudovkin had tempered a long–running and almost debilitating obsession with her former dance partner Yeichi Nimura. Finding herself laughing at "what might be called an ardent love letter" from Nimura, Koner suddenly felt she had found her way. She was determined to "create the first great soviet dance art." Although there were continuing contract problems, conflicts with her pianist, and challenges to Koner's somewhat fragile nerves, that May seems to have been a turning point both in Koner's work and in her relationship with Pudovkin. "Days in the country! Sunlight, grass, trees, water and love!! Yes, days of unbelievable happiness with Kin [Pudovkin]. Without unhappy associations. Days of real beauty and languor. At last I have learned what physical love really is. Kin respects me as a person and as an individual not only as a lover. We share ideas and plans."[75]

One night Pudovkin related to her the plot of the scenario he was working on ("he could have paid me no greater compliment than to have taken me into the midst of his work," she noted). But Koner was not destined to merely play muse to Pudovkin: part of his attraction for her was that their connection fed her creatively, professionally, emotionally, *and* physically. As she became more secure in her relationship with Pudovkin, she also gained more confidence in her own vision:

> As for work, my greatest dream, my desire beyond myself has almost been realized. I shall have a school subsidized by the Russian government. . . . The thing I primarily came to Russia for. To complete what Duncan began. To create a great new art. The "proletarian dance art." To learn myself and help others learn. The school shall not only have dance but shall have courses in all the affiliated arts: music, painting, sculpture, and literature. We shall make from the red style Russian ballerina a creative intelligent person who shall know dancing not as a trick but as an art.[76]

She was invited to dinner at the home of Andrei Goncharov, a portraitist. Pudovkin was at the dinner, but so was his wife, Anna Nikolaevna Zemtsova, a prominent film critic and actress. Koner found her attractive and intelligent, but did not feel threatened. "Instead I was exceptionally gay, happy and confident in the matter of comparison." Pudovkin hardly spoke all evening. "I compared youth against age—sparkle against dullness, litheness against bluntness, life against lethargy," Koner noted in her diary.[77]

On June 26, in Sverlovsk, Koner turned twenty-three. "Years are adding up and yet for twenty three I have already seen and done a great deal," she told herself. Koner's youthful exuberance both heightened her hopes and may have softened the blow when she determined her Moscow dance school was not to be. While still waiting for word about it, Koner received an invitation to teach dance at the Lesgaft Physical Culture Institute in Leningrad, whose program had the closest thing to modern dance in Russia.[78]

"Physical culture" (*fizkul'tura*) in the Soviet Union was one of the only arenas for movements that in the United States might be classed as modern dance, especially as nearly all private dance studios (Duncan's was one of the few exceptions) were closed in April 1924 as part of an effort to centralize instruction. Physical culture emphasized the cultural dimensions of movement, especially gymnastics, which "taught not only discipline and control but also synchronization through group exercises believed to be capable of integrating and uniting individuals."[79]

Koner was torn for weeks about whether to take the position at Lesgaft, because it meant giving up or at least delaying plans for opening her own school; it also meant being apart from Pudovkin. One night she called Pudovkin for advice and he, feeling unwell, asked her to come to his house. She wound up spending the evening with Pudovkin and his wife, telling them about her troubles, ultimately finding herself laughing hysterically at the whole situation. "Anna Nikolaevna felt so sorry for me and didn't know the half of it," she remarked to her diary.[80] She decided to accept the appointment in Leningrad because it would allow her to develop as a dancer and a teacher. In fact, Koner's real development as a choreographer in the Soviet Union began only once she became involved with the Lesgaft Institute. What Koner didn't realize was that the appointment put her squarely within the Stalinist project of militarizing Soviet youth.[81]

Physical Culture and the "New Soviet Dance"

The Lesgaft Institute was named for the father of physical education in Russia, Pyotr Lesgaft, a biologist, social reformer, and education theorist who gave special attention to sport as a vehicle for "women's social emancipation." The institute's program embodied the hybrid projects of physical culture and women's empowerment under Stalin. A principal aim of the institute was to determine ways to "utilize physical exercise rationally to improve productivity," which evolved to encompass, by the mid-1930s, military preparation. Physical culture was simultaneously a tool for cultivating "an individual with the harmonious development of mental and bodily strengths," an instrument for building workers' labor capacity, and a means of inculcating discipline and fitness for battle.[82]

Dance taught under the rubric of physical culture was to be collective, vigorous, and easily intelligible to the masses; these ideas inspired elements of the revolutionary dance movement in the United States but also echoed the totalitarian mass dances of Nazi Germany, which converted *ausdruckstanz* (expressive dance) into political spectacles. In the Soviet Union, mass spectacles became increasingly commonplace as a "new outbreak of festivity" accompanied intensification of "the purges and political repression of the Soviet elite."[83]

Especially by the mid-1930s, Stalinism fostered women's identities in what Westerners might construe as two competing arenas. On the one hand, women were encouraged to embrace motherhood and marriage. On the other hand, stories of women's successes—in such varied fields as "aviation, defense, agriculture, industry, and sports"—helped define the country's modernity. Young women were widely celebrated in Stalinist culture as full partners in industrialization and mobilization for a war that seemed increasingly imminent. Women's displays of strength, agility, flexibility, and rhythm in physical culture parades can be seen as scripted but deeply felt performances of the new Soviet woman.[84] That is to say, massive demonstrations of collective unity under Stalin could have expressed genuine feelings, even as they were orchestrated by authorities. Koner's own compositions for Lesgaft students are telling in this regard.

The work at Lesgaft was all-consuming and exhausting but also incredibly stimulating. Koner's teaching incorporated film as well as excursions to museums and concerts. Students were paid a stipend and were thus not distracted by the need to work. They seemed fully present, energetic, and full of excitement. They seemed, indeed, like new people. "The pupils of Leningrad are young and fresh, a new type of youth, Soviet youth. Full of enthusiasm, life and energy, full of a desire to work and strength to accomplish. They are bubbling with ambition." The women were especially inspiring. Koner, not much older than her students, was likely enthralled by the "cult of the heroine" that showcased the new Soviet woman "as an emancipated representative of progress and modernization."[85]

A Russian newspaper describes Koner teaching Foregger-inspired machine dances, but photographs show that Koner also embraced a more organic vision for the "new Soviet dance." Images from what appears to be a rehearsal on the Leningrad beach show young people in bathing suits moving in unison or posed in evocative tableaux vivants. Their collective gestures suggest freedom, joy, possibility, and dynamism, recalling the style cultivated by German *Ausdruckstanz* and also echoing Pudovkin's shots of expansive spaces with grasses swaying in the wind.[86] Formations incorporate a primitively fashioned bow and arrow, sheets, and a crown of flowers worn by Koner. Dancers reach toward the sky, their arms gesturally repeating the leafy branches that several students grasp. Koner also dances solo, improvising for her students or perhaps for the photographer: she stretches, reaches, lunges, twists, kicks, bends, leaps, and even spirals in midair. Here we see something like an accommodation between Duncan-style "plastic dance" and Soviet physical culture.

The Lesgaft students inspired Koner to choreograph her first "Soviet" dance: "The theme is the triumphant joy the victory and hope of the new Russian Soviet life. My subject is the red flag. I do not dance one who sees carries or feels the flag, no, I dance the flag itself. All its movement and all for which it stands," she noted, in language reminiscent of the American Pledge of Allegiance. Years later, Koner remembered the composition as "awful," complaining she was too busy stimulating others to be genuinely creative herself, but this memory may have been colored by recognition that she had become increasingly mired in the question of what the "new Soviet dance" would, or should, be.[87]

Her goal was to express "the quintessence of emotional realism" through dance. But her notes are choppy, confused: "Find the definite themes such as the hope the health the youth the happiness of Soviet form ... feeling of vigor delight of the new generation their desire to learn to grow to go ever higher and accomplish more. Yes that is the proper line to take." Koner's momentary certitude seems to crumble as she admits,

Fig. 5.3 Pauline Koner with her students from the Lesgaft Physical Culture Institute. Pauline Koner papers, Jerome Robbins Dance Division, The New York Public Library for the Performing Arts, Astor, Lennox and Tilden Foundations.

Fig. 5.4 Pauline Koner dancing on the beach in Leningrad. Pauline Koner papers, Jerome Robbins Dance Division, The New York Public Library for the Performing Arts, Astor, Lennox and Tilden Foundations. This image was used on the cover of Koner's dance textbook, *Elements of Performance* (1993).

almost in the same breath, that her emotional state is "very bad." The work at Lesgaft was not enough to distract Koner from realizing the "impossibility" of her love for Pudovkin.[88]

Resigned to let go of their relationship, Koner threw herself into work with renewed vigor. She was invited to propose a program for a 70,000-person physical culture parade, a visible manifestation of youthful fitness and discipline. She spent two days and nights working on what was her first attempt at "group choreography," and her plan was accepted. "Hurrah! It means working like the devil but it will be worth it. I'm set to work twenty hours a day." She recognized that the chance to "show this work to the highest government officials" could mean "the beginning of an important phase in my career." But more important, she told herself, "it means interesting work for myself."[89]

Koner's memoir says almost nothing about the actual performance of her "Dance of the New Youth," and her Russia diary ends before the performance amid her struggle over the "ideological correctness" of having the dancers create a star formation. "I felt it symbolized the force [of] the new generation. . . . But everyone was extremely wary of chancing criticism," she lamented years later. She came up with an alternative that consisted, she claimed, of "just some brilliant movement that would catch the eye."[90] But this description is not entirely credible, as evidenced by several newspaper clippings in a scrapbook that Koner kept.

The Leningrad sports newspaper, *Spartak*, features a photo of the Lesgaft students' performance beneath Stalin's famous words, now evoked only as an ironic reminder of his regime's duplicity: "Life has become better comrades. Life has become joyful." A clipping from *Pravda* goes into greater detail, describing dancers in white, blue, yellow, orange, and red jerseys whirling and then freezing in place on a giant Soviet emblem of unspecified shape. The performance is said to take on "new power" as "the famous American dancer Pauline Koner" joins the students: "On the square rose a border pole. Suddenly there arrives a detachment of defenders of the Soviet borders. Unexpectedly, from an enclosure jumps a saboteur unit. With baited breath, all of the square expressed, through bayonets, the fervent courage of Soviet border guards. Here already gathered a handful of brave souls. The saboteurs rush the Soviet territory, but the new detachment of border guards turns out to cruelly resist them. The enemy is beaten. His pathetic remnants flee, etc. The victorious thunder 'Oora!'"[91]

A month before the most famous Moscow show trials, an idealistic young woman trying to build her career and discover her true self in a foreign land choreographed and participated in a militaristic spectacle showing defenders of the Soviet borders crushing supposed saboteurs. "I had heard rumors that there were political trials going on, but knew very little about them," Koner writes in her memoir, which suggests dissociation from political machinations. Later, she mentions the "Stalin purge" but says almost nothing about it.[92]

In an article Koner wrote for the left-wing *New Theatre* shortly after her return to New York, she mentions the title of the dance and the size of the parade, but claims that she was "sure of my viewpoint" and "firm against all opposition." She never mentions that Stalin himself was in the audience. She also says nothing about the actual dance other than that her students were full of "the joy of life" and that the success of the parade had led to government orders that Lesgaft continue its work, thereby eliminating "a great chunk in the wall of opposition to the modern dance." In her memoir all she says is that "the performance on the great Palace Square was quite a spectacle, and the newspaper reviews were excellent."[93]

Koner left the Soviet Union shortly after the physical culture parade. She had planned to return to Lesgaft after a two-month holiday with her family in the United States, but when it came time to go back, she was denied a visa. Fewer foreigners were being admitted to the Soviet Union, and the climate was rapidly changing. Koner was disappointed, but she recognized that the real draw for her was Pudovkin, who could never fully give himself to her.[94]

Koner is not usually remembered as having any affiliation with the Left. But her Russian days clearly made their mark on her. She is open in her memoir about having had positive experiences in the Soviet Union, and the cover of her popular dance technique textbook shows her dancing, seemingly hanging midair, on the Leningrad beach, implying that this place and this moment was the culmination of her technical development. The FBI kept a file on her, but it noted only a handful of performances she gave in the late 1930s and early 1940s in the United States supporting the Soviet Union or Spain.[95]

What, then, do we make of the massive performance for Stalin, or her desire to create the "new Soviet dance"? Perhaps this entire project was, for her, another ethnographic act, an experiment in performing another persona, undertaken not as an expression of faith but as a chance for "interesting work" that would advance her career. Or maybe she found actual inspiration in the Stalinist project. Koner's gravity-defying leaps on the Leningrad beach seem to defy the weight of the history they embody.

Isadora Duncan and the American modern dancers who followed her to the Soviet Union went with tremendous hopes that in witnessing a new society they themselves would be transformed, and that they could share with this society, particularly its young women, movement and techniques attuned to a revolutionary new era. Despite very different successes and disappointments, both Duncan and Koner cited their time in Russia and the Soviet Union as crucial to their work and their social conscience. But neither woman publicly acknowledged the personal or ethical concessions that were necessary to finding love and dancing revolution in Soviet Russia.

In between Duncan's and Koner's Russian days, a group of African Americans, eight women among them, would likewise come to Moscow to perform. Although their planned performance was called off, sharing in the drama of Soviet life was a deeply moving experience for them.

Black and White—and Yellow—in Red

Performing Race in Russia

On June 15, 1932, a group of twenty-two African Americans, including eight women, set sail on the SS *Europa* from New York City. They were headed to Moscow to perform in an English-language film, *Black and White*, that would offer the first "authentic picture of Negro life in America." The group included just one full-time, professional actor; the rest were students or professionals, including two social workers, two salesmen, a lawyer, three journalists, and a couple of writers. Less than nine days earlier, before driving from California in an old Ford with two other cast members, poet Langston Hughes had dashed off a telegram to Louise Thompson, the trip's organizer: "Hold that boat," he said. "Cause it's an ark to me." Loaded down with "a huge assortment of baggage, including a typewriter, record player, and a big box of jazz records," Hughes barely scrambled on board before the ship left.[1]

Dorothy West, a young writer and, like Hughes, participant in the Harlem Renaissance, found every leg of the journey thrilling. "Everybody adores me in my boating outfit, the sailor cap and all," West wrote her mother from the ship. Each day group members met to discuss some aspect of Russia. Thompson spent most of her time with Hughes and Loren Miller, an attorney and city editor of the Los Angeles–based *California Eagle*, sitting on the deck while talking or looking out at the sea. West began paying attention to Hughes as well. One night Hughes and West "went out and looked at the stars. The moon was big and friendly. The sea was calm." West went back to her cabin and wrote, "My porthole is open. The sea air blows in and is a tonic." Another evening she stayed up late with him and Mollie Lewis, a student at Columbia Teachers College, wearing her "black dress with the yellow top" and drinking champagne. Hughes was "swell fun."[2]

Prominent liberal African Americans Alain Locke and Ralph Bunche were on the same ship, but in a higher-class cabin; Thompson, who knew Locke from her days teaching at the Hampton Institute, gave him the "cold shoulder" and described Bunche as a "frightful bore."[3]

The ship stopped in Berlin, where the *Black and White* group was delayed by the fact that the Russian consulate had no visas waiting for them, or any knowledge that they were coming. Thompson straightened things out and the ship proceeded across the Baltic Sea, "the sun never setting, always on the horizon, the pink flush of dawn." In Helsinki the group boarded a train for what Thompson called "the last lap of our journey to the Promised Land." The train stopped briefly when it crossed the Russian border; Hughes jumped off and handed Thompson and several others "a first handful of Russian soil."[4]

In Leningrad Lovett Fort-Whiteman, an African American Communist and former Shakespearean actor who had been living in the Soviet Union since 1928 (and who helped translate the original script for the film), met them with a brass band playing "The Internationale." At their hotel, cast members were treated to "a sumptuous banquet—chicken, ice cream, and everything one would not expect to find in Russia." An overnight train brought them to Moscow, where they were greeted by members of the African American community, including Robert Robinson, an auto worker from Detroit, as well as Corretti Arle-Tietz and Emma Harris, singers who had been in Russia since before the revolution. Taken to the Grand Hotel ("it really is a grand hotel," West reported

Fig. 6.1 Langston Hughes and Dorothy West on the SS *Europa*. Langston Hughes papers, Yale Collection of American Literature, Beinecke Rare Book and Manuscript Library.

to her mother), they found a special breakfast prepared for them. Other than the hiccup in Berlin, it was an auspicious beginning to a Soviet adventure.[5]

African American women, like Euro-American women, came to the Soviet Union to explore new ways of being in the world, to see these ways enacted, and to embody new selves in a land where racism had been outlawed. Each of the eight women who made their way to Moscow to take part in *Black and White* had her own particular reasons for going, but in some fundamental way each believed that being in the Soviet Union would be a transformative experience, and might even influence hearts and minds in the United States.

Participants were right that the experience would be transformative for those involved: not only did it give them a chance to experience the vibrant life of Moscow and its environs; it also took most of them to the far corners of the Soviet Union. Here they witnessed firsthand how the lives of Soviet national minorities, and minority women in particular, had been transformed by the revolution. However, the film itself was never made: it was canceled about six weeks after the group arrived in Moscow and began performing—though not in front of a movie camera.

While African Americans were officially honored as key figures in the world proletarian struggle, historically, Black performances in Russia and the Soviet Union revealed a deep ambivalence among Russians about racial others. In some cases, as with the Afro-Chinese dancer Sylvia Chen, whose time in Moscow overlapped with that of the *Black and White* group, racial performances could be liberating for both performers and audiences. But just as often they hinted at fissures between performances and underlying realities. And even as many African Americans insisted that there was no race consciousness in the USSR, in Russia they constantly performed their Blackness.

Black and White may be among the most famous films never made, but it has not been considered in terms of the performances it *did* produce, or in the context of Soviet performances of race and gender more generally. The Soviets interpreted their Black visitors' daily, quotidian acts through a political lens that heightened the significance of African Americans as social actors on a stage that made them "hypervisible."[6]

African American Performance in Russia and the Soviet Union

The promoters of *Black and White* were not entirely accurate in asserting that this film would be the "first authentic picture" of African American life. But it is true that as performers the cast would be especially welcome in Russia, which had a long tradition of hosting Black entertainers from the United States. In the United States, especially after the Civil War, African American theatre productions geared toward Black audiences produced realistic portrayals of African American life and often took on racial violence as a subject. In US films, too, in the 1920s, African American pioneers like Oscar Micheaux began challenging lynching and Jim Crow while exploring African American life.[7]

However, most depictions of African Americans in US popular culture were either negative or at the very least stereotyped. Before the Civil War, African American performances predominantly took place either for the pleasure of white slave owners, who insisted on demonstrations of slaves' happy state, or in abolitionist melodrama. The latter form treated Blackness as a tragic condition or employed minstrelsy's "darky fanfare" as comic relief in dramas depicting slavery's evils. White audiences' obsession with Blackness made the practice of racial drag—almost always in the form of whites performing in blackface—among the most popular forms of American entertainment at the turn of the century. But performances by real African Americans, whose Blackness represented "the prohibited and the repressed," had unique appeal.[8]

At the turn of the twentieth century, W. E. B. Du Bois asserted that African Americans lived behind a "veil" that both separated and to some degree protected them from whites. As critical race scholar Patricia Williams has noted, "the real lives of real blacks unfold outside the view of many whites," while whites indulge in a "fantasy of black life as a theatrical enterprise." Black women, historically, have experienced this twice over: not just through their race but also through their gender. Seen as subject to the white male gaze, either as actual property or as sexual objects, African American women had few arenas in which to be authentically themselves.[9]

Even before the revolution, Russians were used to seeing African Americans as performers, whether stage actors like Ira Aldridge, or the

Fisk Jubilee Singers, or dancers like Olga Burgoyne, who performed the cakewalk throughout Russia and studied acting in Saint Petersburg. African American performers appealed to Silver Age intellectuals in Russia for many of the same reasons Isadora Duncan did: they seemed to possess the vibrancy and life force that a decadent, repressive society lacked. (Duncan herself was explicit about distinguishing her ecstatic, Dionysian dance from "the sensual convulsion of the Negro.") Saint Petersburg "was a center for black performers" between 1904 and 1909, precisely the years that Duncan made her initial tours of Russia. Black singers and chorus girls Ida Forsyne, Mattie Wilkes, and Laura Bowman all based themselves for extended stretches in Russia during these years, performing the cakewalk and other "Negro" dances, which spread to the general population of rebellious youth in Russia.[10]

In 1912 a Ukrainian orchestra performed "A Negro's Dream," and a Russian music publisher offered scores for cakewalks entitled "The Creole Girl," "The Negro Dance," and "The Holiday of the Negroes." A Saint Petersburg candy maker even issued ragtime hits (recognizable as "Black" music) on records "pressed into disks of hard baker's chocolate." Music and dances derived from African American culture were presented to the Russian public as "exotic, earthy, and blatantly lascivious" and were eagerly lapped up. Images on sheet music "conjured up uninhibited savages wailing erotic melodies under a tropical moon."[11]

The small number of African Americans remaining in Russia through World War I and the revolution were both highly visible and often beloved among Russians. The daughter of Georgia slaves, Emma Harris, by some accounts the "eldest American resident of Moscow," had come to Moscow in 1901 with a troupe known as the Louisiana Amazons, which had toured Europe singing "Southern negro folk songs and spirituals." The troupe was especially popular in Moscow and Saint Petersburg, and it stayed in Russia for several months before disbanding. Harris made a career onstage in Moscow and Saint Petersburg as "the Black Nightingale." "Wherever she was, she had the ability to hold center stage," Langston Hughes recalled.[12]

Corretti Arle-Tietz, née Coretta Alfred, had come to Russia with a "negro theatre troupe" prior to the revolution and wound up staying on, taking Soviet citizenship and marrying noted musician Boris Borisovich Tietz. In the midst of revolutionary ferment, she performed in a vaudeville program set up by workers at a factory as the front for an antigovernment meeting. The performance brought her popularity with Russian workers, who embraced Tietz as a voice of the revolution.[13]

Given this long tradition, and the shared histories of oppression represented by slavery and serfdom—both of which were ended at nearly the same moment—the Soviet Union was ripe to embrace African Americans, although those we usually hear about were men. Claude McKay, the West Indian–born poet and fiction writer and fixture of the Harlem Renaissance, spoke in 1922 at the Fourth Congress of the Comintern on the "Negro Question." In addition, a set of "theses," presented by Rose Pastor Stokes and passed under McKay and Otto Huiswood's advisement, recognized the American Negro's crucial role "in the liberation struggle of the entire African race," defined "black liberation as a key part of the global struggle against capitalism and imperialism," and explicitly directed American Communists "to fight for black-white unity."[14]

Ruth Kennell and her comrades at the Kuzbas colony had performed a "negro play," *Aftermath*, about a year after McKay's trip to Moscow. Originally published in the Communist *Liberator* in 1919, this play by the African American playwright, drama teacher, and activist Mary Burrill portrays the return of a World War I veteran who discovers that his father has been lynched.[15] Photographs suggest that at least one African American woman numbered among the Kuzbas colonists, but one wonders whether colonists performed the play—which presumes an all-Black cast—in blackface. Doing so certainly would have affected the play's impact and its antiracist intent. Then again, even African American members of the Chocolate Kiddies, the group credited with bringing authentic Black jazz to the Soviet Union, performed in blackface.

Jazz was first popularized in Russia by the futurist poet, Dadaist, and surrealist Valentin Parnakh, a Jew who formed a New Orleans–style jazz band in Moscow in the fall of 1922. Although much of the Soviet elite viewed jazz as an expression of bourgeois decadence, it had credibility as an African American musical expression. Parnakh's band was enormously popular.[16]

Aiming to capitalize on the jazz craze, a Russian émigré impresario made his way to Harlem to recruit performers. Eubie Blake and Noble Sissle's *Chocolate Dandies*—the show that started the Charleston craze and launched Josephine Baker's career—had just closed, and several members of the cast were available. The Chocolate Kiddies was born. The twenty-five-person all-Black song-and-dance revue included Lottie Gee (the female lead in the landmark Black musical *Shuffle Along*), Margaret Simms (who had been "the toast of Broadway" at eighteen), the acrobatic team Bobby and Baby Goines, and eleven chorus girls. Sam Wooding's eleven-piece orchestra, "all the rage" in New York, was booked, too; a young Duke Ellington composed several of the program's tunes. After successful runs in Germany, France, Italy, Turkey, Czechoslovakia, Tunisia, and Spain, the Russian Philharmonic Society booked the group.[17]

Acts in the Kiddies' "Negro Operetta" included "At the Plantation before the Setting Sun," "Jungle Nights in Dixie," "Harlem in New York," and a "Negro Concert" showcasing jazz, blues, and spirituals. All in all the program was typical of the Black variety stage, many of whose numbers, designed for white audiences, offered "a fantastical rendition of a strange and mythical Southland," mixing a happy Old South with primitive "jungle nights." In the Soviet Union, the performance conjured up a complicated mix of Western decadence, African primitivism, and the specter of colonialism. Orchestra member Garvin Bushell recalled, "They'd always give the same reason to have jungle music: tom-toms and hoochie-coochie," which added a sexual dimension to the performance. Not coincidentally, Josephine Baker's "banana dance," in which Baker performed with Black "natives" wearing loincloths and playing tom-toms, titillated audiences in Paris and Berlin the same year as the Kiddies tour.[18]

The Kiddies played at the Moscow Circus in February 1926 and then at the Leningrad Music Hall, remaining in Russia for three months, and consistently packing audiences. Scenes from the Kiddies' performance used in Dziga Vertov's film *One Sixth of the World* show scantily clad, frenetic, brown female performers interspersed with wealthy white concertgoers wearing furs and looking bored, images of naked Africans emerging from a thatched hut and Soviet workers in a steel factory. A special issue of the magazine *Tsirk* devoted to the Chocolate Kiddies

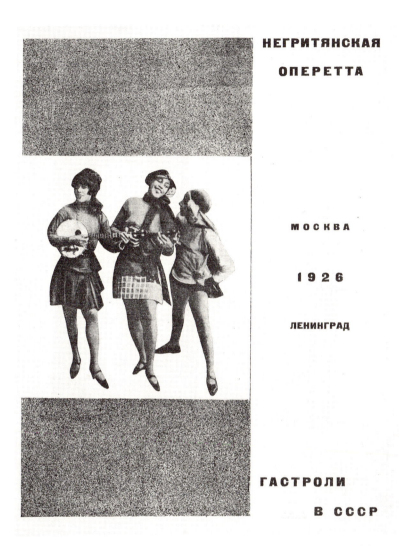

НЕГРИТЯНСКАЯ

ОПЕРЕТТА

МОСКВА

1926

ЛЕНИНГРАД

ГАСТРОЛИ

В СССР

Fig. 6.2 Chocolate Kiddies, in *Tsirk*, 1926. Image courtesy of Amherst Center for Russian Culture.

includes images in the montage style characteristic of Soviet avant-garde art of the period as well as reviews from prominent Russian directors, critics, and intellectuals. Here and in other promotional material, "Chocolate Kiddies" is translated as "Shokoladnie Rebiata," or, literally, "Chocolate Children" or "Chocolate Gang." Cover photographs show performers standing in a line wearing top hats and tuxedoes. Another page shows three women wearing short skirts and cloche hats; one woman plays a banjo, another plays a ukulele, and the third stands with her hands on her hips, legs spread, leaning forward, as if in conversation with the other two. On another page, Baby Goines, wearing overalls, stands smiling, in a gender-bending image of the happy southern laborer. In still another image, the Black performers are gathered together at tables as though in a jazz club, with musicians in the back and, in the foreground, a female dancer doing a split and showing her legs while being held in a man's arms.[19]

Although the numbers clearly drew on racist traditions of minstrelsy, there were good reasons for Black performers to join these traveling troupes. They were paid well and treated with respect. Though not especially enthusiastic about communism, Bushell was moved by his treatment at the hands of Russians: "Russia was the first country I'd ever been in where I was considered a human being—a person like anybody else."[20]

Ruth Kennell, writing her mother from Moscow in April 1926, mentioned the Chocolate Kiddies and described their show as "the hit of the season." "Negroes are the fashion now here," she added, noting that one woman's millinery shop in Moscow had a "negro lady" mannequin in the window as a model. In an earlier letter, Kennell had bragged about her personal contacts with African Americans, marveling at the way in which spending time in the Soviet Union had forced her to rethink her views concerning race:

> Speaking of "niggers," you would be shocked to see me walking on
> the street with a real black one, or entertaining four of them at once in
> my room. I can't remember when I wrote you last, I think I must have
> mentioned the four negroes who are attending the Eastern University,
> preparing themselves to be C.[Communist] leaders in America. They are
> nice fellows, but old prejudices are not easily overcome. However, I am
> getting over them, because I am ashamed of them. I have only to close
> my eyes and picture the horrors in America, the impossible color lines in
> the south, the persecution and lynching of the negroes, and I open them
> again, breathe deeply and thank God for the opportunity of meeting
> these people of the black race as human beings.[21]

Prominent Russian critics greeted the Chocolate Kiddies with decidedly mixed reviews that point to ambivalent perceptions not just of jazz but also of African Americans. Stanislavsky praised the performers' rhythm and "wonderful, plastic bodies," but he found the rest of the performance "naïve" and "interesting only from the point of view of representing the national color and exotics." Madame Lunacharskaya said the performance reflected a decadent European civilization using the "acute plastic abilities" of "a fresh and vigorous primitive people" as "a drug for its dull nerves."[22] Beyond obvious stereotypes, the conflation of Africans with African Americans and of Europe with the United States in these reviews (associating the former two with primitivism and the latter two with bourgeois decadence) had a parallel in Soviet policy. For example, African Americans usually attended KUTV, the Communist University of the Toilers of the East (along with people from Africa and the Middle East), rather than the Lenin School, which otherwise served Communists from the West.

While the Chocolate Kiddies' three-month run in Russia had an indelible impact, it was not the only staged performance of Blackness in Soviet Russia prior to 1932. One of the showcase productions of the Moscow Theatre for Children, *The Negro Boy and the Monkey*, a play for six- to eight-year-olds by Natalia Sats and Sergei Rozanov, ran for over a decade, beginning in 1927. Critics cite the play's enormous significance in the history of Soviet theatre, pointing to its popularity and formal innovations like combining live-action pantomime with animated film projections, as well as the score by avant-garde composer Leonid Polovinkin. But more striking from a contemporary perspective—beyond the obvious fact of a (Black) boy-monkey friendship and implicit equivalence, all under the rubric of what was billed as a "true story"—are the gender-bending performances of Blackness in the play.[23]

The three main characters—the "Negro Boy," Nagua; the monkey, Yirka; and the Nice Negro Girl/Woman (Dobraia Negra)—were all played by white women in blackface. And although the story is ostensibly set in Africa (prior to Yirka's capture by Europeans, Nagua's search for him, and their happy reunion in the Soviet Union when Nagua spies his friend in a circus), the Nice Negro girl (the only one with a speaking part) appears to be an odd caricature of a southern mammy.[24]

Photographs point to the odd visual effect of the performers' racial, gender, species, and generational drag: The actress playing Nagua appears in blackface, body paint, and a black bodystocking, a skirt-like thing around her waist, adorned with what look like cave paintings. Squatting in a pose that would seem to replicate that of Nagua's monkey friend, she wears hoop earrings and a necklace made from shells, and sports feathers that seem to sprout from the top of her head. The Nice Negro Girl is also in blackface, with white lines over her eyebrows and around her mouth. She wears a clownish, billowing dress with giant polka dots, ruffled sleeves and collar, and hoop skirts under a much-too-small apron, with what appear to be slippers on her feet.[25]

The African American social worker Thyra Edwards featured the play in a discussion of Moscow's Theatre for Children: "The children never tire of this one. . . . They crowd backstage to meet the little Negro boy and to see if the monkey is a real monkey or only the actress Claudia Koreneva all 'monkeyed up.'" Despite the conflation of Africans and African Americans, and the caricaturing and feminizing of both, some African Americans apparently appreciated the play's self-consciously anticolonial message, and it's clear that Soviet authorities encouraged them to see the play. Hughes did not go ("so crowded was the theater") but reported later: "The handsome little Negro boy was presented most sympathetically, I was told." Eslanda Robeson noted how fortuitous it was that her one visit to a children's theatre turned out to be "about how life in an African village was disrupted by greedy white hunters." At the play's intermission, "a little boy rushed up to her husband, the actor/singer Paul Robeson, hugged him around the knees, and begged him to stay in the Soviet Union—'You will be happy with us,'" the boy insisted.[26]

From the "Negro Question" to Scottsboro: Performing Soviet Antiracism

Soviet policy and rhetoric was officially anti-imperial, anticolonial, color-blind, and in favor of self-determination. Indeed, the Soviet Union vigorously welcomed into its fold people of color and oppressed minorities, especially African Americans.[27]

The 1922 theses on the "Negro Question" in effect put race issues on the agenda not just in the Soviet Union but also in the United States. Even more significantly, in 1928 the Sixth Comintern Congress declared African Americans to be an "oppressed nation within a nation" with the right to self-determination. They identified rural, southern African Americans as "the germ of a 'national revolutionary movement,'" effectively making them "indispensable in the battle to change the world." Soviet policies presumed that "'backwardness' [was] the result of sociohistorical circumstances and not of innate racial or biological traits," and that "all peoples could 'evolve' and thrive in new Soviet conditions." On the one hand, this meant that members of any racial group who conformed to Bolshevik policy could be citizens of the Soviet Union. On the other hand, in the 1920s, "Soviet leaders and experts endeavored to *wipe out* the languages, cultures, and separate identities of hundreds of clans and tribes in order to 'help' them 'evolve' into officially sanctioned nationalities."[28]

Even so, African Americans found much to praise in Soviet policy toward not only African Americans but also Soviet national minorities. The liberal African American press was receptive to Soviet messages about race relations. The *Crisis* (journal of the NAACP), for instance, published Claude McKay's glowing report on his 1922 visit, "Soviet Russia and the Negro," in which he insisted that "despite the lack of knowledge or interest in the Negro" in much of Europe, "there is one great nation with an arm in Europe that is thinking intelligently on the Negro as it does about all international problems." He said he encountered no prejudice in Russia, only "friendly, refreshing" "curios[ity]." McKay noted that Russian women workers showed great interest in "the working conditions of the colored women of America," and then went on to describe, more generally, "the new status of the Russian women gained through the revolution of 1917." A decade later, *Black and White* cast member Henry Lee Moon (also writing for the *Crisis*) affirmed McKay's portrait of Soviet womanhood, noting that both Soviet and African American women have been "viciously maligned and misrepresented" in the United States, and that both are more economically independent than other women in the world.

So too, both "have been less defiled by the hypocrisy of Nordic Puritanism," a reference to supposedly more liberated attitudes about sex among both Soviet women and African American women. But unlike African American women in the United States, the Soviet woman "is barred from no field of endeavor and from no honor or position for which she is able to fit herself."[29]

Such rhetoric may have helped make the Soviet Union more attractive to African American women, but aside from those who came with musical or theatrical troupes, the number who managed to get to Russia was quite small. Thus the few African American women who enrolled in Comintern schools were highly visible. Maude White Katz, who spent three years studying at KUTV in the mid-1920s, recalled that she was "always at the center of attention." Williana Burroughs, a prominent figure in the New York Communist Party, became a symbol of Black womanhood in the Soviet Union. The educated, articulate, and by some accounts strikingly beautiful daughter of former slaves, Burroughs had been a teacher in the New York City schools, before being dismissed for defending the actions of a (white) colleague in her union. She'd been an active member of the Communist Party since 1926, teaching in the Harlem Workers' School, serving as secretary for the American Negro Labor Congress (ANLC, a Communist organization), and even running for lieutenant governor of New York on the Communist Party ticket. In 1928 she traveled to the Soviet Union for two months to attend the Sixth World Congress of the Comintern and to find a school for two of her children, Charles and Neal (aged nine and six). She was able to enroll the boys in "an elite Moscow school for the children of Soviet and foreign Communists" (Paul and Eslanda Robeson would later do the same for their son, likewise believing that he would get a better and less alienating education in the Soviet Union). Like Katz, once in Moscow Burroughs found herself immediately in the limelight: a photograph of Burroughs (not named) with a mammy-style bandana on her head, flanked by her two boys wearing the red scarves of the Young Pioneers, appeared on the front page of *Trud*, the newspaper representing the All-Union Central Council of Trade Unions, during the Comintern Congress.[30]

Fig. 6.3 Williana Burroughs and her two sons. The picture appeared on the front page of *Trud*, the newspaper of the All-Union Central Council of Trade Unions. Information courtesy of Meredith Roman. Soyuzphoto, in Langston Hughes papers, Yale Collection of American Literature, Beinecke Rare Book and Manuscript Library.

Soviets invested deeply in promoting ideological solidarity with African Americans. Following the 1928 Comintern resolution on the "Negro question," the CPUSA began organizing in the US South with the explicit goal of recruiting African Americans. One such organizer, Myra Page, a party member from Virginia, had organized Blacks and whites in southern cotton mills before going to Moscow from 1931 to 1933. While there, she reported for the Communist press and wrote her novel *Moscow Yankee*, which centers on a group of Detroit auto workers who relocated to Moscow during the Five-Year Plan. Drawing from actual instances of racial conflict among Americans in the Soviet Union, Page's novel describes how the red-headed, "hundred percent [American]" Andy Anderson and his friends are surprised to find themselves working side by side with an African American, Ned Folsom (whom Page presents as intelligent and articulate, but also musically inclined and athletic). At least some of the white American (male) workers learn to respect Ned—just as they learn to expect and respect women in the factory.[31]

Page was in Moscow when the case of the Scottsboro Boys, "perhaps the most infamous and celebrated racial spectacle of the 1930s," exploded in the Soviet Union. On March 25, 1931, nine Black young men, aged thirteen to twenty, who had been riding the rails in search of work, were arrested on a freight train in Paint Rock, Alabama, after two white women, Ruby Bates and Victoria Price, aged seventeen and twenty, were also discovered in one of the cars. The women, unemployed mill-workers and sometime prostitutes, were dressed in overalls; Bates was drunk. And "only after a pointed talk with the local authorities" did the women claim the Black youths had raped them. Within two weeks, eight of the nine "Scottsboro Boys" (a moniker that both diminished them and brought them sympathy) were sentenced to death.[32]

The piece Page wrote on the case for the *Moscow News*, "Help Us or We Burn!"—like most of the publicity surrounding the case in the USSR—suggested that the Soviets had a crucial role to play in saving the Scottsboro Boys from an American judicial system that was deeply biased against African Americans and the working class more generally. "If white Alabamians had meant to stage the Scottsboro prosecution as a show trial to prove the bestiality of African Americans, the Communists used it as a show trial to prove their commitment to racial equality," historian Glenda Gilmore has asserted. As soon as news of the arrests hit, the International Labor Defense (ILD), a Communist organization that had taken a strong stance against lynching in the South, volunteered its services to the defendants' families and began publicizing the case. The liberal National Association for the Advancement of Colored People (NAACP), at least at first, cautiously avoided getting involved. The CPUSA led a wave of protests, which soon spread all over the world, as "workers and activists rallied in Latin America, Asia, the Middle East, and Africa, across Europe and the United States, in parts of the British Empire and its dominants, and in the farming collectives of Russia, in an unprecedented attempt to create sympathy for the victims of racial injustice."[33]

Protests on behalf of the Scottsboro Boys became an almost constant fixture of public life all over the Soviet Union, where nine illiterate, unemployed youths were rhetorically transformed into "champions of interracial proletarian unity." Sadie Tanner Mossell Alexander and her husband, Raymond Pace Alexander, prominent African American attorneys who had been active in Scottsboro defense efforts, traveled to the Soviet Union in the summer of 1931 and were thrilled to see how much interest the case had generated there. Ada Wright, the mother of two of the defendants, who took an ILD-sponsored tour through Europe on behalf of the "Boys," declared "that it was the Russians who saved her sons."[34]

By February 1932, building on the momentum generated by Scottsboro defense efforts, the Comintern's Executive Committee labeled the struggle for Black equality "THE MOST IMPORTANT TASK of the American Party," calling for the CPUSA to eliminate "every manifestation or even slightest echo within its own ranks of the ideology of white chauvinism." That same month, Ruby Bates recanted her accusations and joined Scottsboro defense efforts. And by March plans for a Soviet-produced film to showcase American race relations were under way.[35]

The Making and Unmaking of *Black and White*

In the spring of 1932, promotional material distributed by the "Cooperating Committee for Production of a Soviet Film on Negro Life" described plans by the "Meschrobprom [*sic*] Film Company of Moscow" to make "the first authentic picture of Negro life." The film would "trace the development of the Negro people in this country, their work, their play, their progress, their difficulties—devoid of sentimentality as well as of buffoonery," using "professional and non-professional actors" from the United States, and "Negro writers from America," so as "to assure a picture true to the life of the American Negro." There were many good reasons to believe that such a film was more likely to come out of Moscow than Hollywood, among them Soviet policy toward African Americans and national minorities, as well as the fact that "Hollywood producers continue to manufacture sentimental and banal pictures, and particularly cling to traditional types in portraying the Negro." Would-be African American recruits were presented not just with the chance to visit the Soviet Union on the cheap. They were also going to be part of a technically, artistically, and socially groundbreaking film: as promoters noted, the Soviet Union "is receiving world-wide acclaim for new technical and artistic developments in film production." (Cast members had to pay their own passage to Moscow, which limited the group to professionals rather than the laborers filmmakers hoped to feature.)[36]

Mezhrobpom Studio was based in Moscow but headquartered in Berlin: What began as an arm of Workers International Relief, an aid organization formed in September 1921 by German Communist Willi Müzenberg to provide famine relief, eventually became one of the most significant film studios operating in the Soviet Union. The film was being directed by Karl Junghans, a German who had never visited the United States, spoke poor Russian and poor English, and knew almost nothing about African Americans (he was chosen, in part, because he had recently made a film about Africans). Based on a script that the Russian scenarist Georgii Grebner, known for making historical documentaries, wrote in consultation with Lovett Fort-Whiteman, *Black and White* was to employ the latest sound technology and technique. Plans for the film generated considerable publicity both in the United States and in the Soviet Union.[37]

The cooperating committee sponsoring the film on the US end included an interracial assemblage of prominent cultural figures, whose names brought credibility to the project; among them were writers Floyd Dell and Malcolm Cowley; educator George Counts; journalist and editor Whittaker Chambers; Rose McClendon, perhaps the leading African American Broadway actress of the 1920s; and musician John Hammond. James Ford, an African American who had recently launched his campaign as Communist Party candidate for vice president of the United States, had been directed to recruit African Americans to help make the film. Ford, in turn, asked Louise Thompson to spearhead this effort.[38]

A Chicago-born African American, Thompson had grown up in California. After obtaining a degree in economics at Berkeley, she taught at the Hampton Institute in Virginia, where she supported a student strike against the white administration. Moving to New York in 1928 to study social work on a fellowship from the Urban League, Thompson found the approach too palliative. Seeking other ways to effect change, she obtained a position with the Congregational Education Society, which dealt with race relations, labor relations, and social issues. She also became involved in the Harlem Renaissance milieu in part through a short-lived marriage to the writer Wallace Thurman; the couple divorced after just six months, as Thurman's sexual preference for men made him a less-than-ideal husband. Through an introduction, provided by Alain Locke, to the white patron Charlotte Osgood Mason, Thompson became secretary for Zora Neale Hurston and Langston Hughes, both recipients of Mason's largesse.[39]

In New York Thompson attended classes at the Marxist downtown Workers' School, where she got her first exposure to works by Marx and Lenin. She also organized the Vanguard Club with the artist Augusta Savage for Black intellectuals and artists to discuss political and cultural issues. The Scottsboro case propelled Thompson into involvement with the National Committee for the Defense of Political Prisoners and growing awareness of Soviet attention to African Americans. After founding a Harlem chapter of the Friends of the Soviet Union, Thompson caught the attention of James Ford, who appointed her corresponding secretary for the cooperating committee; she embraced the work of recruiting the *Black and White* cast with gusto, writing to friends and acquaintances, helping them gather the ninety dollars necessary for passage, and seeking assurances that they could be ready to leave by mid-June 1932, for filming was scheduled to begin July 1.[40]

Among the final group who signed on, only a handful had actual stage experience. Wayland Rudd, who had appeared in *Emperor Jones*, *Porgy and Bess*, and other Broadway plays, was the most prominent and the only real professional actor in the group. Sylvia Garner, a singer, had played with Ethel Barrymore in *Scarlet Sister Mary*. Juanita Lewis was a member of the Hall Johnson Negro Choir and also a "dramatic reader." Thurston McNairy Lewis was a member of two amateur theatre companies and had appeared in a play called *Ham's Daughters*. Dorothy West had been a supernumerary in *Porgy and Bess* and part of the production's London tour.[41]

Despite publicity in the Soviet Union hailing the arrival of Negro "workers," just about everyone in the group was solidly middle class. Most were in their twenties and thirties. Dorothy West was known less for her stint in *Porgy* and more as a young and promising Harlem Renaissance writer. McNairy Lewis (by some accounts the only actual Communist Party member in the group) and Allen McKenzie were salesmen; Mildred Jones was an art student; George Sample was a law student; Constance White, Katherine Jenkins, and Leonard Hill were social workers; Lloyd Patterson was a paper hanger, and Henry Lee Moon, Ted Poston, and Homer Smith were journalists.[42]

Fun in Moscow

The *Black and White* group arrived in Moscow in early July. In their first few days, they participated in a Scottsboro demonstration at the Park of Culture and Rest featuring speeches by Emma Harris. According to Hughes, Harris was always introduced as "our own beloved Negro comrade, Emma, who before she came to the Soviet motherland, knew the stinging lash of race hatred in her native America." Harris had come to Russia long before it was the Soviet Union, so she was not exactly rescued from American race hatred by the Soviets. But she was a trained actress, and "she could denounce race prejudice in no uncertain terms, in long sentences, in fluent Russian, without taking a breath. At the end of her speech, she would hail the workers of the world, the Soviet Union, and Stalin, in traditional form, eyes blazing in her dark face, and walk off the platform to bravos. Had she been in a play, she would have taken a half-dozen bows after each speech," Hughes recalled.[43]

For the *Black and White* cast—like plans for the film itself, and like the elaborate meals, the brass band that met them in Leningrad, and the celebrity treatment they received throughout their stay—this demonstration was yet one more stirring act in an ongoing display of the Soviets' commitment to challenging racism, indeed, to transforming human nature itself. The latter theme plays out in a Soviet film shown to the group early in their visit: *Road to Life* showcases a camp that turns young orphans, runaways, and thieves into good Soviet citizens. "I was so thrilled by it," Thompson reported to her mother after seeing the film.[44]

As it turned out, the group had plenty of time to go to demonstrations and see movies. Despite insistence that they arrive by early July, the studio was not actually ready with the script, which still needed to be translated. This proved mildly annoying for cast members, but they were getting paid and glad to enjoy the sights. For their part, the film's producers were not entirely pleased with the group of well-dressed, articulate, mostly light-skinned African Americans who looked nothing like the poor, illiterate, dark-skinned Scottsboro Boys, whose faces had become so pervasive in Soviet propaganda that some Russians assumed all African Americans looked like them. Further, "most of the group knew no Negro folk songs, [and] some could not carry a tune nor dance a step."[45]

Thompson was so different in appearance from the Soviet notion of an "American Negro" that most people she met did not even know she was a foreigner: "Whenever I go by myself I feel like a dumb animal," Thompson wrote her mother. "Anyone of my complexion is not taken for a Negro unless he is with darker people, so they assume that I should know what they are talking about and it is most amusing." But if she felt foolish for not knowing Russian, mostly it was tremendously liberating to be served in any restaurant, to be treated not simply like a human being but, quite often, like the movie star she might have been. "Everywhere we go we are treated as honored guests, given enthusiastic ovations and offered the best," Thompson told her mother with evident relish. "It will really be difficult to scramble back into obscurity when we return to the old USA I suspect."[46]

All the cast members, in fact, seemed to be enjoying themselves, at least at first. The rooms were comfortable. They were allotted a loaf of bread each day, and as foreigners they had access to special stores with more and better food than was available to native Russians. They attended theatrical and musical productions at places like the Meyerhold Theatre, the Kameny Theatre, the Stanislavsky Theatre, and the Moscow Music Hall. They wandered around the city, they went to nightclubs, and they swam in the Moscow River. West reported that Emma Harris was doing laundry for her and Jones—and was "going to be in the picture too." West was probably not exaggerating when she told her mother, "Life continues to be a grand holiday."[47]

Once Fort-Whiteman finished translating the script, Hughes was given the task of revising what he later claimed was a nearly unworkable scenario, rife with misconceptions about African Americans and Black-white relations in the South. By mid-July, weeks after the group had arrived, they still hadn't started working on the film. "Russian time is worse than CPT [colored people time] and tomorrow may mean next week or next month," Thompson complained to her mother. But she didn't seem all that concerned: they were "living like royalty."[48]

Meanwhile, the other cast members spent time "working up some songs." Sylvia Garner, the only professional singer in the group, got herself a gig singing spirituals on Radio Moscow, finding creative ways to avoid using the words "*God, Lord, Christ* or *Jesus*." Whether the cast members could sing or not, they apparently still recognized and willingly obliged Russians' expectation that they would do so. At a workers' rest home the group was "greeted most enthusiastically and on every hand groups of workers would run to meet us." Thompson reported, "We joined them in their group games and also sang for them at their evening's concert."[49]

At another demonstration in the Park of Culture and Rest, they were honored guests. The high point came when, after wagons of vegetables from various collective farms were paraded in front of the group, one wagon drove up on the platform and "a real peasant woman descended, and before the many thousands of people began to relate how she had gone about raising these things on the collective farm. It was real drama," Thompson reported. "She was very bashful and would stop frequently and the applause of people would force her to continue. Gee, it was a marvelous moment and also an excellent example of the way in which the Soviets dramatize their social programs."[50]

Thompson never mentioned the famine that was at that time ravaging large swaths of the Soviet Union, primarily in areas where peasants had resisted collectivization and were essentially starved by the government as retribution. Years later, Hughes admitted that Emma Harris had mentioned a famine in the Ukraine, "where, she said, the peasants had refused to harvest the grain." Though hard for these well-fed visitors to fathom, "down in Kharkov," Harris supposedly said, "people's so hungry they are slicing hams off each other's butts and eating them!" Maybe not everyone had heard Harris's colorful, chilling tales, but several members of the group would flatly deny to the US press the "manufactured stories about 'starvation and famine.'"[51]

The drama of everyday people celebrating their new life—as well as the dramatic changes that the Soviet system had brought to national minorities and to women—is probably what most impressed Thompson during her four-month stay. Describing the tram cars, Thompson noted, "And you should see the way in which women here hop on these cars on the run." Women weren't just running *after* the tram cars; they were literally running them: "Many of the conductors and motormen [*sic*] are women," she continued. "In fact, women do everything here. Work on building construction, on the streets, in factories of course, and everywhere." She acknowledged their shabby appearance but also said that people believed things would get better and felt that the work they were doing was meaningful. Even leisure was edifying in the Soviet Union, Thompson insisted, comparing Moscow's Park of Culture and Rest to Coney Island. West, similarly, noted women's presence in the Red Army, acknowledging that "some of them look silly" doing their drills, "but some of them are very serious and straight and strong, and when at last they are full fledged soldiers, and you see them in uniform, they are truly a splendid sight."[52]

As members of the *Black and White* group watched the Russians, the Russians also watched them, quite intently. One evening at a party hosted by the film director Sergei Eisenstein that included dancers from the Bolshoi Ballet, Eisenstein approached Dorothy West and said "in the kindest, coaxing voice, 'Will you dance for me?'" Half amused and half taken aback, West answered, "politely and pleasantly, 'I don't dance.'" Eisenstein kept insisting and West kept refusing. This lasted for about fifteen minutes, until Eisenstein finally became angry, stood up, "and bellowed . . . in a voice like God's, 'I am the great Sergei Eisenstein, and you *will* dance for me.'" West "burst into tears and fled the room," racing down the stairs of the building.[53]

It turns out that someone had played a joke on West. She recalled, "Word of my dancing achievements—I couldn't even tap—was passed from mouth to mouth until it got way out of bounds, and I became an event, the reigning jazz dancer in America, known in every major city.

Fig. 6.4 *Black and White* cast members on the beach. Langston Hughes papers, Yale Collection of American Literature, Beinecke Rare Book and Manuscript Library.

But I had one fault, I was so excessively modest when not onstage that I would never dance off-stage when asked. Indeed, I would deny that I could dance." Later, West was invited to a dinner party and found herself seated at a table beside Eisenstein. Having heard that in Russia one can achieve anything by drinking five shots of vodka in quick succession, she did so and then redeemed herself with Eisenstein. In fact, he was the one to apologize for so readily assuming that this Black woman *must* be able to dance.[54]

Mostly the Russians' interest in their Black visitors played to the visitors' advantage. Men in the group enjoyed "cavorting nude among the nude Russians" by the Moscow River and also having their pick of Russian women after long being told that white women in their home country were off-limits. (Thompson complained, "Their attitude toward the Russian women was so obvious as to seem absolute proof of all the things white Americans say about Negro men and white women.") At least some of the women in the group likewise felt freer sexually in this revolutionary context, despite an increasing climate of sexual restraint in the Soviet Union.[55]

Sylvia Garner got into her first lesbian relationship with cast member Connie White (who subsequently left her for a Russian woman, prompting Garner to attempt suicide). West, who had been flirting with Hughes during the voyage over, found herself also drawn to the beautiful Mildred Jones, who was involved with at least two adoring Russian men during her stay but seems to have preferred West above either of them. And in the midst of his on-again, off-again flirtation with West, Hughes met Sylvia Chen, a dancer of Caribbean and Chinese background whose Charleston had made her a sensation in Moscow. Hughes later referred to Chen as "my girl friend at the moment." Hughes himself is thought to have been gay, or bisexual, or perhaps asexual, a possibility given credibility in correspondence between him and Chen—which suggests that his professions of affection primarily came at a distance ("why can't you say all those nice things when I'm near enough to react?")—and in a series of unanswered letters from West to Hughes that point to his discomfort with the level of intimacy both of these women sought.[56]

The Film and Its Unmaking

While the imported Black cast members waited for filming to begin, volunteers from the American community were solicited to audition for *Black and White*. Junghans called for "real Americans, with American accents and American clothes." He seems to have had trouble finding them, though the American community in Moscow at this time was significant and growing by the day. For instance, the part of the hard-headed labor organizer who endangers his life by organizing Black and white workers together in the South was going to be played by John Bovington, a vegan nudist dancer in the Duncan style. When Hughes complained to the director, Junghans reportedly responded, "Vot ist matter? Bovington nich look like American worker?"[57]

In mid-August most of the group went on a trip to the Black Sea, visiting Kiev, Sebastopol, Yalta, Batum, Odessa, and several other ports with the understanding that filming would actually begin in Odessa. But in Odessa they were met by a representative from Mezhrobpom who told them the film was being postponed indefinitely because of technical problems. Almost at the same moment, Henry Lee Moon, who had been delayed in Moscow, showed up with a copy of the *New York Herald Tribune* announcing the film's cancellation; Moon proclaimed, "Comrades, we've been screwed!" In a bar in Moscow, Moon had heard the chief engineer on the Dnieper dam, Colonel Hugh Cooper, explain that he'd vowed to withdraw his support for US recognition of the Soviet Union if the film project went forward.[58]

The group quickly divided between a majority, which included Thompson, West, Hughes, Miller, and Jones, who at least publicly accepted the official version of why the film had been "postponed," and a few dissenters. The latter group, consisting of Moon, Ted Poston, McNairy Lewis, and Lawrence Alberga, quickly made plans to return to the United States. Moon and Poston happened to be journalists, and they almost immediately sold their side of the story to American newspapers, whose editors were eager to publish sensational stories about helpless Negroes stranded in the Soviet Union. Members of the majority were upset too, but did not air their grievances publicly; they did, however, express their frustration to Mezhrobpom, noting the "grave political repercussions" that abandoning the film would have, not only among African Americans, but also among "the other darker colonial peoples of the world." They even appealed directly to the Comintern, arguing that the script was "essentially true to Negro life in America" and could, "in the hands of a competent director," be the basis of "a powerful film."[59]

Although Hughes later claimed that the script could never have been made into a film, both Grebner's Russian script and the English version (written by Junghans with assistance from Hughes) seem workable. Each begins with a historical overview showing Africans being captured and sold into slavery, and then moves to small-town Alabama, roughly the area indelibly associated with Scottsboro.[60] Blacks are working in the worst jobs, while whites have all the positions of power. Two interwoven plot threads echo the Scottsboro case: first, there is growing unrest in a factory among both Black and white laborers over working conditions, especially after an African American worker dies on the job. The other plotline concerns the alleged rape of the chief engineer's fiancée, Phyllis (described by Junghans as "the vamp type") by a Black teenager, Shine, a houseboy at her estate. In reality she was verbally and physically abusing him on the job and when he resisted her blows she cried rape.

The film's depiction of women is arguably the most problematic thing about it, but there is no evidence that it ever elicited complaints (Hughes's criticism was that the script showed no understanding of Black life). There is one positive female character, the wife and daughter of white labor organizers and an ally in that struggle. Other women, Black and white, are cast as temptresses or victims, or as selfish and lacking class consciousness. For instance, an African American woman, whose husband is a worker, resists donating the money he has just brought home to help with expenses for the dead worker's funeral; her husband chides her and gladly contributes.

Other Black female characters are stereotyped but are at least sympathetic. Emma, the wife of the fallen Black worker, is left bereft and helpless (but still full of rhythm) after losing her husband: in one scene she sits at the edge of her dead husband's bed, eyes filled with tears as "the rhythmic movements of her body are accompanied by groans of sorrow." At an upscale party for bosses, "the Negro girl, Babe, serves drinks to a group of men in library. They joke with her and ask her to dance for them. One dials the radio until he finds some hot music." The camera cuts from Babe, surrounded by a circle of white men, to Shine (who has been captured by a white lynch mob, which included the chief engineer), "tied to a tree in the forest" as he "moans, twists, and turns, also encircled by a group of white men." The men proceed to burn Shine at the stake, while white women watching from their cars crowd and crane their necks, trying to get a better look. As men douse Shine's body with gasoline and the flames leap higher, the camera cuts to Babe, now asleep in bed with a white man. Throughout this sex- and violence-charged thread, the film cuts to a strike at the factory that is led by white workers but gradually gains support from the African Americans as well. The script ends with an interracial group of marchers holding banners pushing through the factory gates and then disappearing into the smoke as police spray tear gas at them.

Whether the film was workable or not, the Comintern pulled the plug on *Black and White*. Thompson issued a press release to the Crusader

News Agency, a Black syndicate with ties to the Communist left, calling the stories published by Moon and others about the diplomatic concerns "completely false." She also wrote to other papers and directly challenged reports they'd published by the dissenters. The majority also sent out a statement to people thought to be sympathetic to the Soviet Union challenging "all slanderous charges and rumors concerning the postponement of the film." How much traction that got them is not clear: photographer Margaret Bourke-White asked her secretary, "Do we have to do anything about this?"[61]

Thompson told her mother, "Aside from any disappointment at not making the picture there is nothing that any of us have to complain of, besides having a trip that we could not have had for a thousand dollars had we come here as tourists. We have had first class accommodations every where we have gone and these people have lived and dined in places they would not even dare to stick their heads into in America." In her mind, the group's first-rate treatment in the Soviet Union ought to impress the American public: "Here we come from a country where everything is denied us—work, protection of life and property, freedom to go where we will and to live where we will—where we are despised and humiliated at every turn. And here we are accorded every courtesy—free to go where we will and eagerly welcomed—given every opportunity to enjoy ourselves and to travel, free to pursue any work that we choose."[62]

Witnessing Transformation in Soviet Central Asia

Despite the film's outcome, none of the women who came to the Soviet Union to act in *Black and White* ultimately regretted making the trip. All of them elected to stay on for several months, and all except Sylvia Garner eagerly accepted the chance to take a government-sponsored tour of Soviet Central Asia to study Soviet national minorities. For women like Louise Thompson, the drama of women's transformation under Soviet socialism was compelling enough, but to see women of color casting off their veils (in the case of Muslim women), bobbing their hair, and entering public life was astonishing; indeed, for Thompson the trip to Soviet Central Asia represented a "turning point in her life."[63]

During the trip, Thompson focused her attention on the changing position of women, something even men in the group could not help noticing. In fact, this undoubtedly was emphasized by the group's Soviet guides, as just a few years earlier "women's liberation was selected as the crucial strategy to find Bolshevik allies among the indigenous peoples of Central Asia."[64] At the center of this project was the unveiling of Muslim women, the object of a massive campaign undertaken in 1927 by members of the Zhenotdel, or women's branch of the Communist Party, sometimes at gunpoint.

In Tashkent the group visited a Woman's Club, with its literacy classes, nursery rooms in which children sang for the group, and other facilities. Most striking, though, were the women themselves. There was Halima Kazakova, a forty-two-year-old mother of five children, unveiled since 1925, literate for only two years; Bakhri Guliamova, unveiled in 1926, married in 1927 at fifteen, member of city Soviet, hair bobbed; and Rosa Balabaeva, unveiled in 1928, previously married at fourteen to an old man and now unable to have children. She left her husband and came to Tashkent without telling her family. After studying at the textile technicum, she found work and was later promoted to the city Soviet. Now she was "head of women's work in trade unions" and married to a party man.[65]

In city after city and village after village, group members heard about how the revolution had transformed women's lives, giving them economic independence, education, and freedom. They visited a silk factory that had been built in 1928 specifically to liberate women: most of its 1,200 employees were women and nearly all were national minorities (Bukhara Jews and Uzbeks). Furnished with a nursery, kindergarten, dining hall, hospital, and housing cooperative, the factory had become a model for the region. Several Uzbek women were in leadership positions. "Not a single woman with paranja" (the Central Asian version of a burqa), Thompson noted.[66]

Jahah Obidova, vice president of the Central Committee of Soviets of Uzbekistan, told the group her story: she came from an extremely poor family, and at the age of eleven had been sold to a rich peasant as his fourth wife. After the revolution, she left her husband, attended school, and became literate. She joined the Komsomol, was elected a delegate, and began organizing other women. She joined the Communist Party in 1924. And in 1929, at the all-Uzbekian Congress of Soviets, she was elected vice president. Obidova now wore her hair bobbed and dressed in European clothing.[67]

At the end of their stay in Bukhara, the "Negro delegation" gave an address to "the Workers and Peasants of Uzbekistan Socialist Soviet Republic," praising what they had seen of "the emancipation of women, the complete elimination of national antagonisms, the stimulation of national proletarian culture, [and] the proletarianization and collectivization of workers and poor peasants." They promised "as members of an oppressed national minority," to tell members of the American working class— "especially the Negro"—about the Soviets' "complete solution of the national problem" as well as "the successes of socialist construction."[68]

The trip through Soviet Central Asia was tremendously "liberating" for Thompson, for here were "people of color, oppressed national minorities, women" for whom the state was actively working. Many years later, Thompson's daughter recalled stories about a man imprisoned for beating his wife after she unveiled, and remarked, "That trial symbolized the double or triple oppression . . . that it could be dealt with, very concretely." In a region where wife-beating had been common practice and socially accepted, now men were being imprisoned for it.[69]

"There is a tremendous upheaval taking place, undisturbed for so many hundreds of years, under Soviet guidance," Louise Thompson wrote her mother during that trip. "The peasant and artisan are being emancipated from their ancient ways of doing their work through collectivization and proletarianization in colhoz (collective farm) and factory. . . . Religion, ignorance, and the lack of anything in the way of modern tools with which to work are being rapidly overcome. The women are discarding, and for the most part have already, the pranja [sic], which was the symbol of their slavery."[70] If the musings of one woman writing a private letter to her mother read like published propaganda, it is because the experience felt larger than life, like history in the making.

Of the paranja (a full-body covering, including a veil of horse hair that a woman had to peer through in order to see, and which women had been murdered for discarding), Thompson insisted, "a woman dressed like that could never work in a factory or anywhere else, for that matter." The notion of the veil, of course, resonated explicitly with African Americans' feeling of "double consciousness," that is, of living behind a veil. But if Thompson and others would hail women who risked violence from husbands and brothers and fathers for unveiling, they overlooked the violence represented by Soviet pressure on national minorities to unveil. Indeed in reaction to the Bolshevik campaign against the veil, for some women in Soviet Central Asia, "wearing a veil became more than a narrowly religious or moral matter; for many people it also became an act of political and national resistance to an outside colonial power."[71]

Dorothy West had been ill when the group left and so was only able to join them in Baku after several weeks. West brought from Moscow American newspapers carrying sensational stories about how the *Black and White* group was "stranded" in Russia. She herself had more pressing concerns. While the group was gone, she'd missed both Jones and Hughes "and I did not know who I wanted to see most," she admitted to Hughes in a letter. When West arrived in Baku, Jones came running to her. It was "such a happy meeting," West acknowledged. And yet her "eyes searched everywhere" for Hughes. Learning that he was no longer with the group, she felt that "nothing in the world seemed to matter quite so much." She was bereft. "Do you forgive my folly?" West asked him. "That brightness that was beginning with us, can I make it shine again? Oh Lank, I want to crawl. What I have done [with Jones?] is not unforgiveable. But what I have missed of you—three months in this marvelous country!—I shall regret as long as I live." She said she'd never stopped loving him, and "after my first feelings for M[ildred] had passed, my love for you grew very steadily and steadily." In her letter to Hughes, she claimed that though she remained fond of Mildred, "I do not want her as she wants me."[72]

Hughes would stay on in Central Asia for several months, spending Christmas in Tashkent with the family of Oliver Golden and Bertha Bialek. Golden had studied at Tuskegee and was recruited in the mid-1920s to study at KUTV. Returning to the United States, he joined the Communist Party and also met his Jewish wife, Bertha Bialek. With the help of George Washington Carver, Golden had recruited a group of Black agronomists to join him in an effort to develop the Soviet Union's cotton industry; Hughes later recalled both the bone-chilling journey to their experimental cotton farm and the wonderful Christmas day he shared with several families, complete with pumpkin pie and "all the American-style dishes that those clever Negro wives could concoct over there in Uzbekistan."[73]

While Hughes stayed on in Central Asia, the others returned to Moscow. Thompson reflected on the train, "It is interesting to notice how many members of our group who came to Russia without a single idea in their heads have been stimulated to read and to question and desire to know more about Russia and communism. The enthusiasms of the workers and peasants we meet everywhere, the amazing changes that are taking place could not help but affect this change in them. What is this new thing that is building factories and electrical stations in barren steppes, that is taking primitive peoples from illiterate, isolated life and placing them on the level of other people, that is bringing together Russian and Uzbek, Jew and Armenian, countless other peoples to fight and work for the same thing?"[74]

Thompson makes clear why the trip was so powerful for their group. Speaking of their time in Tashkent she wrote, "There in 1932, I actually saw people leaping into a whole new world, industrially and culturally, and it was fascinating. The people looked like many of us. They were brown; a number of them were very dark brown. The only thing they didn't have that we had was curly hair."[75]

Back in Moscow: Dancers, Lovers, and Circuses

In November Thompson sailed home to be with her ailing mother. Several of the men made plans to remain in the Soviet Union permanently. Both West and Jones decided to stay at least another six months in Moscow: "I have been living furiously, and learning very much," West wrote to friends. "This has been an invaluable experience. . . . If fortune continues to favor me I'll stay in this grand, experimental country until I have absorbed all its virtues and cast aside all my vices."[76] Jones got a job working on the *Moscow News*, and West got a position at Mezhrobpom, apparently having not given up on the idea of appearing on the Soviet silver screen.

In March Hughes, Jones, and West were having various misadventures in Moscow. Jones was involved with the Russian writer Boris Pilnyak (who just months earlier had been confessing his love to Margaret Bourke-White), after breaking the heart of Constantine Oumansky from the Commissariat for Foreign Affairs.[77] The exact character of West and Jones's involvement with one another at this point is unclear, but they were still roommates. Hughes came by one evening and brought West to meet Sylvia Chen. West clearly smelled a rival. "She is one of the better known dancers here," West wrote her mother. "She belongs to the new school of the dance, of course, and is thought very clever. She is half Chinese and half West Indian negro. Her features are somewhat Negroid but her hair is beautiful and slightly curly. She has nothing of the American negro in her and talks in an English accent." West had waited eagerly for Hughes to arrive, standing near the door in her hat and overshoes. They "danced and drank tea and ate cake and candy. It was a pleasant evening, because Sylvia is very interesting, though she shows off a little."[78]

Chen, at this point in her life, was in a groove, professionally and personally. Chen was a classically trained dancer whose exotic looks had helped her land a variety of ethnic roles as a child; if Pauline Koner had taken such roles to show her versatility, Chen had taken them by necessity. Sylvia Chen's father, Eugene Chen, had been a close advisor to Sun Yat-Sen and served as China's foreign minister after Sun's death; Chen's family, along with Anna Louise Strong and Mikhail Borodin, had fled China after Communists were expelled in 1928, moving to Moscow, where she finally found her own style. In Moscow Chen had studied with a variety of teachers, first making a splash with audiences by performing the Charleston at the annual recital of Vera Maya's school at the Kameny Theatre. Chen's Charleston played into the craze for authentic Black jazz, earning her accolades and even a prize at Moscow's only nightclub and a cameo role in Leonid Obolensky's *Merchants of Glory: The Dead Do Not Return* (1929).[79]

Although Chen could draw audiences through titillating performances choreographed by Kasian Goleizovsky, whose works were notoriously fused with eroticism (during the intermission at one of her shows, Anna Louise Strong rushed into Chen's dressing room, "panting, 'Sylvia, you've created a sensation!'"), Chen came to conclude that true success as a dancer in the Soviet Union meant rejecting an outworn aesthetic that associated her with a world in decline. Advised to study the movements of common people, to try to "understand the great new emotions being born so that you can give spontaneous expression to them," Chen, in addition to "ethnographic material," began to create dances of protest that incorporated elements of her African and Chinese heritage: doing so not only brought her more enduring success in the Soviet Union but also strengthened her sense of connection to an ethnic and racial heritage that she had heretofore mostly ignored. With her new repertoire and new consciousness, Chen was hailed as "the first Soviet modern dancer."[80]

Milly Bennett, who had known Chen since both of them were in China, praised Chen's "rare miming ability" in an extended review published in the *Moscow News* in January 1932. Bennett maintained Chen had, five years earlier, "danced well. But her art was the expression of her own lively spirit. It was lacking in social consciousness." Based on Chen's most recent performance at the Kameny Theatre, Bennett insisted, "her development is phenomenal." In particular, "'The American Negro' (a protest) was Sylvia Chen in her new development, that of a socially conscious artist. She danced before the silhouette of a gallows tree, from which hung the body of a murdered Negro. Every gesture was a cry against the brutal oppression of the Negro."[81]

By the time Chen met Hughes, she was touring three months of the year, spending the rest of her time working on programs and performing in and around Moscow. She had begun working at TRAM, the Theatre of Working Youth, where she taught dance classes for factory workers and created movements for plays "concerned with some urgent political or industrial subject, like anti-Semitism in a university or the preparation of a new machine in a factory." She had been told the work would "help in breaking my bourgeois background." This was an ongoing concern for Chen who, though from a distinguished revolutionary family, had grown up in privilege and, up until her political awakening in Moscow, had taken little interest in politics herself.[82]

Fig. 6.5 Sylvia Chen performing Turkoman dance. Writing on the back of the photograph reads:
"Sylvia Chen is a Chinese dancer, working in the Soviet Union, where she is not only uncovering
a mass of ethnographic material, as in this Turkoman dance, but is also making great
strides towards an expression of revolutionary themes." Sylvia Chen papers, Tamiment
Library, New York University. Used with permission from Elena Pinto Simon.

During a tour of Crimea in the summer of 1931, Chen's accompanist
brought a friend, the actress Lyubov Orlova, who sang along with piano
and violin while Chen danced. Chen also began taking classes at KUTV.
Chen was the only woman in her class, the only person with a bourgeois
background, "and the only one who had never worked for a living, at

least in the sense that they understood working." All of this had made her especially interested in the *Black and White* project. And more aware of her own racialized performances.[83]

West, complaining that Chen "shows off," probably felt threatened by this more seasoned performer, who seemed to capture Hughes's imagination. But Chen found herself ultimately frustrated by Hughes's half-hearted attentions ("Will you kiss me next time or not? Heh? You better! What nationality would our baby be anyhow? Just so long as he or she is anti-fascist!" he wrote in one letter). As of December 1934, Chen was still telling Hughes, "I want to be with you Langston, not necessarily as a wife, but just to be with you." In truth, however, she was already involved with the American filmmaker and scholar Jay Leyda, a protégé of Eisenstein whom she met in Moscow and married in 1936. "I don't remember whether I ever wrote telling you about my American husband, yes, I got tired of waiting for you to propose so I got myself a consort."[84]

So Chen and West both gave up on Hughes. West also gave up on acting. What is ironic is the role for which West was finally cast: a rich woman's maid in a film whose name seems lost to history. The director, as West recalled, had told her that she had talent, indeed, the makings of an excellent actress. He asked, directly, if she wanted to act for a living. West was taken aback: her response was that no, she did not want to act, she wanted to write. After that day, she decided not to return to the set and told her translator to make up an excuse for her. Years later, she claimed that she was embarrassed by the director's praises. Perhaps it was also that she did not want to play the role of a maid, a role she would likely play again if cast in American films. Indeed, it was the lack of good parts for African American performers in the United States (as well as Russia's reputation for stellar theatre) that had prompted actors like Wayland Rudd and Frances E. Williams to come to the Soviet Union; in a sense this was what motivated the whole *Black and White* cast to come.[85]

Chen came to conclude that racial performances—of her own design—were a route to more authentic selfhood. Moving to the United States, she changed her appellation from the "Sylvia" she had used for so many years to her birth name, Si-Lan, and joined the radical dance movement. She continued to emphasize Chinese and African American themes in her work, and consciously contrasted American attitudes about race with those she experienced in the Soviet Union. Although it took living in the Soviet Union for Chen to gain appreciation for the Chinese and African parts of herself, she was also lucky enough to leave in 1936 with her American husband.[86]

A further irony is that a 1936 Soviet blockbuster that did offer sharp commentary on American race relations, *The Circus*, featured only one very small part for an African American woman: the nanny for the white circus performer, Marian Dixon (played by Lyubov Orlova), who is trying to hide her dark-skinned child from the public. The role is not credited, but some sources say it was Frances E. Williams, which would, indeed, be ironic, given her desire for roles that broke with Black stereotypes. In the film, Dixon's secret gets out, but that turns out to be a gift more than a curse, as she's able to see how much the Russians love her little Black boy.[87]

The same year that *The Circus* was released, Williana Burroughs began working as the voice of Radio Moscow in English, with Lloyd Patterson, a member of the *Black and White* cast, whose son played the biracial child in *The Circus* (and with whom Frances Williams was staying). Burroughs had made her fourth and final visit to the Soviet Union in 1934, traveling on the same ship as Anna Louise Strong and Frances Williams, the former most likely helping her land a job as copy editor on the *Moscow News*. Sometime later, she literally assumed the voice of Americans in Moscow. Under the name "Ooma Percy," Burroughs's race was invisible as her disembodied voice echoed across oceans.[88]

Although the Soviet Union's record on matters of race was spottier and less enlightened than Soviet leaders would ever acknowledge, for many of the people of color who visited, including most of those who came to perform in *Black and White*, the experience was not only positive but even life changing. Dorothy West would remember her year in Moscow as perhaps the happiest of her life: "I will have a nostalgia for Moscow as long as I live," she wrote in 1934, in sentiments she confirmed later in life. "There is my lost youth and all things lovely. There is my bright adventure."[89]

PART IV

TRIALS, TRIBULATIONS, AND BATTLES

"There was much else, but one cannot remember everything."

Mikhail Bulgakov, *The Master and Margarita*[1]

Anna Louise Strong's *Wild River* (1943) is "a novel of the people who built the Dnieper Dam and then destroyed it in the battle for the world." Strong also describes it as a "distilled essence of my twenty years in Soviet Russia."[2] The principal protagonists are famine orphans and street children who form a collective not unlike the John Reed Colony, of which Strong had been "shef," or patron. Members of Young Plowman, which later becomes the collective farm Red Dawn, grow up to construct the great Dnieper Dam, along the way themselves becoming new men and new women and dedicating their lives to Soviet socialism. The book climaxes with the Second World War, during which, as in reality, many of those who spent years building the dam deliberately destroy it to save it from Nazi control. Strong's epic tale largely skips over the late 1930s. As for the story of the American new woman and the Soviet dream, its narrative tropes, hitting a disjuncture in the mid-1930s, revived and climaxed during the Second World War before ultimately collapsing.[3]

What elements of the late 1930s must be taken into account to understand the new Soviet woman's reappearance in American media during the Second World War, and her subsequent disappearance during the Cold War? In August 1935 the Seventh Congress of the Communist International endorsed a "Popular Front" strategy that called for Communists to tone down their revolutionary rhetoric and make alliances with all enemies of fascism. In the United States, the Popular Front manifested as an unofficial coalition among Communists, independent radicals, and New Deal liberals. As representatives of the American Communist Party declared that "Communism is twentieth-century Americanism," the CPUSA worked to broaden its appeal, shifting from a focus on (male) industrial workers to a more capacious category of "the people."[4] Roughly coinciding with the purges and radically new messages about gender and motherhood in the Soviet Union, the Popular Front brought new visibility and acceptability to Communism in American life. But it also brought a new cadre of critics, now on the Left as well as on the Right. An anti-Communist coalition formed in the wake of the Moscow Trials and the Great Terror that followed them, the Nazi-Soviet pact (which suggested that the Soviet government cared more about self-preservation than about actually defeating Hitler), and the Soviet invasion of Finland. Anti-Stalinists pointed to the sins of the Soviet Union in ways that predicted not just the unraveling of the Popular Front but also the rise of McCarthyism and the demise of the new Soviet woman as a viable role model.

In the mid-1930s, the American Communist publication *Working Woman* was renamed *Woman Today*, and it began addressing the home-maker/mother's concerns—as well as those of professional women—along with those of women in factories and fields. The *Daily Worker* started a women's page, with recipes, advice, and tips for frugal home-makers. Although women working outside the home remained visible in Popular Front discourses, emphasis shifted toward women in more traditional roles. "Soviet Women return to homemaking," declared an article in the *Christian Science Monitor* in January 1938, and an article in the *Literary Digest* highlighted a new emphasis on feminine beauty and a boom in cosmetics in the Soviet Union. *Soviet Russia Today* emphasized the Soviet Union as a "land of healthy childhood" and celebrated the strength of the Soviet family, provided for by the state, and bound by bonds of affection rather than economic need: "In the sharing of the fruitful and stimulating experiences of Soviet life, family relationships are strengthened and enriched," one article noted. Sources emphasized that because of the public welfare system, the Soviet mother was able to have interests outside the home. By economic necessity, she usually worked as well, but what later feminists would call women's "double burden" could also be seen as evidence of women's emancipation—what we would now call "having it all."[5]

In May 1936, Strong published an article, "Free Women," remarking on Soviet women's progress and celebrating women who are committed to their work, to a system that will bring social justice, and to forming relationships based on comradely love.[6] Photographs accompanying the article show, among others, "C. Freiberg, woman meteorologist; member of the arctic expedition at Tixie Bay," "Miravaeva, the first girl parachutist of Uzbekistan, with her proud grandmother," "and Klavdia Pavlova, woman ship captain and fishing brigade head," the latter with her binoculars pointed out at the sea but her weather-beaten, knowing face turned toward the camera.

Echoing Louise Thompson, Strong discussed women in Soviet East Asia and their liberation from the veil. She noted women's share of work in industrial labor and in politics, celebrating "heroines of production" like Marie Demchenko, who began her career working on a kulak's (land-owning peasant's) farm and only with collectivization "discovered her talents." After learning to read, she spent years studying and then developing new methods of beet cultivation; she then joined a congress of farm leaders in Moscow where she personally promised Stalin to increase output. "Let us flood the land with sugar," she told him.

The focus of Strong's article is Soviet women's ability to resolve the "clashing claims of marriage and career which form so much of the content of feminist discussion under capitalism." Although Soviet women expect to marry, she wrote, "most of them expect to keep on with work after marriage; no law compels them to this, but they find it economically advantageous and socially more interesting. They expect the state to help them keep on with their work, by providing special care in childbirth and help in rearing children." She hailed women's right to decide whether to have children, made possible through legal and free birth control or through abortions.

In this heroic tale, what Strong did not mention is that the new Soviet family law of 1936, drafts of which were being circulated at the time of her writing, would dramatically limit women's rights—most significantly, legal and free abortion and easy divorce. Abortion was outlawed in the Soviet Union in June 1936; this was accompanied by strong pronatalist measures, including stipends for new mothers, bonuses for having large families, and longer maternity leaves paid for by the state (along with other supports such as prenatal services and expansion of childcare facilities). Accompanying restrictions on divorce were greater penalties for men who refused to pay child support.[7]

In some fundamental ways, the new conservative messages vis-à-vis gender challenged the very essence of the new Soviet woman as she had been seen since the revolution. For the first time, as historian Barbara Engel has noted, "the home itself, such as it was, and woman's role within it assumed an unequivocally positive dimension." Along with greater emphasis on feminine beauty, women were also praised as loyal wives and mothers, and a movement of wife-activists, which began in 1936, emphasized the social role that housewives could play in Soviet society (outside the workforce). These women "organized kindergartens, nurseries, and camps for children; they furnished workers' dormitories and barracks, supervised factory cafeterias, planted trees and flowers, and set up discussion circles."[8]

The irony in this change did not escape Strong's more cynical comrade, Milly Bennett. "She [Valery, Bennett's alter ego] was to see in Moscow in 1936 along with a fat abundance, a great revival of home cooking," Bennett wrote in her unpublished autobiographical novel. "Witness a page of *Komsomolskaya Pravda* given over to letters from embarrassed brides asking for a 'good Soviet cookbook'—and read how 'My husband and I were married six months ago and are very much in love with each other and we got along fine until he began laughing at the dinners I cook for him.' " Whereas *Pravda* (and the *Moscow News*) had once boasted of all the meals that factory kitchens were supplying so that women could focus on their work, now, Bennett remarked, the paper was hailing women who cooked for their husbands, had children, and made their homes comfortable.[9]

The new abortion law seemed to many Russian women like a huge step backward. "Hundreds, thousands of Soviet women in meetings, in letters to the newspapers had protested against the abortion law when it was projected, most of them because of the housing shortage," Bennett wrote. Markoosha Fischer, the Russian-born wife of the American journalist Louis Fischer, confirmed both the unpopularity of the law and many people's assumption that it would not be passed: "The draft was open for discussion; people were asked to express their opinion, and since it was clear that the country was opposed we were sure it would not be enacted." But it was. An old Bolshevik explained to Bennett, "There will be natural birth control when people have other means of self-expression than the bed."[10]

Passage of the abortion law against popular opposition was an indication not just of the shift toward more conservative gender politics but also the shift toward a more repressive government. "The government's control over spirit and mind constantly grew tighter," Fischer recalled of the mid-1930s. Efforts were being made to actively separate tourists from ordinary Soviet citizens, and the community of foreign residents was shrinking, in part through people leaving voluntarily and in part through people disappearing, as arrests became common.[11]

By 1938 visits to the Soviet Union by foreigners, the majority of whom were American, were down to one-third of the number just two years earlier. Those who did come as tourists in this period tended to report a far less rosy picture. However, the state's attention to women (and children) during these years became something that enthusiasts of the Soviet regime could still praise.[12]

Foreign residents of the Soviet Union often were forced to choose between leaving and taking Soviet citizenship. Most elected to leave; many of those who stayed were swept up in the purge, during which all foreigners were suspect. The former Detroit auto worker Robert Robinson noted, "Every single black I knew in the early 1930s who became a Soviet citizen disappeared from Moscow within seven years. The fortunate ones were exiled to Siberian labor camps. Those less fortunate were shot."[13]

Following Kirov's assassination in December 1934, an ostensible hunt for the leaders of a conspiracy to execute him became an obsessive search for enemies of the state. Especially after the public trials of original Bolshevik revolutionaries that began in Moscow in the summer of 1936 (eventually encompassing almost the entire leadership of the Communist Party), millions of Soviet citizens were arrested, the majority for political reasons. So many people were arrested in 1937 and 1938 that the labor camps were unable to feed, clothe, or house all of them. An atmosphere of fear and mistrust came to permeate the entire culture.[14]

Markoosha Fischer described how people got into the habit of calling one another to ask, "in disguised form," whether friends and family were okay. Assuming that phones were bugged, they would ask, "'Is Kolya's throat better? Didn't I forget my umbrella at your house? Aren't you late for work?' or similar questions the answers to which were thoroughly unimportant. The important thing was to hear a friend's voice over the phone and to know that nothing had happened during the night."[15]

Several from the staff of the *Moscow News* were arrested and killed, including Rose Cohen, a British Communist whose avidness and "eternal bloom" had made her the butt of jokes between Milly Bennett and Ruth Epperson Kennell when they worked on the paper.[16] Mary Leder, who worked in the Foreign Languages Publishing House, recalled that several coworkers disappeared in the late 1930s; one was actually taken away while on the job: "Everyone in the office went on doing whatever they had been doing, stony-faced, not reacting." She was asked to serve as an informer and felt she had no choice but to agree. Still, even though she was active in the Komsomol (Young Communist League) and by her own account (at that point) a "true believer," she avoided giving any useful information to her contact. At the same time, she started watching her every word, realizing that many of the people she knew had probably also become informers.[17]

Friends began breaking off relations with one another, either because of suspicion or to avoid tarring others. Vigilance was the new watchword.

Fischer was asked to spy on fellow Americans, with the implication that this would help her get a visa to leave the country. At one point two women were sent to her house specifically to test whether she would accurately report on her interactions with them. "If I did, then I was probably telling the truth all along, and was not seeing anyone secretly. Though how I could have done this is a mystery. There was a man in front of our house 24 hours a day; the janitors, handymen, maids, all 'reported.' "[18]

If the Terror was intended to purge enemies of the state, it in fact had the effect of turning many deeply loyal citizens into critics of the regime. "Hardly a day passed without a new heartache and another hope shattered," Fischer wrote of the period before she entirely gave up hope. "I desperately fought against complete disillusion. I imagined a mental scale: I could find that all was not lost yet. I was always more eager to fill the positive than the negative scale. I looked for people who were untouched by the purge and who had reason to be happy. I found plenty of them." But as "fear and insecurity dominated every field of life," it ultimately became impossible for her, as for others.[19]

Peggy Dennis, a Party member and the wife of a high official in the CPUSA, Eugene Dennis, returned to Moscow in the spring of 1937—after having been stationed there from 1931 to 1935—and found the atmosphere entirely different. Calls to several old friends "brought only strange voices saying, '*Ne sdez*,'—not here." When she went to look at the room she and Gene had been assigned in the Lux Hotel, she discovered that "heavy webbing crisscrossed over the doors, knobs and keyholes. . . . In three separate places on each door were heavy wax seals that gleamed red in the dim light from the small communal kitchen directly across the narrow hall." When Peggy asked another tenant "what infectious disease had been quarantined here, and how long had the fumigation seals been on," the neighbor "gave a mirthless cackle," responding "You *are* a new one, aren't you?"[20]

More men than women were arrested, mainly because there were more men in positions of power, but plenty of women were arrested as well. Eleanor Lipper's chilling account, *My Eleven Years in a Soviet Prison*, describes the many "revolutionaries or the wives of revolutionaries whom I met in prison and camp. All of them, after more or less brutal interrogations, were given long prison sentences, whether or not they had renounced their husband, whether or not they had lived with them during the years before their arrest, whether or not they had children or were pregnant. They were convicted and sentenced even when their husbands had committed suicide a year before their arrest." A committed Communist when she came to the Soviet Union in 1937, Lipper was arrested only two months after her arrival. "Nothing I had done, said or planned could have justified my arrest," she insisted. "My only fault was my boundless naiveté in imagining that the Soviet Union was the realization of my ideals." Deep belief made Lipper assume that her arrest was an aberration and that she would soon be released. Moved from one collective cell to another, in a prison that held thousands of other women, she eventually picked up Russian "and heard my fellow prisoners' stories. Each new story that I heard made me see more and more, until at last I realized what I vainly tried not to realize: that all these people were as innocent as I was. Then my own suffering began to merge into the vast suffering of them all." Other women apparently had the same experience.[21]

Although Fischer, terrorized, stayed home every morning in case the phone rang for her at 11:00 a.m., at which point she would answer any question her contact asked, her reports were apparently not deemed useful enough. She was denied a visa to join her husband in the United States. Like Leder, she was trapped. Utterly panicked, Fischer finally sent an SOS to her husband, who appealed directly to Eleanor Roosevelt. Almost immediately she was told she could have a visa anytime she wanted.[22]

And then, on the night before Fischer and her two sons were to depart, the phone rang at midnight. It was Andrei, her contact. She was asked to meet him in a car outside her apartment. Silent, Andrei drove her before stopping, "to my horror," Fischer wrote, "at GPU [secret police] headquarters." After many hours, Fischer found herself in the office of Lavrenti Beria himself, the head of the secret police and one of the chief architects of the purge. Beria's right-hand man explained to Fischer that she could be useful to the Soviet Union if she would simply report on Europeans she encountered who were looking to "harm the Fatherland." Fischer's terror turned to cynicism as she realized that the entire meeting was a ruse to save face "now that the American President was interested in my case." She was polite, and they were polite, and she got out as fast as she could, without looking back.[23]

As Strong's fictional *Wild River* suggests, once the United States and the Soviet Union entered into an alliance in what many felt was a battle to save the world, the best way to make Americans feel sympathy toward the Soviet Union was to relate the Soviets' epic tale of socialist construction up to the mid-1930s then jump straight to the war, with ongoing rumors of sabotage implicitly justifying the years between.

Strong herself was not actually in the Soviet Union for the Second World War, and this may be why her *Wild River*, its publication clearly an artifact of the wartime alliance between the United States and the Soviet Union, is not really a war story. In the fall of 1940, Strong's husband had advised her to leave the country before a Nazi attack. Strong had been dividing much of her time between China, the United States, and Spain— the antifascist destination of choice in the late 1930s—as the atmosphere of fear and suspicion that pervaded life in Moscow became hard to tolerate, even for a loyalist like Strong. She was there to witness the famous trials of the "United Trotskyist-Zinovievite Center" in August 1936, in which the sixteen defendants "recounted various plots to kill Stalin and other party leaders." Like many foreigners, Strong found evidence of their guilt convincing. In reality, the confessions, "extracted under torture and duress," were all false. Strong was disturbed by the many "unjust arrests and executions" that followed as the hunt for enemies became all consuming; indeed, she recalled later that the staff members purged from the *Moscow News* were among the hardest workers and the most dedicated to the Party.[24]

Wild River is dedicated to Strong's late Russian husband, Joel Shubin, "who in living and in dying made clear to me the Soviet way of life." Strong's husband had not, in fact, died fighting for the Soviet motherland, as the dedication—and his 1942 death—seem to imply. Strong was told Shubin died of lung disease, which is certainly possible, but it's also possible that he was swept up in the Terror: a Jew, a member of the Party faithful, partner to a foreigner, he certainly fit the profile of many who were purged.[25]

When war came to Russia—and especially once the Soviet Union became a US ally—showing the American public a more positive side of Soviet life seemed necessary to winning the war. And now, machine gun in her hand, the new Soviet woman resurged with a vengeance in American popular culture. After the war, her longtime admirers—along with many other radicals and progressives—would become keenly aware that, by almost all accounts, their loyalties had been misplaced.

Heroines and Heretics on the Russian Front

About a third of the way through the film *The North Star* (1943)—based on a screenplay by Lillian Hellman—we see in the distance a scout on horseback riding into hills on the horizon. The camera zooms in to reveal that the scout is a strikingly beautiful, young woman. Shot from below, making her seem larger than life, the woman's upright, determined form appears in silhouette against a mottled sky at dawn. Spying a convoy of Nazi trucks in the distance, she pauses, turns her horse around, and gallops away, presumably to warn her people. Similarly, Margaret Bourke-White's *Shooting the Russian War* (1942) contains a description of a Russian scout named Tanya: she had "widely spaced blue eyes, honey-colored curls that spilled down shoulder length, and a strong, chunky little body." Bourke-White's admiration for Tanya is palpable: "She knew every footpath, and at night, as soon as it grew completely dark, she would buckle on her sidearms and go crawling on her hands and knees through the long grass and low shrubbery, across to the German lines." Behind the lines, Tanya would learn everything she could about the enemy's movements and armaments and then come back before dawn to report. "Then she would sleep a few hours, go to the hospital tent to help tend the wounded, and at night if she was needed she would be off again."[1]

Hellman and Bourke-White were the most visible American women to visit and create popular images of the Soviet Union during World War II.[2] Both were among the few foreigners—and may have been the only foreign women—to make it to the Russian front. And their writings, photographs, radio talks, speeches, films and other work shaped public views of the Soviet Union during the war in ways that highlighted women's significance as authors and as objects of pro-Soviet discourse. Reactions to Bourke-White and Hellman and their Soviet work also point to ways in which that discourse was reaching its limit.[3]

Margaret Bourke-White went to the Soviet Union in the spring of 1941 with her husband, the writer Erskine Caldwell, on assignment for *Life* magazine. They arrived less than two months before the German invasion; she was the only foreign photographer there when it came, and despite a government ban on photography, she managed to get permission to shoot, just as she had been the first foreigner to gain permission to take photographs in the Soviet Union twelve years earlier. She had visited in 1930, 1931, and 1932, publishing her first book, *Eyes on Russia* (1931), and a series of newspaper articles. She had also made two cinematic travelogues, illustrated materials by others, and exhibited her photographs in prestigious venues. Bourke-White's groundbreaking photographs of the new Russia were critical to establishing her reputation as a photographer, offering the first postrevolution images of Russian people and industry at a moment when American interest was at its height. And Bourke-White's visits to the USSR not only propelled her career; they also aroused her social conscience.[4]

At the start of Bourke-White's 1941 visit, the photographs and articles she published in *Life* were outliers. But once the United States and the Soviet Union officially became allies, American popular culture was full of pro-Soviet messages. And in many ways, the photographs Bourke-White shot before that time set the visual terms for American depictions of the Russian front.[5]

Lillian Hellman first visited the Soviet Union in 1937 to attend the Moscow Theatre Festival. Unlike many Americans, Hellman claimed to have been unimpressed. Even so, she forged warm relationships with luminaries of Soviet theatre and film. She also visited a collective farm and later claimed this visit made it possible for her to authentically depict one in *The North Star*.[6]

During the war, Hellman and the director William Wyler got permission to go to the Soviet Union to make a documentary film for Samuel Goldwyn, who'd been encouraged by President Roosevelt to make such a film: "The Russian news was very bad that winter of 1942, but all of America was moved and bewildered by the courage of a people who had been presented to two generations of Americans as passive slaves," Hellman wrote later. Although the documentary fell through because Wyler enlisted in the military, Goldwyn convinced Hellman to make a feature film on Russia's wartime youth with the Russian-born director Lewis Milestone.[7]

Hellman was unhappy with changes that Milestone made to her original script. ("It could have been a good picture instead of the big-time, sentimental, badly directed, badly acted mess it turned out to be," she declared later.) Still, the film was relatively well received in the Soviet Union: "When I got to Moscow I found they thought *North Star* a great joke, but I guess outside Moscow there were some simple peasant folk glad to find themselves so noble on the screen," she noted. Hellman's plays, *Watch on the Rhine* and *The Little Foxes*, were in rehearsal in Moscow, and she was sent as a kind of goodwill ambassador and temporary substitute for a second front, which Roosevelt had still not delivered.[8]

Both Bourke-White and Hellman were beneficiaries of US government support for their work on and in Russia, even as that work made them targets of FBI surveillance. And both were larger-than-life figures: Bourke-White is often called the most outstanding photographer of her era (certainly the most outstanding female photographer): she was the first to portray the artistry of industry, the first to capture the essence of the times through her images. Hellman is described as the outstanding— sometimes the *only*—female playwright of her era. Yet both women's reputations were plagued by questions about their veracity, honesty, careerism, and authenticity in ways that cannot be separated from their engagement with the Soviet Union.

Hellman's memoirs have generated as much if not more attention than her plays, mainly from critics who have argued that she could not have done many of the things she said she did: most famously, Hellman claimed to have carried money from Moscow to Nazi resisters in Germany in 1937.[9] Bourke-White, for her part, not only managed to get her name on the photos she published in *Fortune* and *Life*—when few others did—but insisted on telling everyone how she scaled skyscrapers, or narrowly escaped bomb blasts, or gained permission to photograph Stalin. *Eyes on Russia* is clearly about *Bourke-White's* eyes on Russia, and *Shooting the Russian War* arguably says more about Bourke-White than about the war itself.

From a critical perspective, both women have as often been scorned or even hated by critics as they were revered by the general public. The writer James Agee famously "despised" Bourke-White for her 1937 book with Erskine Caldwell, *You Have Seen Their Faces.* The critic Caleb Crain has noted, "Bourke-White lay in wait for her subjects with a flash, and wrote with pleasure of having them 'imprisoned on a sheet of film before they knew what had happened.' The resulting portraits are by turns sentimental and grotesque, and she and Caldwell printed them with contrived first-person captions." Mary McCarthy, among many others, similarly condemned Lillian Hellman's dishonesty with a vehemence that suggests something beyond mere artistic differences: "Every word she writes is false, including 'and' and 'but.' "[10]

In both cases the criticisms recall critiques by the anti-Stalinist Left. These critiques are both political—condemning the communist Left's acceptance of the Moscow Trials, the Stalinist purges, the Nazi-Soviet pact, and more—and aesthetic: the Popular Front hollowed out art, creating middlebrow, sentimental substitutes that "destroy[ed] the intellectual and moral content of experience."[11] This critique accused artists of the Left of being not just soft on Communism but fuzzy and "soft" overall, that is, feminine. Criticisms of Bourke-White and Hellman are emblematic of this turn. Their visibility during the war also helps us understand the ways in which the Second World War temporarily revived the new Soviet woman as a role model for American women, as well as why that revival could only be temporary.

Women, Uneasy Alliances, and Wartime Propaganda

When the United States and the Soviet Union became wartime allies in December 1941, American popular opinion of the Soviet Union was at an all-time low. Although the full extent of the Terror remained invisible to most Americans, anyone who kept up on the news knew an overreaching "purge," ostensibly of internal enemies, had taken place. Add to this the controversial Nazi-Soviet pact in August 1939 (which dramatically diminished Communism's popularity in the United States, especially among Jews), and the Soviet invasion of Finland several months later, and it is no surprise that in June 1942 only 41 percent of Americans believed that the Soviet Union could be trusted as an ally.[12]

The wartime alliance legitimized some degree of sympathy toward the Soviet Union, with the government supporting and even encouraging efforts to disseminate positive images of the Soviets. Some of the most striking of these were portrayals of the new Soviet woman. A 1943 *Woman's Home Companion* article, "Free Women of Russia," showed female snipers, bomber pilots, guerilla fighters, and wireless operators in the Soviet Union; an article from *Colliers* on the "fearless women of Russia" told a "girl guerilla's story." In *Survey Graphic* Rose Maurer pointed out that "it did not take Hitler to make Julia Plyakova a metallurgical engineer or Anna Shchetinina the captain of a sea-going ship." However, "the need to defeat 'women's greatest enemy' was back of it when Maria Nikitenko took over her husband's job of breaking semi-wild horses on a stud farm in Central Asia and back of it when Maria Popova became a 'Tugboat Annie' whose all-woman crew on the Volga read fan mail from grateful Red Army men to whom they have passed the ammunition." Still other women, Maurer noted, were on the front lines, fighting and dying for their country.[13]

In Soviet-themed films made by American studios during the war, female leads were no longer "slated for conversion or liberation," as in several popular films of the late 1930s (*Ninotchka* [1939] is perhaps the most famous example). Rather, in *Mission to Moscow* (1943), *The North Star* (1943), *Song of Russia* (1944), *Days of Glory* (1944), *Three Russian Girls* (1943), and others, the Soviet woman was attractive, committed, and prepared to fight for her country in ways that suggest the bravery and ardor of the Russian people generally.[14]

As the examples of *The North Star* and Tanya suggest, Soviet women who served as scouts and partisans assumed legendary status, perhaps no one more than Zoya Kosmodemyanskaya, called "the Joan of Arc of Russia today." Caught setting fire to German headquarters in her village, Zoya was dragged through the streets, tortured, and then left hanging for several weeks in the town square wearing a placard that read "Incendiary of Homes." She became a staple of wartime and postwar popular culture, and the subject of artwork, a 1944 Soviet film, and monuments that stand to this day. *Time* magazine featured her story in March 1942, describing a young woman who quit the tenth grade to join a guerilla band: "Hair cropped, in men's clothes, tall, 18-year old Zoya proved an apt recruit: before the Germans captured her, she had cut a German field-telephone wire, fired on German troop quarters, destroyed a 20-horse enemy stable." After she was captured, the Nazis tortured her for information: "They flogged her with a leather belt, punched her with their fists. They held lighted matches to her chin. They scraped a saw across her back. They walked her, at bayonet point, barefoot through the snow." When they finally took her to the gallows for execution, Zoya taunted her captors: "I am not alone," she is said to have told them. "There are 200,000,000 of us. You won't hang everybody. I shall be avenged."[15]

Reports of Soviet women's violent resistance to the German enemy were legion in American media. The National Council of American Soviet Friendship, for instance, as part of a campaign to publicize the activity of Soviet women in the war, disseminated a letter a Red Army officer received from his sister describing the death of several female comrades who'd been taken into a house "to satisfy the bestial lust" of fourteen German officers: "When a German lieutenant colonel seized Tanya, she picked up a fork from the table and gouged out his eyes. Zina upset a tankful of benzene standing near the door and hurled a lighted cigarette on the floor. Vera locked the door and threw the key into the stove. The

Fig. 7.1 "Behind the Enemy Lines in Belorussia: Taisa, a partisan girl." Photo by M. Trakhman, Soviet Information Bureau Photo Service, in scrapbook of National Council of American Soviet Friendship, Tamiment Library, New York University.

drunken fascists were trapped. The girls perished with them. Of the four-teen officers only two escaped."[16]

The late 1930s had dramatically redefined women's place in Soviet life to mostly conservative ends, with new government policies and pro-paganda emphasizing their roles as wives, mothers, and homemakers. However, during the war, the presence of Soviet women in combat—to a degree unprecedented in history—suggested possibilities for women akin to those that had animated some of the most utopian phases of So-viet history. One million women served in the Red Army on the East-ern Front, and another twenty-eight thousand fought with the partisans. Many women in combat were highly trained and among the "professional and technical elite of the armed forces. Serving as machine and mortar gunners, snipers, artillery fighters, combat pilots, and junior command-ing officers in male, mixed, and female units, they constituted more than 120,000 of half a million women in the field army during the war." And despite the purges of the late 1930s, most of these women were eager to fight for their country. Moreover, they saw armed service "as an expres-sion of their new liberated Soviet womanhood."[17]

Despite its repressive nature and mixed messages, the Stalinist system benefited many women. Young women who were loyal to the regime, and who accepted restrictions on their personal autonomy, found real opportunities for education and professional advancement in the late 1930s and during the war. The war in particular allowed women to see themselves as future mothers *and* citizen-soldiers—making possible a "profound reimagination of the female self."[18]

To a far greater degree than Rosie the Riveter and her sisters on the wartime assembly lines of American factories, Soviet women assumed roles in the traditionally masculine bastion of war that fundamentally challenged the "war system," and, by extension, the gender system that underlies it.[19] Both the Soviet women on the frontlines and the American women documenting and celebrating their achievements were disrup-tive in ways that thrilled some people and terrified others. The mixed re-action to the US-Soviet alliance and to the gender dynamics it made vis-ible speaks to the awkward but insistent place of the new Soviet woman in American popular culture. Not only did the war make it fashionable to put aside reservations about the Soviet Union; it engendered the most far-reaching and carefully orchestrated campaign to create positive views of the Soviets, a campaign in which women figured prominently as both subjects and authors.

These efforts stretched beyond the United States. Thanks to the war, positive images of Soviet life became part of everyday popular culture in Britain too. From London, May O'Callaghan wrote to Ruth Kennell, a close friend from the days when both women worked in the English-language section of the Comintern together, "People who never heard of that country are now listening to lectures and quite interested—at least they are getting to know a little of the real state of affairs, which was not the case in pre-war days." Indeed, she said, "It's rather a topsy turvy world we are living in, especially the volte-face in regard to the USSR and the people who have come out as admirers who were at one time the worst critics. But who could see what the Red Army is doing and not be impressed?"[20]

Approximately twenty-five pro-Soviet films were produced in the United States during the war, as were numerous works of nonfiction, novels (such as Strong's *Wild River*), collections of poetry, children's books, posters, and other media. In many of these works, the new Soviet woman and her particular concerns, as well as the bravery of Russian women and girls, are prominently featured. In *Wild River*, the male pro-tagonist, Stepan, grows up and becomes a Soviet "new man" in large part because of the women in his life, particularly Anya, the star beet farmer. When she returns from a trip to Moscow in which her achievements have been publicly recognized by Stalin himself, she is full of pride, ex-citement, and renewed commitment to her work. However, she finds Stepan threatened by her new prominence and afraid of losing her. She scolds him, asking "What has this talk of losing or going beyond to do with comradeship? Must you have either possession or worship? I think that equal companionship between man and woman is the best relation of all, and the hardest to reach." Anya sees her marriage as inseparable from a broader set of commitments that drive her; Stepan, however, clearly finds Anya's work "only a hindrance to their marriage." Strong's book suggested that the gender battles playing out among Soviet men and women—which would certainly have resonated with educated and professional women in the United States—were indelibly tied to the Soviets' larger goals in fighting.[21]

A number of children's books, from Vera Edelstadt's *Young Fighters of the Soviets* (1944) to the collection *Youth Replies I Can: Stories of Resistance* (1945), highlight the bravery of Soviet children; others simply use the occasion of the war to portray Soviet life in a positive light. Many of these books give particular attention to girls. In Henry Gregor Felsen's *Struggle Is Our Brother* (1943), a girl in her early teens risks her life to avoid disclosing the whereabouts of partisans. The title story in Ruth Kennell's *That Boy Nikolka and Other Stories of Soviet Children* (1945) actually focuses on a young female refugee from Germany, Elsa, who offers shelter to forty Nazi soldiers in a root cellar, then plugs the air vent.[22]

Other stories for children, like the Junior Literary Guild Selection for 1945, *Ilenka*, focus not on war or politics but instead emphasize the expanded field of possibility for young women in the Soviet Union. In this charming picture book, Ilenka cannot decide what she wants to be when she grows up: "a farmer or an engineer or a fireman or a painter or a dancer or a singer or a tailor or a streetcleaner or a nurse or a doctor." In a country where "girls can be anything they want to be," Ilenka's indecision reminds readers of all the possibility open to her, in contrast to the United States, where a girl's future possibilities were limited. Even the course of Ilenka's typical day challenges American norms, for in the Soviet Union time spent in nursery school is not only naturalized but also shown to be beneficial. In the United States, day care centers—a number of which were opened by the federal government so that women could work in support of the war effort—were condemned as threatening to the family and bad for children.[23]

Both the US government itself, through the Office of War Information (OWI) and its subsidiaries, and independent organizations, perhaps most notably Russian War Relief and the National Council of American Soviet Friendship, promoted positive images of the Soviet Union.[24] The OWI worked with Hollywood, libraries, museums, media outlets, and other agencies, such as the American Library Association, with whom it would cosponsor an information program on Russia in May 1944. The OWI's Bureau of Motion Pictures (BMP) became especially active in efforts to overcome Americans' hostility toward their Soviet allies. The BMP's head, Lowell Mellett, worked closely with Hollywood producers, directors, and screenwriters—many of whom, like Hellman, were already supporters of the Soviet Union—to help them navigate the tricky path between US wartime rhetoric that "portrayed the war as a movement for the global extension of freedom, democracy, and regulated capitalism" and the need for interallied cooperation. As historian Todd Bennett has noted, "Performing intellectual gymnastics, publicists responded by generally avoiding the sensitive issues of socialism and Stalin, rationalizing past Soviet behavior, suggesting the Soviet Union was evolving into a less revolutionary state, and focusing on the heroic wartime efforts of the Soviet people."[25]

The US government also gave tacit approval of and support to independent, pro-Soviet organizations that were less conflicted about celebrating the Soviet system. Russian War Relief (formed in 1941) worked to build popular sympathy for the Soviets and to provide material support to the war-torn country and people. It published dozens of books and pamphlets, from the *Russian Cook Book for American Homes*, to a collection of Soviet war posters that had been exhibited at the Metropolitan Museum of Art, to children's books like *Igor's Summer* and Kennell's *That Boy Nikolka*.[26]

Also founded in 1941, the National Council of American Soviet Friendship (NCASF) drew prominent individuals ranging from Popular Front figures in the cultural world (e.g., Charlie Chaplin, Norman Corwin, and Aaron Copland) to progressives and liberals in a range of fields (e.g., Colonel Hugh Cooper, the education pioneer Lucy Sprague Mitchell, Helen Keller, Senator Claude Pepper, university professors, scientists, and more). The NCASF sponsored publications, exhibitions, films, programs and conferences, educational curricula, and various other efforts. In 1944 alone, the council sent 282 exhibits to 157 locales, among them schools, colleges and universities, libraries, army camps, department stores, and church groups. The council's Committee on Education worked with schools to influence curricula, promoted Soviet and Soviet-themed children's books and films, and examined aspects of Soviet schooling. Exhibits and programs focused on the Soviet Union's wartime contributions as well as its welfare programs and culture, both of which attracted liberals who were less enthusiastic about Soviet politics or its economic system. Other committees focused on more specific dimensions of Soviet culture or society. A dance committee, for instance, included the critic John Martin, as well as dancers Pauline Koner, Agnes De Mille, Katherine Dunham, Doris Humphrey, and Helen Tamiris; this group prepared and sent to the Soviet Union materials on American dance, ranging from films to reviews and programs. An art committee sponsored a traveling exhibit of Soviet children's art, which started at the Museum of Modern Art. A theatre committee worked to promote productions of Soviet plays in the United States.[27] The roster of prominent members and sponsors of the NCASF and its successful outreach efforts attest to the extent to which positive images of the Soviet Union became mainstream during the war.

Probably the most active component of the NCASF aside from the Committee on Education was the Committee of Women.[28] The latter group's members and/or sponsors included the suffrage pioneers Carrie Chapman Catt and Alice Stone Blackwell; African American activist Mary McLeod Bethune (who, at an NCASF rally, hailed the Soviet Union's "complete elimination of the minority problem"); Sidonie Gruenberg, head of the Child Study Association; Mrs. Hugh Cooper (wife of the Dnieper Dam's chief engineer); Dr. Alice Hamilton; Clara Savage Littledale, editor of *Parents* magazine; fashion designer Elizabeth Hawes; Mrs. Sidney Hillman, wife of the prominent labor leader; Jessica Smith (the committee's educational director); settlement house leader Mary K. Simkovitch; authors Katherine Anne Porter, Genevieve Taggard, Muriel Rukeyser, and Anna Louise Strong; several professors; and other public figures.[29] The committee forged partnerships with groups such as the National Council of Negro Women, the Children's Bureau, the National Federation of Women's Clubs, the Congress of Women's Auxiliaries of the Congress of Industrial Organizations, and the American Association of University Women.

Beyond working to involve more women in the NCASF, the Committee of Women aimed to publicize "the achievements of the women of the Soviet Union through an educational program about their methods of childcare, their family and social relationships, the experience of Soviet women in the many fields of work they have entered, and their heroic exploits in the war"; to promote exchange between women in the two countries; and to draw more women into the war effort and postwar plans.[30] The committee sponsored exhibits and materials that it sent directly to the Soviet Union, as well as publications such as Rose Maurer's pamphlets *Soviet Children and Their Care* and *Soviet Women*.

The committee's efforts often had a (circumscribed) feminist dimension. Thelma Nuremberg, a committee member originally from the Soviet Union, spoke to the *New York World Telegram* on "Russian feminine opinion" and reported that Russian women had questioned American women's lack of substantive representation in the professions, and they believed their American counterparts were "shamefully held down in our war efforts," as "the first to be fired when jobs are scarce," whereas "their own economic gains are permanent." The *New York Times* report on an event the committee sponsored, headlined "Part Time Jobs for Women Urged," noted that a Barnard College dean, addressing the NCASF Committee of Women, "says Russians may lead Americans in combining home and career." The article quoted Jessica Smith, explaining why changes in Soviet law that made divorce more difficult did not undermine women's gains: "The early easy divorce laws were an inevitable reaction not against marriage but against the enslaving kind of marriage that existed in old Russia." Now that women were economically independent, and marriages were "founded only on considerations of real love and comradeship, easy divorce laws were no longer necessary."[31]

The women's committee's work built on an exchange between Soviet and American women that had been fostered by the American Council on Soviet Relations (ACSR). Among the numerous statements by prominent women that are featured in an ACSR pamphlet encouraging the cooperation of American and Soviet women in the fight against fascism, Lillian Hellman's stands out, in part because she was not known for speaking out on anything having to do with women, and in part because it was so representative of all the women's comments. "There are many times when one feels good about being a woman," Hellman wrote. "One of those times, for all of us who watch your magnificent fight against fascism, must be tonight when you speak not only in the great name of Russian women, but for all women everywhere."[32]

Hellman became a member of the NCASF in 1944 and in November 1945 spoke at a program on American-Soviet cultural cooperation. Later, she claimed she'd never had any association with the organization. Bourke-White's association with the NCASF is unclear, but in cooperation with Russian War Relief, the council published her photo essay booklet *Meet Some of the Russian People*. She was also on their mailing list.[33]

Brave Women and Children

Among the wide range of materials created to promote Soviet-American friendship, Bourke-White and Hellman created some of the most influential ones: *Life* magazine, which featured Bourke-White's photographs of Russia for several months in 1941, had, around this time, "a circulation of 2.86 million, with a high 'pass-along rate,' multiplying its actual audience." Bourke-White's photographs and writings about wartime Russia also appeared in *Harpers* and *Vogue* and were collected into the volume *Shooting the Russian War*. And Bourke-White (with Erskine Caldwell) had a virtual monopoly on live radio broadcasts from Moscow that weren't coming from the staff of Radio Moscow itself. For Hellman's part, *The North Star* became "the most commercially successful wartime propaganda film" and was nominated for several Academy Awards. Samuel Goldwyn spent over $2 million on the set, creating "a complete modern Russian village covering ten acres," and outfitted with "hundreds of authentic Russian pieces, furniture, clocks, samovars, newspapers, posters, pictures," based on Sovfoto agency pictures. He hired Bourke-White to take photos of film scenes, which were published in *Life*, "as if her onsite documentation of the Soviet war magically conferred authenticity on a built Soviet set," historian Beth Holmgren has commented. In the wake of *The North*

Star's success, it seemed as though Hellman's every utterance was news-worthy, and her accounts of her trip to the Soviet Union—from the time and years later—also received a great deal of attention.[34]

While it would not be accurate to assert that Bourke-White or Hell-man had a feminist agenda per se, by virtue of their visibility as American women on the Russian front, they were de facto vehicles for "women's perspective" on the Soviet Union. Bourke-White claimed to have rejected all assignments that asked her to provide the "woman's angle" on the war, but she did give attention to women's contributions, striking as they were. The left-wing journalist Ella Winter, covering Russia's home front (rather than "the military story") for the *New York Post*, devoted a chapter of her book *I Saw the Russian People* to "heroines at close range": "They were tank commanders, partisans, peasants, girls deported to Germany who had escaped and fought in the woods, women who had stayed at their benches and lathes through bombing and terror and hunger." Even dis-cussions of the "home front" could not avoid a discussion of women's ser-vice at the battlefront: almost by definition, women in battle blurred the distinction between the domestic realm and the front.[35]

In fact, Bourke-White consistently gave attention to women's role in the war effort, noting women "massing in the fields" to replace male farmers who had gone to battle, the coeds who were now getting trained to drive tractors, and chambermaids in her hotel who had "voted to re-place the waiters and porters so that they might be freed to go to the front," meaning that the women would all be working two jobs. Although Bourke-White noted women's eagerness to go to the front, she apparently did not anticipate that they would actually see combat. On the script of one of her radio addresses, the Russian censor crossed out a line follow-ing Bourke-White's claim that "all the girls want to go [to the front]": "~~but are being told that it is Soviet practice not to send women to the front except for those with medical training who will have duties there.~~" It's not clear whether the censor knew women would wind up serving in battle or if it was simply Soviet practice to avoid publicly acknowledging any limits on women's possibility. In actual fact, by June 1941, hundreds of thousands of Soviet women were entering the military.[36]

Bourke-White made much of the fact that she and Caldwell were able to do these live radio addresses, noting that NBC "had been paying a man's salary for three years just to keep him on the spot, negotiating a live broadcast." While she did have to show her scripts to the censors, she was trusted not to stray from them. Otherwise, she claimed, the voice of Radio Moscow was entirely the voice of Soviet citizens.[37]

Bourke-White did note that "several American expatriates" were "on the staff of Radio Center" and had "taken out Soviet citizenship ten years before." She worked most with two "Negroes: Mr. Whittaker, from Harlem, and a South Carolina colored mammy, whose name we never heard." Whittaker would announce Bourke-White and Caldwell to New York, at which time the station would move to a "nation-wide hookup." As for "Comrade Mammy," as Bourke-White put it, "our relations . . . consisted in shoving her gradually off the bench in front of the microphone as our time approached, and being in turn shoved off by her as our time ended and hers, to read from her government-prepared script, began again."[38]

The "colored mammy" has to have been Williana Burroughs (working under the name "Ooma Percy"), who was college-educated, articulate, and neither from South Carolina nor a Soviet citizen—it's unlikely that Bourke-White had bothered to ask where Burroughs was from since she had not even gotten her name.[39] ("Whittaker" was probably Lloyd Patterson, who likely also used an alias.) Bourke-White's appreciation for women's role in the war and her efforts to connect the Soviet Union's interests with those of the United States apparently did not translate into any genuine commitment to the "double victory" campaign that made ending American racism, long a target of Soviet criticisms, a priority equal to destroying fascism.

Shooting the Russian War says a great deal about women's contributions. They are shown, for instance, defusing bombs: "the process is known as liquidating the fire." They are pictured in "sanitary training": one young woman bandages the head of another; in the background, on shelves, are mannequin heads wearing a variety of bandages. We see women keeping the night watch, as in the photograph of an elderly peasant, kerchief on her head, photographed from a low angle so that she seems to be towering beside the wooden door to a bomb shelter over which she presides. Another photograph shows women rushing to gather the harvest before the Nazis could get to it: we see Ukrainian farm women massed together, all wearing white kerchiefs on their heads, holding their rakes aloft. Also shot from a low angle, the women's bodies fill almost half the photograph. The caption notes that they are voluntarily working three times as hard now that their men are gone, and that "these collective-farm women could no longer merely walk to work; they marched. They even began referring to their tools as agricultural weapons."[40]

In *Shooting the Russian War*, Bourke-White tells of her visit to a crèche in a technical school. Nursing mothers studying there got regular breaks to feed their children: "In the nursery hung the typical ten-times-life-size picture of Stalin, holding a smiling child on his knee. Slogans bordered the picture—for example: 'Long live women of the U.S.S.R., to whom Article 122 of the Constitution has brought equal rights with men.'" An accompanying photograph, captioned "The Stairway of a Typical Creche," is shot from above and shows half a dozen smiling women wearing clean lab coats and kerchiefs on their heads. We are told that the women are nurses and graduates of the Medical Institute but that mothers wear similar white robes and handkerchiefs when they come in from the factory to breast-feed their children. A woman in the foreground is holding a bannister and seems to be coming up the stairs, as though to invite the viewer into the photograph. The entire background is taken up by a huge painting in socialist realist style of Stalin holding a smiling little girl behind a huge vase of flowers; the picture is surrounded by various slogans celebrating the Soviet Union's gifts to women and children. Largest of all is a sign reading, "Thank you Comrade Stalin for our Happy Childhood," a slogan that Soviet children were required to recite regularly.[41]

Bourke-White has a vivid writing style, and *Shooting the Russian War* contains more text than photographs. Most of the photographs require lengthy captions, and there is much that she did not capture on film. There is, for instance, only a written description of Tanya the scout, who Bourke-White says is "the person whom I remember the most vividly among the Russians I came to know."[42]

While Bourke-White consciously rejected calls to give a woman's angle, Lillian Hellman, brash, outspoken, and unwilling to identify as a

Fig. 7.2 Margaret Bourke-White, "Ukrainian Farm Women." From *Shooting the Russian War* (New York: Simon and Schuster, 1942), 165. Photo © Estate of Margaret Bourke White. Licensed by VAGA, New York, NY.

feminist, would have self-consciously resisted any implication that her approach was somehow "limited" to a women's perspective. On the other hand, Hellman's extensive research notes for *The North Star* point to her awareness of Soviet women's significant role on the front; however, their contribution as fighters in the Red Army is not touched on in the film or in any of her published writings about the Soviet Union during the war, and in Hellman's original script the scout we see on the horizon is male. Still, there is no evidence that she objected to a suggestion that the scout be female, unlike so many of the other changes that Milestone made. And although women are not shown in *The North Star* as enlisted soldiers, young women, who are among the film's core protagonists, are shown arming themselves and fighting in the woods.[43]

The brave women and girls in Hellman's screenplay come in all ages, but those most prominently featured are young. The film centers on Russian children, who were part of a longer-running left-feminist discourse in the United States vis-à-vis the Soviet Union. As we have seen, Soviet children represented, on the one hand, hope for a socialist future and, on the other, the need to protect that future.

In writing *The North Star*, Hellman consulted a large number of books and articles on Soviet education, family life, and children's wartime roles, among them articles from *Soviet Russia Today*, Anna Louise Strong's *The Soviets Expected It*, speeches clipped from the *Moscow News*, and Bourke-White's *Shooting the Russian War*. She also took note of contemporary children's books that portrayed the Soviet Union in a positive light, books like Kennell's *That Boy Nikolka* and Arkady Gaidar's *Timur and His Gang*, a Russian children's book, also published in the United States, portraying children who helped families of soldiers.[44]

Both Hellman's script and the cinematic version of *The North Star* revolve around a group of young people, ranging in age from perhaps eleven to nineteen, from a Ukrainian collective farm called "The North Star" (the film never explicitly identifies it as a collective).[45] The name evokes the Underground Railroad as well as biblical references, suggesting a prophetic role for the Soviet Union. At the core of the film are Damian (Farley Granger), star pupil at the collective's school, and his girlfriend Marina (Anne Baxter). These idealistic, patriotic teenagers are in love and planning to marry. Several friends and siblings join them on a hiking expedition to Kiev, a journey that sets them apart from their community. In the midst of their excursion, German bombs begin dropping, breaking up the idyll. Although the group emerges from this initial bombing unscathed (but shaken), a young child they've met on the road is injured and subsequently dies in their midst. The scene shifts back to North Star, where Marina's younger sister is killed in a bombing raid. Her mother (Ann Harding) gathers the child in her arms with a look of rage in her eyes. Later Harding's character lets the occupying Nazis break her arm and leg rather than reveal where village men are hiding in the woods planning to launch an attack. She and other women are also shown setting fire to their homes so nothing will be left for the Nazis, as happened under Stalin's "scorched earth" policy.

The bravery and resilience of the Soviet youths makes the film ultimately hopeful rather than tragic. For Hellman this was a tricky balance. Part of what frustrated her about the film that was actually made was its visual style and musical numbers. As Dan Georgakas's critical discussion of changes to Hellman's original vision notes, "most devastating to Hellman's conception was Goldwyn's notion that the American public had to be warmed up to the Russkies with some music." Indeed, "this singing, dancing, and storytelling goes on for nearly a third of the film. Folksy peasants pure of mind, body, and spirit romp about like so many Kansas cornhuskers in Eastern European drag. They love their land, their children, their spouses, and their village in the simple way peasants always do." Hellman herself called it an "extended opera bouffe, peopled not by peasants, real and alive, but by musical comedy characters without a thought or care in the world."[46]

But Hellman's script had itself called for music, though not necessarily along the lines of what was finally used in the film. The finished film includes a score for balalaika by Aaron Copeland with Ira Gershwin lyrics, lending a folksy, show-tunes feeling to much of the film. One scene shows a celebration at the farm "replete with bounteous food, faux Russian couplets poking gentle fun at those present, and a choreographed dance in which peasant lasses flirtatiously waved their handkerchiefs and peasant lads squatted down to show off Cossack kicks." However, an early scene at the collective's school showing children singing "The Internationale" was in the original script.[47]

Hellman had wanted to create something that seemed, at least to her, "honest": "Neither of us wants to have anything to do with the fashionable trend of cashing in on the Russian fight," she wrote to Goldwyn in October 1942, defending her script. "I want to do a *Russian* picture and, I hope, so do you. We cannot pull rabbits out of hats: there is the war and we must face it and write about it. I don't know what audiences want to see: guessing is usually fruitless and inaccurate." She contended that audiences would come to see a good picture that was also "honest." Hellman deliberately tried to show children's vulnerability as well as their bravery. In the film, the greatest tragedy is also the most treacherous Nazi act: taking blood from the community's children to use for the German army, an act for which Hellman found documentation.[48]

It was, in the end, the lack of honesty and authenticity that not only Hellman but also her critics would complain about. Mary McCarthy, whose criticisms cannot be separated from her own avowed anti-Stalinism, called the film "political indoctrination" in a review that may have been the first shot in her efforts to discredit a rival. McCarthy criticized Hellman for depicting a "peace loving hamlet" instead of showing "the terror which held the country in domestic siege long before the first German company moved across the frontier." McCarthy called the film "a tissue of falsehoods woven of every variety of untruth."[49]

Propaganda, Lies, and the Line Between Sentiment and Sentimentality

Only a few years after it premiered, *The North Star* was one of several films highlighted at hearings of the House Committee on Un-American Activities (HUAC) as evidence of Communist infiltration of Hollywood, and was specifically cited as "not a true picture" of the Soviet Union. Other films named in those hearings were *Mission to Moscow* (1943) and *Song of Russia* (1944). *Mission to Moscow*, which drew smaller audiences and more criticisms than *The North Star*, parroted Soviet rhetoric that rationalized both the Moscow Trials and the purges as necessary efforts to rout internal enemies and strengthen the Soviets against the Nazis.[50]

Song of Russia, for which Anna Louise Strong served as an uncred-
ited "technical advisor," features a romance between John Meredith, an
American conductor on tour in the Soviet Union, and a beautiful Russian woman, Sonia, who has traveled from her collective farm in the very
musical village of Tchaikovskoy to beg him to come to their village. Sonia winds up winning John's heart through her beauty, marvelous skill at
piano, and both fortitude and commitment such as he has never before
seen in a woman. Strong suggested that Sonia should "not betray her political and social convictions for love." Even if the American male protag-
onist believes that "love should be woman's whole existence," Strong argued, "Sonia should not be content to be secure and wealthy as Mrs. John
Meredith and nothing else." Her notes on the script insist that "she tells
John that she could never be happy with a comfortable life in America
while her people are fighting."[51] When John travels to Sonia's village to
assure her of his true love, Sonia is shown driving a tractor in the fields;
later she and several other women learn to fire a machine gun.

Ayn Rand, in HUAC testimony on *Song of Russia*, maintained that
almost everything about that film was dishonest, from its "manicured
starlets driving tractors and the happy women who come in from work
singing" to the idea that the heroine would rather stay in Russia to "fight
the war" than live comfortably in the United States. *The North Star* was
subject to similar criticisms: in HUAC testimony James McGuinness, an
editorial supervisor at MGM and a member of the Executive Board of
the Motion-Picture Alliance for the Preservation of American Ideals, a
group of high-profile, conservative members of the Hollywood film industry organized to combat Communist influence, said that both *The
North Star* and *Song of Russia* falsely "represented Russia as a never-never
land, flowing with milk and honey." But McGuiness played down the
significance of these descriptions, claiming he "never regarded them too
seriously since they were made during the war. In fact, I looked at them
as a form of intellectual lend-lease."[52]

Was it possible to make an "honest" pro-Soviet film, indeed, an honest
pro-Soviet anything, during the war? Despite Hellman's criticisms, it is
unfair to blame Lewis Milestone for all the ways in which *The North Star*

Fig. 7.3 Susan Peters as Nadya Stepanova firing a machine gun in *Song of Russia* (1944, dir. Gregory Ratoff, MGM).

fails. However, Hellman had strongly desired to communicate certain truths with the film, which Milestone undercut: "I have tried hard in the picture to stay away from sentimentality and oppose it with sentiment," she told him. "Sentimentality is rotted nonsense and true sentiments are the only things that really matter to anybody." Sadly, she complained of one scene, "you have taken a big moment and made it a sentimental one."[53]

Hellman was especially concerned about the portrayal of Clavdia, the immature, romantic, and self-conscious friend of Marina who exhibits nothing but terror when the other young people conclude that they should be prepared to fight the Nazis. Although she constantly struggles against her own fear, Clavdia does, in the end, assist in attacking a Nazi convoy. In that climactic scene she trembles with dread, whispering a kind of prayer to her grandparents for strength to do the right thing as she creeps through the darkened woods, holding a gun and moving toward the road where German vehicles are passing. Mustering her courage as a line of motorcycles begins to pass, she raises her gun and fires, killing a Nazi, but also setting off a chase in which she, tragically, is killed.

Hellman felt strongly that characterization of Clavdia remain consistent throughout the film, so that her acts at the end would be that much more powerful; indeed, because she was a *child*, and felt like a child. "I meant Clavdia to be a little girl for whom anything unpleasant is desperately hard," Hellman wrote Milestone, who had made Clavdia pluckier. "Thus, when I wrote the scene in which she is tearing up bandages [for the wounded child], I had her head turned away as if she is about to vomit. If she is a girl who takes the initiative and who is able to function under bad circumstances, she is *not* the girl who has to struggle with herself to go forward to her death."[54]

Lowell Mellett, head of the Office of War Information's Bureau of Motion Pictures, told Hellman he preferred her original vision, but still had positive words for the film. Hellman herself, despite all her frustrations, nonetheless thought the film "a valuable and good picture which tells a good deal of the truth about fascism." So did critics: *The North Star* was nominated for six Academy Awards, and *Life* named it "Movie of the Year." The *Washington Post* called the film "a moving, human drama," and *Variety* called it "one of the most spectacular productions of the season." Even the morning edition of Hearst's conservative *New York Mirror* praised *The North Star* as "one of the most vivid of war dramas." But after Frank Quinn's review had hit the stands, all Hearst newspapers were ordered to condemn the film as "Bolshevik propaganda." The afternoon edition panned it.[55]

Bourke-White and Hellman in the War Zone

Hellman's experience in wartime Russia has interesting parallels to—and differences from—Bourke-White's several years earlier. They met many of the same people, including Sergei Eisenstein, Vsevolod Pudovkin, and Gregorii Alexandrov, probably best known for directing *The Circus*. They both visited the front. But while Hellman was admittedly frightened by being in a war zone, Bourke-White seems to have relished it. This fearless-

Fig. 7.4 Margaret Bourke-White and Erskine Caldwell's Christmas greeting for December 1941. Margaret Bourke-White papers, Syracuse University Libraries' Special Collections Research Center. Photo © Estate of Margaret Bourke White. Licensed by VAGA, New York, NY.

ness, combined with a single-minded focus on work, gave her photographs power but diminished any sense of a human connection to her subjects. John Scott, an American who worked for several years in Soviet industry, found in *Shooting the Russian War* "a sense of almost eerie detachment from the violence and sudden death which surrounded Miss Bourke-White while she manipulated her camera." Bourke-White's single-minded focus on work helped break up her marriage to Erskine Caldwell not long after the Russia trip. A photograph of the couple in Siberia had served as their Christmas card for 1941; after they'd split up, Bourke-White, not one to waste a good photograph, cropped Caldwell out and used the picture of herself in publicity for *Shooting the Russian War*.[56]

Bourke-White rationalized her refusal to heed the American ambassador's advice to evacuate Moscow: "Anybody would know that I would start throwing my lenses like hand grenades at anyone who tried to carry me away from a scoop like this." As the only American photographer in the entire Soviet Union, she was determined to make the most of it. She regularly defied orders to take shelter in the subway station during the nightly raids: when inspectors came to evacuate the rooms in her hotel, she hid under the bed, then snuck out after the inspectors left. Her photographs of the bombings are striking, but perhaps more striking are her aestheticized descriptions of the way they looked (like art) and sounded (like music): "I had not realized that there is so much music with an air raid," she noted later. "The most beautiful sound is the echo of the guns, which returns on a deeper note, like the bass of a Beethoven chord. The total effect is as though two types of music were being played together—formal chords with overtures of jazz thrown in. The peculiar whistle, which one soon learns to recognize, of bombs falling in the neighborhood is like a dash of Gershwin against a classic symphonic background."[57] (Bourke-White was not alone in making this comparison. Ella Winter's chapter on Soviet war heroines takes its title from a comment by Tank Commander Eugenie Kostrikova, daughter of Sergei Kirov: "I love the symphony of the music of the tanks!"[58] But Bourke-White's description suggests her detachment from war's true horror.)

Bourke-White practically begged to go to the front and seemed to give no thought at all to her own safety. Once there, she single-mindedly pursued the shots she wanted. After an early morning bombing in a village, she discovered a family of four in the doorway of their home, "in contorted positions and very still," and began snapping pictures. Acknowledging that this impulse might seem strange, she noted, "It is a peculiar thing about pictures of this sort. It is as though a protecting screen draws itself across my mind and makes it possible to consider focus and light values and the technique of photography, in as impersonal a way as though I were making an abstract camera composition. The blind lasts as long as it is needed—while I am actually operating the camera. Days later, when I developed the negatives, I was surprised to find that I could not bring myself to look at the films."[59]

Her photograph, "Death Comes to Vyzama," is hard to look at. Harder, still, is imagining Bourke-White taking it. Two or more mangled bodies lie amid rubble and wires. One man lies prostrate, his body covered with blood and debris and crisscrossed by cables. By his right foot, in the lower corner of the photograph, is someone's hand and just a bit of a sleeve. A young woman is crouched in the right-hand corner, her legs exposed. A blanket is draped over her shoulders, almost as though she is sleeping, and her head rests on something too difficult to make out, possibly a young child she was trying to protect. Two hands are visibly protruding from the area close to her body, although it is not clear whether both are hers.[60]

Bourke-White admitted to having been stirred, briefly, when she heard the moans of a mother discovering her daughter, dead, "with dust-filled yellow hair," among the bombed group. "As I focused my camera on this vision of human misery it seemed heartless to turn her suffering into a photograph," Bourke-White noted, adding "But war is war and it has to be recorded."[61]

Bourke-White described the devastation with more fascination than horror, noting odd objects on the battlefield at Yelna days after the Germans had evacuated: a piece of fabric, a spoon, a moldy loaf of bread that blew apart when she accidentally hit it with her foot. "When we drove into [Yelna's] ruined streets I knew that here at last I had the pictures I wanted, pictures that would look like war." The only moments that made Bourke-White cry were when she was kept from taking a picture she really wanted.[62]

Hellman, in contrast, was open about her terror at going to the front and went only because she saw no way to refuse the invitation. She was also clearly shocked by the devastation to the landscape, in contrast to Bourke-White's detachment. Interestingly, though, at the front she lost all her fear, despite the sounds of shooting all around her. "I don't know how close we were to anything, but I wasn't scared, but exhilarated and confident," she wrote in her diary. The landscape reminded her alternately of her own farm in Westchester and of *War and Peace*. She found the Red Army men with whom she encamped completely delightful. "These are warm, strong men," she noted, and she mentioned flirting with General Chernov, who gave her an engraved cigarette lighter as a memento. Over dinner she began joking with the men:

I said that I thought I was dining with more generals than any woman since Catherine the Great and they were over-delighted with this. We drank a great many toasts,—to Pres. Roosevelt, to the Red Army, and so many to my health that I began to wonder if I looked ill. Russian men, almost all of them, have a very attractive quality; they are men who know they are men and like all such act with simplicity and tenderness. Especially these men who are happy to see a foreigner and a woman—each has told me this with every glass of vodka—and anxious to show me that war has not roughened them. I think every little girl, when she is about thirteen, has a dream of being grown up and going to the ball. A whole room of handsome gentlemen in uniform turn as one and move toward her to do her bidding for the rest of the evening. That dream never came true for me, and I never thought about it again until this dinner. When I did think about it I began to laugh.[63]

Stalin(ism), Patriotism, and Disloyalty

Hellman reported in *An Unfinished Woman* (1969) that she left Moscow a week early to avoid having to talk to Stalin, who granted her an interview though she had not asked for one. She did write a warm letter to him upon departing, apparently in response to a message from him. She thanked Stalin for "the truly wonderful three months I have had in your country," and added that it was difficult to find words that expressed the depth of her feeling: "All of my country feels great respect and admiration for the Soviet Union: I would like now to try to tell them about the warmth, the good-nature, the humor, and the true human tenderness that I have seen everywhere."[64]

The warmth that Hellman felt toward the Russian people was real, and the feeling seems to have been mutual, judging by the many letters she received from Russians, ranging from actors who had performed in her plays, to directors like Pudovkin, Eisenstein, and Alexandrov, to women she came to know during her stay. At the end of a diary that Hellman kept during her trip, she mentions someone's comment that her visit to the Soviet Union had done more good than anyone else's. Quite possibly this feeling came from the direct, human connections she was able to establish with a significant number of individuals.[65]

That Hellman did not, and supposedly did not want to, meet Stalin directly would not shield her from the charges of Stalinism that nagged her for the rest of her life. Indeed, these charges were fundamental to claims about her "dishonesty." In *An Unfinished Woman*, she says that when she went to the Moscow Theatre Festival in 1937, "I did not even know I was there in the middle of the ugliest purge period." Even if she had known, it might not have made a difference: in 1938 she signed a statement published in the communist *New Masses* supporting the Moscow trials. By 1969 Hellman had clearly changed her position on the purges. But she also, at that point, claimed to have written in her diary in 1944 (on pages that I did not find in the Russian diaries in her archive) that "great honour must and will be paid those who did protest the criminal purges. It is hard to judge those who tossed about in silent doubt and despair, but it is even harder to believe that they did not understand what was happening."[66]

Turning a blind eye to the purges came to represent the worst of Stalinist willed ignorance in the eyes of the Popular Front's critics. However, in the context of the Second World War, such blindness could be made into a patriotic gesture, as it was in *Mission to Moscow* and Genevieve Taggard's *Falcon: Poems on Soviet Themes* (1942). The latter is a collection of poems Taggard wrote over twenty-five years, and many are from her 1936–1937 visit to the Soviet Union, where she socialized with Moscow residents like Markoosha Fischer, who, as we have seen, wrote later about the atmosphere of fear at that time. But in a poem like Taggard's 1937 "Black Sea Rest Home," there is only hope. The poem recalls the history and legend tied to this part of the world: Jason and the Golden Fleece, "ancient peoples," and advancements achieved through "the bent backs of slaves." Now, "what no man saw on earth before, never before, new and like rock to stay: / wealth in a just scale, the start without finish, the Soviet." Here, "the skilled worker rests." Here, "makers of the next great age strip themselves and swim."[67] Other poems in the collection celebrating wartime heroism implicitly rest on foundations laid during this time period. Maybe Hellman—and Taggard—truly did not realize the purges were going on. Or maybe they convinced themselves that whatever was happening represented progress.

Some of Hellman's critics claimed that her depiction in *The North Star* of a prosperous collective farm in Ukraine, whose members valiantly resist the Nazis, was done at the bidding of the Soviet government. The Soviet government had starved Ukrainian peasants as punishment to the kulaks (or land-owning peasants) for resisting collectivization a decade earlier; once war came, many Ukrainians actually collaborated with the Nazis, not the Soviets. Then again, Bourke-White's photographs document Ukrainian collective farmers mobilizing against the Nazis.[68]

Beyond the film itself, many of Hellman's positions suggested acquiescence to the Soviet line. In 1945 the journalist Eric Sevareid asked her to comment on Finland (whose invasion had been widely condemned in the United States). She replied, "Well, really I can't remember anyone even mentioning the Finns. Particularly since they feel the Finns are guilty of some of the worst atrocities. I think they've been given generous peace terms." And then she changed the subject.[69] Although this response might suggest she simply followed the Communist "line," Hellman's plays were consistently antifascist, even during the Nazi-Soviet pact (during which time Communists essentially abandoned their antifascist rhetoric). Indeed, Communists had criticized her play *Watch on the Rhine* when it first came out for just this reason.

Bourke-White seems to have been more aware of Stalin's purges while in Moscow but also less concerned about them. That sense of distance may have helped her escape charges of Stalinism. Not only did Bourke-White actually meet Stalin; she compulsively petitioned Soviet authorities for the chance to photograph him. One photograph of Stalin she shot subsequently became an iconic image of the US-Soviet alliance, appearing on the cover of *Life*. In *Shooting the Russian War* and in at least one published article, she describes her efforts to get to the man and her unexpected success at getting a hint of a smile out of him: she dropped to her knees to photograph Stalin from a low angle, and then put his interpreter to work holding flashbulbs for her. She wanted to photograph Stalin sitting down or talking, "but I don't know what you can do with a dictator when he thinks he wants to stand in the middle of the rug," she writes. Of the man himself, she notes, in words that echo Anna Louise Strong's a decade earlier: "He looks like a completely strong person, immobile and unemotional, but through it all one gets the distinct impression of a person with a great deal of charm and a magnetic personality."[70]

In *Shooting the Russian War*, Bourke-White acknowledges that "whatever dissension existed during the last few years was wiped out. Thus no organized opposition is left." She says the "drastic measures" helped explain the Soviet Union's strength, but "did leave a wake of fear. Even among the patriotic and loyal, this fear was noticeable." She implies that those purged were, in fact, guilty or at least that rightness prevailed. Her story about her Moscow secretary, Tatiana, is instructive here. Tatiana, whom Bourke-White describes as "the kindest person who ever stepped into a human skin," had been arrested "during the time of the purge, in early 1938," but had been amazed rather than frightened when it happened. "'I didn't worry,' she said. 'I knew I had done nothing wrong.'" Tatiana spent two years in Central Asia on a prison farm and six months in a Moscow prison, but all along, she said, "I had faith that I would be set free." She was released when it was revealed that a saboteur "had been maneuvering to get the most efficient office workers imprisoned" to slow up work. "He was liquidated and all the people he had attempted to incriminate were set free," she explained. By Bourke-White's telling, Tatiana felt no resentment toward the government. She was reinstated in her old job, with back pay for the work she had missed, and even was given a new apartment, "much bigger than my last and looking out over a park," as compensation.[71] If Tatiana's experience was at all representative, it would appear that there may have been a few mistakes in the flurry to find enemies of the regime, but the mistakes—necessary costs of a necessary effort—had mostly been rectified. Certainly this is the picture the Soviet government would have presented.

Wartime work in praise of the Soviet Union would later dog both Hellman and Bourke-White—along with many others. Hellman was blacklisted from Hollywood after her "unfriendly" testimony before the House Committee on Un-American Activities. However, she would continue to work as a playwright. Bourke-White was cited by HUAC but never called to testify. Her FBI file is nearly as long as Hellman's, and *Life*'s editors had to fend off complaints about their "red" photographer. Still, as one scholar has noted, "the witch hunt did not harm her professional career nor damage her respected position among photography greats." Bourke-White submitted a statement to the Secretary of Defense in January 1951, in which she insisted that she had never been a Communist, had never knowingly supported Communist organizations, and had "never been sympathetic to the Communist Party or Communist ideology." Although Bourke-White supported numerous left-wing organizations, it is doubtful that she was ever an actual member of the Communist Party; Hellman almost certainly was, even if she was notoriously bad at following the party line.[72]

In her 1951 statement, Bourke-White claimed the trip she and Caldwell took to Russia in 1941 had been taken at the initiative of higher-ups in the Luce empire. In truth, she and Caldwell had been corresponding since at least 1936 with Soviet cultural figures—first Sergey Dinamov, a member of the International Association of Revolutionary Writers (MORP), and then, after Dinamov was purged in 1938, Mikhael Appletin, who became director of MORP. In April 1939 Caldwell wrote Appletin expressing hope that he and Bourke-White could come to Russia in about six months.[73] The trip had not been instigated by Luce. Neither woman was entirely honest about her Soviet experiences. But given that they were simultaneously encouraged and condemned by different branches of the US government for their interest in the Soviet Union, this lack of full disclosure should not come as so great a surprise.

In the end, what revelations come from looking at Hellman and Bourke-White together, in relation to the war, and in relation to the Soviet Union? Although their intentions were repeatedly questioned by critics, the two women came by their hatred of Nazis honestly: Hellman was Jewish and Bourke-White was half Jewish, though they did both have problematic relationships to Judaism.[74] The animosity the two women aroused from various quarters is rooted in the fact that they were women who succeeded, dramatically (if not without compromises), in male terrain. But the Soviet dimension is also key. In the context of the war effort, making the Russians look good was necessary to upholding an alliance that was always fragile, and never especially popular in the United States. But neither woman went to the Soviet Union or documented its war efforts merely (if at all) as expressions of patriotic duty. As independent women committed to their creative vision, their careers, and their freedom to love as they wished and to generally resist norms of femininity, Hellman and Bourke-White would have found Soviet defiance of bourgeois gender roles—most strikingly in sending women to the front—deeply appealing. These same factors, as Ayn Rand's HUAC testimony suggests, were part of what made the Soviet Union so threatening to some Americans, particularly once traditional gender roles took on new importance during the Cold War.[75] No wonder, then, that Hellman's and Bourke-White's missions to Moscow were subject to so much debate.

Ironically, neither Bourke-White nor Hellman were deeply invested in Stalin or in Soviet ideology. Both were impressed by the level of Soviet resistance to Nazism, and were attracted to many other aspects of life in the Soviet Union, not least of which was Soviet appreciation for *them*. Anna Louise Strong, by contrast, was deeply loyal to Stalin, but she was never fully appreciated in the Soviet Union. Moreover, while both Hellman and Bourke-White enjoyed commercial if not always critical success in the United States, few of Strong's books—other than her autobiography— ever sold particularly well, nor were they hailed by critics.

Near the end of Strong's *Wild River*, one of the boys from Stepan's old gang, who had joined Red Dawn farm with him and had built the Dnieper Dam with him, wonders aloud, as they destroy the dam and as Anya and her comrades burn the farm in order to leave nothing for the Nazis, if they are back right where they had started. Stepan replies: "No, Ivan, we're not back where we started. We're two hundred million lifetimes ahead. We built not only the Red Dawn Farm and the Dnieper Dam. We built the people that burned the farm and blew up the dam in the war to save the world." Although *Wild River* received a number of positive reviews, a negative one is particularly telling. Bertram Wolfe, in the *New York Times*, called the book interesting primarily "as a document of psychological self-revelation." Strong, Wolfe said, is "a symbol of a whole generation of worshipful pilgrims—whose 'reports' tell more of their will-to-believe than of what they saw in Moscow."[76]

If during the Second World War there was room in the most distinguished arenas of popular culture to praise the Soviet Union—and particularly the new Soviet woman—in Academy Award–nominated films, in *Life* magazine, and in novels that earned at least a modicum of serious attention and acclaim, it was already becoming very clear that the American love affair with Soviet Russia was near its end. Thus one reviewer could praise Markoosha Fischer for discussing the Great Terror in her 1944 book *My Lives in Russia*—given the fact that "it is not very fashionable, or even tactful, at the moment to write critical books about the internal affairs of the Soviet Union"—and yet also condemn the "utopian blindness" that made her continue to hope that the Soviet Union would one day be democratic.[77]

The US-Soviet alliance was a marriage of convenience. At the end of the war, the Stalinist terror that preceded the war, and to a degree continued after it, made many truths about Soviet achievements—including the new Soviet woman, who was hailed in novels like *Wild River*, in exhibits created by the NCASF, in Bourke-White's photographs and writings, and in films like *The North Star* and *Song of Russia*—seem like wishful lies.

Red Spy Queens?

On May 21, 1942, the American writer Josephine Herbst, living in Washington, DC, and—like many antifascist creative types—doing propaganda work in support of the war effort, returned from a lunch break to find herself greeted by a uniformed security guard. The guard "padlocked her desk and locker, pawed over her handbag, and escorted her unceremoniously from the building."[1] Taken to "a big, impersonal room" with "clean tables, shiny chairs, and vacant windows opening on a wispy sky," Herbst found herself having to justify the course of her adult life. "It is Reported that in 1930 you went to the Soviet Union," a man said. More accusations, all apparently inseparable from this one, followed. As she described it:

> The voices of the men, in ritualistic devotion to the recurring phrase, *It is Reported*, began to sound like an incantation and to cast a spell. . . . I might say that in the whirlwind of events, doors had slammed. The vagabond road to the twenties was blocked. The inquiring journeys of the thirties . . . had ended

in this office. . . . Should I call up, from the debris of the twenties, Rilke's impassioned line "Choose to be changed. With the flame be enraptured!" Too literary for the present customers. But it had ignited the flambeau of the thirties, "Change the world," and no doubt about it, the world had changed. So had I.[2]

This particular investigation, which ended with Herbst losing her job, came relatively early in a long line of investigations that destroyed Popular Front efforts to create a more equitable social order and to promote a "left-feminist" agenda that included "interest in labor, poverty, housing, public health, health insurance, consumer rights, and international peace." That agenda also included more-personal concerns: access to abortion, birth control, and divorce; the ability to have both a career and a family; and an ideal of comradely love, free from economic incentives. During the Cold War, all of these things seemed to resonate too closely with Bolshevik rhetoric and practice. And advocating them marked a person as potentially subversive.[3]

As Herbst confronted passive-voiced accusations, which her questioners gleaned from a surveillance system that seems quaint by today's standards, she tried to square her own memories with the litany of "facts" they recited. "Should I try to go back to the crossroads where my own history intersected with the history of our time? But every crossroads is a split second. And what would it get me?"[4]

She had acted out of conscience, but in the minds of her interrogators she was disloyal, a traitor, possibly even dangerous. The "facts" they reported back to her now sounded like falsehoods, bereft of the context in which they occurred. The gap between her memories and their accusations made it seem to Herbst as if the men were speaking a foreign language. "What I understood very well was that the dry rattle of all these *It is Reporteds* might be calculated to reduce some of my best yesterdays to outworn slogans; telephone numbers of people who were no longer there, or were dead; and foxed files." She tried to answer with her own question: "Why do you keep saying *It is Reported*, when it is a fact?" But then she caught herself wondering what to do with the really essential question: "What is a *fact?* Who is to interpret it? What ideas ride on its back? And a protean Me wanted to break the cords that bind, and to soar, if only back to my attic, where there was some hope of getting to the source of things."[5]

What might she find in her attic? Old newspapers. Publications like "the *Little Review*, which I had carried to classes at Berkeley in 1917 instead of a ball of wool to knit a sock for a soldier boy." She had not knitted soldiers socks. Even this was damning. *The Masses.* Photographs. Oh, those could be very damning. There was one of her and the writer Nathanael West, he holding a hammer, she holding a sickle, "crossed, as duelists had once crossed swords." Most damning of all, a photograph of Herbst in Moscow: "portrait of the Author in a round cap, three-quarter view; eyelashes sloping downward over serious, downcast eyes; hand on table, open like an open book, expression watchful, listening, tender and intense."[6]

I returned to this essay from Herbst's memoirs after reading a scathing portrait of her in Stephen Koch's *Double Lives: Spies and Writers in the Secret Soviet War of Ideas against the West* (1994). Koch concedes that there is "no evidence that [Herbst] herself was personally active in the Washington [espionage] apparatus." But he immediately qualifies this acknowledgement, noting that her "propaganda assignments" for Willi Müzenberg and Otto Katz, that is, "working as a 'journalist' in Spain, Berlin, and Latin America, clearly made her, for all intents and purposes, an agent of the Comintern." Even if she was not guilty of espionage per se, "at the very least," he says, she "had guilty knowledge of the Washington espionage operations."[7]

Herbst had been on my radar, to a degree, but I had not done extensive research on her, given that her 1930 trip, lasting only a few weeks, to attend the Kharkov writers' congress seems to have been her only visit to the Soviet Union. Still, the contrast between the woman who emerges in Herbst's memoir and the one described by Koch—a woman not just treacherous but also "domineering, abusive, and foul-mouthed"— seemed a fitting entry point for considering some of the thorniest issues haunting this book. "It is hard to retain a sense of proportion about espionage," Ellen Schrecker and Maurice Isserman have noted. "Merely to evoke it risks killing off any attempt at intellectual fine shading. Who, after all, wants to take a position that even appears to be sympathetic to that benighted creature, the spy?"[8]

But in a book like this one, could I really avoid the issue of espionage? My concern with the attraction that Russian revolutionary ideology held for American new women did not necessarily lead me to spies, but it did, from the beginning, raise the question of loyalty. Loyalty to one's country, a set of ideas, one's own experience, one's sense of justice, a party, a lover, a community. For whom, or for what, should one sacrifice, believe, trust? All of these things—and fear that critics would accuse me of hiding or denying something if I didn't go there—finally made me start actively looking for spies. If nothing else, I wanted to be able to explain why the people I was looking at were different from those murky, dangerous figures beyond the pale of history.

By the logic of both McCarthyism and present-day right-wingers, the lines between upper- or lowercase "c" communist, "progressive," "fellow traveler," and "New Deal liberal" blend together. Do these labels cloud or reveal deeper truths? The contrast between the very human and sympathetic woman in Herbst's own accounting and the deceptive shrew Koch describes repeats in many other instances. Usually the contrast is between a flattened or distorted description from the perspective of a political opponent and a very different portrait in the writings of friends or in a person's own words.[9] On the other side of the coin, there are examples like Tony Hiss's loving memoir about his father, which was meant to exculpate him from charges of treason. The memoir proves that Alger Hiss was a good father. But does that mean he wasn't a spy?[10]

In my effort to identify "spies," I discovered many more shades of gray than a Cold War–inflected discourse—which places spies somewhere near pedophiles on the spectrum of social acceptability—admits. My search led me to the Comintern archives in Moscow, where I discovered in the *lichnoe delo*, or "personal file," of Anna Louise Strong that Milly Bennett, after she moved to Madrid in 1936 to cover the war, regularly sent information back to Moscow about volunteers in Spain.[11] Was that spying?

What was I to make of the long autobiographical statement by Myra Page, whom I knew to be a member of the Communist Party of the United States (CPUSA)?[12] John Earl Haynes, an expert on Soviet spying, told me this kind of statement was generally a prelude to doing underground or illegal work for the party. But Haynes had also told me that I wouldn't be given access to any *lichnie dela* in Moscow. Did someone at the Russian State Archive of Socio-Political History, which did grant me access to just about every *lichnoe delo* I requested, surmise that I would interpret these files differently than the conservative Haynes? How *should* I interpret them?

Sylvia Chen, before moving to the United States from Moscow, submitted a memo to the Comintern stating that her aim in going was "to work for C.P. in America through my dance, or in any other capacity which the party thinks suitable for me." What did she mean by this? Could her memo make her a traitor to her adopted country, even in light of the fact that she was denied American citizenship and constantly risked being deported because her Chinese heritage made her ineligible for naturalization?[13] Similar exceptional circumstances make it less simple to condemn African Americans' attraction to the Soviet Union.

Mary Leder, in the course of trying to get a visa that would allow her to return home to the United States to be with her family, agreed to spy for the Soviets without much hesitation. She spent nearly eighteen months at a special, secret school, learning foreign languages, shortwave radio operation, microphotography, and Morse code, and studying history and current events, after which she prepared to go to the United States to await further instructions. As it turned out, her assignment was called off before she could go: there had been too many arrests and the entire agency was at risk.[14] Had she carried out her assignment, she would have been a traitor to her homeland. But there was no other path to going home. Reading her memoir, one finds it hard not to sympathize with her predicament.

I am less interested in the question of spying per se than in legacies, and loyalties. In 1969 Ruth Epperson Kennell published *Theodore Dreiser and the Soviet Union, 1927–1945*. "There may be a timely message for our rebellious youth and their troubled elders in these pages," Kennell wrote in the book's introduction. Those "rebellious youth" called themselves the "New Left" in part because they rejected the Old Left's loyalty to the Soviet Union. As Kennell saw it, "two generations of students have been brainwashed. Their textbooks have been purged of meaningful facts about the Russian Revolution, the causes of World War II, and the decisive role of the Red Army in our common victory." Now an old woman, trying to redeem her own past while reassessing Dreiser's legacy, Kennell was in a difficult position. She dedicated her book "To the Memory of Sergey Dinamov, 1901–1939," described as "a beloved friend of Theodore Dreiser during his stay in Moscow." A prominent literary critic and loyal Party member, Dinamov had been shot in the purges of the original Bolsheviks. This dedication may have been Kennell's attempt to condemn the Soviet Union's excesses without forgetting its achievements.[15]

About a year after Kennell's book was published, Jessica Smith sent her a letter apologizing for having been out of touch for almost four decades.[16] Much had happened between Kennell's breezy *American Mercury* pieces (which Kennell told Smith she regretted writing) and the wistful letters she and Smith exchanged nearly forty years later. An FBI informant claimed that Kennell's former lover, the journalist Junius Wood, had identified her (in letters recovered after his death) as an OGPU (Soviet secret police) agent. I find this doubtful, but not altogether impossible.[17]

Smith had testified in the 1950s before the Senate Judiciary Committee (and HUAC) but refused to answer most of the committee's questions, especially those concerning her first and second husbands: before dying in a car accident in 1935, Harold Ware allegedly cultivated covert Soviet operatives within the Roosevelt administration, and John Abt, a member (along with Herbst's former husband John Herrman) of the so-called Ware group, was also a suspected spy. Smith herself allegedly passed various kinds of information to Soviet authorities.[18]

Like Josephine Herbst, Smith apparently felt that she and her questioners were talking past each other: "If you really wanted to find out any information, I would think that you would question me about our magazine, about the work through which we have reached the public and done our best . . . to create a basis for decent understanding between nations, for the ending of atomic war, and for peace [she was editor of the *New World Review*, successor to *Soviet Russia Today*, which she'd also edited].... Why have you not . . . if this is an honest investigation, tried to question me along such lines?" Interrogators repeatedly asked Smith whether she had ever been a member of the Communist Party—as if they didn't already know, and as if that would reveal everything there was to know about her. To Smith's complaints, one of the men replied, "I am assuring you that this is not a witch hunt, and it is nothing that anyone enjoys. We are here representing the American people in a job that is given to us."[19] Was Smith disloyal to the United States? I don't think she believed herself to be. Was she dangerous? By the standards of the 1950s social order, she was, but that's not saying much.

Louise Thompson, who married the Civil Rights leader and Communist Party activist William Patterson in 1940, emerged as a leader in the party by the late 1930s. The FBI and J. Edgar Hoover himself closely monitored Thompson Patterson until the mid-1970s. Reports repeatedly returned to the fact that she had traveled to the Soviet Union "in 1932 or 1933." They also highlighted her involvement in organizations like the National Negro Congress, the American League Against War and Fascism, the Council on African Affairs, the International Labor Defense, the Civil Rights Congress, and the Sojourners for Truth and Justice. Admittedly, all or most of these organizations had Communist connections, but their goals—promoting civil rights, peace, the rights of labor, and so on—were not exactly un-American. Thompson Patterson, at one time or another, had written for *Working Woman* (a Communist magazine) and had edited the *Harlem Liberator* (ditto, sort of). At a Colored American Day celebration, she'd spoken against the torture of Lluang Ping, a Chinese working-class leader. She'd made speeches condemning lynching and had toured the country with lynch victims' wives. She'd even been arrested for "vagrancy" in Birmingham in 1934, undoubtedly when she was working on the defense of the Scottsboro Boys. She'd "criticized President Truman's Point Four Program [a technical assistance program for developing countries] as an attempt to shackle the African people to Wall Street's program." She was "interested in Negro History week." She'd written to

UNESCO, "urging the conference to direct attention to discrimination against Negro women in jobs and education." Yes, she was a Communist. But the fact that Patterson's work on behalf of civil rights, women's rights, and labor, and against fascism, lynching, and colonialism—the bulk of activity referenced in her FBI file—justified calling her a "security risk" in the eyes of the United States government demonstrates why this very formulation, especially during the Cold War, was highly problematic, serving to limit legitimate dissent and movements for social justice.[20]

What motivated women who almost certainly *did* pass information to the Soviets or the CPUSA? They had differing motivations, ranging from opposition to fascism or colonialism, to genuine admiration of the Soviet Union, to the desire for approval, love, or power.[21] Martha Dodd, daughter of the American ambassador to Germany, apparently began spying to prove her love for a Soviet diplomat who'd been instructed by the KGB to win her affections. She also had a friend in the German resistance, Mildred Harnack (who also became a spy), whom she greatly admired. She went further than most devoted activists in trying to aid the Soviet Union, yet nothing she gave Moscow, including reports on conversations overheard in the American embassy, seems to have been of critical importance for US security. Dodd spent only a couple of weeks in Russia, but her writings emphasize the ways the Soviet system benefited women. In this respect she also seems very much like other American women who noted the very same things.[22] What, then, to make of that crucial difference?

Dodd eluded a subpoena by fleeing to Mexico (and Cuba, and Czechoslovakia). Anna Louise Strong also lived out her final years in a Communist country, China. In Strong's case, this was not because she was hiding from the law, but because she felt rejected by both her native land and her adopted homeland, the USSR. In 1949, following various conflicts related to her work in China, Strong was arrested in the middle of the night. She was taken to Lubyanka prison, where "her belongings were confiscated, [and] she was led to a small cell and told to strip naked." After several inquisitions, it became clear that the Soviets believed she was spying. She was expelled from the land to which she'd devoted nearly all her energies and hopes for the past thirty years. Back in the

United States, Strong became a pariah among American Communists, even as the FBI questioned her loyalty.[23] Five years later, she was cleared by the Soviets, but her reputation in the American Left had already been irreparably damaged.

Still, in some deep way, Strong continued to believe in the Soviet Union. In *The Stalin Era* (1956)—published the same year Khruschev made public the horrors enacted under Stalin—she acknowledged that innocent people had been purged in what she said were necessary efforts to rout a Nazi fifth column, but she implied that most of them didn't have it so bad. She described a friend who was arrested as a "wife of an enemy of the people" and exiled to a small town in Kazakhstan, where she worked as a teacher. "Once a month she had to report to a local GPU [secret police] official, an intelligent man with whom she had many interesting discussions." Later she was released.[24] The connotation is that this was a typical scenario.

Of course Stalin was paranoid, Strong wrote in the same book, for "the enemy had penetrated into the citadel of leadership" and "nobody knew who was loyal." After several good workers at the *Moscow News* were arrested, Mikhail Borodin had assured Strong that innocent people would eventually be released. But then Borodin himself was arrested and died in a labor camp in the Far East.[25]

The worst Strong would say of Stalin was that he violated rights that he had guaranteed to Soviet citizens, though he "thought he was saving the revolution thereby." The lesson from this was "that no man should be deified as Stalin was. . . . Eternal vigilance is the price of liberty and justice, not only under capitalism, but even more under socialism." Like Kennell, Strong held out hope for the younger generation: as an elderly woman in the 1960s, she sent money to Students for a Democratic Society and offered praise for the Black Panthers. Today she barely merits a glance from historians. "Ubiquitous Stalinist hack" apparently says it all.[26]

That term, "Stalinist," has been applied to anyone on the Left who did not publicly condemn the Soviet Union. If revelations from Soviet archives and decoded Venona cables have been hailed as cause to rethink historians' denunciations of McCarthyism, I'm wondering what can be said about (and from) our current moment as we look through the lens of those no longer new revelations to and through the lens of women in the 1960s and 1970s. In 1978, Lillian Hellman admitted that she "was, indeed, late to believe the political-intellectual persecutions under Stalin" but still insisted that she had been "nobody's girl." Her memoirs revisit trips to the Soviet Union with the suggestion that she possessed more critical faculties than she in fact exercised at the time.[27]

And so it is for Herbst who, in recalling thirty years later her visit to the Kharkov writers' congress, said she was disturbed by the number of outstanding writers who were missing and by the emphasis on ideological correctness over literary quality. These criticisms are nowhere in the report she published on the conference in 1930, right after it happened.[28] Recognizing this, I still find myself moved by her words:

> But who of our literary generation was not a Crime Snob of a sort? Who did not lean toward the underdogs, peddlers, thieves, prostitutes, beyond the call of duty; all the underbelly of the world, which looked so fat and smug on top? Perhaps we had gone to Russia because it had been so almost universally despised by the cautious and the respectable. . . . Who of us had not dreamed of freedom, limpid affections, intensity above all, passionate friendships; and had not become, as well, demanding, possessive? We wanted the universe; we wanted ALL. And leaning out from our traveling trains to wave Farewell, Goodbye, we rounded that long curve, back to war again.[29]

After the Second World War, after the Cold War, after everything, what remains for those who have been reluctant to acknowledge the Soviet Union's place in the legacy of the Left in general, or "left feminism" in particular? Both the Soviet Union and Communism itself are largely taboo subjects, despite their outsized influence on many individuals—because, it seems to me, to be even a small "c" communist was be disloyal, and if disloyal, a traitor, and if a traitor, a potential spy, and if that, all discussion stops.

These days, as we try to distinguish refugees from terrorists and legitimate dissent from security threats, and as women continue to struggle with the same things they struggled with in the 1920s, 1930s, and

1940s (balancing a career and motherhood; working to attain equity with men in the political, economic, and domestic spheres; finding a romantic relationship that is truly a partnership of equals), there is much to be learned—about desire, faith, human fallibility, and lost possibility— from the hopes and failures of yesteryear's new women, women for whom a "Russian chapter" once seemed as if it might rewrite the entire story.[30]

ACKNOWLEDGMENTS

As a child of the Cold War (I was born in 1968 and graduated from college in 1990), I had long felt an inexplicable fascination with the Soviet Union. In my senior year of high school my history teacher, Mr. Elges, assigned *The Communist Manifesto*, and I felt a thrilling kind of subversive pleasure in reading it. Communism, we all knew, was something taboo, but we didn't have the kind of fear of it that the older generation seemed to have. I'd also grown up with an appreciation for Russian culture: at a young age my grandfather took my sister and me to see the Russian circus in Madison Square Garden; later he would send me books by Tolstoy, Gogol, Chekhov, Turgenev, and other great Russian authors. In college I thought of double-majoring in Russian studies and American studies, but Russian did not come easily to me, and besides, there was so much I wanted to learn about my own country. Years later, however, Russia haunted my scholarship. Studying the US Left for my first book, I began to feel like the Soviet Union was the great elephant in the room; liberal and left-wing magazines from the 1930s are rife with positive portraits of the Soviet Union, with special attention devoted to women and children. Yet other than folks seeking to prove there really was a Communist conspiracy to create a "Soviet America," American fascination with the Soviet experiment has not received very much attention.

Throughout the process of writing this book, I kept coming back to the nesting dolls that my grandparents brought back from a visit to the Soviet Union when I was six or seven. I can still recall my intense desire to pry open the last tiny doll hidden within the others, as if that would reveal some fundamental truth. This book, in a sense, is my attempt to open that doll.

To properly acknowledge everyone who has helped this book come into being during its more than ten-year gestation would take up too much space in a book that is already long enough, but I should at least mention the names of institutions, organizations, and especially individuals without whose help it never would have happened.

The Children's Literature Association funded a fateful trip to Eugene, Oregon, which unexpectedly shifted my attention from Ruth Epperson Kennell's children's books to her two years living in an American colony in Siberia. Once my topic came into focus, I received funding for this project from the National Endowment for the Humanities, the Schlesinger Library at Harvard University, the Sophia Smith Collection at Smith College, New York University's Center for the Study of the Cold War, the Jay C. and Ruth Halls Visiting Scholar Award at the University of Wisconsin, the Harry Ransom Humanities Center, the University of Texas's College of Liberal Arts (in the form of a Humanities Research Award and, most recently, a subvention grant to offset publication costs for this book), UT's vice president for research (in the form of two Special Research Grants), the UT Graduate School (in the form of a Summer Research Assignment), and UT's Center for Russian and Eastern European Studies. I also received funding from UT that allowed me to present my work at conferences. I am also grateful for a UT Humanities Institute Faculty Fellowship and an Honorary Fellowship from the Institute for Research in the Humanities at the University of Wisconsin.

I'm indebted to all the Russian teachers at UT and at the University of Wisconsin who let me sit in their classes: Hyoungsup Kim, Jennifer

Tishler, Amanda Murphy, Filip Zachoval, Bella Jordan, Alexei Lalo, and Gil Rappaport. The American Studies Department at the University of Texas at Austin has supported me in numerous ways; I owe special debts to chairs Steve Hoelscher and Elizabeth Englehardt and support staff Stephanie Kaufman and Ella Schwartz.

I'm also grateful for the access and support I received at numerous libraries and archives: (including, but not limited to) the University of Oregon Special Collections (especially Linda Long), the Tamiment Library (the late Michael Nash, Peter Filardo, Kevyne Baar, Andrew Lee, Kate Donovan, and Sara Moazeni), the New York Public Library for the Performing Arts (Susan Kraft, Charles Perrier, and Cassie Mey), the New York Public Library's Arts and Humanities Branch Special Collections (Tal Nadan), the Wisconsin Historical Society, the University of Washington Special Collections (Nicole Bouche and James Stack), the Sophia Smith Library, the Schlesinger Library (Sarah Hutcheon and Ellen Shea), the Hoover Library, the Westover School Archives (Muffie Green), the Beinecke (Adrienne Sharpe and Mary Ellen Budney) and Sterling Libraries at Yale University, the Harry Ransom Humanities Center, the Syracuse University Library (Nicolette Dobrowolski), Emory University Library (Kathy Shoemaker), the International Institute for Social History in Amsterdam, the American Friends Service Committee Library (Don Davis), the Swarthmore College Peace Collection, Haverford College Special Collections, the Friends Library in London (Josef Keith), the Biblioteque Nationale de France, the Bodleian Libraries at the University of Oxford (Colin Harris), the Wellcome Library, the Marx Memorial Library in London, the Library of Congress (John Earl Haynes), the University of Illinois Special Collections (Mark Bullock), the Huntington Library (Sue Hodson), the Minnesota Historical Society, UCLA Special Collections, the American Foundation for the Blind (Helen Selsden), the Brooklyn Museum (Beth Kusner), Occidental College Special Collections (Ann Marr), the University of Pennsylvania Special Collections (Daniel Traister), the Seeley G. Mudd Manuscript Library at Princeton University, the Federal Bureau of Investigation (David M. Hardy), the National Archives, the Amherst College Center for Russian Culture (Stanley Rabinowitz), Reuther Library at Wayne State University, and the University of Texas

Libraries, especially Interlibrary Loan Services. And, in Moscow, where archival adventures are unlike anything I've ever experienced, the State Archive of the Russian Federation (GARF), the Russian State Archive of Literature and Art (RGALI) (Vlada Gyduk), the Russian State Archive of Socio-Political History (RGASPI) (Svetlana Rosenthal), and, especially, the Center for Preservation of Records of Personal Collections, now part of the Central State Archive of the City of Moscow (TsGA) (Victoria Smolentseva). Thanks for help with navigation go to Ani Mukherji, Sean Gillen, Andy Spencer, and Marina Sorokina. I can't imagine Moscow without Joan Neuberger or Lisa Kirschenbaum.

I received invaluable research assistance in Moscow from Liubov Puhova and Daria Lotareva, with additional guidance from Sergei Zhuravlev, as well as translation assistance from Galina Belokurova. In the United States, I received research assistance of various kinds from Alyse Camus, Peter Carlson, Andi Gustavson, Christina Hood, Melody Ivins, Rebecca Onion, Annie Petersen, Matthew Prickett, and Camille Ricketts, and translation assistance from Andrey Bredstein, Irina Levshina, and Katya Cotey. And also Kevin Platt. For very kind assistance with general research or practical queries, thanks go to Julia Allen, Francis Beckett, Allison Blakely, Eliot Borenstein, James Boylan, Donna Kornhaber, Bertrude Patenaude, Karen Petrone, Jennifer Polk, Ishtiak Rahman, Thomas Riggio, Meredith Roman, Rigmaila Salys, David Shneer, Tracy Strong, Bethany Wiggin, and Andrew Wilbur.

For fruitful discussions, suggestions, and feedback that helped me think through the work, thanks go to Bob Abzug, Joyce Antler, Molly Arboleda, Marina Balina, Benjamin Balthaser, Sabrina Barton, Erin Battat, Kate Brown, Russ Castronovo, Mary Chapman, Choi Chatterjee, Cherene Cherrard-Johnson, Jason Andrew Cieply, Judy Coffin, Ann Cvetkovich, Susan David-Bernstein, Leslie DeBauche, Joe Dorinson, David Engerman, Susan Ferber, Sheila Fitzpatrick, Estelle Freedman, Andrea Friedman, Susan Stanford Friedman, Melanie Getreuer, David Goldstein, Dayo Gore, Ellen Gruber-Garvey, Linda Henderson, Cheryl Higashida, Dan and Helen Horowitz, Pernille Ipsen, Will Jones, Alice Kessler-Harris, Elizabeth Woodbury Kasius, Lisa Kirschenbaum, Kathryn Kish-Sklar, Aaron Lecklider, Steve Lee, Bob Lockhart, Elaine Tyler May, Lary May, Erik

McDuffie, Tony Michels, Bill Mullen, Joan Neuberger, Ginger Janet Pinkard, Marina Potoplyak, Riv-Ellen Prell, Jennifer Ratner-Rosenhagen, Ann Reynolds, Kim Reynolds, Jane Rosen, Karen Sanchez-Eppler, Brian Sandberg, Avery Slater, Landon Storrs, Jeremi Suri, Anastasia Ulanowicz, Maya Vinokour, Lise Vogel, Alan Wald, Hannah Chapelle Wojciehowski, and Jack Zipes. At the University of Wisconsin, Fran Hirsch and David McDonald allowed me to sit in on their graduate seminar and meet world-class scholars who took my work in important directions. Lauren Fox and Elizabeth Woodbury Kasius offered moral support at key moments.

Carola Burroughs, Victor Garlin, Joan Holden, MaryLouise Patterson, and Emily Socolov graciously granted interviews. Part of chapter 2 appeared (in an earlier version) in Julia L. Mickenberg, "Suffragettes and Soviets: American Feminists and the Specter of Revolutionary Russia," *Journal of American History* (vol. 100, no. 4, March 2014, pp. 1021–51). Material on Pauline Koner in chapter 5 appeared (in an earlier version) in *Lineages of the Literary Left: Essays in Honor of Alan Wald*, ed. Howard Brick, Robbie Lieberman, and Paula Rabinowitz (University of Michigan Press, 2015).

For reading my work and giving feedback, thanks go to Bettina Aptheker, Howard Brick, Janet Davis (who read the whole manuscript), Nan Enstad, Madeline Hsu, Helen Kinsella, Randy Lewis, Robbie Lieberman, Jeff Meikle, Mary Neuberger, Rob Oppenheim, Paula Rabinowitz, Sue Ridgley, Rebecca Rossen, and Miranda Spieler. I received especially valuable advice on making the book more readable from my amazing sister, Risa Mickenberg. And special thanks to Glenda Gilmore and an anonymous reader at the University of Chicago Press, my agent Geri Thoma, my wonderful editor Tim Mennel, and copyeditor Kelly Finefrock-Creed.

Deep thanks go to my family: my parents, Yvette Mickenberg and Ira Mickenberg; stepmother, Pat Fahey; in-laws Dean and Janet Birkholz; and sister, Risa Mickenberg—all of whom have taken care of my children while I was doing research and supported me in too many ways to enumerate. The memory of my grandparents, Eddie and Fannie Mickenberg, sustains much of my work. My daughters, Lena and Edie Birkholz, have been living with this book for most of their lives. They've traveled with me to New York City, Eugene, Amsterdam, and Boston; tolerated my leaving them for weeks at a time for various research trips; and otherwise allowed a project that has often consumed me to affect their lives in all sorts of ways. What I most appreciate is all the times they've made me slow me down, made me laugh, and reminded me of everything else in the world besides this book. Dan Birkholz has been there all along, listening, reading, editing, inspiring, encouraging, loving, and being super-husband-father. Thank you.

ABBREVIATIONS

ACSR	American Council on Soviet Relations
AFSC	American Friends Service Committee
AIK	Autonomous Industrial Colony of Kuzbas
ALS	Anna Louise Strong
ARA	American Relief Administration
ARC	American Red Cross
ASB	Alice Stone Blackwell
ASW	Anna Strunsky Walling
AWEC	American Women's Emergency Committee
BFWVRC	British Friends War Victims Relief Committee
BMP	Bureau of Motion Pictures
CPUSA	Communist Party of the United States
FSR	Friends of Soviet Russia
GARF	State Archive of the Russian Federation (Moscow)
GPU/OGPU	Joint State Political Directorate (Soviet secret police)
HRC	Harry Ransom Humanities Center (Austin, TX)

HUAC	House Un-American Activities Committee
IISH	International Institute of Social History (Amsterdam)
ILD	International Labor Defense
IWW	Industrial Workers of the World
JDC	Jewish Joint Distribution Committee
JRC	John Reed Colony
KUTV	Communist University of the Toilers of the East
LTP	Louise Thompson Patterson
MORP	International Association of Revolutionary Writers
NAACP	National Association for the Advancement of Colored People
NCASF	National Council of American Soviet Friendship
NEP	New Economic Policy
NWP	National Woman's Party
NYPL	New York Public Library (New York City)
OWI	Office of War Information
PSR	Partia sotsialistov-revoliutsionerov (Socialist Revolutionary Party)
REK	Ruth Epperson Kennell
RGALI	Russian State Archive of Literature and Art (Moscow)
RGASPI	Russian State Archive of Socio-Political History (Moscow)
SAFRF	Society of American Friends of Russian Freedom
SR	Socialist Revolutionary
STASR	Society for Technical Aid to Soviet Russia
TRAM	Theatre of Working Youth
TsGA	Central State Archive of the City of Moscow
VOKS	All-Union Society for Cultural Relations with Foreign Countries
WKT	Wilbur K. Thomas

NOTES

INTRODUCTION

1. Milly Bennett, "American Girls in Red Russia," *EveryWeek*, May 28–29, 1932, 4.

2. The phrase "red Jerusalem" comes from Ruth Kennell and Milly Bennett, "They All Come to Moscow," *American Mercury*, Dec. 1931, 394.

3. The British comparisons are most self-evident, especially when it comes to the attraction to Russia among feminists; here Sylvia Pankhurst is a key figure. See, for example, Katherine Connelly, *Sylvia Pankhurst: Suffragette, Socialist and Scourge of Empire* (London: Pluto Press, 2013). Also see Christine Fauré, "The Utopia of the New Woman in the Work of Alexandra Kollontai and Its Impact on the French Feminist and Communist Press," in *Women in Culture and Politics: A Century of Change*, ed. Judith Friedlander, Blanche Wiesen Cook, Alice Kessler-Harris, and Carroll Smith-Rosenberg (Bloomington: Indiana University Press, 2006), 376–89.

4. Emma Goldman, *Living My Life*, abridged ed. (New York: Penguin Classics, 2006), 27; Pauline Koner diary, May 1–31, 1935, box 1, folder 14, Pauline Koner papers, New York Public Library (NYPL) for the Performing Arts; Margaret Bourke-White, *Eyes on Russia* (New York: Simon and Schuster, 1931), 23.

5. See Lewis S. Feuer, "American Travelers to the Soviet Union, 1917–32: The Formation of a Component of New Deal Ideology," *American Quarterly* 24 (1962): 119–49.

6. Eugene Lyons, *Assignment in Utopia* (New York: Harcourt, 1937), 329–30.

7. Hence what Thomas Schaub refers to as the "liberal narrative" of youthful idealism in the interwar years followed by "realism" in the postwar era. Thomas H. Schaub, *American Fiction in the Cold War* (Madison: University of Wisconsin Press, 1991). For just a few well-known examples, see Elizabeth Bentley, *Out of Bondage: The Story of Elizabeth Bentley* (New York: Devin-Adair, 1951); Whittaker Chambers, *Witness* (New York: Random House, 1952); Hede Massing, *This Deception* (New York: Duell, 1951); George S. Counts and Nucia Perlmutter Lodge, *The Country of the Blind: The Soviet System of Mind Control* (Boston: Houghton Mifflin, 1949). The phrase "evil empire" came from Ronald Reagan in the 1980s, but the sentiment nevertheless applied earlier. Also see Vivian Gornick, *The Romance of American Communism* (New York: Basic Books), 1977.

8. The term "darkest Russia" may have come from a play of that title first published in 1890 to expose violence against Russia's Jews; the term remained in popular usage. See Henry Grattan Donnelly, *Darkest Russia [A Play in 4 Acts]* (New York, 1891).

9. Winifred Harper Cooley and Carrie Chapman Catt, quoted in Nancy Cott, *The Grounding of Modern Feminism* (New Haven, CT: Yale University Press, 1987), 15, 14.

10. Christine Stansell, *American Moderns: Bohemian New York and the Creation of a New Century* (New York: Metropolitan Books, 2000), 43, 227, 321 (quotation). On the immigrant character of socialism, see Tony Michels, *A Fire in Their Hearts: Yiddish Socialists in New York* (Cambridge, MA: Harvard University Press, 2005). The phrase "new people" is a rough translation of the popular Soviet ideal of a *novy sovetsky chelovek*, or new Soviet person. For further discussion, see Kate A. Baldwin, *Beyond the Color Line and the Iron Curtain: Reading Encounters between Black and Red, 1922–1963* (Durham, NC: Duke University Press, 2002), 18.

11. Barbara Alpern Engel, *Women in Russia, 1700–2000* (New York: Cambridge University Press, 2004), 142 (quotation). The Lenin quotation is from a 1920 interview with Clara Zetkin; see http://sfr-21.org/zetkin.html (accessed Apr. 6, 2011). Wendy Z. Goldman, *Women, the State, and Revolution: Soviet Family Policy & Social Life, 1917–1936* (Cambridge: Cambridge University Press, 1995), 51. On the "General Decree on Wages," see Elizabeth A. Wood, *The Baba and the Comrade: Gender and Politics in Revolutionary Russia* (Bloomington: Indiana University Press, 1997), 50. The decree may have been passed as early as December 1917, but certainly by 1920. E. P. Frenkel', *Polovye prestupleniia* (Odessa: Svetoch, 1927), 12.

12. Engel, *Women in Russia*, 142–47; Wood, *The Baba and the Comrade*, 30–36, 51 (quotation); Nikolai Lenin, speech delivered at fourth Moscow City Conference of Non-Party Women Workers (Sept. 1919), in V. I. Lenin, *Women and Society*, Little Lenin Library (New York: International Publishers, 1938), 16. Examples of feminist journals covering Soviet Russia include Ellen Hayes, "Woman, Bolshevism, and Home," *Woman Citizen* 3, no. 47 (Apr. 19, 1919): 1002; John Rockman, "The Alleged 'Nationalization' of Women," *International Woman Suffrage News* 13, no. 8 (May 1919): 110–11; "As We Unfortunately Get No Direct News from the Women of Russia," *International Woman Suf-*

frage News 19, no. 2 (Nov. 1924): 19; Ruby A. Black, "Women in Russia," *Equal Rights* 11, no. 50 (Jan. 24, 1925): 395; "Russia Becoming Feminist," *Equal Rights* 11, no. 50 (June 24, 1925): 394; "An Enviable Record," *Equal Rights* 12 (May 2, 1925): 92; Ella Rush Murray, "Women under the Soviet," *Weekly News* (New York League of Women Voters) 7, no. 2 (Apr. 13, 1928):1; "Enter the Woman Warrior," *Modern Review* 30, no. 5 (Nov. 1921): 549 (quotation).

13. Madeleine Z. Doty, *Behind the Battle Line, around the World in 1918* (New York: Macmillan, 1918), 34, 36, 40–41.

14. Thompson to mother, July 4, 1932, box 1, folder 1, Louise Thompson Patterson papers, Emory University.

15. Florence Luscomb, Russia diary, pp. 61–62, box 12, folder 291, Florence Luscomb papers, MC 394, Schlesinger Library, Harvard University.

16. Benjamin Sawyer, "Shedding the White and Blue: American Migration and Soviet Dreams in the Era of the New Economic Policy," *Ab Imperio* 1 (2013), esp. 70–71. Also see Seth Bernstein and Robert Cherny, "Searching for the Soviet Dream: Prosperity and Disillusionment on the Soviet Seattle Agricultural Commune, 1922–1927," *Agricultural History* 88, no. 1 (2014): 22–44.

17. On NEP, see Richard Stites, *Revolutionary Dreams: Utopian Vision and Experimental Life in the Russian Revolution* (New York: Oxford University Press, 1989); Sheila Fitzpatrick, Alexander Rabinowitch, and Richard Stites, *Russia in the Era of NEP: Explorations in Soviet Society and Culture* (Bloomington: Indiana University Press, 1991). On visitors' comments, see Anna Louise Strong, *The First Time in History: Two Years of Russia's New Life (August, 1921 to December, 1923)* (New York: Boni and Liveright, 1924), 210; Markoosha Fischer, *My Lives in Russia* (New York: Harper & Brothers, 1944), 12, 13, 15; Lynn Mally, *Culture of the Future: The Proletkult Movement in Revolutionary Russia* (Berkeley: University of California Press, 1990); Magdeleine Marx, "The New Russian Women," *Nation* 117 (1923): 508–10. The quotations are from Fischer and Marx.

18. Robert Robinson, for instance, who was earning $140 a month at Ford in Detroit, was offered a salary of $250 a month, free transportation to Russia, thirty days of vacation, a maid, and free living quarters in the Soviet Union. Tim Tzouliadis, *The Forsaken: An American Tragedy in Stalin's Russia* (New York: Penguin Press, 2008), 39.

19. N. L. Kornienko, "Razvitie internatsional'nykh sviazei sovetskogo rabochego klassa v gody pervoi piatiletki" *Istorija SSSR* 6 (1979): 170; Tim Tzouliadis, *The Forsaken: An American Tragedy in Stalin's Russia* (New York: Penguin Press, 2008), 35–37; Meredith L. Roman, "Racism in a 'Raceless' Society: The Soviet Press and Representations of American Racial Violence at Stalingrad in 1930," *International Labor and Working-Class History* 71 (2007): 199n3; Sergei Zhuravlev, *"Malen'kie liudi" I "bol'shaia istoriia": Inostrantsy moskovskogo electrozavoda v sovestkom obshchestve 1920-kh-1930-kh gg* (Moscow: Rosspen, 2000), 29–31. Records of Intourist, the Soviet travel office established in 1929 to coordinate with foreign travel agencies, indicate that the number of foreign visitors increased steadily until the mid-1930s. Of the nearly twenty-five thousand tourists in 1936,

29.1 percent came from the United States (Britain was second at 13.5 percent). After 1936 the numbers dropped quite precipitously as Soviet efforts to cultivate foreign allies were replaced by an overwhelming fear of foreigners. Walter Duranty, "Immigration Now an Issue in Soviet," *New York Times*, Mar. 14, 1932, 8. On Intourist numbers, see f. 9612, op. 2, d. 146, State Archive of the Russian Federation (GARF), Moscow.

20. Engel, *Women in Russia*, 166; G. Friedrich, *Miss U.S.S.R.: The Story of a Girl Stakhanovitc* (New York: International Publishers, 1930); Choi Chatterjee, *Celebrating Women: Gender, Festival Culture, and Bolshevik Ideology, 1910–1939* (Pittsburgh, PA: University of Pittsburgh Press, 2002), 106.

21. Michael David-Fox, *Showcasing the Great Experiment: Cultural Diplomacy and Western Visitors to the Soviet Union* (New York: Oxford University Press, 2011), 16.

22. VOKS records, f. 5283, op. 3, d. 39, l. 146 (1927); f. 5283, op. 3, d. 1003, l. 14, 30, (1937); f. 5283, op. 3, d. 1001, l. 11 (1937). All in GARF, Moscow.

23. Dean MacCannell, *The Tourist: A New Theory of the Leisure Class* (Berkeley: University of California Press, 1999), 7; Elizabeth Hawes, *Fashion Is Spinach* (New York: Random House, 1938), 292; Maria Diedrich, *Cornelia James Cannon and the Future American Race* (Amherst: University of Massachusetts Press, 2011), 219–20; Landon R. Y. Storrs, *The Second Red Scare and the Unmaking of the New Deal Left* (Princeton, NJ: Princeton University Press, 2013), 38–40; Peter H. Oberlander, Eva Newbrun, and Martin Meyerson, *Houser: The Life and Work of Catherine Bauer* (Vancouver: UBC Press, 1999), 146–47.

24. Sheila Fitzpatrick, "Foreigners Observed: Moscow Visitors in the 1930s under the Eyes of Their Soviet Guides," *Russian History/Histoire Russe* 35, no. 1–2 (2008): 224–25; Jessica Smith, *Woman in Soviet Russia* (New York: Vanguard Press, 1928), 166 ("scientific study" and "bright faced peasant woman"); Rebecca Reyher, Russia/Palestine diary, box 12, folders 3+4, Rebecca Reyher papers, Schlesinger Library, Harvard University.

25. Frances E. Williams, "To Hell with Bandanas," interview by Karen Anne Mason and Richard Cándida Smith, 1992–1993, transcript, pp. 236–37, UCLA Oral History Program, Bancroft Library, University of California, Berkeley, accessed Oct. 21, 2015, https://archive.org/details/tohellwithbandan00will.

26. Paul Hollander, *Political Pilgrims: Travels of Western Intellectuals to the Soviet Union, China, and Cuba, 1928–1978* (New York: Oxford University Press, 1981; repr., 1983, New York: Harper and Row), 141; Fitzpatrick, "Foreigners Observed"; Michael David-Fox, "The Fellow Travelers Revisited: The 'Cultured West' through Soviet Eyes," *Journal of Modern History* 75, no. 2 (2003): 300–35; David-Fox, *Showcasing the Great Experiment*; Ludmila Stern, *Western Intellectuals and the Soviet Union, 1920–40: From Red Square to the Left Bank* (New York: Routledge, 2006).

27. Sanora Babb, "There Are No Fences in Russia: Collective Farm" (typescript), p. 3, box 30, folder 14, Sanora Babb papers, Harry Ransom Humanities Center, University of Texas. Photographs in box 68, folders 7–8. Babb's book *Whose Names Are Unknown*

(written in the 1930s but not published until 2004) chronicles the plight of the migrant farmer in America.

28. Julia Allen, *Passionate Commitments: The Lives of Anna Rochester and Grace Hutchins* (Albany: State University of New York Press, 2013), 120–123; Ruth Gruber, *I Went to the Soviet Arctic* (New York: Simon and Schuster, 1939), quoted in Charlotte Nekola and Paula Rabinowitz, *Writing Red: An Anthology of American Women Writers, 1930–1940* (New York: Feminist Press at the City University of New York, 1987), 236.

29. David-Fox, *Showcasing the Great Experiment*, 25–26.

30. Hallie Flanagan, "Three Russian Women" (typescript), Hallie Flanagan papers, NYPL for the Performing Arts. Partially published as "Two Russian Women," *Tanager*, Sept. 1932.

31. Ros Pesman, *Duty Free: Australian Women Abroad* (Melbourne: Oxford University Press, 1996), 140; Lillian D. Wald, *Windows on Henry Street* (Boston: Little, Brown, 1934), 262.

32. Jochen Hellbeck, *Revolution on My Mind: Writing a Diary under Stalin* (Cambridge, MA: Harvard University Press, 2006), 5–6. As Hellbeck and others have attempted to demonstrate through the use of Soviet diaries as well as theoretical tools borrowed largely from Michel Foucault, "Soviet power did not merely repress and efface the individual and his thoughts, but actually created individuals, both as objects of knowledge to be molded and perfected (individuation), and as subjects capable of action and agency (individualization)." Choi Chatterjee and Karen Petrone, "Models of Selfhood and Subjectivity: The Soviet Case in Historical Perspective," *Slavic Review* 67, no. 4 (2008): 978.

33. Hellbeck, *Revolution on My Mind*; Koner diary, Dec. 16, 1934.

34. Massing, *This Deception*, 51 ("lifted us"); Hellbeck, *Revolution on My Mind*, 10 ("to escape"); Isadora Duncan quoted in Irma Duncan and Allan Ross Macdougall, *Isadora Duncan's Russian Days and Her Last Years in France* (New York: Covici Friede, 1929), 66.

35. Rose Pastor Stokes, "Impressions of Russia," microfilm 67, sec. 24, Rose Pastor Stokes papers, Tamiment Library, New York University (NYU).

36. Allen, *Passionate Commitments*, 120. The phrase "rhetoric of the whole person" referred to the notion that all parts of their lives, from their writing to their intimate relations to their clothing, must contribute "to their revolutionary aims." Ibid., xi.

37. The phrase "magic pilgrimage" comes from Claude McKay's description of his 1922 trip to the Soviet Union in McKay, *A Long Way from Home*, ed. Gene Andrew Jarrett (New Brunswick, NJ: Rutgers University Press, 2007), 118. Daniel Soyer, "Back to the Future: American Jews Visit the Soviet Union in the 1920s and 1930s," *Jewish Social Studies* 6, no. 3 (2000): 125 ("class and political solidarity"); Robert Weinberg, *Stalin's Forgotten Zion: Birobidzhan and the Making of a Soviet Jewish Homeland: An Illustrated History, 1928–1996* (Berkeley: University of California Press / Judah L. Magnas Museum, 1998), 13. Pauline Koner barely comments on Jewish things in her Russia diary, despite having just spent several months in Palestine, although she mentions seeing *King Lear* at

the Moscow State Yiddish Theatre. Koner diary, Mar. 4, 1935. Photographs suggest that she may have also performed one of her "Jewish dances" in Russia. Box 31, Pauline Koner papers, NYPL for the Performing Arts. On African Americans and the Soviet Union, see Baldwin, *Beyond the Color Line and the Iron Curtain*; Joy Gleason Carew, *Blacks, Reds, and Russians: Sojourners in Search of the Soviet Promise* (New Brunswick, NJ: Rutgers University Press, 2008); Glenda Elizabeth Gilmore, *Defying Dixie: The Radical Roots of Civil Rights, 1919–1950* (New York: W. W. Norton, 2008); Erik S. McDuffie, *Sojourning for Freedom: Black Women, American Communism, and the Making of Black Left Feminism* (Durham, NC: Duke University Press, 2011); Mark I. Solomon, *The Cry Was Unity: Communists and African Americans, 1917–1936* (Jackson: University Press of Mississippi, 1998); Meredith L. Roman, *Opposing Jim Crow: African Americans and the Soviet Indictment of U.S. Racism, 1928–1937* (Lincoln: University of Nebraska Press, 2012); Allison Blakely, *Russia and the Negro: Blacks in Russian History and Thought* (Washington, DC: Howard University Press, 1986); Maxim Matusevich, "Journeys of Hope: African Diaspora and the Soviet Society," *African Diaspora* 1 (2008): 53–85.

38. Mary M. Leder and Laurie Bernstein, *My Life in Stalinist Russia: An American Woman Looks Back* (Bloomington: Indiana University Press, 2001). For more on American victims of Stalin, see Tzouliadis, *The Foresaken*. Also see John Earl Haynes and Harvey Klehr, *In Denial: Historians, Communism & Espionage* (San Francisco: Encounter Books, 2003), 235–47.

39. Jessie Lloyd to Lola Maverick Lloyd, July 30, 1927, box 32, folder 2, Lola Maverick Lloyd papers, Archives and Manuscripts Division, NYPL.

40. Bennett to Florence [last name unidentified], Jan. 27, 1932, box 2, folder 1, Milly Bennett papers, Hoover Library; Emma Goldman, *My Disillusionment in Russia* (Garden City, NY: Doubleday, Page, 1923).

41. Luben to CPUSA, Oct. 13, 1926, f. 515, d. 773, microfilm reel 55, CPUSA papers, Tamiment Library, NYU.

42. Sawyer, "Shedding the White and Blue," 67; Christina Looper Baker and Myra Page, *In a Generous Spirit: A First-Person Biography of Myra Page* (Urbana: University of Illinois Press, 1996), 125; Fitzpatrick, "Foreigners Observed," 234. For Jessica Smith, Mary "Mignon" Garlin, and Louise Thompson, their time in the Soviet Union likely persuaded them to become fellow travelers or even Communists, although only Thompson either admitted to membership in the Communist Party or acknowledged that her time in the Soviet Union convinced her to join. Louise Thompson Patterson oral history, recorded Nov. 16, 1981, Oral History of the American Left collection, Tamiment Library, NYU. Hede Massing claimed that her time in the Soviet Union had the opposite effect. Massing, *This Deception*, 98. Massing's claims here are complicated by the fact that she continued to spy for the Soviets after one and then another negative experience in the Soviet Union.

43. On the new everyday life, or *novyi byt*, see Christina Kiaer and Eric Naiman, eds., *Everyday Life in Soviet Russia: Taking the Revolution Inside* (Bloomington: Indiana University Press, 2006).

44. E. P. Frenkel', *Polovye prestupleniia* (Odessa: Svetoch, 1927), quoted in Dan Healey, *Homosexual Desire in Revolutionary Russia: The Regulation of Sexual and Gender Dissent* (Chicago: University of Chicago Press, 2001), 129. See also Laura Engelstein, *The Keys to Happiness: Sex and the Search for Modernity in Fin de Siecle Russia* (Ithaca, NY: Cornell University Press, 1992); Gregory Carleton, *Sexual Revolution in Bolshevik Russia* (Pittsburgh, PA: University of Pittsburgh Press, 2005); Sheila Fitzpatrick, "Sex and Revolution: An Examination of Literary and Statistical Data on the Mores of Soviet Students in the 1920s," *Journal of Modern History* 50, no. 2 (1978): 252–78; Igor Semenovich Kon, *The Sexual Revolution in Russia: From the Age of the Czars to Today* (New York: The Free Press, 1995); Eric Naiman, *Sex in Public: The Incarnation of Early Soviet Ideology* (Princeton, NJ: Princeton University Press, 1997).

45. Alexandra Kollontai quoted in Barbara Evans Clements, "Emancipation through Communism: The Ideology of A. M. Kollontai," *Slavic Review* 32, no. 2 (1973): 336; Fitzpatrick, "Sex and Revolution," 255; Smith, *Woman in Soviet Russia*, 126.

46. Clara Zetkin, "Lenin on the Woman Question," last update Feb. 29, 2004, accessed Aug. 3, 2016, https://www.marxists.org/archive/zetkin/1920/lenin/zetkin1.htm.

47. Clements, "Emancipation through Communism," 336 ("wingless eros"); Alexandra Kollontai, "Make Way for the Winged Eros," in *Modernism: An Anthology of Sources and Documents*, ed. Vassiliki Kolocotroni (Chicago: University of Chicago Press, 1998), 232–37 ("winged eros").

48. Ella Winter, *Red Virtue: Human Relationships in the New Russia* (New York: Harcourt, Brace, 1933), 6.

49. Ibid., 116.

50. Barbara Foley, *Radical Representations: Politics and Form in U.S. Proletarian Fiction, 1929–1941* (Durham, NC: Duke University Press, 1993); Henry James Foreman, "Sex in the Civilization of the Twentieth Century," *New York Times Book Review*, June 9, 1929, BR8 ("Karl Marx"); V. F. Calverton, "Sex and the Social Struggle," in *Sex in Civilization*, ed. V. F. Calverton and Samuel D. Schmalhausen (New York: Macaulay, 1929), 276–79; Maurice Hindus, *Humanity Uprooted* (1929; repr., New York: Blue Ribbon Books, 1932), 90.

51. Myra Page, *Moscow Yankee* (New York: G. P. Putnam's Sons, 1935), 16; Kirsten Delegard, *Battling Miss Bolsheviki: The Origins of Female Conservatism in the United States* (Philadelphia: University of Pennsylvania Press, 2012), 28–29. The *Woman Patriot*, a rightwing magazine, has numerous articles supposedly attesting to the Bolshevik "nationalization of women" and condemning Alexandra Kollontai.

52. Dorothy Thompson, *The New Russia* (Henry Holt, 1928), 263–64, 274; Goldman, *Women, the State, and Revolution*, 109.

53. Anne O'Hare McCormick, *The Hammer and the Scythe: Communist Russia Enters the Second Decade* (New York: A. A. Knopf, 1928), 166.

54. Nadine [last name unidentified] to West, sent from Boston, July 15, 1932, carton 1, folder 9, Dorothy West papers, Schlesinger Library, Harvard University; Ruth Kennell, "Soviet Satisfied with 'Free Love': Prudery and Hypocrisy Ended, Says American Woman,"

San Francisco News, n.d., ca. 1928, clipping, box 6, folder 16, Ruth Epperson Kennell (REK) papers, University of Oregon, Eugene; Kennell to Sam Shipman, Mar. 20, 1926, box 9, folder 3, REK papers, University of Oregon, Eugene.

55. Hindus, *Humanity Uprooted*, 97; Jessie Lloyd, "A Flapper in Russia" (unpublished manuscript), p. 22, box 88, folders 10–15, Jessie Lloyd O'Connor papers, Smith College.

56. Healey, *Homosexual Desire in Revolutionary Russia*; Bennett to Elmer Roesinger, Sept. 28, 1934, box 4, folder 22, Milly Bennett papers, Hoover Library.

57. Margaret Bourke-White, "Silk Stockings in the Five-Year Plan," *New York Times*, Feb. 14, 1932, SM4.

58. Hindus, *Humanity Uprooted*, 288.

59. Johnson to West, Oct. 1932, carton 1, folder 9, Dorothy West papers, Schlesinger Library, Harvard University. For further discussion, see, for instance, Lois Scharf and Joan M. Jensen, *Decades of Discontent: The Women's Movement, 1920–1940* (Boston: Northeastern University Press, 1987); Barbara Melosh, *Engendering Culture: Manhood and Womanhood in New Deal Public Art and Theater* (Washington, DC: Smithsonian Institution Press, 1991).

60. Hallie Flanagan, "Blood and Oil: In Russia Drama Is Made to Serve Man's Welfare in Unprecedented Ways," *Theatre Guild Magazine* (1930): 28.

61. Goldman, *Women, the State, and Revolution*, 96.

62. Engel, *Women in Russia*, 150–53.

63. McCormick, *The Hammer and the Scythe*, 159; Chatterjee, *Celebrating Women*, 139 (on factory and agricultural conditions); Engel, *Women in Russia*, 172 (on Ukraine).

64. Engel, *Women in Russia*, 180–85.

65. Cornelia Cannon, Russia diary, Aug. 17, 1935, box 12, folder 9, Cornelia Cannon papers, Schlesinger Library, Harvard University.

66. National Security Council, "NSC-68: United States Objectives and Programs for National Security," Apr. 15, 1950, accessed Sept. 4, 2015, http://fas.org/irp/offdocs/nsc-hst/nsc-68.htm. On the relationship between the Old Left and the New Left, see Maurice Isserman, *If I Had a Hammer: The Death of the Old left and the Birth of the New Left* (New York: Basic Books, 1987); John Patrick Diggins, *The Rise and Fall of the American Left* (New York: W. W. Norton, 1992). There are exceptions to this: for example, a significant number of African Americans traveled to the Soviet Union in the 1950s and 1960s following Khruschev's support for African decolonization movements. Carew, *Blacks, Reds, and Russians*, 200–207.

67. Lauren Berlant, *Cruel Optimism* (Durham: Duke University Press, 2011); Joan Scott, "Fantasy Echo: History and the Construction of Identity," *Critical Inquiry* 27, no. 2 (2001): 289.

68. Betty Friedan, *The Feminine Mystique* (New York: Norton, 1963). On postwar gender roles and sexual mores, see Elaine Tyler May, *Homeward Bound: American Families in the Cold War Era* (New York: Basic Books, 1988). On Cold War dynamics as a defining feature of US-Soviet relations since the Bolshevik revolution, see Susan Buck-Morss, *Dreamworld and Catastrophe: The Passing of Mass Utopia in East and West* (Cambridge, MA: MIT Press, 2000).

69. Sheryl Sandberg and Nell Scovell, *Lean In: For Graduates* (New York: Alfred A. Knopf, 2014); Arianna Stassinopoulos Huffington, *Thrive: The Third Metric to Redefining Success and Creating a Life of Well-Being, Wisdom, and Wonder* (New York: Harmony Books, 2014); Amy Chua, *Battle Hymn of the Tiger Mother* (New York: Penguin Press, 2011); Hanna Rosin, *The End of Men: And the Rise of Women* (New York, New York: Riverhead Books, 2012).

PART I

1. On the rise of international reporting, see Giovanna Dell'Orto, *Giving Meanings to the World: the First U.S. Foreign Correspondents, 1838–1859* (Westport, CT: Greenwood Press, 2002). On increasing American awareness of and attention to Russia, see David C. Engerman, *Modernization from the Other Shore: American Intellectuals and the Romance of Russian Development* (Cambridge, MA: Harvard University Press, 2003). On the rise of a modern (international) feminist movement, see Nancy Cott, *The Grounding of Modern Feminism* (New Haven, CT: Yale University Press, 1987); Leila J. Rupp, *Worlds of Women: The Making of an International Women's Movement* (Princeton, NJ: Princeton University Press, 1997). On women's involvement with progressive reform, see Robyn Muncy, *Creating a Female Dominion in American Reform, 1890–1935* (New York: Oxford University Press, 1991). On "progressive internationalism," see Alan Dawley, *Changing the World: American Progressives in War and Revolution* (Princeton, NJ: Princeton University Press, 2003), 7 (quotations).

2. Anna Strunsky, "Revolutionary Lives" (unpublished manuscript), box 32, folder 388, Anna Strunsky Walling papers, Yale University; Lillian Wald, *The House on Henry Street* (New York: Henry Holt, 1915), 248.

3. Mary Winsor, "The Status of Women in Soviet Russia" (typescript), 1927, Mary Winsor papers, Schlesinger Library, Harvard University.

4. Jane H. Hunter, "Women's Mission in Historical Perspective: American Identity and Christian Internationalism," in *Competing Kingdoms: Women, Mission, Nation, and the American Protestant Empire, 1812–1960*, ed. Barbara Reeves-Ellington, Kathryn Kish Sklar, and Connie A. Shemo (Durham, NC: Duke University Press, 2010), 26, 29 (quotation); Amy Kaplan, "Manifest Domesticity," *American Literature* 70, no. 3 (1998): 585–86.

5. Jonathan Frankel, *Prophecy and Politics: Socialism, Nationalism, and the Russian Jews, 1862–1917* (Cambridge: Cambridge University Press, 1981).

CHAPTER 1

1. Anna Strunsky, "Woman and the Russian Revolutionary Movement," *California Woman's Magazine* 5, no. 12 (Aug. 1905), 1–2, in Anna Strunsky Walling papers, Special Collections, Bancroft Library, University of California Berkeley. The image of a woman standing "in the gray dawn of freedom" echoes Ivan Turgenev's 1878 poem "On the Threshold," written just after the revolutionary Vera Zasulich shot the governor of Saint Petersburg

in retribution for his brutal flogging of an jailed comrade. The shooting made Zasulich a folk hero; indeed, her defense so moved a Russian jury that she was not punished.

2. Choi Chatterjee, "Transnational Romance, Terror, and Heroism: Russia in American Popular Fiction, 1860–1917," *Comparative Studies in Society and History* 50, no. 3 (2008): 669. For pre-1917 romantic and heroic portrayals of Russian revolutionaries, see, for example, Abraham Cahan, "Russian Revolutionists," *World's Work* 8 (1904), 5311–15; W. L. Howard, "In Prison and Exile: The Experience of a Russian Student," *Arena* 33 (1905), 600–608; I. Okuntsoff, "Martyrs of the Revolution," *The Independent* 62 (1907): 1120–23.

3. Israel Zangwill, *The Melting Pot: A Drama in Four Acts* (New York: Macmillan, 1909); *Beneath the Czar*, American Film Institute Catalog, accessed Mar. 22, 2010, http://www.afi.com/members/catalog/DetailView.aspx?s=&Movie=13570 (with thanks to Leslie DeBauche).

4. "Russian Girl Glories in Death of Tyrant; Mlle Spiridonova Tells Her Tale of Wrongs; Happy in Her Martyrdom," *New York Times*, Apr. 30, 1906, 6; Kellogg Durland, "'Red Reign' as Seen By an American: A Widespread Revolutionary Movement, in Which Are Many Women Leaders," *New York Times*, Oct. 13, 1907, SM8. On rates of women's participation in Russian revolutionary and terrorist activity, see Amy Knight, "Female Terrorists and the Russian Socialist Revolutionary Party," *Russian Review* 38, no. 2 (1979): 139–59. On revolutionary women in Russia, see Barbara Engel Alpern and Clifford N. Rosenthal, eds., *Five Sisters: Women against the Tsar* (New York: Random House, 1975); Margaret Maxwell, *Narodniki Women: Russian Women Who Sacrificed Themselves for the Dream of Freedom* (New York: Pergamon Press, 1990); Vera Broido, *Apostles into Terrorists: Women and the Revolutionary Movement in the Russia of Alexander II* (New York: Viking, 1977).

5. Leroy Scott, "Women of the Russian Revolution," *The Outlook* 90 (1908): 915, 917.

6. My thinking about the importance of personal connections for the creation of empathy comes from Gregory Shaya, "Empathy and Modernity: With Evidence from the Visual Culture of the Railway Disaster in Nineteenth Century France" (paper presented at Global France seminar, May 10, 2012, Paris). The papers of the Socialist Revolutionaries contain hundreds of letters to Breshkovsky from American women. Partija Socialistov Revoljucionerov (PSR) papers, International Institute for Social History, Amsterdam (hereafter cited as PSR papers). Note that the standard Library of Congress transcription of the original Russian, Партия социалистов-революционеров, looks slightly different, as per reference in the text.

7. Jane E. Good and David R. Jones, *Babushka: The Life of the Russian Revolutionary Ekaterina K. Breshko-Breshkovskaia (1844–1934)* (Newtonville, MA: Oriental Research Partners, 1991), 7–31; Alice Stone Blackwell (hereafter cited as ASB), *The Little Grandmother of the Russian Revolution: Reminiscences and Letters of Catherine Breshkovsky* (Boston: Little, Brown, 1917), 39 (quotation). For Breshkovsky's biography, I draw on Good and Jones, *Babushka*; ASB, *Little Grandmother of the Russian Revolution* (including

the sketch by Abraham Cahan); Ekaterina Konstantinovna Breshko-Breshkovskaia and Lincoln Hutchinson, *Hidden Springs of the Russian Revolution* (London: H. Milford, Oxford University Press, 1931); and Anna Strunsky, "Catherine Breshkovsky" (unpublished sketch), box 33, folder 396, Anna Strunsky Walling (ASW) papers, Yale University.

8. On the movement "to the people," see Franco Venturi, *Roots of Revolution: A History of the Populist and Socialist Movements in Nineteenth Century Russia* (London: Weidenfield and Nicholson, 1960), 62–70.

9. Frederick F. Travis, *George Kennan and the American-Russian Relationship, 1865–1924* (Athens: Ohio University Press, 1990), 26. The diplomat and Cold War architect George F. Kennan was a distant cousin and namesake of this older Kennan.

10. George Kennan to Anna Dawes, quoted in ibid., 111–12.

11. Kennan quoted in ibid., 129–30.

12. Ibid., 177, 178 (Mark Twain quotation). On Kennan's appearance in the rags and shackles of a prisoner, see Jane Good, "America and the Russian Revolutionary Movement, 1888–1905," *Russian Review* 41, no. 3 (1982): 274.

13. On Stepniak, see Charles A. Moser, "A Nihilist's Career: S. M. Stepniak-Kravchinskij," *American Slavic and East European Review* 20, no. 1 (1961): 55–71.

14. ASB, *Little Grandmother of the Russian Revolution*, 125.

15. Mary Heaton Vorse's earliest political memory was of reading George Kennan's *Siberia and the Exile System* with her mother as a child. Mary Heaton Vorse, *A Footnote to Folly: Reminiscences of Mary Heaton Vorse* (New York: Farrar & Rinehart, 1935), 22. Also see Emma Goldman, chap. 28 in *Living My Life* (New York: Alfred A Knopf, 1931), https://theanarchistlibrary.org/library/emma-goldman-living-my-life#toc30.

16. Manfred Hildermeier, *The Russian Socialist Revolutionary Party before the First World War* (New York: St. Martin's Press, 2000), 52; Anna Strunsky, "Revolutionary Lives" (unpublished manuscript), box 32, folder 388, p. 39 (quotation), ASW papers, Yale University.

17. Emma Goldman, *Living My Life*, abridged ed. (New York: Penguin Classics, 2006), 359–60; Hippolyte Havel, introduction to Emma Goldman, *Anarchism and Other Essays* (New York: Mother Earth Publishing Association, 1917), 12 ("shoulder to shoulder"); Emma Goldman, *Living My Life* (Mineola, NY: Dover Publications, 2003), 1:24 ("guiding stars").

18. Peter Kropotkin, quoted in Ana Siljak, *Angel of Vengeance: The "Girl Assassin," the Governor of St. Petersburg, and Russia's Revolutionary World* (New York: St. Martin's Press, 2008), 50 ("black woolen dress"); Richard Stites, *The Women's Liberation Movement in Russia: Feminism, Nihilism, and Bolshevism, 1860–1930* (Princeton, NJ: Princeton University Press, 1978), 99–100 ("manners"). Nikolay Gavrilovich Chernyshevsky, *What Is to Be Done?*, trans. Michael R. Katz (Ithaca, NY: Cornell University Press, 1989). On the dissemination of Chernyshevsky's ideas, see Steven Cassedy, "Chernyshevskii Goes West: How Jewish Immigration Helped Bring Russian Radicalism to America," *Russian History* 21, no. 1 (1994): 1–21.

19. Goldman, *Living My Life* (Dover), 1:51. On which Chernyshevsky characters inspired men and women, see Siljak, *Angel of Vengeance*, 75.

20. Goldman, *Living My Life* (Dover), 1:360–61.

21. Ibid., 1:362.

22. On the philosophy underlying the settlement house movement, see Allen F. Davis, *Spearheads for Reform: The Social Settlements and the Progressive Movement, 1890–1914* (New Brunswick: Rutgers University Press, 1987). On the antimodernist impulse at the turn of the twentieth century, see T. J. Jackson Lears, *No Place of Grace: Antimodernism and the Transformation of American Culture, 1880–1920* (Chicago: University of Chicago Press, 1994). On women in settlement house work, see Kathryn Kish Sklar, *Florence Kelley and the Nation's Work* (New Haven, CT: Yale University Press, 1995); Robyn Muncy, *Creating a Female Dominion in American Reform, 1890–1935* (New York: Oxford University Press, 1991); Molly Ladd Taylor, *Mother-Work: Women, Child Welfare, and the State, 1890–1930* (Urbana: University of Illinois Press, 1994).

23. Goldman, *Living My Life* (Dover), 1:362; Goldman to Breshkovsky, Dec. 12, 1904, folder 690, PSR papers.

24. Lillian Wald, *The House on Henry Street* (New York: Henry Holt, 1915), 231, 239–40. On Wald's biography, see Marjorie N. Feld, *Lillian Wald: A Biography* (Chapel Hill: University of North Carolina Press, 2008).

25. For Tolstoy's influence on Addams, see Jan C. Behrends, "Visions of Civility: Lev Tolstoy and Jane Addams on the Urban Condition in *Fin de Siècle* Moscow and Chicago," *European Review of History/ Revue europeenne d'histoire* 18, no. 3 (2011): 335–57. Breshkovsky confided to a comrade, "[Addams] gave me a warm welcome, and tomorrow there will be a meeting under her patronage, and yet she is afraid, and looks with suspicion. Personally she accepts me, and treats [me] with respect—but as a good manager, she knows that being too close with Russian revolutionaries can reduce the funds donated by Chicago capitalists, which she doesn't want." Breshkovsky to Felix Volkhonsky, Jan. 28, 1905, folder 691, PSR papers. Translation by Andrey Bredstein. There is a large file of correspondence between Breshkovsky and Ellen Gates Starr in the papers of Hull House. On Dudley, see ASB, *Little Grandmother of the Russian Revolution*, 123.

26. Self-description in ASB to Catherine Breshkovsky, Dec. 9, 1904, folder 688, PSR papers.

27. ASB to Peter Kropotkin, Mar. 11, 1904, f. 1129, op. 2, d. 615, State Archive of the Russian Federation (GARF), Moscow. In fact, Stone Blackwell had been involved with the SAFRF since its founding in 1891, and she had worked with her parents on behalf of Boris Gorow, an exile who lectured in the United States in 1884. ASB, *Little Grandmother of the Russian Revolution*, 124. Shannon Smith, "From Relief to Revolution: American Women and the Russian-American Relationship, 1890–1917," *Diplomatic History* 19, no. 4 (1995): 610–11. Charlotte Perkins Gilman, "Our Attitude toward Russia," *Woman's Journal* 35 (Mar. 19, 1904), 90. African American newspapers tended to voice support for "Russian Freedom" precisely because of obvious parallels to African Americans' predicament. Examples of such articles include "The Revolution Subdued; Drastic Methods Employed

by Russia in Poland. Thousands are Victims to Government's Policies," *Wichita Searchlight*, Dec. 22, 1906, 3; "The Underground Railroad in Russia: Extracts from Dr. Booker T. Washington's Forthcoming Book the Man Farthest," *Savannah Tribune*, Jan. 20, 1912, 3. Also see Lawrence S. Little, *Disciples of Liberty: The African Methodist Episcopal Church in the Age of Imperialism, 1884–1916* (Knoxville: University of Tennessee Press, 2000). In 1909 several Americans active in support of Russian revolutionaries, including the Wallings and Lillian Wald, helped found the National Association for the Advancement of Colored People (NAACP); Stone Blackwell also became active in the organization.

28. ASB to Breshkovsky, Jan. 3, 1905, folder 688, PSR papers. Rather than translating from the original, Blackwell would rework a literal translation to preserve its poetic essence. For an example, see ASB, ed. and trans., *Songs of Russia* (Dorchester: MA: published by the author, 1906).

29. Barrows to "My Dear Isaac" [Hourwich?], Mar. 29, 1905, folder 688, PSR papers. June Barrows Mussey, the teenage grandson of Isabel Barrows, would tour Europe as the magician Haji Baba and visit Breshkovsky and her protégé, George Lazarev, in exile in Prague. Letters from June Barrows Mussey and Mabel Barrows Mussey to George Lazarev, f. 5824, op. 1, d. 258, l. 256, Lazarev papers, GARF, Moscow.

30. ASB diary, Dec. 11, 1904, box 2, microfilm reel 3, ASB papers, Library of Congress; ASB to Lazarev, Feb. 13, 1913, f. 5824, op. 1, d. 436, Lazarev papers, GARF, Moscow. On October 27, 1904, Stone Blackwell noted in her diary that Kitty (Barry Blackwell) had scolded her about consorting with Emma Goldman, and on March 16, 1905, two days before Breshkovsky left the United States, Stone Blackwell noted that she "told Aunt Isabel who E. G. Smith is."

31. On the frequency of Breshkovsky's speaking engagements, see ASB, *Little Grandmother of the Russian Revolution*, 123. On the Faneuil Hall event, see "Cradle Rocked for Free Russia," *Boston Herald*, Dec. 15, 1904, and *Woman's Journal*, Dec. 17, 1904, quoted in ASB, *Little Grandmother of the Russian Revolution*, 112. During her first week in Boston, Breshkovsky addressed the New England Women's Club, the Brookline Woman Suffrage Association, guests at a Denison House reception, the Boston Friends of Russian Freedom, students and teachers at Wellesley College, a meeting in Boston's Jewish quarter, and the Twentieth Century Club. ASB, schedule of engagement for Breshkovsky, Nov. 20, 1904, folder 688, PSR papers.

32. A copy of Breshkovsky's Faneuil Hall speech is in folder 697, PSR papers. It's also reprinted in ASB, *Little Grandmother of the Russian Revolution*, 112–18, as part of a reprinting of an account of the event from *Woman's Journal*, Dec. 17, 1904. "Cradle Rocked for Free Russia," *Boston Herald*, Dec. 15, 1904.

33. Goldman, *Living My Life* (Dover), 1:221.

34. Breshkovsky to Felix [Volkhonsky?], Jan. 28, 1905, Chicago, folder 687, PSR papers. Translation by Andrey Bredstein.

35. "Describes Life in Dark Russia," [name of paper obscured], Jan. 3, 1905, Camden, NJ; "Russian Woman Cheered: Madame Breshkovsky the Star of Enthusiastic Meeting," *Philadelphia Record*, Mar. 6, 1905. Both articles in folder 701, PSR papers.

36. Speeches collected in folder 703, PSR papers.

37. On the rush to see Breshkovsky speak, see "Hear Slav Agitator," [name of newspaper cut off], Jan. 23, 1905, Chicago, folder 701, PSR papers. On Breshkovsky's fundraising, see Good and Jones, *Babushka*, 87–89; Candace Falk, ed. *Emma Goldman: A Documentary History of the American Years*, 3 vols. (Urbana: University of Illinois Press, 2005), 2:158.

38. ASB to Breshkovsky, Jan. 27, 1905, folder 688, PSR papers.

39. Dudley to Breshkovsky, Dec. 21, 1904; Starr to Breshkovksy, Mar. 5, 1905; and Todd to Breshkovsky, n.d. All three letters are in folder 688, PSR papers. For further discussion, see Julia L. Mickenberg, "Suffragettes and Soviets: American Feminists and the Specter of Revolutionary Russia," *Journal of American History* 100, no. 4 (2014): 1021–51.

40. Goldman, *Living My Life* (Dover), 1:372.

41. Isadora Duncan, *My Life* (New York: Boni & Liveright, 1927; repr., New York: W. W. Norton, 1995), 119; Tony Michels, *A Fire in Their Hearts: Yiddish Socialists in New York* (Cambridge, MA: Harvard University Press, 2005).

42. James R. Boylan, *Revolutionary Lives: Anna Strunsky and William English Walling* (Amherst: University of Massachusetts Press, 1998), 92.

43. Ibid., 92–93.

44. Anna Strunsky, fragment (manuscript), box 37, folder 415, ASW papers, Yale University.

45. Strunsky to her father, Jan. 19, 1906, box 5, ASW papers, Yale University; Boylan, *Revolutionary Lives*, 96.

46. Graham Phelps Stokes, known as the "millionaire socialist," married Rose Pastor, who interviewed Stokes for the Yiddish *Forward*, and Leroy Scott married Miriam Finn, an early childhood education specialist whose first job was managing the University Settlement's playground. The Scotts followed English and Anna to Saint Petersburg in 1907. Rose Pastor Stokes was among the founding members of the Communist Party of the United States. The Stokes set up a small colony on Caritas Island off of Stamford, Connecticut, so the families could all live close to one another. See "Stokes Plans a Utopia," *New York Times*, Dec. 17, 1909, 8. Also see Keren McGinty, *Still Jewish: A History of Women and Intermarriage in America* (New York: New York University Press, 2009), 19–62. On Rose Pastor Stokes, see Arthur Zipster and Pearl Zipster, *Fire and Grace: The Life of Rose Pastor Stokes* (Athens: University of Georgia Press, 1989).

47. Boylan, *Revolutionary Lives*, 94–95. The quotation is from Strunsky, "Revolutionary Lives," 15, which is also quoted in Boylan, *Revolutionary Lives*, 95.

48. Bykov, *In the Steps of Jack London*, accessed May 8, 2012, http://www.jacklondons.net/writings/Bykov/ihs_chapter14.html. Anna Strunsky to Mr. and Mrs. Elias Strunsky, July 1, 1906, ASW papers, Yale University, quoted in Leon Fink, *Progressive Intellectuals and the Dilemmas of Democratic Commitment* (Cambridge, MA: Harvard University Press, 1997), 158 (quotation).

49. Strunsky's diary reveals consistent insecurity about Walling's feelings for her. ASW papers, Yale University. Strunsky, "Revolutionary Lives," 2. On the significance of

Russia's Message, see David S. Foglesong, *The American Mission and the Evil Empire: The Crusade for a 'Free Russia' since 1881* (New York: Cambridge University Press, 2007), 38–39.

50. "Alleged Morals of Gorky Cause Panic: Statement Made That Companion Is Not His Legal Wife," *Los Angeles Times*, Apr. 15, 1906, 11; "Timely Exposure of Gorky," *Washington Post*, Apr. 18, 1906, 6; Filia Holtzman, "A Mission That Failed: Gorky in America," *Slavic and East European Journal* 6, no. 3 (1962): 227–35; Arthur William Thompson, "The Reception of Russian Revolutionary Leaders in America, 1904–1906," *American Quarterly* 18, no. 3 (1966): 452–76.

51. Vorse, *Footnote to Folly*, 34 (quotation). On the A-Club, also see Christine Stansell, *American Moderns: Bohemian New York and the Creation of a New Century* (New York: Metropolitan Books, 2000), 65–66; Gerald W. McFarland, *Inside Greenwich Village: A New York City Neighborhood, 1898–1918* (Amherst: University of Massachusetts Press, 2001), 120–28; Boylan, *Revolutionary Lives*, 126. On Twain and Gorky, see Arthur William Thompson with Robert A Hart, *An Uncertain Crusade: America and the Russian Revolution of 1905* (Amherst: University of Massachusetts Press, 1970), 129–31.

52. Goldman, *Living My Life* (Dover), 1:36; Siljak, *Angel of Vengeance*, 73. For further discussion, see Stansell, *American Moderns*. The marriage vows of Madeleine Z. Doty and Roger Baldwin, close watchers of revolutionary Russia, are representative. Aiming to model "the new brotherhood," they would be "bound by no laws, subjected to no force, dominated wholly by love." Box 1, folder 4, Madeleine Z. Doty papers, Sophia Smith Collection, Smith College.

53. Strunsky, "Revolutionary Lives," 47–48.

54. Boylan, *Revolutionary Lives*, 134–35; Strunsky, "Revolutionary Lives," 360–70; Rose Strunsky, "Siberia and the Russian Woman," *Forum* 44 (1910): 139.

55. Barrows to Lillian Wald, Feb. 28, 1909, box 1, microfilm reel 1, Lillian Wald papers, Columbia University Special Collections; Isabel Barrows, "The Island Palace," *Outlook* 14 (Aug. 1909): 888–89.

56. Tchaikovsky lived in exile for many years but was caught by authorities not long after his return to Russia in 1907. On Tchaikovsky and the revolution, see, for example, "Americans Active for Tchaykovsky, 500 Prominent Men Petition Stolypin for a Fair Trial for Him and Mme. Breshkovsky," *New York Times*, Dec. 2, 1909, 6.

57. Elsa Barker, "Breshkovskaya," *New York Times*, Mar. 13, 1910, 10, reprinted in *Current Literature* 48 (May 1910): 564–65.

58. "Sociological Conditions in the Far East: Miss Lillian Wald, the Famous Settlement Worker of New York, Tells Her Impressions during Extended Trip around the World," *New York Times*, July 10, 1910, SM11.

59. Strunsky, "Siberia and the Russian Woman," 139.

60. Catherine Breshkovsky to Ellen Gates Starr, Sept. 26, 1913, quoted in ASB, *Little Grandmother of the Russian Revolution*, 207. On Dudley's relationship with Vida Scudder, see Sklar, *Florence Kelley and the Nation's Work*, 373n48. On Stone Blackwell's relationship with Kitty Barry, see Lillian Faderman, *To Believe in Women: What Lesbians Have Done for*

America—a History (Boston: Houghton Mifflin, 1999), 37–39. On Starr's relationship with Jane Addams, see ibid., 118. Victoria Bissell Brown notes a lack of clear evidence that they had an erotic relationship. Victoria Bissell Brown, *The Education of Jane Addams* (Philadelphia: University of Pennsylvania Press, 2004), 361. At the turn of the century, the Christian socialist and homosexual Edward Carpenter argued for "the existence of a sexual minority—a third sex—defined not only by same-sex erotic choice but also by a heightened commitment to social justice and to alliance, in the name of social justice, across difference." Robin Hackett, foreword to Julia M. Allen, *Passionate Commitments: The Lives of Anna Rochester and Grace Hutchins* (Albany: State University of New York Press, 2013), xi–xii.

61. Isabel Barrows to Mary Hilliard, Dec. 1912, Westover School Archives, Middlebury, CT.

62. Breshkovsky to ASB, May 27–June 9, 1911, in ASB, *Little Grandmother of the Russian Revolution*, 180; Breshkovsky to ASB and Helena Dudley, Oct. 13, 1910, box 5, microfilm reel 4, National American Women's Suffrage Association papers, Library of Congress; Breshkovsky to Westover School, c/o Miss Lucy Pratt, Apr. 1916, Westover School Archives, Middlebury, CT.

63. Mabel Hay Barrows Mussey to George Lazarev, Apr. 6, 1914, f. 5824, op. 1, d. 258, GARF, Moscow; Grace Abbott, John Sorensen, and Judith Sealander, *The Grace Abbott Reader* (Lincoln: University of Nebraska Press, 2008), 5–6; Mabel Barrows Mussey to George Lazarev, June 26, 1915, f. 5824, op. 1, d. 256, GARF, Moscow. On Sukloff, see Marie Sukloff, *The Life Story of a Russian Exile* (New York: Century, 1914). Also see "The Making of a Russian Terrorist," *Century* 89 (Mar. 1914), 93–105.

64. *Golden Valley Chronicle* (Billings, MT), Nov. 12, 1915; *Seattle Star*, Nov. 1915, 4; *Washington Herald* (Washington, DC), Jan. 18, 1916. All three are available at http://chroniclingamerica.loc.gov/search/pages/results/?state=&date1=1915&date2=1916&proxtext=Kollontai&x=0&y=0&dateFilterType=yearRange&rows=20&searchType=basic (accessed July 2, 2015). Alexandra Kollontai, *Autobiography of a Sexually Emancipated Woman* (1926), trans. Salvator Attansio (New York: Herder and Herder, 1971), accessed July 2, 2015, https://www.marxists.org/archive/kollonta/1926/autobiography.htm. *Daily Ardmoreite* (Ardmore, OK), Apr. 26, 1916, 6; *Bismark (ND) Daily Tribune*, May 9, 1916, 5. Lela B. Costin, *Two Sisters for Social Justice: A Biography of Grace and Edith Abbott*, 1st pbk. ed. (Urbana: University of Illinois Press, 2003), 144–45. There are dozens of references to Kollontai in the right-wing *Woman Patriot*, most of them attempting to tie her to US feminism and social welfare. See, for instance, "Kollontay and Our Children's Bureau," *Woman Patriot* 9, no. 9 (1925): 66. Kim E. Nielsen, *Un-American Womanhood: Antiradicalism, Antifeminism, and the First Red Scare* (Columbus: Ohio State University Press, 2001), 107.

65. Wald to ASB, Mar. 1917, microfilm reel 2, Lillian Wald papers, Columbia University Special Collections.

66. "Little Grandmother, Exile in Siberia, Adopted by Westover School," *Sunday Republican*, Feb. 16, 1919; A. J. Sack, "Back from Siberia: Our Dear Grandmother," *New York Sun*, Aug. 6, 1917, 6; ASB, *Little Grandmother of the Russian Revolution*, 314 (quotation).

67. ASB, *Little Grandmother of the Russian Revolution*, 330.

68. "Mme. Breshkovsky's Last Days Vividly Pictured in Letter: Alice S. Blackwell Produces Epistle Written Shortly before Revolutionist's Death; Her Demise Is Confirmed," *Women's Press* 2, no. 12 (Nov. 23, 1918): 3a; ASB, "When Babushka Came," *Woman Citizen* 3, no. 37 (1919): 759.

69. "Some Memories of Mme. Breshkovsky's Visit to Westover" (typescript), Westover School Archives, Middlebury, CT.

70. ASB to George Lazarev, Feb. 22, 1920 and May 28, 1922, f. 5824, op. 1, d. 190, GARF, Moscow; Wald to Catherine Breshkovsky, Feb. 27, 1919, box 93, folder 1.1, Lillian Wald papers, Columbia University Special Collections.

71. Louise Bryant, *Six Red Months in Russia* (New York: George H. Doran, 1918), 111.

72. Boylan, *Revolutionary Lives*, 265; Strunsky, "Catherine Breshkovsky," n.p. (quotations).

73. See Emma Goldman, *My Disillusionment in Russia* (Garden City, NY: Doubleday, Page, 1923).

CHAPTER 2

1. Louise Bryant, "Serge" (unpublished manuscript), 1918, box 12, folder 52, Louise Bryant papers, Yale University.

2. Michael Barnett, *Empire of Humanity: A History of Humanitarianism* (Ithaca, NY: Cornell University Press, 2011), 6. Leon Trotsky, *Sputnik kommunista* (Mosow), no. 3 (Sept. 4, 1921), 15, quoted in Benjamin M. Weissman, *Herbert Hoover and Famine Relief to Soviet Russia, 1921–1923* (Stanford, CA: Stanford University, Hoover Institution Press, 1974), 15.

3. Floyd Dell, "Were You Ever a Child?," *The Liberator* 1, no. 6 (1918): 5–9; V. F. Calverton and Samuel D. Schmalhausen, eds., *The New Generation: The Intimate Problems of Modern Parents and Children* (New York: Macaulay, 1930), 10 (quotation); Isadora Duncan, "I Will Go to Russia," in *Isadora Speaks*, ed. Franklin Rosemont (San Francisco: City Lights Books, 1981), 63.

4. Evelyn Sharp diary, Jan. 7, 8, and 16, 1922, mss. Eng. misc. e. 632-3, Evelyn Sharp papers, Bodleian Library, Oxford University.

5. Helen Keller, "Helen Keller for Soviet Russia," in Nadezhda Krupskaya, Jessica Smith, and William F. Kruse, *Children at Work and Play in School Communes* [pamphlet] (New York: Friends of Soviet Russia, 1923), 7.

6. See Julia L. Mickenberg, "Suffragettes and Soviets: American Feminists and the Specter of Revolutionary Russia," *Journal of American History* 100, no. 4 (2014): 1021–51.

7. Norbert H. Gaworek, "From Blockade to Trade: Allied Economic Warfare against Soviet Russia, June 1919–January 1920," *Jahrbücher für Geschichte Osteuropas Neue Folge* 23, no. 1 (1975): 39–69. The United States was not officially part of the Allied blockade, but the United States nonetheless effectively restricted all exports to and communications with Soviet Russia. David S. Foglesong, *America's Secret War against Bolshevism:*

U.S. Intervention in the Russian Civil War, 1917–1920 (Chapel Hill: University of North Carolina Press, 1995), 248–52. For an example of the AWEC's appeals, see "Bitter Cry of the Children," *Survey* 43 (Dec. 20, 1919): 252.

8. "Police Fail to Stop Protest for Russia: Reserves Go to the Commodore but Women Hold an Orderly Sidewalk Parade," *New York Times*, Nov. 2, 1919, 18; Dwinelle Benthall, "From Occoquan to Cream Puffs" (newspaper clipping marked 1919), Lucy Branham papers, Library of Congress.

9. Bryant, speech delivered by Mrs. Bennett, box 16, folder 110, Louise Bryant papers, Yale University; "Halt Russian Protest: Police Seize, Then Release, Leader of 35 Women in Wall Street," *New York Times*, Dec. 13, 1919.

10. *Survey* 43, no. 8 (Dec. 20, 1919), 251.

11. For instance, Lucy Branham took part in AFSC meetings on Russian relief on February 4 and 17, 1921. AFSC papers, AFSC central office, Philadelphia (hereafter cited as AFSC papers). E-mail from archivist Don Davis to author, Sept. 23, 2013. *Relations with Russia: Hearing before the Committee on Foreign Relations, United States Senate* 66th Cong. 96 (1921) (statement of Harriet Stanton Blatch, American Women's Emergency Committee).

12. *Relations with Russia* 66th Cong. 101 (1921) (statement of Lucy G. Branham). On Branham's appointment with the AFSC, see "Minutes of a Meeting of Committee on Work in Poland and Russia Held Wednesday, Dec. 29, 1921," AFSC papers. In a 1941 application for federal employment with the war board, Branham claimed to have worked with the AFSC as a "famine investigator" between August 1921 and April 1922. Lucy Branham papers, Library of Congress. She traveled through Russia in the summer of 1921 with the pro-Soviet industrial magnate Armand Hammer, a close family friend. Joseph Finder, *Red Carpet* (New York: Holt, Rinehart, and Winston, 1983), 22. Arthur J. Watts, "The Care of Children in the Russian Socialist Federated Socialist Republic (A Preliminary Survey)," Oct. 1920, box 7, parcel 3, British Friends War Victims Relief Committee (BFWVRC) papers, Library of the Religious Society of Friends, London (hereafter cited as BFWVRC papers). A condensed version of Watts's report, entitled "The Provision for Children in Soviet Russia" (1921), is in general files (Russia), AFSC papers. On Watts's arrival in Moscow, see Richenda C. Scott, *Quakers in Russia* (London: M. Joseph, 1964), 229. Unbeknownst to Branham, Blatch, or the congressmen before whom they testified, Watts was strongly predisposed in favor of the Soviet government. A British Quaker and labor activist who had been imprisoned as a conscientious objector during World War I, Watts ultimately immigrated to Soviet Russia, where he lived until his death in 1958. "Dictionary of Quaker Biography" (typescript), Library of the Religious Society of Friends, London.

13. Margaret Barber, *A British Nurse in Bolshevik Russia: The Narrative of Margaret H. Barber, April, 1916–December, 1919* (London: A. C. Fifield, 1920), 47–48; Jerome Davis, "Friends among the Children in Russia," *New Republic* 28 (1921): 375–77; Louise Bryant, "Russian Children" (typescript), 1921, box 13, folder 64, Louise Bryant papers, Yale University, also published in *Portland Oregonian*, Aug. 31, 1921, 1.

14. Bertrand Patenaude, *The Big Show in Bololand: The American Relief Expedition to Soviet Russia in the Famine of 1921* (Stanford, CA: Stanford University Press, 2002), 26; Michael Asquith, *Famine (Quaker Work in Russia 1921–23)* (London: Oxford University Press, 1943), 9.

15. Wendy Z. Goldman, *Women, the State, and Revolution: Soviet Family Policy & Social Life, 1917–1936* (Cambridge: Cambridge University Press, 1995), 67; Weissman, *Herbert Hoover and Famine Relief*, 522.

16. Friends of Soviet Russia, *The Russian Famine: Appeals, Photographs* (New York: Friends of Soviet Russia, 1921). See figure 2.5 in the pamphlet, which contains this and at least one other image from the BFWVRC collections.

17. Anna Haines, *The Story of a Quaker Woman in Russia* (New York: Russian Famine Fund [Distributing through the American Friends], [1921]), n.p.

18. "Starri-Gumerova: We Stop at One of the Richer Villages," [Feb. 18, 1923], Jessica Smith reports, Hoover Library, Stanford. An undated (but original) copy is in publicity files (Russia), AFSC papers.

19. Louise Bryant, *Six Red Months in Russia* (New York: George H. Doran, 1918), 258.

20. Thomas W. Laqueur, "Bodies, Details, and the Humanitarian Narrative," in *The New Cultural History*, ed. Lynn Hunt (Berkeley: University of California Press, 1989), 177; Susan Sontag, *Regarding the Pain of Others* (New York: Farrar, Straus and Giroux, 2003), 18.

21. Mary Heaton Vorse paraphrased in Dee Garrison, *Mary Heaton Vorse: The Life of an American Insurgent* (Philadelphia, PA: Temple University Press, 1989), 178. Vorse, a labor journalist active with the FSR, was given special dispensation to enter the famine district with Bessie Beatty and several Soviet representatives (177). George Bernard Shaw quoted in Philip E. Veerman, *The Rights of the Child and the Changing Image of Childhood* (Leiden, Neth.: Martinus Nijhoff Publishers, 1992), 88.

22. Julia F Irwin, *Making the World Safe* (New York: Oxford University Press, 2013), 2. Jennifer Ann Polk, "Constructive Efforts: The American Red Cross and the YMCA in Revolutionary and Civil War Russia, 1917–1924" (PhD diss., University of Toronto, 2012), 23, 60. On the JDC, see Michael Beizer, "The Joint Distribution Committee, American Government, Jewish Community, Soviet Authorities and Russian Jewish Public, 1920–1924" (paper delivered at the 44th Conference of the American Association for Jewish Studies, Chicago, Dec. 16–18, 2012), accessed Aug. 2, 2013, pluto.huji.ac.il/~beizer /files/JDC%201920-1924.pdf; Tom Shachtman, *I Seek My Brethren: Ralph Goldman and "The Joint": Rescue, Relief and Reconstruction* (New York, 2001); Oscar Handlin, *A Continuing Task: The American Jewish Joint Distribution Committee, 1914–1964* (New York, 1964).

23. Ruth Fry, *A Quaker Adventure: The Story of Nine Years' Relief and Reconstruction* (London: Nisbet, 1926). xvii–xviii (first two quotations); Ilana Feldman, "The Quaker Way: Ethical Labor and Humanitarian Relief," *American Ethnologist* 34, no. 4 (2007): 692–93 (final two quotations).

24. Feldman, "The Quaker Way," 692–93.

25. Weissman, *Herbert Hoover and Famine Relief*, 29.

26. M. Il'in, *New Russia's Primer*, trans. George S. Counts and Nucia P. Lodge (Cambridge, MA: The Riverside Press, 1931), 150 ("red-cheeked"); Lucy L. W. Wilson, "The New Schools in the New Russia," *Progressive Education* 5, no. 3 (1928): 253, 254 ("capable, happy, and eager children"); Anna Louise Strong (hereafter cited as ALS), "Education in Modern Russia," *Progressive Education* 1, no. 3 (1924): 157–59 ("self-reliant" and "first socialist commonwealth").

27. Isadora Duncan to Ivor Novello, Sept. 4, 1921, box 2, folder 18, Isadora Duncan collection, UCLA. Emphasis in original.

28. Patenaude, *The Big Show in Bololand*, 50.

29. Scott, *Quakers in Russia*, 32; Haines to Henry Cadbury, June 1, 1917, Anna Haines personnel file, AFSC papers (quotation); *Register of Alumnae and Former Students, Bryn Mawr College* (Bryn Mawr: The College, 1917), 75.

30. Anna J. Haines, "Children of Moscow," *Asia* 22 (1922): 216.

31. Anna J. Haines, "Across the Steppes of Russia," in Edward Thomas, *Quaker Adventures: Experiences of Twenty-Three Adventurers in International Understanding* (New York: Fleming H. Revell, 1928), 114–15.

32. Smith to Mrs. Eliza M. Cope (on Intercollegiate Socialist Society letterhead), Dec. 28, 1920. Smith's original letter of application to the AFSC for work in Russia is dated July 6, 1919. Both items in Jessica Smith personnel file, AFSC papers (hereafter cited as Smith personnel file).

33. Dorothy Detzer, note on Jessica Smith, box 2, Dorothy Detzer papers, Swarthmore College Peace Collection; E. Carleton McDonald, letter of recommendation for Jessica Smith's application to the AFSC, Apr. 18, 1921, Smith personnel file.

34. Jessica Smith, application blank for Women for Service in Russia, July 6, 1919, Smith personnel file. The application was later updated.

35. Haines to Ruth Fry, June 18, 1919, box 7, parcel 1, folder 9, BFWVRC papers.

36. Haines was scheduled to sail on October 30, according to BFWVRC minutes, Oct. 13, 1920, BFWVRC minutes, vol. 1, 1918–1921, BFWVRC papers; Bryant, "Russian Children."

37. Watts to London office, Dec. 16, 1920, box 7, parcel 3, folder 4, BFWVRC papers.

38. Bryant, "Russian Children"; Haines and Watts to Ruth Fry, Feb. 17 and Mar. 24, 1921, box 7, parcel 3, folder 4, BFWVRC papers.

39. Bryant, "Russian Children"; Watts and Haines to London office, Dec. 30, 1920, box 7 parcel 3, folder 4, BFWVRC papers.

40. Haines and Watts to Ruth Fry, Jan. 20, 1921 (regarding the ARC), and Watts to London office, Oct. 21, 1920 ("bourgeois philanthropists"). Both letters in box 7, parcel 3, folder 4, BFWVRC papers. Meeting minutes, Nov. 20, 1920 (on American committee response to idea of statement), and excerpt from letter from Watts, Mar. 2, 1921, meeting minutes from Mar. 9, 1921 (on Save the Children). Both are in the BFWVRC papers; the former is from BFWVRC minutes, vol. 1, 1918–1921, and the latter BFWVRC minutes, vol. 2, 1921–1923. The Save the Children Fund was established in the UK in 1919 as an outgrowth of the Fight the Famine Council, which put pressure on the British govern-

ment to end the blockade of Russia. The former split off because of political disagreements. Rodney Breen, "Saving Enemy Children: Save the Children's Russian Relief Organisation, 1921–1923," *Disasters* 18, no. 3 (1994): 221–37.

41. Haines to Ruth Fry, Apr. 21, May 5, and June 14, 1921, box 7, parcel 3, folder 4, BFWVRC papers.

42. Watts and Haines report to Ruth Fry, Jan. 20, 1921, box 7, parcel 3, folder 4, BFWVRC papers; telegram from Watts and Haines to Ruth Fry, Aug. 9, 1921, box 7, parcel 3, folder 4, BFWVRC papers; Scott, *Quakers in Russia*, 229, 231.

43. Gorky quoted in David McFadden and Claire Gorfinkel, *Constructive Spirit: Quakers in Revolutionary Russia* (Pasadena, CA: Intentional Productions, 2004), 59; Patenaude, *The Big Show in Bololand*, 31–32.

44. Haines and Watts to Ruth Fry, Mar. 14, 1921, box 7, parcel 3, folder 4, BFWVRC papers, quoted in Weissman, *Herbert Hoover and Famine Relief*, 40; Patenaude, *The Big Show in Bololand*, 38; Haines to Ruth Fry, Apr. 21, 1921, box 7, parcel 3, folder 4, BFWVRC papers. ALS to Sydney Strong, Dec. 31, 1921, box 3, folder 12, ALS papers, accession no. 1309-001, University of Washington (hereafter cited as ALS papers).

45. Herbert Hoover to Rufus Jones, quoted in McFadden and Gorfinkel, *Constructive Spirit*, 72.

46. Anna Haines visited the famine region in August to survey conditions and bring supplies; Strong followed a few weeks later. Telegram from Watts to Ruth Fry, Aug. 9, 1921, box 7, parcel 3, BFWVRC papers. Garrison, *Mary Heaton Vorse*, 177.

47. ALS, *I Change Worlds* (Seattle: The Seal Press, 1979), 5, 13, 21 (quotation); Tracy B. Strong and Helene Keyssar, *Right in Her Soul: The Life of Anna Louise Strong* (New York: Random House, 1983), 15.

48. ALS, *I Change Worlds*, 39–43.

49. Ibid., 69, 71.

50. On Strong's arranging of Bryant's speaking tour, see Virginia Gardner, *"Friend and Lover": The Life of Louise Bryant* (New York: Horizon Press, 1982), 153. Louise Bryant to John Reed, "Saturday on the Train" (1919), quoted in ibid, 155. ALS, *I Change Worlds*, 89. ALS to Wilbur K. Thomas (hereafter cited as WKT), dated Feb. 7, 1920, but marked as received Feb. 14, 1921, with 1920 circled in red pencil (so 1920 was probably a typo); ALS to WKT, Feb. 20, 1921. Both letters are in ALS personnel file, AFSC papers.

51. ALS to WKT, Apr. 30, 1921; WKT to ALS, May 2, 1921; ALS to WKT, May 7, 1921; letter from R.I.G., copying letter from John H. Roberts dated June 1, 1921. All in ALS personnel file, AFSC papers.

52. ALS, *I Change Worlds*, 91–92.

53. Ibid., 91, 93, 94.

54. McFadden and Gorfinkel, *Constructive Spirit*, 64 (emphasis in original).

55. Ibid., 69.

56. ALS, *I Change Worlds*, 101 (quotations), 127; ALS to Carr, Feb. 6, and Mar. 1, 2, and Mar. 10, 1922, f. 515, op. 1, d. 120, microfilm reel 7, CPUSA papers, Tamiment Library, New York University (NYU).

57. ALS, *I Change Worlds*, 101–2.

58. Watts to Ruth Fry, Sept. 9 and 24, 1921, box 7, parcel 3, folder 4, BFWVRC papers; ALS, *I Change Worlds*, 111–12.

59. ALS, *I Change Worlds*, 112 ("without mattresses"), 104 ("creators in chaos").

60. Ibid., 109.

61. Watts to Ruth Fry, Sept. 24, 1921, box 7, parcel 3, folder 4, BFWVRC papers.

62. Ibid. Cable from Watts to Ruth Fry, Aug. 12, 1921: "SEND DEPUTATION TO AROUSE ENGLISH PUBLIC SYMPATHY BY VIVID INFORMATION DESIRE ONE QUAKER MEMBER CAN YOU ACT OR SHALL WE SEND QUAKER FROM HERE REPLY URGENT." Box 7, parcel 3, folder 4, BFWVRC papers.

63. ALS, *I Change Worlds*, 95, 90; Watts to Ruth Fry, Oct. 7, 1921, box 7, parcel 3, folder 4, BFWVRC papers.

64. Watts to Ruth Fry, Oct. 14, 1921, box 7, parcel 3, folder 4, BFWVRC papers. He explained that she had volunteered to do temporary work for the ARA "without consulting us" (ibid.). ALS, *I Change Worlds*, 115. Scott, *Quakers in Russia*, 251.

65. Marvin R. Weisbord, "Famine on the Steppe," in *Some Form of Peace: True Stories of the American Friends Service Committee at Home and Abroad*, ed. Marvin R. Weisbord (New York: Viking, 1968), 68–69.

66. Evelyn Sharp diary, Jan. 16, 1922.

67. ALS to Sydney Strong, Dec. 31, 1921, box 3, folder 12, ALS papers (quotation); Ruth Fry to Watts, Sept. 16, 1921, box 7, parcel 4, folder 1, BFWVRC papers. Thomas noted in a letter to volunteer Robert Dunn, a socialist, his own attraction to "radical movement work" and confessed that he would probably "throw my lot in with that work" if not for "home obligations." WKT to Dunn, Jan. 15, 1919, Robert Dunn personnel file, AFSC papers.

68. That man was Harold Ware, an agricultural expert and one of the founding members of the American Communist Party. On Strong's attraction to Harold Ware, see Strong and Keyssar, *Right in Her Soul*, 93.

69. Smith to WKT, Jan. 20 and 24, 1922; Smith to WKT, n.d., stamped as received Jan. 21, 1922. All three letters are in Smith personnel file.

70. Smith to WKT, Feb. 4, 1922; Jessica Smith, addendum to application, Jan. 23, 1922. These two items are in Smith personnel file.

71. Robert Dunn citing comments by Jessica Smith, in "Need for Famine Relief Continues," *Soviet Russia Pictorial*, Sept. 15, 1922, 162–63.

72. *Sorochinskoya Nightingale*, May 2, 1922, box 6, folder 40, Labor Research Association papers, Tamiment Library, NYU.

73. Dunn to family, Thursday, July 28, 1922, box 6, folder 40, Labor Research Association papers, Tamiment Library, NYU; Jessica Smith, "Efim's Vocabulary Increases," Feb. 1923, publicity files (Russia), AFSC papers.

74. Smith to WKT, Dec. 26, 1922, Smith personnel file.

75. Jessica Smith, "In the Monastery at Shar," Feb. 18, 1923, Sorochinskoye, Jessica Smith reports, Hoover Library; Jessica Smith, "In the Children's City," Feb. 1923, Gamaleyevka, Russia, publicity files (Russia), AFSC papers.

76. The quotation within Smith's commentary is from Henry Noel Brailsford, *The Russian Workers' Republic* (London: Allen and Unwin, 1921), 17.

77. Jessica Smith, "Why They Suffered So," Feb. 15, 1923, Sorochinskoye, Russia, publicity files (Russia), AFSC papers.

78. Harold Ware's wife, Clarissa, became ill during the trip. Shortly after her return home, she was admitted to the hospital for surgery and died on the operating table. Lement Harris, *Harold M. Ware (1890–1935): Agricultural Pioneer, USA and USSR*. Occasional Paper 30 (New York: American Institute for Marxist Studies, 1978), 19, 16–17. Ella Reeve Bloor, *We Are Many: An Autobiography by Ella Reeve Bloor* (New York: International publishers, 1940), 187, 268–72. Strong and Keyssar, *Right in Her Soul*, 95.

79. WKT to Smith, Sept. 20 and Dec. 10, 1923, Smith personnel file.

80. Jessica Smith, "Quaker Mission Worker Disputes Spewack's Views," letter sent by Robert W. Dunn, associate director of the American Civil Liberties Union, in *New York World*, date not visible, clipping, box 6, folder 40, Labor Research Association papers, Tamiment Library, NYU; Jessica Smith, "In the House of the Sugar King," *Nation* 117 (1923); "House of Sugar King," *Soviet Russia Pictorial*, Feb. 1924, 40–41.

81. Alice Hamilton, *Exploring the Dangerous Trades: The Autobiography of Alice Hamilton, M.D.* (Boston, MA: Northeastern University Press, 1985), 319, 337. Hamilton does not name Smith, but Dorothy Detzer, one of Smith's covolunteers from the Quaker mission, citing Hamilton's "extraordinary description of Jessica Smith," said that "any one reading it who had been in our unit would know at once who she was referring to." Dorothy Detzer Denny to Andree Aelion Brooks, Mar. 28, 1977, box 1, Andree Aelion Brooks papers, Tamiment Library, NYU.

82. Smith to WKT, Nov. 18, 1924, Smith personnel file; Ruby A. Black, "Women In Russia," *Equal Rights* 11, no. 50 (1925): 395 (quotation). The book was Jessica Smith, *Woman in Soviet Russia* (New York: Vanguard, 1928).

83. There was speculation in Moscow's American community to this effect. Strong and Keyssar, *Right in Her Soul*, 92–93.

84. ALS to Dr. Kunz [*sic*] and Yavorskaia, Feb. 8, 1926, box 6, folder 13, ALS papers. (Dr. Charles Kuntz was a founder of the Birobidjian colony.) On the situation with homeless children, see Goldman, *Women, the State, and Revolution*, 59.

85. ALS, *I Change Worlds*, 192.

86. Ibid., 193; ALS to Sydney Strong, May 17, 1924, box 3, ALS papers; Edward K. Balls to Alice Nike, Friends International Service, July 7, 1924, box 8, parcel 3, folder 1, BFWVRC papers (on hesitation to support Bolshevik colonies). On the lingering mistrust of Strong in Philadelphia, see Thomas's response to her request to hold meetings there to enlist support for the JRC. He said there were already "several Russian meetings" happening and there probably wasn't room for another. WKT to ALS, Feb. 10, 1925, ALS personnel file, AFSC papers.

87. ALS to Sydney Strong, June 7 (quotation) and Aug. 2, 1924, box 3, folder 24, ALS papers. Also listed on the letterhead are Harry Stevens, a former BFWVRC volunteer; Rose Cohen and Gertrude Haessler (British and American Communists, respectively);

and Marie [Sukloff] Yarros, the famed revolutionary and author of *The Story of a Russian Exile* (1915). ALS to Sydney Strong, Aug. 2, 1924. On Strong's deteriorating friendship with Smith, see Strong and Keyssar, *Right in Her Soul*, 103.

88. ALS to "Bob," sent from Lux Hotel, Moscow, May 5, 1924, box 3, folder 24, ALS papers.

89. ALS, "A Children's School-Commune," *Soviet Russia Pictorial* 9, no. 10 (Oct. 1924): 274–77; ALS, *A Children's Colony on the Volga* [pamphlet] (London: Friends International Service, 1924), in box 3, folder 26, ALS papers.

90. ALS to Sydney Strong, Sept. 16, 1924, box 3, folder 25, ALS papers.

91. Ibid. (on plans to take over Alexievka); ALS , "A Children's School-Commune," 277.

92. ALS to Sydney Strong, Nov. 13, 1924, box 3, folder 26, ALS papers.

93. ALS to Sydney Strong, Nov. 21, 1924, box 3, folder 26, ALS papers; ALS to Sydney Strong, Aug. 12, 1925, box 3, folder 28, ALS papers.

94. ALS to Sydney Strong, Oct. 10, 1924, box 3, folder 26, ALS papers. See also ALS, *Back from Our Children's Colony* (pamphlet), Oct. 15, 1924, box 6, folder 17, ALS papers.

95. ALS to Sydney Strong, Dec. 5, 1924, box 3, folder 26, ALS papers. On the American vocational school, see ALS, "Report on John Reed Children's Colony" to Comrades Oanzhenski and Konovalof, Sept. 2, 1925, box 3, folder 28, ALS papers.

96. ALS to Ellen Hayes, Aug. 25, 1925, box 6, folder 13, ALS papers.

97. Ibid.

98. ALS, "Report on John Reed Children's Colony."

99. Ibid. (quotations); ALS to Ada [Flomenbaum] and Vivian [Wilkinson], June 26, 1925, box 6, folder 12, ALS papers (on the toilets).

100. ALS to Ellen Hayes Aug. 25, 1925, box 6, folder 13, ALS papers.

101. ALS, "Present Prospects for Our Children's Colonies," May 15, 1925, box 6, folder 11, ALS papers. The playgrounds movement of the early twentieth century reflected a strong faith that the development of children's bodies was closely related to the development of their minds. See Dominick Cavallo, *Muscles and Morals: Organized Playgrounds and Urban Reform, 1880–1920* (Philadelphia: University of Pennsylvania Press, 1981).

102. ALS to Ellen Hayes, Aug. 25, 1925, box 6, folder 13, ALS papers; ALS, "John Reed Colony Has a Tractor and Needs Now a Social-Center-School: Recent Visit by Anna Louise Strong" [publicity mailing], June 25, 1925, box 6, folder 17, ALS papers.

103. ALS to Sydney Strong, Aug. 17, 1925; ALS to Hayes Aug. 25, 1925. Both are in box 6, folder 13, ALS papers. ALS, "John Reed Colony Has a Tractor."

104. Strong and Keyssar, *Right in Her Soul*, 101.

105. ALS to Ada [Flomenbaum] and Vivian [Wilkinson], June 26 1925, box 6, folder 12, ALS papers.

106. ALS, *Wild River* (Boston: Little, Brown, 1943), 26–27.

107. ALS, "John Reed Colony Has a Tractor"; ALS to Dr. Kunz [sic] and Yavorskaia, Feb. 8, 1926, box 6, folder 13, ALS papers. The subsequent chronology of events and quotations detailing ALS's break with the JRC are from this letter.

108. ALS, *I Change Worlds*, 198; Strong and Keyssar, *Right in Her Soul*, 358 (giving up on the JRC).

109. Assistant secretary, AFSC, to Dorothy Detzer, June 26, 1924, Dorothy Detzer personnel file, AFSC papers. On Marc Cheftel, see Andrée Aelion Brooks, *Russian Dance: A True Story of Intrigue and Passion in Stalinist Russia* (Hoboken, NJ: John Wiley & Sons, 2004), 128–51. An example of Haines's continued support for Soviet causes is the fact that she was a signer of a petition to Franklin Roosevelt urging Russian recognition in 1933. "Amity with Russia Urged in Petition," *New York Times*, May 15, 1933, 7.

110. Smith, *Woman in Soviet Russia*, 77.

111. On the closing of the Quaker offices, see Zachary Oelschlegel, "Bolshevism and Christianity: The American Friends Service Committee in Russia, 1919–1933" (master's thesis, Temple University, 2012). On the Quaker house as a social center for Americans, see Jessie Lloyd diary, box 90, folder 4, Jessie Lloyd O'Connor papers, Smith College. On *New Russia's Primer*, see Julia Mickenberg, "The New Generation and the New Russia: Modern Childhood as Collective Fantasy," *American Quarterly* 62, no. 1 (2010): 103–34.

PART II

1. Ruth Epperson Kennell, "The New Innocents Abroad," *American Mercury* 17 (1929): 10; Statute of Organization & Provisions on the Basis of the Agreement with the Soviet of Labor and Defence, n.d., f. 515, op. 1, d. 4296, l. 57, microfilm reel 324, CPUSA papers, Tamiment Library, NYU; Martin, "A Letter from Siberia," *Kuzbas Bulletin*, Nov. 20, 1922, 8.

2. Benjamin Sawyer, "Shedding the White and Blue: American Migration and Soviet Dreams in the Era of the New Economic Policy," *Ab Imperio* 1 (2013): 70.

3. Andrea Graziosi, *A New, Peculiar State: Explorations in Soviet History, 1917–1937* (Westport, CT: Praeger, 2000), 226; Sawyer, "Shedding the White and Blue," 69, 72; Seth Bernstein and Robert Cherny, "Searching for the Soviet Dream: Prosperity and Disillusionment on the Soviet Seattle Agricultural Commune, 1922–1927," *Agricultural History* 88, no. 1 (2011): 22–44.

4. Graziosi, *A New, Peculiar State*, 226; Sawyer, "Shedding the White and Blue," 73 (first quotation); "Lies and Free Love Cure U.S. Reds in Russia," *Chicago Daily Tribune*, Apr. 7, 1923, quoted in Sawyer, "Shedding the White and Blue," 65–66 (on sensationalist claims); Kennell, "The New Innocents Abroad," 14 (third quotation).

5. Ruth Kennell and Milly Bennett, "They All Come to Moscow," *American Mercury*, Dec. 1931, 394–401. "The Red Jerusalem" is on pages 394–97. "Martyr from the South" is on pages 398–99. On the controversy in the United States following the article's publication, see Evelyn Seeley, "Her Article on Russia Aroused Protest Here, but Soviet Officials Laughed and Let Her Stay," *New York World Telegram*, Jan. 16, 1932.

6. Ruth Epperson Kennell and Milly Bennett, "American Immigrants in Russia," *American Mercury*, 1932, 463.

7. Sixteenth Party Congress quoted in Graziosi, *A New, Peculiar State*, 226; Tim Tzouliadis, *The Forsaken: An American Tragedy in Stalin's Russia* (New York: Penguin Press, 2008), 6–7.

8. Seema Rynin Allan, *Comrades and Citizens* (London: V. Gollancz, 1938), 28–30.

9. Margaret Bourke-White, "Silk Stockings in the Five-Year Plan: Despite the Soviet Drive and the New Order of Things, Russia's Women Are Still Feminine," *New York Times*, Feb. 14, 1932, SM14.

10. The unseemly contrast between Bourke-White's expensive clothes and those of the poor folk she sometimes made good money photographing was the subject of legendary critique by James Agee in *Let Us Now Praise Famous Men* (1941). For further discussion, see Paula Rabinowitz, *They Must Be Represented: The Politics of Documentary* (New York: Verso, 1994), 68.

11. Allan, *Comrades and Citizens*, 18–19.

12. Eugene Lyons, *Assignment in Utopia* (New York: Harcourt, 1937), 229–31 (ellipsis in original).

CHAPTER 3

1. Ruth Epperson Kennell (hereafter cited as REK), "Kuzbas, a New Pennsylvania," *Nation* 116 (1923). The only book in English on the American colony in Kuzbas was published by the Communist Party. See J. P. Morray, *Project Kuzbas: American Workers in Siberia (1921–1926)* (New York: International Publishers, 1983). Also see William Thomas Smith, "The Kuzbas Colony, Soviet Russia, 1921–1926: An American Contribution to the Building of a Communist State" (PhD diss., University of Miami, 1978); Martha Ann Evans, "Kuzbas Colony, 1921–1927" (master's thesis, College of Saint Catherine, 1976); and Vincent E. Bakers, "American Workers in the Soviet Union between the Two World Wars: From Dream to Disillusionment" (master's thesis, West Virginia University, 1998). A segment of the Russian documentary series *Soblazhennye Stranoi Sovetov* (Seduced by the land of the Soviets) (dir. Tat'iana Malova, 2007) entitled *Nash Malen'kii Internasional v Sibiri* (Our little international in Siberia) deals with the American colony in Kuzbas. Theodore Dreiser gives a version of Kennell's experience in Kuzbas in "Ernita," in vol. 1 of *A Gallery of Women*, 2 vols. (New York: Horace Liveright, 1929).

2. REK, "Kuzbas: A Romantic Chronicle" (unpublished memoir), p. 8, REK papers, University of Oregon, Eugene (hereafter cited as REK papers). Where not otherwise noted, for the sequence of events described in this chapter, I am drawing on Kennell's unpublished memoir and Dreiser's "Ernita" sketch.

3. REK, "Kuzbas: A Romantic Chronicle," 8–16. See also Alan Michelson and Katherine Solomson, "Remnants of a Failed Utopia: Reconstructing Runnymede's Agricultural Landscape," *Perspectives in Vernacular Architecture* 6 (1997): 3.

4. REK, "Kuzbas: A Romantic Chronicle," 23. On the Industrial Workers of the World, see Melvyn Dubofsky, *We Shall Be All: A History of the Industrial Workers of the World*, 2nd ed. (Urbana: University of Illinois Press, 1988); Salvatore Salerno, *Red November, Black November: Culture and Community in the Industrial Workers of the World* (Albany: State University of New York Press, 1989).

5. REK, "Kuzbas: A Romantic Chronicle," 21.

6. Michael Gold, "Wanted, Pioneers for Siberia!," *The Liberator* 5, no. 3 (1922): 1, 6. On Calvert's work at Ford as preparation for work in Russia, see Herbert S. Calvert and Mellie M. Calvert, "The Kuzbas Story: History of the Autonomous Industrial Colony Kuzbas," 1973, Herbert S. Calvert papers, Wayne State University.

7. Herbert Calvert, "Economic Reconstruction," Apr. 1921, quoted in Calvert and Calvert, "Kuzbas Story" (first two quotations); "Kuzbas: An Opportunity for Workers and Engineers," flier, Tamiment Library, New York University (NYU) (advertisement/prospectus quotations); "The Cooperatives of Kuzbas," f. 515, d. 4304, microfilm reel 325, CPUSA papers, Tamiment Library, NYU (on the imagined dinner). On Lenin's cautious support, see his note to Molotov (Oct. 12, 1921), in which he considered the benefits and drawbacks of the Kuzbas colony as he weighed the issue of whether to offer it funding:

> For: if the Americans keep their word, it will be of tremendous benefit. In that case, we shall not grudge the 600,000 gold rubles.
>
> Against: will they keep their word? Haywood is half-anarchist. More sentimental than business-like. Rutgers may succumb to Leftism. Calvert is highly garrulous. We have no business guarantee whatever. Enthusiastic people, in an atmosphere of unemployment, may recruit a group of "adventurous spirits" who will end up in squabbles. We may then lose part of our 600,000 gold rubles . . . and risk losing up to 1 million gold rubles more.
>
> *No small risk.*

Lenin, *Collected Works*, 45:304, quoted in Nemmy Sparks, "Lenin and the Americans at Kuzbas," in *For Dirk Struik: Scientific, Historical, and Political Essays in Honor of Dirk Struik*, ed. Robert S. Cohen, John J. Stachel, Marx W. Wartofsky (Dordrecht; Boston: D. Reidel, 1974), 618.

8. S. J. Rutgers quoted in "Industrial Labor Colony Kuzbas: Economic Reconstruction in Soviet Russia," clipping, f. 626, op. 1, d. 11, Russian State Archive of Socio-Political History (RGASPI), Moscow (hereafter cited as RGASPI); comments by "Comrade Pearson," Aug. 27, 1922, Kuzbas meeting, f. 515, op.1, d. 4299, l. 145–47, microfilm reel 324, CPUSA papers, Tamiment Library, NYU.

9. Charles W. Wood, "H. S. Calvert's Giant Task in Industry: Once a Worker in a Ford Factory, He Has Engaged to Develop a Russian Territory Bigger than New Jersey," *New York World*, Sunday, Feb. 12, 1922, f. 626, op. 1, d. 12, Comintern files, RGASPI. Letter from Haywood, Oct. 13, 1921, f. 515, op. 1., d. 4298, microfilm reel 324, CPUSA papers, Tamiment Library, NYU. Quotation regarding pioneer women from Gold, "Wanted: Pioneers for Siberia!," 7. Gold seems to have drawn on Wood's article in his discussion.

10. V. I. Lenin, "A Great Beginning," speech delivered to Fourth Moscow City Conference of Non-Party Women Workers, Sept. 23, 1919, reprinted in V. I. Lenin, "Women in Soviet Russia," *Nation* 110 (Feb. 1920): 185–86.

11. Statute of Organization & Provisions on the Basis of the Agreement with the Soviet of Labor and Defence, n.d., f. 515, op. 1, d. 4296, l. 57, microfilm reel 324, CPUSA

papers, Tamiment Library, NYU. Also see the version dated Nov. 1921 in "Kuzbas," *Nation* 114 (June 14, 1922): 730–32. Application for colonists, f. 626, op. 1, d. 13, Comintern files, RGASPI.

12. REK to Heber Epperson, Apr. 7, 8, and 13, 1924, box 6, folder 33, REK papers.

13. Dreiser, "Ernita," 326.

14. REK, "Kuzbas: A Romantic Chronicle," 37 (quotation); REK to Ella Epperson, July 25, 1922, box 9, folder 5, REK papers. All letters between REK and Ella Epperson are in box 9, folder 5, of the REK papers. Subsequent citations provide names and dates only.

15. "More Pioneers Leave for Siberia," *Kuzbas Bulletin*, Aug. 20, 1922, 9 (on the group's composition); REK, "Kuzbas: A Romantic Chronicle," 36; REK to Ella Epperson, July 25, 1922; REK, "Kuzbassers Enjoy Themselves on the Atlantic," *Kuzbas Bulletin*, Oct. 20, 1922, 9.

16. REK, "Kuzbas: A Romantic Chronicle," 37, 39.

17. Ibid., 39–40.

18. REK to Ella Epperson, Aug. 19, 1922 ("desolate place"); REK, "Kuzbas: A Romantic Chronicle," 40 (on the landscape).

19. REK, "Kuzbas: A Romantic Chronicle," 41.

20. Ibid. (quotation); Helen Calista Wilson and Elsie Reed Mitchell, "A Light Running Utopia," *Asia* 28 (1928): 1035.

21. Wilson and Mitchell, "A Light Running Utopia," 961–62.

22. *Kuzbas Bulletin*, Apr. 1, 1923, 4 (emphasis in original).

23. Morray, *Project Kuzbas*, 95.

24. Haywood quoted in Morray, *Project Kuzbas*, 100.

25. REK, "A Kuzbas Chronicle," *Nation* 116, no. 3000 (1923): 9.

26. REK, "Kuzbas: A Romantic Chronicle," 42.

27. Ibid., 45.

28. Ibid., 46. On the roles women occupied in the Kuzbas colony, see material collected by Mellie Calvert, compiled by Ruth Kennell, and then sent by Rutgers's daughter to Moscow, f. 626, op. 1, d. 13, Comintern files, RGASPI.

29. Wilson and Mitchell, "A Light Running Utopia," 960.

30. REK, "A Kuzbas Chronicle," 9.

31. REK, "Kuzbas: A Romantic Chronicle," 48.

32. REK to Ella Epperson, Sept. 24 (quotation) and 29, 1922. "It is through sexual desire that the longing for unity is most powerfully expressed, a longing that pervades the divided, alienated, fragmented human condition." Catriona Ni Dhuill, *Sex in Imagined Spaces: Gender and Utopia from More to Bloch* (Oxford: Legenda, 2010), 18.

33. REK, "Kuzbas: A Romantic Chronicle," 46.

34. Ibid., 59–60, 65.

35. Ibid., 54–56.

36. Smith, "The Kuzbas Colony," 192–93. On the New Economic Policy (NEP), see Sheila Fitzpatrick, Alexander Rabinowitch, and Richard Stites, *Russia in the Era of NEP: Explorations in Soviet Society and Culture* (Bloomington: Indiana University Press, 1991).

37. Sparks, "Lenin and the Americans at Kuzbas," 623.

38. REK, "Kuzbas: A Romantic Chronicle," 67; REK diary, Jan. 15, 1923, box 2, folder 2, REK papers.

39. REK to Ella Epperson, Dec. 20, 1922.

40. REK, "Kuzbas: A Romantic Chronicle," 75–77 (ellipsis added).

41. "Starved, Robbed, Back from Russia." *New York Times*, Apr. 7, 1923, 16 (quotation); "Kuzbas Prisoners Plea Not Guilty," *New York Times*, Apr. 25, 1923, 44; "Lerner Is Freed of Bomb Charge," *New York Times*, May 24, 1923, 11; "Eight Kuzbas Indictments Dropped," *New York Times*, Sept. 27, 1923, 5.

42. Smith, "The Kuzbas Colony," 86.

43. Tom Barker, "Hell in Siberia," *New Masses* 2, no. 1 (Nov. 1926): 15.

44. Although the article was published in the May 2 issue, it is dated February 12.

45. *Kuzbas Bulletin*, Apr. 1, 1923, quoted in Paula Garb, *They Came to Stay: North Americans in the U.S.S.R.* (Moscow: Progress Publishers, 1987), 19 (quotation). The *New York World* articles are discussed in Herbert S. Calvert, "Indictment of the Organizing Committee," chap. 8 in Calvert and Calvert, "Kuzbas Story," 2. "Kuzbas Tells Its Own Story," *Nation* 117 (Aug. 8, 1923): 145–47. REK, "Lenin Called to Us: A Kuzbas Chronicle," draft of article sent to Jessica [Smith] Nov. 1971, p. 12, box 2, folder 5, REK papers (Sussman comment).

46. "The Promised Land," *New York Times*, Apr. 28, 1923, 12; REK to Ella Epperson, June 11, 1923. Although Kennell's article was in the May 2 issue of the *Nation*, it must have come out a few days before that, as the *Times* article makes direct reference to it.

47. *Kuzbas Bulletin*, May 7, 1923 (quotations); Garb, *They Came to Stay*, 20.

48. REK diary, May 5, 1923, quoted in REK, "Kuzbas: A Romantic Chronicle," 83.

49. REK diary, May 27, 1923, quoted in REK, "Kuzbas: A Romantic Chronicle," 85; REK to Ella Epperson, July 1, 1923.

50. REK, "Kuzbas: A Romantic Chronicle," 89.

51. Ibid., 90.

52. Ibid., 92; *Kuzbas Bulletin*, Aug. 30, 1923, 9, 7; REK to Frank Kennell, Aug. 23, 1923, box 9, folder 1, REK papers. All letters between REK and Frank Kennell cited here are in box 9, folder 1, of the REK papers. Subsequent citations provide names and dates only.

53. REK to Frank Kennell, Sept. 4, 1923.

54. REK, "Kuzbas: A Romantic Chronicle," 94.

55. Ibid., 97.

56. REK to Heber Epperson, Jan. 2, 1924, box 6, folder 33, REK papers.

57. REK to Ella Epperson, Oct. 4, 1923.

58. REK to Ella Epperson, Oct. 4, 1923.

59. REK diary, Oct. 22, 1923; REK to Ella Epperson, Oct. 24, 1923.

60. REK to Heber Epperson, Apr. 13, 1924, box 6, folder 33, REK papers.

61. REK to Frank Kennell, undated fragment [probably Nov. 30 or Dec. 4, 1923].

62. REK to Frank Kennell, Nov. 30, 1923; REK to Ella Epperson, Oct. 24, 1923.

63. Ella Epperson to REK, Dec. 3, 1923; REK diary, Nov. 30 and Dec. 7, 1923.

64. Quotation about Dr. Nikitina from Wilson and Mitchell, "A Light Running Utopia," 1037; REK diary, Jan. 14, 1924. For birth control she had a notation system in her diary: a dot marked the day her menstrual cycle began each month and asterisks or XXs signaled intercourse. Clearly the system was unreliable.

65. Edward Carpenter, *The Drama of Love and Death; a Study of Human Evolution and Transfiguration* (London: G. Allen, 1912), 12; REK diary, Jan. 24, 1924; REK, "Kuzbas: A Romantic Chronicle," 114; REK to Frank Kennell, Jan. 6, 1924.

66. REK diary, Dec. 30, 1923, and Jan. 3, 1924; REK to Frank Kennell, Jan. 6, 1924; Wilson and Mitchell, "A Light Running Utopia," 1036.

67. Wilson and Mitchell, "A Light Running Utopia," 1035–36; REK, "Kuzbas in 1924," *Nation* 119 (1924): 568.

68. REK, "Kuzbas in 1924," 568; REK diary, Mar. 29, 1924; REK to Frank Kennell, May 4, 1924.

69. REK, "Kuzbas: A Romantic Chronicle," 60 (Russian wives), 85 ("primitive people"); REK to Frank Kennell, Sept. 4, 1923 (bathhouse description). Anna Preikshas, in contrast, later claimed that the colonists' relations with Russians were overwhelmingly positive, but she was speaking then as a Soviet citizen and thus was unlikely to describe the situation in more negative terms. See Garb, *They Came to Stay*, 20.

70. REK diary, Mar. 8, 1923, and Mar. 8, 1924; REK, "Lenin Called to Us: A Kuzbas Chronicle," 15; material supplied by REK to Dr. Tinchter-Rutgers, who sent it to Comintern, Jan. 17, 1966, f. 626, op. 1, d. 13, Comintern files, RGASPI.

71. Frank Kennell to REK, Jan. 8, 1924; REK to Frank Kennell, Jan. 6, 1924.

72. Frank Kennell to REK, May 3 and 15, 1924.

73. Frank Kennell to REK, May 25, 1924, and REK correspondence, box 9, folder 1, REK papers.

74. REK to Ella Epperson, Aug. 5, 1924.

75. Ibid.; REK diary, Aug. 13, 1924.

76. REK to Frank Kennell, Aug. 15, 1924.

77. Frank Kennell to REK, Sept. 27, 1924; and REK to Frank Kennell, Oct. 17, 1924.

78. REK diary, Dec. 31, 1924; REK to Ella Epperson, Nov. 4, 1924 (on Sam's leaving); Frank Kennell to REK, Sept. 7 and 27, Oct. 17, and Dec. 6, 1924. Frank's December 6 letter indicates having sent cable and departure plans.

79. REK, "Kuzbas: A Romantic Chronicle," 174 (quotation). Dreiser, "Ernita," 350 (quotation). REK to Ella Epperson, Mar. 9 and Apr. 6, 1925. REK to Shipman, Mar. 5, 1925; Shipman to REK, Mar. 13, 1925 (quotation); REK to Shipman, Aug. 23, 1926 (on Russian Reconstruction Farms). All three letters are in box 9, folder 3, REK papers. REK, "Kuzbas: A Romantic Chronicle," 191 (quotation).

80. Ruth mentions her hopes that Helen will be interested in Frank in a letter to her mother, Ella Epperson, on May 18, 1925. The description of the fallout surrounding Frank's affair with Helen is drawn from Ruth's letter to her mother dated August 30, 1925.

81. REK, "Kuzbas: A Romantic Chronicle," 201.

82. REK to Ella Epperson, Aug. 30, 1925.

83. REK to Ella Epperson, May 28, 1926.

84. REK to Shipman, Dec. 31, 1926, box 9, folder 3, REK papers.

85. REK, "The End of Kuzbas," *Nation* 128 (Feb. 6, 1929): 170–72; REK to Nina Chutonovova, Oct. 20, 1967, notes, "The American woman in my account who suffered a terrible experience at the hands of one of Korbokin's staff, sent to take charge of the Moscow office, is myself, but I have never revealed this." Box 1, folder 19, REK papers.

86. REK, "The End of Kuzbas,", 171–72.

87. On "Ossip," see REK to Ella Epperson, Apr. 16, 1927. Ruth also had extensive correspondence with Junius Wood; see box 7, REK papers.

88. O'Callaghan, a founding member of the Communist Party of Great Britain, and her lover Nellie Cohen Rathbone managed the office of the *Workers Dreadnought*, the newspaper founded by British suffragist Sylvia Pankhurst, who herself became a supporter of Lenin. Records of Kennell and O'Callaghan's correspondence, which point to the nature of the latter's relationship to Rathbone in the 1920s, extend into the 1970s. See box 7, REK papers. Also see Barbara Winslow and Sheila Rowbotham, *Sylvia Pankhurst: Sexual Politics and Political Activism* (London: UCL Press, 1996), 118. On Dreiser and Kennell as lovers, see Thomas P. Riggio, ed., *Dreiser's Russian Diary* (Philadelphia: University of Pennsylvania Press, 1996), 10.

89. Koz'ko, Nina Timofeevna, and Evenia Antonovna, *Zagadka Ernity* [The story of Ernita] (Kemerovo, Russia: Kemerovskoe Knizhnoe Izdvo, 1979). Also see "One Who Was Not Afraid to Love," *Molodoi Kommunist*, Apr. 1970. REK to Theodore Dreiser, June 9, 1928, copy, box 6, folder 32, REK papers. In addition to journalistic pieces, Ruth began writing stories for children about the new Russia as well as juvenile books. Although she changed the names of many characters, Ruth never published her memoir, "Kuzbas: A Romantic Chronicle," most likely as a concession to Frank.

90. Dreiser, "Ernita," 357–58.

91. Ni Dhuill, *Sex in Imagined Spaces*, 166–67, 5.

92. There was a major trial in 1937 following a 1936 explosion in one of the Kemerovo mines and charges of Trotskyist wrecking. See Robert Conquest, *The Great Terror: Stalin's Purge of the Thirties*, rev. ed. (New York: Macmillan, 1973). Donald A. Filtzer, *A Dream Deferred: New Studies in Russian and Soviet Labour History* (New York: Peter Lang, 2008), 213. For figures on colonists sent to the gulag and subsequent deaths, I am drawing on the documentary film *Soblazhennye Stranoi Sovetov* (Russia, 2007).

93. Wilson and Mitchell, "A Light Running Utopia," 956.

CHAPTER 4

1. Walter Benjamin, "Moscow," in *Walter Benjamin, Selected Writings*, ed. Michael W. Jennings, Howard Eiland, and Gary Smith (Cambridge, MA: Harvard University Press, 1999), 22. The phrase "eyes on Russia" is from Margaret Bourke-White, *Eyes on Russia* (New York: 1931).

2. Norman E. Saul, *Friends or Foes? The United States and Soviet Russia, 1921–1941* (Lawrence: University Press of Kansas, 2006); David C. Engerman, *Modernization from the Other Shore: American Intellectuals and the Romance of Russian Development* (Cambridge, MA: Harvard University Press, 2003); Harold Dorn, "Hugh Lincoln Cooper and the First Détente," *Technology and Culture* 20, no. 2 (Apr. 1979): 322–47.

3. Russ Castronovo, "Propaganda, Prenational Critique, and Early American Literature," *American Literary History* 21, no. 2 (2009): 184; Jochen Hellbeck, *Revolution on My Mind: Writing a Diary under Stalin* (Cambridge, MA: Harvard University Press, 2006), 9–10.

4. Anna Louise Strong (hereafter cited as ALS), *I Change Worlds* (Seattle: The Seal Press, 1979), 11; Joan Scott, "Fantasy Echo: History and the Construction of Identity," *Critical Inquiry* 27, no. 2 (2001): 288. My use of Scott was inspired by Lisa Kirschenbaum, "Exile, Gender, and Communist Self-Fashioning: Dolores Ibárruri (La Pasionaria) in the Soviet Union," *Slavic Review* 71, no. 3 (2012): 566–89.

5. ALS, *I Change Worlds*, 126 ("creator in chaos").

6. See Michel Foucault, "About the Beginnings of the Hermeneutics of the Self: Two Lectures at Dartmouth," *Political Theory* 21, no. 2 (1993): 198–227; and Jean Marie Lutes, *Front Page Girls: Women Journalists in American Culture and Fiction, 1880–1930* (Ithaca, NY: Cornell University Press, 2006). Given that female journalists typically included themselves in the news stories they wrote (lending their work immediacy though less credibility as "objective" news), the female reporter becomes an ideal vehicle for thinking about the way in which American women crafted public selves, and by extension private selves, in relation to their experiences.

7. Whitman Bassow, *The Moscow Correspondents: Reporting on Russia from the Revolution to Glasnost* (New York: W. Morrow, 1988), 311.

8. On female journalists' choice of subject matter, see Choi Chatterjee, " 'Odds and Ends of the Russian Revolution,' 1917–1920: Gender and American Travel Narratives," *Journal of Women's History* 20, no. 4 (2008): 10–33. For examples of women reporting from the Soviet Union at least through the mid-1930s, consider the following: Margaret Ashmun, "Russia through Women's Eyes," *Bookman* 48 (Feb. 1919): 755. Bessie Beatty returned to the Soviet Union to continue her reporting in 1921, and Lucy Gwynne Branham went in 1922 as a reporter for the *New York Herald Tribune.* During the fifteen months she spent in Moscow from 1927 to 1928, Jessie Lloyd wrote (without a byline) for the *London Daily Herald* and filled in for Walter Duranty on the *New York Times* (also without a byline), and Kennell, as we know, sent reports to the *Nation* and elsewhere from Moscow. There are too many others to mention.

9. John Elfreth Watkins, general manager at the *Philadelphia Public Ledger*, to Bryant, May 10, 1918, box 6, folder 83, Louise Bryant papers, Yale University; Zena Beth McGlashan, "Women Witness the Russian Revolution: Analyzing Ways of Seeing," *Journalism History* 12, no. 2 (1985): 65–61.

10. ALS to Bryant, Jan. 13 and Dec. 16, 1918, box 7, folder 101, Louise Bryant papers, Yale University.

11. ALS, *I Change Worlds*, 109, 126.

12. Ibid., 127; Strong (in Poland) to Carr (representing the US Communist Press in Moscow), Mar. 1, 2, and 22, 1922, requesting assistance in obtaining a passport and volunteering to write for them, f. 515, op. 1, d. 120, microfilm reel 7, CPUSA papers, Tamiment Library, New York University.

13. Daniela Spenser, *The Impossible Triangle: Mexico, Soviet Russia, and the United States in the 1920s* (Durham, NC: Duke University Press, 1999).

14. ALS, *I Change Worlds*, 224.

15. Ibid., 110.

16. ALS to Sydney Strong, July 6, 1930, box 4, folder 9, ALS papers, accession 1309-001, University of Washington (hereafter cited as ALS papers); ALS, *I Change Worlds*, 200–301; Dan N. Jacobs, *Borodin: Stalin's Man in China* (Cambridge, MA: Harvard University Press, 1981), 314–15. Borodin appears in memoirs and letters by several women in this study, including Isadora Duncan, Sylvia Chen, Anna Louise Strong, and Milly Bennett, and he is uniformly described in positive terms. Where not otherwise noted, for the chronology of events surrounding the *Moscow News*, I am drawing on Strong's *I Change Worlds* and correspondence in Strong's papers.

17. ALS to Sydney Strong, July 6 and Aug. 4, 1930, box 4, folder 9, ALS papers; "Plan for a Weekly Newspaper Issued in Moscow," n.d., box 6, folder 18, ALS papers.

18. "Plan for a Weekly Newspaper Issued in Moscow," n.d., box 6, folder 18, ALS papers.

19. ALS, *I Change Worlds*, 302.

20. Both Lyons and Fischer did write articles; Duranty may have as well.

21. ALS, *I Change Worlds*, 305.

22. Ibid., 305 (quotation). The censor cut several paragraphs of a humorous column by Ed Falkowski about housing conditions in Moscow; Strong conceded that perhaps his mockery did go too far. *Moscow News*, Oct. 5, 1930, 7. There is no archive for the *Moscow News*. For another discussion of the newspaper and its staffers, see Lisa A. Kirschenbaum, *International Communism and the Spanish Civil War: Solidarity and Suspicion* (New York: Cambridge University Press, 2015), 52–79.

23. Walter Duranty, "First American Paper Appears in Moscow," *New York Times*, Oct. 6, 1930, 5; S. J. Taylor, *Stalin's Apologist: Walter Duranty, the New York Times's Man in Moscow* (New York: Oxford University Press, 1990).

24. *Moscow News*, Oct. 5, 1930; *Moscow News*, Oct. 10, 1930.

25. William Stott, *Documentary Expression and Thirties America* (Chicago: University of Chicago Press, 1986).

26. "Equality an Actuality," *Moscow News*, Oct. 15, 1931, 8; "Birth Control Scientifically Handled by the State," *Moscow News*, Oct. 30, 1931, 3.

27. ALS, *I Change Worlds*, 305.

28. This was one of many "wrecker" trials undertaken beginning in 1928 to weed out technical personnel who were supposedly directly sabotaging Soviet construction or indirectly impeding it through an outlook characteristic of the old regime. See Mark R.

Beissinger, *Scientific Management, Socialist Discipline, and Soviet Power* (Cambridge, MA: Harvard University Press, 1988).

29. ALS to Sydney Strong, Apr. 4, 1931, box 5, folder 11, ALS papers.

30. Richard Hyer, Freda Utley, Marian Merriman, and Warren Larude quoted in Tom Grunfeld, editor's introduction to Milly Bennett, *On Her Own: Journalistic Adventures from San Francisco to the Chinese Revolution* (Armonk, NY: M. E. Sharpe, 1993), xv. Joan Holden (daughter of Seema Allan) mentioned to me in an interview on October 25, 2012, Bennett's husky laugh and the fact that she always told people she had great legs.

31. Milly Bennett, "The Girl with the Whistling Eye" (typescript), box 14, folder 1, Bennett papers, Hoover Library (hereafter cited as Bennett papers). For the articles mentioned, see, box 6, folder 5, Bennett papers. In *On Her Own*, Bennett claims to have been hired fresh out of high school, although her archive suggests that she didn't actually start on the paper full-time until she had completed two years of college. See "Register of the Milly Bennett Papers, 1915–1960" (collection guide), Online Archive of California, accessed Aug. 10, 2016, http://www.oac.cdlib.org/findaid/ark:/13030/tf6n39n837 /admin/#bioghist-1.7.4.

32. Bennett, *On Her Own*, xii. It's possible Strong and Bennett met earlier.

33. Strong knew that Meshlauk would be aboard this ship, and she thought it wise for Bennett to make contact with a man who could presumably guarantee her employment. ALS to Bennett, Feb. 15, 1931, box 5, folder 10, Bennett papers.

34. Ruth Epperson Kennell (hereafter cited as REK) to Ella Epperson, Nov. 7, 1924, Jan. 1925, box 9, folder 5, REK papers, University of Oregon, Eugene (hereafter cited as REK papers). All letters between REK and Ella Epperson are in box 9, folder 5, of the REK papers. Subsequent citations provide names and dates only.

35. From the Jessie Lloyd O'Connor papers, Smith College (hereafter cited as O'Connor papers): ALS to Jessie Lloyd O'Connor, Mar. 2, 1931, box 64, folder 24. For references and examples of her articles, see box 91. Jessie Lloyd diary, Nov. 5, 1927, box 90. On the apartment, see Lloyd diary, July 10, 1928. Also see Jessie Lloyd O'Connor, statement granting ALS power over attorney over the apartment, June 2, 1931, box 90, folder 2.

36. ALS to Jessie Lloyd O'Connor, May 20, 1931, box 64, folder 24, O'Connor papers.

37. Dreiser to REK, Mar. 18, 1928 (sending edits on *Vanya*), Mar. 20, 1929 (noting publishers who had read the MS), box 6, folder 32, REK papers. Dreiser and H. L. Mencken were friends, and Dreiser was a regular contributor to the *American Mercury*. Frank Kennell to REK, Aug. 18, 1929, box 9, folder 2, REK papers.

38. REK to Ella Epperson, Mar. 1, 1931. Kennell's romantic involvement with Wood from approximately 1928 to 1930 is documented in their correspondence; see box 7, folder 11, REK papers.

39. REK to Ella Epperson, Mar. 1, 1931. Correspondence and the fact that Wood had left for Moscow the prior August suggest the baby was Frank's.

40. Bennett to unidentified recipient, Apr. 2, 1931; Bennett to Holly [last name unknown], May 4, 1931. Both in box 1, folder 21, Bennett papers. On Kennell's feelings, see REK to Ella Epperson, Apr. 5, 1931.

41. Bennett to Rosie [last name unknown], Evelyn Seeley, Anne and Gene Cohn, Martinsen [full name unknown], Amaryllis Nichol, and Irma [last name unknown], n.d. [winter 1931], box 1, folder 21, Bennett papers; Tim Tzouliadis, *The Forsaken: An American Tragedy in Stalin's Russia* (New York: Penguin Press, 2008).

42. Bennett to Holly [last name unknown], May 4, 1931; Bennett to Evelyn Seeley, Apr. 2, 1931. Both in box 1, folder 21, Bennett papers. On "ordinary affects," see Kathleen Stewart, *Ordinary Affects* (Durham, NC: Duke University Press, 2007).

43. Bennett to Evelyn Seeley, Apr. 2, 1931, box 1, folder 21, Bennett papers.

44. Milly Bennett, unpublished novel, box 8, folder 8, Bennett papers.

45. Bennett to "Mr. Hoozis," Apr. 22, 1931, box 1, folder 21, Bennett papers.

46. Bennett to Rosie [last name unknown], Evelyn Seeley, Anne and Gene Cohn, Martinsen [full name unknown], Amaryllis Nichol, and Irma [last name unknown], n.d. [winter 1931], box 1, folder 21, Bennett papers.

47. M.M., "The Sidewalks of Moscow," *Moscow News*, Mar. 27, 1931.

48. REK to Ella Epperson, Apr. 5, 1931.

49. REK to Ella Epperson, Apr. 27 and June 22, 1931.

50. REK to Ella Epperson, fragment, n.d. [but 1931]. Ruth mentions still having "inflammation" and being "unable to douche" in a letter to her mother, June 22, 1931.

51. Bennett to Blake [last name unknown], Apr. 12, 1931, box 1, folder 21, Bennett papers.

52. Ibid.; Bennett to Fred [last name unknown], Apr. 8, 1931, box 1, folder 21, Bennett papers.

53. Bennett to Ethel Bogardus, May 4, 1931, box 1, folder 21, Bennett papers; M.M., "In the Marching Lines," *Moscow News*, May 4, 1931, 1–2.

54. Bennett to Betty [last name unknown], May 6, 1931, box 1, folder 21, Bennett papers; Bennett, unpublished novel.

55. REK to family, fragment, n.d. [1931], box 9, folder 5, REK papers; Bennett, unpublished novel; M.M., "May Night in Moscow," *Moscow News*, May 24, 1931, 6.

56. Bennett, unpublished novel.

57. Bennett, unpublished novel. The reference to Alice in Wonderland actually appears with some regularity in writing from this era on Stalinist Russia, signaling how difficult it was to grapple with the situation. Eugene Lyons referred to the "Alice in Wonderland" innocence of foreign writers who dared to mention "subjects like political prisoners and suppression of revolutionary thought," Hubert Hessell Tiltman's 1932 *The Terror in Europe* discussed in a chapter called "Stalin in Wonderland" the October 1930 discovery of "wreckers," and Tim Tzouliadis has referred to the "Alice in Wonderland quality" of the news from the USSR. Eugene Lyons, *Assignment in Utopia* (New York: Harcourt, 1937), 332; H. Hessell Tiltman, *The Terror in Europe* (New York: F. Stokes, 1932); Tzouliadis, *The Foresaken*, 50.

58. Bennett to Evelyn [Seeley], Apr. 2, 1931, box 1, folder 21, Bennett papers.

59. ALS, "Textile Worker Dunia," *Moscow News*, Mar. 15, 1931; ALS, "Flamelike Shadiva," *Moscow News*, Mar. 18, 1931; ALS, "Utsina The Chicken Woman," *Moscow*

News, Mar. 23, 1931; D. Saslavsky, "Complete Equality of Women Is Only Possible under Soviet Conditions," *Moscow News*, Aug. 27, 1931, 4.

60. R.K., "Soviets Run Factory Kitchens to Relieve Women of Drudgery," *Moscow News*, May 29, 1931, 5.

61. M.M., "You Can Eat in Moscow," *Moscow News*, Apr. 17, 1931, 3; Bennett, unpublished novel.

62. Bennett, unpublished novel.

63. Milly Bennett, "Soviet Russia Discovers Home Sweet Home: The New Place of Women in the State Reflected in Stricter Social Laws," *New York Times Magazine*, Nov. 10, 1935, 12.

64. REK, "Soviet Family Life, in Theory and Practice" (unpublished draft of "Where Women Are Really Equal"), n.d. [but early 1930s], box 5, folder 80, REK papers; REK, "Where Women Are Really Equal," *EveryWeek*, Feb. 7, 1932, box 6, folder 22, REK papers.

65. The pressures created by collectivization in the countryside, industrialization, and family instability—and the continuing problem of homeless children—made clear the need for stable families to assume burdens that the state was unequipped to shoulder, and industrial and military needs intensified government concerns about declining birth-rates. See Wendy Z. Goldman, *Women, the State, and Revolution: Soviet Family Policy & Social Life, 1917–1936* (Cambridge: Cambridge University Press, 1995), 296–322; Eric Naiman, *Sex in Public: The Incarnation of Early Soviet Ideology* (Princeton, NJ: Princeton University Press, 1997), 290; Igor Semenovich Kon, *The Sexual Revolution in Russia: From the Age of the Czars to Today* (New York: The Free Press, 1995), 78–79; Gregory Carleton, *Sexual Revolution in Russia* (Pittsburgh, PA: University of Pittsburgh Press, 1995), 18.

66. Bennett to Chester [last name unknown], n.d. [but probably mid-Oct. 1931], box 1, folder 21, Bennett papers; Bennett to Elmer Rosinger, Sept. 28, 1934, box 4, folder 22, Bennett papers.

67. Bennett to Elmer Rosinger, Sept. 28, 1934, box 4, folder 22, Bennett papers. Laura Englestein has noted that "privilege" was often associated with "perversion," and men of bourgeois or aristocratic backgrounds were more likely to be picked up for homosexual activity. See Laura Engelstein, "Soviet Policy toward Male Homosexuality: Its Origins and Historical Roots," *Journal of Homosexuality* 29, no. 2/3 (1995): 155–78. Homosexuals were also seen as espionage threats and an attempt was made to associate homosexuals with both bourgeois decadence and fascism. Dan Healey, *Homosexual Desire in Revolutionary Russia: The Regulation of Sexual and Gender Dissent* (Chicago: University of Chicago Press, 2001), 181–195.

68. REK and John Washburne, *They All Come to Moscow*, act 3, p. 35, New York Public Library for the Performing Arts. By all accounts, the play was a flop, closing after just twenty performances. A reporter for the *New York Evening Post* said, "It moved so slowly that it seemed it must have been written on a Five-Year Plan." Scrapbook, box 9, folder 7, REK papers. Playbill, accessed Aug. 11, 2016, http://www.playbill.com/production

/they-all-come-to-moscow-lyceum-theatre-vault-0000007241. David Kennell was born in May 1932.

69. ALS, "We Soviet Wives," *American Mercury*, Aug. 1934, 415–23.

70. ALS, *I Change Worlds*, 310.

71. These dynamics can be seen in Myra Page's *Moscow Yankee*.

72. ALS, *I Change Worlds*, 312. Bennett to Lionel [last name unknown], Sept. 1, 1931, box 1, folder 21, Bennett papers; ALS to O'Connor, July 7, 1931, box 62, folder 24, O'Connor papers.

73. ALS, *I Change Worlds*, 314.

74. Ibid., 316. See ALS, "Stalingrad Entrenched for Fight against Inefficiency," *Moscow News*, Aug. 23, 1931, 5; ALS, "Dnieprostroy: World's Largest Dam Entering Final Stage of Construction," *Moscow News*, Sept. 2, 1931, 4–5; ALS, "The American Worker in Kuzbas: How Pioneers Laid Basis for Present Foreign Workers' Colonies," *Moscow News*, Oct. 21, 1931.

75. REK to Frank and family, Aug. 24, 1931, box 9, folder 2, REK papers. Initially I thought the "kosher" reference was to communists, but given that Bennett, not a communist, was still on the staff, the "chosen race" and "kosher" almost certainly referred to Jews.

76. REK to "Dear family and O'C [her friend May O'Callaghan, whom she'd met in Moscow in the 1920s], Oct. 26, 1931, box 9, folder 5, REK papers. She refers to her need to "get my business straightened out here, treatment in the hospital, perhaps operation finished." Kennell's final *Moscow News* article was "Kuzbas Veterans Still Going Strong in Siberia," published on October 26, 1931.

77. Bennett to Lionel [last name unknown], Sept. 1, 1931, box 1, folder 21, Bennett papers.

78. "Her Article on Russia Aroused Protest Here, but Soviet Officials Laughed and Let Her Stay: Ruth Kennell Returns with Kind Words for O.G.P.U.," *New York World Telegram*, Jan. 16, 1932; REK to Jessica Smith, Nov. 1970, box 7, folder 7, REK papers. Kennell published three *Mercury* articles about Russia, two of them with Bennett, in 1929, 1931, and 1932. See, for instance, Ruth Kennell and Milly Bennett, "They All Come to Moscow," *American Mercury*, Dec. 1931, 394–401.

79. Bennett to REK, Dec. 28, 1931, box 6, folder 29, REK papers. Bennett said Strong was "flattered . . . delighted . . . and pleased!" Bennett to REK, Feb. 19, 1932, box 6, folder 29, REK papers. A 1933 Speakers Bureau flier noted that Strong had become known as the "oldest American resident" of Moscow. ALS papers, Swarthmore College Peace Collection. *Moscow News*, Dec. 18, 1931.

80. Bennett to Florence [last name unknown], Jan. 27, 1932, box 2, folder 1, Bennett papers, Hoover Library.

81. See Bennett to Nelda [last name unknown], Apr. 13, 1932, box 2, folder 1, Bennett papers. She notes that she's no longer employed at *Moscow News*.

82. Jacobs, *Borodin*, 318; ALS, *I Change Worlds*, 333 (quotations).

83. Ibid., 334.

84. The description of Strong's meeting with Stalin (including quotations) is drawn from *I Change Worlds*, 335–43.

85. Tracy B. Strong and Helene Keyssar, *Right in Her Soul: The Life of Anna Louise Strong* (New York: Random House, 1983), 155; ALS, *I Change Worlds*, 353; ALS, "We Soviet Wives," 419. Strong's FBI file says she and Shubin were married in 1932, and her memoir also says they were married after her meeting with Stalin. ALS FBI file, FOIA request #1149391-000.

86. ALS, *I Change Worlds*, 373, 160; ALS, *The Soviets Conquer Wheat: The Drama of Collective Farming* (New York: Henry Holt, 1931). On forced collectivization and famine, see Robert Conquest, *The Harvest of Sorrow: Soviet Collectivization and the Terror-Famine* (London: 1986); and Timothy Snyder, *Bloodlands: Europe between Hitler and Stalin* (New York: 2010).

87. Bennett to REK, Apr. 24, 1932, box 6, folder 29, REK papers; ALS to O'Connor, June 1, 1932, O'Connor papers.

88. Harvey O'Connor to Jessie Lloyd O'Connor, Aug. 25, 1932; Jessie Lloyd O'Connor to Harvey O'Connor, Sept. 1, 1932 (on her misery). Both letters are in box 40, folder 4, O'Connor papers. Seema Rynin Allan, *Comrades and Citizens* (London: V. Gollancz, 1938), 19.

89. Bennett to Bill [last name unknown, but probably Bill Prohme, with whom she'd worked in China], Oct. 3, 1934, box 2, folder 2, Bennett papers.

90. ALS to Bennett, Apr. 24, 1934, box 5, folder 10, Bennett papers.

91. On Bennett's divorce, note that her passport was amended on November 15, 1936, to reflect the fact that she had been divorced; her name was legally changed to Mildred Bremler Mitchell. Milly Bennett FBI file, FOIA request #1149415. Regarding Konstantinov's imprisonment, note that there were at least a few instances of men being acquitted if they could prove that no homosexual behavior had occurred after the antisodomy law was passed, so evidently the law was inconsistently applied. Healey, *Homosexual Desire in Revolutionary Russia*, 192. Kirschenbaum offers a fuller discussion of the circumstances in Spain that may have influenced Bennett's decision to join the Communist Party; she also notes that although Bennett twice applied for membership while in Spain, she does not seem to have followed up on all the necessary procedures, which suggests she remained ambivalent. Kirschenbaum, *International Communism and the Spanish Civil War*, 177–79.

92. Other writings by Strong suggest that *I Change Worlds* accurately depicts her impression of Stalin, so Stalin's edits apparently did not alter its essence. Strong and Keyssar, *Right in Her Soul*, 159–61.

93. ALS, autobiographical statement, f. 495, op. 261, d. 13, l. 205–7, ALS personal file, Russian State Archive of Social and Political History (RGASPI), Moscow (hereafter cited as RGASPI). Translation assistance from Galina Belakurova.

94. Igal Halfin, *Terror in My Soul: Communist Autobiographies on Trial* (Cambridge, MA: Harvard University Press, 2003), 7; ALS, *I Change Worlds*, xxii; Myra Page, autobiographical statement, f. 495, op. 261, d. 2043, l. 5–11, Myra Page, personal file, RGASPI.

95. ALS, *I Change Worlds*, xxii. On the comparisons to Christian as well as ancient Greek rituals of confession, see Halfin, *Terror in My Soul*, 7. John Callaghan and Mark Phythian, "State Surveillance and Communist Lives: Rose Cohen and the Early Communist Milieu," *Journal of Intelligence History* 12, no. 2 (2013); Francis Beckett, *Stalin's British Victims* (Stroud: Sutton, 2004).

96. ALS autobiographical statement.

97. F. 495, op. 261, d. 13, l. 208 (note for discussion and transmission, for Comrade Sherman, from ALS, Dec. 16, 1934), l. 204 (letter to an American comrade), and l. 199 (note on ALS), ALS personal file, RGASPI. The note on ALS is undated, but it's likely from sometime after 1936 (it mentions that she supposedly joined the CPUSA in 1936).

98. "I Change Worlds," *Forum and Century* 93, no. 6 (June 1935): iv; Strong and Keyssar, *Right in Her Soul*, 163 (quotation).

99. Strong and Keyssar, *Right in Her Soul*, 165–72; Kirschenbaum, *International Communism and the Spanish Civil War*.

100. Telephone interview with Joan Holden, Oct. 25, 2012; Margaret Bourke-White, *Eyes on Russia* (film transcript), box 72, Margaret Bourke-White papers, Syracuse University.

101. Benjamin, "Moscow," 22.

PART III

1. Erika Fischer-Lichte, *Theatre, Sacrifice, Ritual: Exploring Forms of Political Theatre* (New York: Routledge, 2005); Louise Bryant, "How the Great Arts Live in Russia" (typescript), n.d., box 13, folder 61, Louise Bryant papers, Yale University. For more on proletarian theatre in the Soviet Union, see Lynn Mally, *Culture of the Future: The Proletkult Movement in Revolutionary Russia* (Berkeley: University of California Press, 1990).

2. Huntley Carter, *The New Theatre and Cinema of Soviet Russia* (London: Chapman & Dodd, 1924), 5.

3. Ibid., 2–3.

4. Diana Taylor, *The Archive and the Repertoire: Performing Cultural Memory in the Americas* (Durham, NC: Duke University Press, 2003), 3, 7; Judith Butler, "Performative Acts and Gender Constitution: An Essay in Phenomenology and Feminist Theory," *Theatre Journal* 40, no. 4 (1988): 519–31, reprinted in Sue-Ellen Case, ed., *Performing Feminisms* (Baltimore, MD: Johns Hopkins University Press, 1990), 270 (original emphasis).

5. Ted Shawn, *Every Little Movement: A Book about François Delsarte, the Man and His Philosophy, His Science of Applied Aesthetics, the Application of This Science to the Art of the Dance, the Influence of Delsarte on American Dance*, 2nd ed. (Brooklyn, NY: Dance Horizons, 1963); Nancy Lee Chalfa Ruyter, "The Delsarte Heritage," *Dance Research: The Journal of the Society for Dance Research* 14, no. 1 (1996): 62–74; John Martin, "Dance as a Means of Communication" and "Metakinesis," in *What Is Dance?*, ed. Roger Copeland (New York: Oxford University Press, 1983), 22–28; Mikhail Yampolsky, "Kuleshov's Experiments and the New Anthropology of the Actor," in *Inside the Film Factory: New*

Approaches to Russian and Soviet Cinema, ed. Richard Taylor and Ian Christie (London: Routledge, 1994), 31–50.

6. Laurence Selenick, introduction to *Wandering Stars: Russian Emigré Theatre, 1905–1940*, ed. Laurence Senelick (Iowa City: University of Iowa Press, 1992), 9 (quotations); Stella Adler, "How I Met Stanislavsky" (typescript), n.d., box 23, folder 13, Stella Adler papers, Harry Ransom Humanities Center (HRC); Stella Adler, "Moscow in the Thirties" (handwritten manuscript and notes, chart of the Stanislavsky method), n.d., box 24, folder 1, Stella Adler papers, HRC; Paul Gray, "Stanislavski and America: A Critical Chronology," *The Tulane Drama Review* 9, no. 2 (1964): 21–60; Christine Edwards, *The Stanislavsky Heritage, Its Contribution to the Russian and American Theatre* (New York: New York University Press, 1965).

7. Julia L. Foulkes, *Modern Bodies: Dance and American Modernism from Martha Graham to Alvin Ailey* (Chapel Hill: University of North Carolina Press, 2002), 9.

8. Devin Fore, "The Operative Word in Soviet Factography," *October* 118 (Fall 2006): 95–131; John Roberts, "The Making of Documentary: Documentary after Factography," in *The Art of Interruption: Realism, Photography, and the Everyday* (Manchester, UK: Manchester University Press, 1998), 58–71. On the popularity of Soviet film in the United States, especially between 1926 and 1936, see Tino Ballio, *The Foreign Film Renaissance on American Screens, 1946–1973* (Madison: University of Wisconsin Press, 2010), 34–35; William Alexander, *Film on the Left: American Documentary Film from 1931 to 1942* (Princeton, NJ: Princeton University Press, 1981).

9. Alma Law and Mel Gordon, *Meyerhold, Eisenstein, and Biomechanics: Actor Training in Revolutionary Russia* (Jefferson, NC: MacFarland, 1996), 4.

10. Hallie Flanagan, *Shifting Scenes of the Modern European Theatre* (New York: Coward-McCann, 1928), 99; Margaret Bourke-White, "Nothing Bores the Russian Audience: At Opera, Play, and Political Meeting the People Are Invariably Intense, Eager and Stirred to Emotion," *New York Times*, Mar. 13, 1932, SM8.

CHAPTER 5

1. Isadora Duncan to A. V. Lunacharsky, spring 1921, quoted in Isadora Duncan and Franklin Rosemont, *Isadora Speaks* (San Francisco: City Lights Books, 1981), 64.

2. Alexander Chepalov, "Nikolai Foregger and the Dance of Revolution," *Experiment/ Эксперимент* 2 (1996): 359–79; Lynn Garafola, *Diaghilev's Ballets Russes* (New York: Oxford University Press, 1989), viii (quotations). Also see Walter Duranty, "Proletarian Dance Invented for Soviet," *New York Times*, Jan. 19, 1927, 7.

3. Havelock Ellis, from *The Dance of Life* (1923), in *What Is Dance?*, ed. Roger Copeland (New York: Oxford University Press, 1983), 494; John Martin, "Dance as a Means of Communication" (1946), in Copeland, *What Is Dance?*, 146; Susan Leigh Foster, *Choreographing Empathy: Kinesthesia in Performance* (New York: Routledge, 2011), 8.

4. Susan Manning, *Ecstasy and the Demon: The Dances of Mary Wigman* (Minneapolis: University of Minnesota Press, 2006), 1; Sally Banes, *Dancing Women: Female Bodies*

on Stage (New York: Routlege, 1998); Isadora Duncan, "The Dance of the Future," in Isadora Duncan, *The Art of the Dance*, ed. Sheldon Cheney (New York: Theatre arts, 1928), 63; Floyd Dell, *Women as World Builders: Studies in Modern Feminism* (Chicago: Forbes, 1913), 49, accessed Nov. 20, 2015, http://www.gutenberg.org/ebooks/33584.

5. Irina Sirotkina, "Dance-*plyaska* in Russia of the Silver Age," *Dance Research* 28, no. 2 (2010): 137, 141; Elizabeth Souritz, "Isadora's Influence on Dance in Russia," *Dance Chronicle* 18, no. 2 (1995): 287–88.

6. W.R.T., "Classical Dancing in England," *T.P.'s Magazine*, May 1911, 119, quoted in Ann Daly, *Done into Dance: Isadora Duncan in America* (Bloomington: Indiana University Press, 1995), 8 (quotation); Isadora Duncan, *My Life* (New York: Boni & Liveright, 1927; repr., New York: W. W. Norton, 1995), 127 (dance as a gateway to the soul); Banes, *Dancing Women*, 75 (quotation).

7. Isadora Duncan, quoted in Daly, *Done into Dance*, 195–96 ("I have constantly danced"); Isadora Duncan, *My Life*, 119 ("down-trodden"), 239 ("on the night of").

8. Duncan, *My Life*, 239; Duncan, *Art of the Dance*, 109 ("a new world"), 62 ("dancer of the future" and "high religious art"), 113 ("ideals of the new world"). On the *Marche Slave* as the "first revolutionary dance," see Fredrika Blair, *Isadora: Portrait of the Artist as a Woman* (New York: McGraw-Hill, 1986), 294.

9. Souritz, "Isadora's Influence on Dance in Russia," 282. On Russia's Silver Age, see John E. Bowlt, *Moscow & St. Petersburg 1900–1920: Art, Life & Culture of the Russian Silver Age* (New York: Vendome Press, 2008), 9–27. On Nietzsche's popularity in Russia and in the United States, see Bernice Glatzer Rosenthal, ed., *Nietzsche in Russia* (Princeton, NJ: Princeton University Press, 1986); Jennifer Ratner-Rosenhagen, *American Nietzsche: A History of an Icon and His Ideas* (Chicago: University of Chicago Press, 2012). On Nietzsche's influence on Duncan and her work, see Kimerer L. LaMothe, *Nietzsche's Dancers: Isadora Duncan, Martha Graham, and the Revaluation of Christian Values* (New York: Palgrave Macmillan, 2006).

10. Sergei Diaghilev quoted in Allan Ross Macdougall, *Isadora: A Revolutionary in Art and Love* (New York: Thomas Nelson & Sons, 1960), 7; Michel Fokine quoted in Blair, *Isadora*, 115; Edward Braun, ed., *Meyerhold on Theatre* (New York: Hill and Wang, 1969), 142; Stanislavsky quoted in Duncan, *My Life*, 122–23.

11. "Novoya Vrema," *New Times* (Saint Petersburg), Dec. 15, 1904, 13–14 ("revolution in choreographic art"); Valerian Svetlov, *Birzhevyie Vedomosti* [Stock exchange journal] (Saint Petersburg), no. 659 (Dec. 15, 1904): 5; *Slovo* [Word], no. 15 (Wed., Dec. 15, 1904): 7; *Slovo*, no. 18 (Sat., Dec. 18, 1904): 7 ("coarse sensuality"). All in folder 17-3, Natalia Roslaveva collection of Isadora Duncan materials, Jerome Robbins Dance Division, New York Public Library (NYPL) for the Performing Arts. Translation by Natalia Roslaveva.

12. Sirotkina, "Dance-*plyaska*," 136.

13. Duncan, *My Life*, 119.

14. Ibid., 122–23, 124 (quotations).

15. Stefanida Dmitrievna Rudneva, *Vospominaniia schastlivogo cheloveka: Stefanida Dmitrievna Rudneva i studiia muzykal'nogo dvizheniia "Geptakhor" v dokumentakh Tsentral'nogo moskovskogo arkhiva-muzeia lichnykh sobranii* (Moscow: Glavarkhiv Moskvy GIS, 2007). On the history of Heptachor, see Sof'ia Nuridzhanova, comp., *K Istorii Geptakhora: Ot Aisedory Dunkan k muzykal'nomu dvizheniiu* (Saint Petersburg: Akademicheskii proekt, 2008); Aida Ailamasian, "The Fortune of Musical Movement," *Ballet International* 4 (1997): 20–23. The archivists at the Center for Preservation of Records of Personal Collections (now Central State Archive of the City of Moscow (TsGA), the Central State Archive of the City of Moscow) were unbelievably helpful in culling and gathering materials related to Rudneva and Duncan.

16. Interview with S. D. Rudneva by V. D. Duvakin, Apr. 28, 1971, quoted in Sirotkina, "Dance-*plyaska*," 142. From the Stefanida Rudneva papers, TsGA: Rudneva, "Memories of Meetings with Duncan, 1904–1907," f. 140, op. 1, d. 1076; Rudneva, draft of a letter to Isadora Duncan, Dec. 1907, f. 140, op. 1, d. 1093.

17. Duncan, *Art of the Dance*, 209.

18. Irma Duncan and Allan Ross Macdougall, *Isadora Duncan's Russian Days and Her Last Years in France* (New York: Covici Friede, 1929), 26–39.

19. Ibid., 45; Ilya Schneider, *Isadora Duncan: The Russian Years*, trans. David Magarshack (New York: Harcourt, Brace & World, 1968), 37 (quotation).

20. Duncan and Macdougall, *Isadora Duncan's Russian Days*, 53.

21. Ibid., 57, 59–60.

22. Ibid., 61.

23. The couple had fled to Paris and even considered renting Isadora's apartment there. Ibid., 72.

24. Natalia Roslavleva, "Prechistenka 20: The Isadora Duncan School in Moscow," *Dance Perspectives* 64 (1975): 9.

25. Review in *Izvestia*, quoted in Duncan and Macdougall, *Isadora Duncan's Russian Days*, 94–95.

26. Leonid Shikhmatov, *Ot Studii k Teatru* (Moscow: VTO, 1970), 144, quoted in Roslavleva, "Prechistenka 20," 12; Duncan and Macdougall, *Isadora Duncan's Russian Days*, 96; Lily Dikovskaya, *In Isadora's Steps: The Story of Isadora Duncan's School in Moscow, Told by Her Favourite Pupil* (Sussex, Eng.: Book Guild Publishing, 2008), 23; Schneider, *Isadora Duncan*, 75.

27. Sim Dreyden, "Lenin Smotrit International" *Musikalnaya Zhizn*, no. 21 (1965), quoted in Roslavleva, "Prechistenka 20," 10; Ivy Litvinov to Isadora Duncan, Dec. 26, 1921, folder 97, Irma Duncan collection of Isadora Duncan materials, Jerome Robbins Dance Division, NYPL for the Performing Arts; Roslavleva, "Prechistenka 20," 11.

28. Roslavleva, "Prechistenka 20," 14, 18.

29. Duncan and Macdougall, *Isadora Duncan's Russian Days*, 97–99.

30. Ibid., 119.

31. Duncan and Rosemont, *Isadora Speaks*, 78.

32. For more on Duncan's 1923 tour of the United States, see Duncan and Macdougall, *Isadora Duncan's Russian Days*, 143–70.

33. Imaginism (or Imagism) was a Russian literary movement cofounded by Esenin and characterized by the use of metaphors as well as arresting images. See Vladimir Markov, *Russian Imagism, 1919–1924*, Bausteine zur Geschichte der Literatur bei den Slawen (Giessen, Ger.: W. Schmitz, 1980).

34. Duncan, *My Life*, 140. For Isadora's relationship with Esenin, I am drawing on Duncan and Macdougall, *Isadora Duncan's Russian Days*; Gordon McVay, *Isadora and Esenin* (Ann Arbor, MI: Ardis, 1980); and Schneider, *Isadora Duncan*.

35. Duncan and Macdougall, *Isadora Duncan's Russian Days*, 133–34; Blair, *Isadora*, 324.

36. Isadora Duncan quoted in Duncan and Macdougall, *Isadora Duncan's Russian Days*, 257.

37. Ailamasian, "The Fortune of Musical Movement," 20.

38. Roslavleva, "Prechistenka 20," 6; Sirotkina, "Dance-*plyaska*," 143–44.

39. V. Iving, "Mimo-dance" (manuscript), n.d., f. 2694, op. 1, d. 4, Russian State Archive of Literature and Art (RGALI), Moscow. Translation by Andrey Bredstein. For examples of others who were critical of Duncan in the 1920s, see Stefanida Rudneva, notes quoting K. Somov (Feb. 13, 1922), from Yu. N. Podkopaeva and A. N. Sveshnikova, comp., *Konstantin Andreevich Somov: Pis'ma. dnevniki. suzhdeniya sovremennikov* (Moscow: Iskusstvo, 1979), 207, Stefanida Rudneva papers, TsGA. Translation assistance by Andrey Bredstein. For further commentary, see T. S. Kasatkina and E. A. Surits, eds., *Aisedora: Gastroli v Rossii* (Moscow: Izdatelstvo Artist, Rezhiser, Teatre, 1992).

40. Duncan and Macdougall, *Isadora Duncan's Russian Days*, 245, 257–60; Isadora Duncan quoted in Roslavleva, "Prechistenka 20," 27.

41. Ann Daly, "The Continuing Beauty of the Curve: Isadora Duncan and Her Last Compositions," *Ballet International* 13, no. 8 (1990): 1596

42. Isadora Duncan quoted in Duncan and Macdougall, *Isadora Duncan's Russian Days*, 264; Daly, "The Continuing Beauty of the Curve," 1687. On the scorn for "Duncanism," see Sirotkina, "Dance-*plyaska*," 146.

43. Sirotkina, "Dance-*plyaska*," 146; Vsevolod Meyerhold quoted in Braun, *Meyerhold on Theatre*, 141–43 (quotation at 142); Vsevolod Meyerhold quoted in David L. Hoffman, "Bodies of Knowledge: Physical Culture and the New Soviet Man," in *Language and Revolution: Making Modern Political Identities*, ed. Igal Halfin (New York: Routledge, 1992), 231.

44. Ellen Graff, *Stepping Left: Dance and Politics in New York City, 1928–1932* (Durham, NC: Duke University Press, 1997), 28.

45. Edith Segal, interview with Lesley Farlow, recorded Jan. 14, 25, and Feb. 1, 1991, Jerome Robbins Dance Division, NYPL for the Performing Arts.

46. Graff, *Stepping Left*, 138 (on Maslow), 49 (on Shapero), 44 (on Spartakiades); "20,000 Pack Garden to Salute Soviet," *New York Times*, Nov. 14, 1937, 39. Shapero's visit to the Soviet Union is noted in the files of VOKS, f. 5283, op. 3, d. 1003, State Archive of the Russian Federation (GARF), Moscow. Thanks to Rebecca Rossen for notes indicating that Shapero performed at the Moscow Theatre Festival.

47. "Mass Dance in the Soviet Union," *New Theatre*, Feb. 1934, 4–5.

48. Maryn Meyers, "The Dance in Moscow," *New Theatre*, Oct. 1934, 25. On Stanislavsky's influence on dancers in the United States, see Graff, *Stepping Left*, 72–75. Segal mentioned learning the Stanislavsky method in her interview with Farlow in 1991. On mass dance, see "Mass Dance in the Soviet Union"; and Jane Dudley, "The Mass Dance," *New Theatre* (Dec. 1934), 17–18.

49. Segal, interview with Farlow, 1991; Anna Sokolow, interview with Barbara Newman, Dec. 1974–May 1975, Jerome Robbins Dance Division, NYPL for the Performing Arts. For more on Sokolow's experience, see Larry Warren, *Anna Sokolow: The Rebellious Spirit* (Princeton, NJ: Princeton Book Co., 1991), 51–60.

50. Victor Garlin (son of Mignon), e-mail to author, Oct. 18, 2012; Irma Duncan, *Duncan Dancer: An Autobiography* (Middletown, CT: Weslyan University Press, 1965), 329–33. Also see Dikovskaya, *In Isadora's Steps*, 161–65.

51. Victor Garlin, telephone interview with author, Jan. 22, 2013; Victor Garlin, e-mails to author, Nov. 14 and Oct. 23, 2012.

52. Mignon Verne, "The Dance," *New Theatre*, Jan. 1934, 15–16; Mignon Garland, "Isadora Duncan," *Daily Cal Arts Magazine*, Feb. 19, 1971; Oakley Johnson, "The Dance," *New Theatre*, Feb. 1934, 17; Hy Glickman, "The New Dance Advances," *New Theatre*, May 1934, 18.

53. Johnson, "The Dance," 17; Emmanuel Eisenberg, "Diagnosis of the Dance," *New Theatre*, July/Aug. 1934, 24–25; A. Prentiss, "Towards the Revolutionary Dance," *Workers Theatre*, May–June 1933, 11.

54. Koner, *Solitary Song*, 2, 18, 23–55, 114 ("socially conscious" dances); Graff, *Stepping Left*, 48; Pauline Koner oral history with Peter Conway, 1975, box 2, Pauline Koner papers, Jerome Robbins Dance Division, NYPL for the Performing Arts (hereafter cited as Koner papers). Koner's papers contain a file devoted to Isadora Duncan. On the extent to which Fokine's work was marked by Duncan's influence, see Elizabeth Souritz, "Isadora Duncan and Prewar Russian Dancemakers," in *The Ballets Russes and Its World*, ed. Lynn Garafola and Nancy Van Norman Baer (New Haven, CT: Yale University Press, 1999), 108–15. On Ito, see the Michio Ito Foundation, accessed Dec. 3, 2013, http://www.michioito.org/, http://www.michioito.org/.

55. Rebecca Rossen, "Hasidic Drag: Jewishness and Transvestism in the Modern Dances of Pauline Koner and Hadassah," *Feminist Studies* 37, no. 2 (Summer 2011): 340. Koner did perform an anti-Hitler dance in 1933 and frequently performed at events sponsored by Jewish groups. See "Pauline Koner, Brilliant 21-Year-Old Dancer, Greatly Incensed at Adolf," *Jewish Examiner*, June 1933.

56. Koner, *Solitary Song*, 68.

57. Ibid., 80.

58. Pauline Koner diary, Dec. 16, 1934, box 1, folder 14, Koner papers. Emphasis in original.

59. Ibid.

60. Ibid.; Koner, *Solitary Song*, 84.

61. "American Artists Warmly Welcomed in Leningrad," *Moscow Daily News*, Jan. 11, 1935, clipping, box 41, folder 11, Koner papers; Koner diary, Jan. 6, 1935.

62. Koner diary, Jan. 26, 1935.

63. Koner diary, Jan. 27, 1935.

64. Koner diary, Jan. 21 and 27, 1935.

65. Koner, *Solitary Song*, 89; Koner diary, Jan. 21 ("all evening") Jan. 29 (other quotations) and Feb. 1 and 12, 1935.

66. Koner diary, Jan. 21, 1935.

67. Koner diary, Mar. 30 and May 1, 1935, Dec. 16, 1934.

68. Koner diary, Feb. 1, 1935; Paul Babitsky and John Rimberg, *The Soviet Film Industry* (New York: Prager, 1955), 122, quoted in Amy Sargeant, *Vsevolod Pudovkin: Classic Films of the Soviet Avant Garde*, vii. An undated letter (1935 or 1936) from Pudovkin to Koner emphasizes the importance of dance ("dance is the most immediate the most inartificial art") and urges her to "view the new victory as your own victory." Box 3, folder 8 (folder labeled ca. 1935–1936), Koner papers.

69. Koner diary, Feb. 2, 3, 6, and 10, 1935.

70. Koner diary, Feb. 14, and 16, 1935; Koner, *Solitary Song*, 91.

71. Koner diary, Feb. 16, 1935.

72. Koner diary, Feb. 20–Mar. 8, 1935.

73. Koner diary, Feb. 20 and 23, and Mar. 8 and 20–21, 1935; Koner, *Solitary Song*, 93.

74. Koner, *Solitary Song*, 94. Koner diary, Apr. 13 and 21, 1935 ("I'm going crazy").

75. Koner diary, Apr. 29 and May 1–31, 1935.

76. Koner diary, May 1–31, 1935.

77. Koner diary, June 5, 1935.

78. Koner diary, June 26 and Sept. 13, 1935.

79. Nicoletta Misler, "A Choreological Laboratory," *Experiment/Эксперимент* 2 (1996): 178, 230 (quotation).

80. Koner diary, Oct. 12, 1935.

81. David L. Hoffman, *Cultivating the Masses: Modern State Practices and Soviet Socialism, 1914–1939* (Ithaca, NY: Cornell University Press, 2011), 110.

82. James Riordan, *Sport in Soviet Society: Development of Sport and Physical Education in Russia and the USSR* (New York: Cambridge University Press, 1977), 20, 53 (quotation), 146 (quotation); Hoffman, *Cultivating the Masses*, 115 (quotation from the 1920 Commissariat of Health report), 10–24.

83. Mary Anne Santos Newhall, "Uniform Bodies: Mass Movement and Modern Totalitarianism," *Dance Research Journal* 34, no. 1 (2002): 27–50; Karen Petrone, *Life Has Become More Joyous, Comrades: Celebrations in the Time of Stalin* (Princeton, NJ: Princeton University Press, 2000), 1 (quotations) (for "new outbreak of festivity," Petrone is quoting Christopher A. P. Binns, "The Changing Face of Power: Revolution and Accommodation in the Development of the Soviet Ceremonial System," pt. 1, *Man*, n.s., 14, no. 4 [Dec., 1979]: 602). Also see Dudley, "The Mass Dance"; Graff, *Stepping Left*; Erika Fischer-Lichte,

Theatre, Sacrifice, Ritual: Exploring Forms of Political Theatre (New York: Routledge, 2005); Manning, *Ecstasy and the Demon*; Hoffman, *Cultivating the Masses*.

84. Choi Chatterjee, *Celebrating Women: Gender, Festival Culture, and Bolshevik Ideology, 1910–1939*, (Pittsburgh, PA: University of Pittsburgh Press, 2002), 140.

85. Koner diary, Dec. 24, 1935; Roger D. Markwick and Euridice Charon Cardona, *Soviet Women on the Frontlines during the Second World War* (London: Palgrave Macmillan, 2012), 7.

86. *Komsomolskaya Pravda*, June 9, 1936, clipping in Pauline Koner scrapbook, box 41 (translation assistance from Alyse Camus), Koner papers; Koner diary, Dec. 24, 1935 ("new Soviet dance"). Thanks to Paula Rabinowitz for suggesting the connection to Pudovkin's films.

87. Koner diary, Dec. 24, 1935; Koner, *Solitary Song*, 104–5.

88. Koner diary, Dec. 24, 1935.

89. Petrone, *Life Has Become More Joyous*, 1; Koner diary, Apr. 9, 1936.

90. Koner diary, n.d. [but under the Apr. 9, 1936 entry—final entry in diary]; Koner, *Solitary Song*, 107.

91. *Spartak* (Leningrad), July 12, 1936, clipping in Koner scrapbook, box 41, Koner papers; "Fizikulturnyi parad v Leningrade," *Pravda*, July 13, 1936, 1. Translations mine.

92. Koner, *Solitary Song*, 108, 110.

93. Pauline Koner, "Russia Dances," *New Theatre*, Oct. 1936, 22–23; Koner, *Solitary Song*, 108, 110.

94. Koner, *Solitary Song*, 110.

95. Koner performed at a Lenin-Liebknecht-Luxemburg memorial sponsored by the Young Communist League on January 15, 1937, and at several other left-wing events. Graff, *Stepping Left*, 48; Pauline Koner FBI file FOIA request #1164057-000; Pauline Koner, *Elements of Performance: A Guide for Performers in Dance, Theatre, and Opera* (Chur, Switz.: Harwood Academic Publishers, 1993).

CHAPTER 6

1. Promotional material; Hughes telegram to Thompson, June 6, 1932, Both in box 12, Louise Thompson Patterson papers, Emory University (hereafter cited as LTP papers); Louise Thompson Patterson, "With Langston Hughes in the USSR," *Freedomways* 8 (1968): 152. On the background of the cast, see box 12, LTP papers, and Langston Hughes papers, box 1, Huntington Library.

2. West to mother, dated "Saturday," from ship, June 1932; and West to mother, dated "Sunday," June 1932. Both in carton 1, folder W, Dorothy West papers, Schlesinger Library, Harvard University (hereafter cited as West papers). Thompson to mother, July 4, 1932 [though letter indicates text from boat was written earlier], box 1, LTP papers.

3. Thompson to mother, July 4, 1932, box 1, LTP papers.

4. West to "Dearest Mummy," June 29, 1932, carton 1, folder W, West papers; Thompson to mother, July 4, 1932, box 1, LTP papers; Louise Thompson Patterson (LTP), memoir (typescript), box 20, LTP papers.

5. Thompson to mother, July 4, 1932, box 1, LTP papers (quotation); Langston Hughes, *I Wonder as I Wander: An Autobiographical Journey* (New York: Hill and Wang, 1956), 82–83; West to mother, June 29, 1932, carton 1, folder W, West papers (quotation).

6. For existing scholarship on *Black and White*, see Glenda Elizabeth Gilmore, *Defying Dixie: The Radical Roots of Civil Rights, 1919–1950* (New York: W. W. Norton, 2008); Joy Gleason Carew, *Blacks, Reds, and Russians: Sojourners in Search of the Soviet Promise* (New Brunswick, NJ: Rutgers University Press, 2008); Kate A. Baldwin, *Beyond the Color Line and the Iron Curtain: Reading Encounters between Black and Red, 1922–1963* (Durham, NC: Duke University Press, 2002); Meredith L. Roman, *Opposing Jim Crow: African Americans and the Soviet Indictment of U.S. Racism, 1928—1937* (Lincoln: University of Nebraska Press, 2012); Mark I. Solomon, *The Cry Was Unity: Communists and African Americans, 1917–1936* (Jackson: University Press of Mississippi, 1998); Steven S. Lee, *The Ethnic Avant-Garde: Minority Cultures and World Revolution* (New York: Columbia University Press, 2015); Claire Nee Nelson, "Black and White," in Cary D. Wintz and Paul Finkelman, eds., *Encyclopedia of the Harlem Renaissance*, 2 vols. (New York: Routledge, 2004), 1:22–24; Allison Blakely, *Russia and the Negro: Blacks in Russian History and Thought* (Washington, DC: Howard University Press, 1986). On the hypervisibility of African Americans, see E. Patrick Johnson, *Appropriating Blackness: Performance and the Politics of Authenticity* (Durham, NC: Duke University Press, 2003), 7.

7. Daphne Brooks, "Black Theatre and Performance Studies: Seminal Critical Essays," in *Cultural Life*, ed. Howard Dodson and Colin A. Palmer, Schomburg Studies on the Black Experience (East Lansing: Michigan State University Press, 2007), 123–80. Also see J. Ronald Green, *Straight Lick: The Cinema of Oscar Micheaux* (Bloomington: Indiana University Press, 2000); Pearl Bowser, Jane Gaines, and Charles Musser, eds., *Oscar Micheaux and His Circle: African-American Filmmaking and Race Cinema of the Silent Era* (Bloomington: Indiana University Press, 2001).

8. Saidiya V. Hartman, *Scenes of Subjection: Terror, Slavery, and Self-Making in Nineteenth-Century America*, Race and American Culture (New York: Oxford University Press, 1997), 26–29.

9. W. E. B. Du Bois, *The Souls of Black Folk* (New York: Dover, 1994); Howard Winant, "Dialectics of the Veil," in *The New Politics of Race: Globalism, Difference, Justice* (Minneapolis: University of Minnesota Press, 2004), 25–38; Patricia J. Williams, "The Pantomime of Race," Reith Lectures, Mar. 4, 1997, BBC Radio 4, accessed Oct. 31, 2015, http://downloads.bbc.co.uk/rmhttp/radio4/transcripts/1997_reith2.pdf. On the sexualization of African American women through the jezebel stereotype (and its counterparts, the mammy and sapphire), see Patricia Hill Collins, *Black Feminist Thought: Knowledge, Consciousness, and the Politics of Empowerment*, 2nd ed., Routledge Classics (New York: Routledge, 2009), 81–86.

10. Jayna Brown, *Babylon Girls: Black Women Performers and the Shaping of the Modern* (Durham, NC: Duke University Press, 2008), 36–38; Isadora Duncan, *My Life* (New York: Boni & Liveright, 1927; repr., New York: W. W. Norton, 1995), 244.

11. S. Frederick Starr, *Red and Hot: The Fate of Jazz in the Soviet Union, 1917–1980* (New York: Oxford University Press, 1983), 32–33. Also see Vladimir E. Alexandrov, *The Black Russian* (New York: Atlantic Monthly Press, 2013).

12. Hughes, *I Wonder as I Wander*, 83; I. D. W. Talmadge, "Mother Emma," *Opportunity: Journal of Negro Life*, Aug. 1933, 245–47. A minor scandal about Harris, who was known as "the Mammy of Moscow," broke out in the *Moscow News* in December 1931 after a piece attempting to capture "local color" made stereotyped references to Harris's "occasional yearning for a dish of hominy or wheatcakes." A letter reminded editors that "no breath of condescension or of patronism hovers about the attitude of Soviet Russia toward those national and racial groups which elsewhere feel the iron heel of imperialist oppression, social ostracism, and contempt." *Moscow News*, Dec. 22, 1931, 2; letter from William Wilson, *Moscow News*, Jan. 1, 1932.

13. L. Nekrassova, "A Negro Artist and Citizen of the USSR," *Soviet Russia Today*, Aug. 1943, 25; Norman E. Saul, *Historical Dictionary of Russian/Soviet Foreign Policy* (Lanham, MD: Rowman & Littlefield, 2015), 30–31.

14. Claude McKay, "Report on the Negro Question" (speech to the Fourth Congress of the Third Communist International, Moscow), accessed Aug. 12, 2016, https://www .marxists.org/history/etol/newspape/internationalist/pamphlets/Com-Int-&-Black -Lib-OptV5.pdf; Solomon, *The Cry Was Unity*, 42; Joyce Moore Turner and W. Burghardt Turner, *Caribbean Crusaders and the Harlem Renaissance* (Urbana: University of Illinois Press, 2005), 104.

15. Kennell to Ella Epperson, n.d. [probably late 1923], box 9, folder 5, Ruth Epperson Kennell (REK) papers, University of Oregon, Eugene; Bernard L. Peterson, "Burrill, Mary," in *Profiles of African American Stage Performers and Theatre People, 1816–1960* (New York: Greenwood Press, 2001), 408; Mary Burrill, "Aftermath: A One Act Play of Negro Life," *Liberator* 2 (Apr. 1919): 10–14.

16. Starr, *Red and Hot*; Sally Banes, "The Moscow Charleston: Black Jazz Dancers in the Soviet Union," in *Writing Dancing in the Age of Postmodernism*, ed. Sally Banes (Middletown, CT: Weslyan University Press, 1994), 298–309.

17. Starr, *Red and Hot*, 55–56; "Negritianskaia Operetta," special issue, *Tsirk* [Circus], 1926 (*Tsirk* was a magazine covering Soviet variety theatre as well as the circus); Floyd Snelson Jr., "Chocolate Kiddies Company Sails for Germany," *Pittsburgh Courier*, May 6, 1925, 10; Bennetta Jules-Rosette, *Josephine Baker in Art and Life: The Icon and the Image* (Urbana: University of Illinois Press, 2007), 178; Margaret Simms obituary, *Jet*, Mar. 21, 1974, 7; A. H. Lawrence, *Duke Ellington and His World: A Biography* (New York: Routledge, 2001), 34; Brown, *Babylon Girls*, 198. On the Chocolate Dandies, see Banes, "The Moscow Charleston."

18. Brown, *Babylon Girls*, 205; Garvin Bushell and Mark Tucker, *Jazz from the Beginning* (Ann Arbor: University of Michigan Press, 1988), 55–56.

19. "Negritianskaia Operetta." On Black bodies as objects of consumption, see Kyla Wazana Tompkins, *Racial Indigestion: Eating Bodies in the Nineteenth Century* (New York: New York University Press, 2012).

20. Bushell and Tucker, *Jazz from the Beginning*, 65–66.

21. Kennell to Ella Epperson, Apr. 2, and Jan. 14, 1926, box 9, folder 5, REK papers, University of Oregon, Eugene.

22. Stanislavsky and Lunacharskaya quoted in "Negritianskaia Operetta." Translation by Katya Cotey.

23. The play traveled to other Soviet republics and beyond the Soviet Union. Party leaders were moved to establish the Central Children's Theatre after seeing the play in 1936. Anastasia Ioanna Kayiatos, "Silence and Alterity in Russia after Stalin, 1955–1875" (PhD diss., University of California, 2012), 75; Boris Wolfson, "Juggernaut in Drag: Theater for Stalin's Children," in *Russian Children's Literature and Culture*, ed. Marina Balina and Larissa Rudova (New York: Routledge, 2008), 173–92. An English-language overview of the Moscow Theatre for Children's work features an image from *The Negro Boy and the Monkey* on its cover and highlights this "play with dance and song, circus interludes, animated cartoons, and running comment by the Nice Negro Girl" as a prime example of the theatre's work. Sergei Rozanov, *The Moscow Theatre for Children* (Moscow: Cooperative Publishing Society of Foreign Workers in the USSR, 1934).

24. Kayiatos, "Silence and Alterity in Russia after Stalin," 77. In the Federal Theatre Project version, a "Negro Mammy," the grandmother of the eponymous "Negro boy," replaces the "Nice Negro Girl" (she has a difficult-to-pronounce African name but tells her audience, "you can call me Mammy, that's what all the pickanninnys [*sic*] call me"). Natalia Sats and Sergei Rozanov, "The Negro Boy and the Monkey: Children's Play in Eight Scenes," music by L. Polovinkin, translated and adapted from the original Russian by Rose Siegel, in George Mason University Federal Theatre Project collection.

25. Rozanov, *Moscow Theatre for Children*, 30–31; Kayiatos, "Silence and Alterity in Russia after Stalin."

26. Thyra Edwards, "The Moscow Theatre for Children," *Woman Today*, Mar. 1937, 7; Hughes, *I Wonder as I Wander*, 200–201, quoted in Kayiatos, "Silence and Alterity in Russia after Stalin," 78; Eslanda Robeson quoted in Martin Duberman, *Paul Robeson: A Biography*, 188. Several African and African American students from KUTV did object to the play as part of a larger resolution condemning negative portrayals of "Negroes" in Soviet "cultural institutions." Kayiatos, "Silence and Alterity in Russia After Stalin," 80; Woodford McClelland, "Africans and Black Americans in the Comintern Schools, 1925–1934," *International Journal of African Historical Studies* 26, no. 2 (1993): 382.

27. Maxim Matusevich, "Black in the U.S.S.R.," *Transition* 100 (2008): 61. For the formulation of "Soviet anti-racism" used in this section, I'm indebted to the discussion in Roman, *Opposing Jim Crow*.

28. Solomon, *The Cry Was Unity*, 8, 146; Francine Hirsch, *Empire of Nations: Ethnographic Knowledge & the Making of the Soviet Union* (Ithaca, NY: Cornell University Press, 2005), 9–10 (original emphasis).

29. Claude McKay, "Soviet Russia and the Negro," pt. 1, *The Crisis* 27 (Dec. 1923): 64; ibid., pt. 2, *The Crisis* 28 (Jan. 1924): 114, 116; Henry Lee Moon, "Woman under the Soviets," *The Crisis* 41 (Apr. 1934): 108.

30. Maude White Katz, interview with Ruth Prago, Dec. 19, 1981, Oral History of the American Left collection, Tamiment Library, New York University (NYU) (quotation); Roman, *Opposing Jim Crow*, 72–73 (Burroughs as signifier of Black womanhood in the Soviet Union); Carola Burroughs, interview with author, Jan. 14, 2015; Harvey Klehr, John Earl Haynes, and Fridrickh Firsov, *The Secret World of American Communism* (New Haven, CT: Yale University Press, 1995), 199 ("elite Moscow school"); Duberman, *Paul Robeson*, 207 (on the Robesons' son). "She was dark brown, with rosy cheeks and deep dimples," Frances E. Williams recalled of Burroughs, and "the first black woman that I ever saw with a natural." Frances E. Williams interview, 1986, box 50, folder 7, John Oliver Killens papers, Emory University. The Burroughs photograph appeared on the front page of *Trud* on August 11, 1928 (information courtesy of Meredith Roman, e-mail to author, Apr. 14, 2016). Burroughs would return to the Soviet Union for ten months in 1930, working as a practicant in the Comintern and then studying at the Lenin School. Williana Burroughs personal file, f. 495, op. 261, d. 3497, l. 11-14, Russian State Archive of Social and Political History (RGASPI), Moscow, from scholar Romy Taylor's notes, e-mailed to author by Carola Burroughs, Jan. 14, 2015; Williana Jones Burroughs obituary from *People's Voice*, date not visible, clipping, Williana Jones Burroughs FBI file, FOIA request #1149393.

31. Robin D. G. Kelley, *Hammer and Hoe: Alabama Communists during the Great Depression* (Chapel Hill: University of North Carolina Press, 1990); Solomon, *The Cry Was Unity*; Roman, *Opposing Jim Crow*, 25–55; Myra Page, *Moscow Yankee* (New York: G. P. Putnam's sons, 1935), 13. Also see Robert Robinson and Jonathan Slevin, *Black on Red: My 44 Years inside the Soviet Union: An Autobiography* (Washington, DC: Acropolis Books, 1988).

32. Susan D. Pennybacker, *From Scottsboro to Munich: Race and Political Culture in 1930s Britain* (Princeton, NJ: Princeton University Press, 2009), 20 (quotations); Gilmore, *Defying Dixie*, 120–21.

33. Myra Page, "Help Us or We Burn!," *Moscow News*, Mar. 14, 1932, 3; Gilmore, *Defying Dixie*, 119 (first quotation); Kelley, *Hammer and Hoe*, 81; James A. Miller, Susan D. Pennybacker, and Eve Rosenhaft, "Mother Ada Wright and the International Campaign to Free the Scottsboro Boys, 1931–1934," *American Historical Review* 106, no. 2 (2001): 388 (second quotation).

34. Roman, *Opposing Jim Crow*, 94–95 (first quotation); "Communism the Only Hope of the Negro People," *Moscow News*, Sept. 17, 1931, 1; Miller, Pennybacker, and Rosenhaft, "Mother Ada Wright," 391, 88, 401 (second quotation).

35. Resolution cited in Roman, *Opposing Jim Crow*, 169–70; letter written in name of Charles R. Walker, Mar. 19, 1932, box 12, LTP papers.

36. Promotional material on letterhead of "Cooperating Committee for the Production of a Soviet Film on Negro Life," n.d., box 12, LTP papers.

37. On Mezhrobpom Studio, see Vance Kepley, "The Workers' International Relief and the Cinema of the Left, 1921–1935," *Cinema Journal* 23, no. 1 (Fall 1983): 7. On Karl Junghans, see Jack El-Hai, "Black and White and Red," *American Heritage* 42, no. 3 (May–

June 1991): 83–92. Junghans had recently directed the film *Strange Birds of Africa* (1932). On publicity surrounding *Black and White*, see press clippings in box 12, LTP papers.

38. Charles Ashleigh, "Black and White: Film of Negro Struggle," *Moscow News* (Weekly Edition), July 5, 1932, 8; names on masthead of "Dear Friend" form letter for "Cooperating Committee for the Production of a Soviet Film on Negro Life," box 12, LTP papers; MaryLouise Patterson, interview with author, Nov. 2014, Los Angeles; Claire Nee Nelson, "Louise Thompson Patterson and the Southern Roots of the Popular Front," in *Women Shaping the South: Creating and Confronting Change* (Columbia: University of Missouri Press, 2006), 204–28; Gilmore, *Defying Dixie*, 134–35.

39. Richard Goldstein, "Louise Patterson, 97, Is Dead; Figure in the Harlem Renaissance," *New York Times*, Sept. 2, 1999, http://www.nytimes.com/1999/09/02/nyregion /louise-patterson-97-is-dead-figure-in-harlem-renaissance.html; Louise Thompson Patterson oral history, recorded Nov. 16, 1981, Oral History of the American Left collection, Tamiment Library, NYU; Eric Garber, "A Spectacle in Color: The Lesbian and Gay Subculture of Jazz Age Harlem," in *Hidden from History: Reclaiming the Gay and Lesbian Past*, ed. Martin Duberman, Martha Vicinus, and George Chauncey Jr. (New York: New American Library, 1989), 318–31; Solomon, *The Cry Was Unity*, 174.

40. Nelson, "Louise Thompson Patterson," 222; Thompson to Henry Moon, June 11, 1932, box 12, LTP papers. The Friends of the Soviet Union was an international organization founded in 1927 and linked to existing friendship societies such as the Friends of Soviet Russia. Louis Nezmer, "The Soviet Friendship Societies," *Public Opinion Quarterly* 13, no. 2 (Summer 1949): 266.

41. "Information on Party of Players En Route to Moscow to Participate in Film on Negro Life in America," June 11, 1932, box 14, Loren Miller papers, Huntington Library; Verner D. Mitchell and Cynthia Davis, *Literary Sisters: Dorothy West and Her Circle, A Biography of the Harlem Renaissance* (New Brunswick, NJ: Rutgers University Press, 2012), 118, 126.

42. MaryLouise Patterson, interview with author, Oct. 2014, Los Angeles; Mitchell and Davis, *Literary Sisters*, 14 (on West); "Information on Party of Players En Route to Moscow," box 14, Loren Miller papers, Huntington Library; "Announce Players for Soviet Picture," *New York Amsterdam News*, June 8, 1932.

43. Hughes, *I Wonder as I Wander*, 84.

44. Thompson to mother, July 4, 1932, box 1, LTP papers. For his work on the film, Nikolai Ekk was given the Venice International Film Festival's Most Convincing Director award. "Nikolai Ekk—Awards," IMDb, accessed Aug. 14, 2016, http://www.imdb.com /name/nm0252388/awards?ref_=nm_awd.

45. Roman, *Opposing Jim Crow*, 113–15; Patterson, "With Langston Hughes in the USSR," 154 (quotation).

46. Thompson to mother, July 14, 1932, box 1, LTP papers.

47. West to "Mummy," June 29, 1932; West to mother, aboard *Abhazia*, n.d. [but on the Black Sea]. Both letters are in carton 1, folder W, West papers. On the cast members' activities, see theatrical programs in West papers; West also discusses drinking tea in their rooms in letters to her mother (carton 1, folder W, West papers); and Homer Smith,

Black Man in Red Russia: A Memoir (Chicago: Johnson, 1964), 28 (on swimming in the Moscow River and going to clubs).

48. Thompson to mother, July 14, 1932, box 1, LTP papers. Hughes describes in his memoir, for instance, a scene in which an upper-class white man asks a Black female servant to dance with him at a party. Given that the film was to take place in 1930s Alabama, anyone familiar with US race relations would know this kind of interaction could never actually take place. Hughes, *I Wonder as I Wander*, 78.

49. Hughes, *I Wonder as I Wander*, 81; Thompson to mother, July 14, 1932, box 1, LTP papers.

50. Thompson to mother, July 14, 1932, box 1, LTP papers.

51. Hughes, *I Wonder as I Wander*, 85; Loren Miller statement (typescript), n.d., box 14, Loren Miller papers, Huntington Library.

52. Thompson to mother, July 14, 1932, box 1, LTP papers; West to Dottie [last name unknown], Apr. 16, 1933, carton 1, box W, West papers.

53. Dorothy West, "An Adventure in Moscow," in *The Richer, the Poorer* (New York: Doubleday Anchor, 1995), 205 (quotations).

54. Ibid., 207–8.

55. Smith, *Black Man in Red Russia*, 28; LTP memoir.

56. On Sylvia Garner, see Gilmore, *Defying Dixie*, 141, 492n185; Hughes, *I Wonder as I Wander*, 88. On Mildred Jones's relationships with Russian men, see Homer Smith, *Black Man in Red Russia*, 28; West to mother, Mar. 6, [1933], carton 1, folder W, West papers. On Jones and West, see references in West to Hughes, Oct. 27, [1932], and May 26, [1933], box 169, Langston Hughes papers, Beinecke Library. Hughes to Carl Van Vechten, Mar. 1, 1933, quoted in Gilmore, *Defying Dixie*, 141 ("girl friend"). Chen to Hughes, June 31, 1934, box 1, Langston Hughes papers, Huntington Library. On the rumors of Hughes's homosexuality and the intimations of queerness in Hughes's poetry, see Shane Vogel, "Closing Time: Langston Hughes and the Queer Poetics of Harlem Nightlife," *Criticism* 48, no. 3 (Summer 2006): 397–425.

57. William C. White, "Americans in Soviet Russia," *Scribner's*, Feb. 1931, 172; Charles Ashleigh, " 'Black and White,' New Film, Illustrates the Class Struggle in USA," *Moscow Daily News*, July 1932 [date not visible but abbreviated version of same article is in weekly edition on July 5, 1932, p. 8], clipping, Mark Solomon collection on African Americans and Communism, Tamiment Library, NYU; Hughes, *I Wonder as I Wander*, 89.

58. Dorothy West oral history, pp. 65–66, Black Women Oral History Project, May 6, 1978, Schlesinger Library, Harvard University; Gilmore, *Defying Dixie*, 146.

59. Stories about the film's cancellation appeared in the mainstream press and in the Black press. See Carew, *Blacks, Reds, and Russians*, 128–29. For the majority's opinion, see press release and statement (signed by fifteen members of cast), box 2, LTP papers.

60. My discussion of the Russian script comes from Steven Sunwoo Lee, "Multiculturalism versus 'Multi-National-Ness': The Clash of American and Soviet Models of Difference" (PhD diss., Stanford University, 2008); Lee, *The Ethnic Avant-Garde*; and Gilmore, *Defying Dixie*, 134–40. Thompson mentions in a letter to her mother dated

August 24, 1932, that there were two versions of the script, one by Grebner and another "as revised by our German director Junghans." Box 1, LTP papers. A copy of one of the *Black and White* scripts is in box 2 of the LTP papers. Some of the names are different in the Russian version. There are other differences as well, but the plots are similar. For further discussion, see Lee, *The Ethnic Avant-Garde*.

61. Regarding Thompson's efforts, there is a letter to the *Pittsburgh Courier* and a response from the *Liberator* in box 1, LTP papers. Also see press releases, press coverage, and statement (signed by fifteen members of cast) in box 2, LTP papers; Margaret Bourke-White's note, box 70, Margaret Bourke-White papers, Syracuse University.

62. Thompson to mother, Aug. 24, 1932, quoted in LTP memoir.

63. MaryLouise Patterson, interview with author, Oct. 2014, Los Angeles.

64. Douglas Taylor Northrop, *Veiled Empire: Gender & Power in Stalinist Central Asia* (Ithaca, NY: Cornell University Press, 2004), 12 (quotation). For examples of how even the male cast members noted the changing position of women, see Hughes commenting on unveiling in Hughes, *I Wonder as I Wander*, 139. Also see Hughes, "Going South in Russia," *The Crisis* 41 (June 1934): 162–63. Hughes's articles from the time period, his book *A Negro Looks at Central Asia* (published in the Soviet Union in a small print run), and his later memoir are some of the only published accounts of this trip.

65. Thompson, notes on Central Asia trip (typescript), box 1, LTP papers.

66. Ibid.

67. Ibid.

68. Document dated Oct. 5, 1932, signed by Langston Hughes, Loren Miller, Louise Thompson, Matt Crawford, Alan McKenzie, Mildred Jones, Kathryn Jenkins, George Sample, Mollie Lewis, Constance White, and Juanita Lewis, box 1, LTP papers.

69. MaryLouise Patterson, interview with author, Oct. 2014, Los Angeles.

70. Thompson to mother, Oct. 7, 1932, quoted in LTP memoir.

71. Thompson to mother, Sept. 25, 1932, quoted in LTP memoir; Northrop, *Veiled Empire*, 13. Also see Baldwin, *Beyond the Color Line and the Iron Curtain*, 120.

72. West to Hughes, Oct. 27, 1932, box 149, Langston Hughes papers, Beinecke Library.

73. Yelena Khanga, *Soul to Soul: The Story of a Black Russian American Family, 1865–1992* (New York: Norton, 1992), 48–49, 72–78; Hughes, *I Wonder as I Wander*, 180.

74. Thompson to mother, Oct. 18, 1932, box 1, LTP papers.

75. LTP memoir.

76. West to Grace and Marie Turner, Nov. 22, 1932, West papers, Boston University. Thanks to Erin Battat for the reference.

77. West mentions Jones's involvement with Pilnyak in a letter to her mother dated March 6 [1933]. Carton 1, folder W, West papers. On Pilnyak's love for Bourke-White, see, for example, Boris Pilnyak to Margaret Bourke-White, Apr. 10, 1931, Margaret Bourke-White papers, Syracuse University. On Oumansky's attraction to Mildred Jones, see Smith, *Black Man in Red Russia*, 28.

78. West to mother, Mar. 6 [1933], West papers.

79. When Sylvia showed the trophy that she and her brother Jack had won in a Charleston competition to Borodin, instead of congratulating the pair, Chen recalled, he "subjected us to a deflation process that helped to change our lives." He told the chastened siblings that "the only medals that won respect here were awarded for more vital victories. Were we to be content with an audience composed of those bourgeois elements feeding on the NEP policy, or were we interested in a greater, more purposeful audience?" Leyda, *Footnote to History*, 105. On the film, see "Torgovtsy slavoi / [Merchants of Glory]," Oct. 11, 2012, *Antti Alanen: Film Diary* (blog), accessed Sept. 11, 2016, http://anttialanenfilm diary.blogspot.com/2012/10/torgovtsy-slavoi-merchants-of-glory.html; and Leyda, *Footnote to History*, 118.

80. Leyda, *Footnote to History*, 139, 147; Jack Chen to Sylvia Chen, July 10, 1931, Sylvia Chen Leyda papers, Tamiment Library, NYU (hereafter cited as Leyda papers).

81. Milly Bennett, *On Her Own: Journalistic Adventures from San Francisco to the Chinese Revolution* (Armonk, NY: M. E. Sharpe, 1993), 304; Mildred Mitchell, "Sylvia Chen Dances," *Moscow News*, Jan. 17, 1932, clipping, Leyda papers.

82. Leyda, *Footnote to History*, 151–52.

83. Ibid., 160–61.

84. Hughes to Chen, Oct. 18, 1934, box 29, folder 4, Leyda papers; Chen to Hughes, Aug. 16, 1936, box 43, folder 770, Langston Hughes papers, Beinecke Library. On her frustration with him, see Chen to Hughes, May 11 and June 26, 1934, box 43, folder 770, Langston Hughes papers, Beinecke Library.

85. West oral history, 71. On this as Williams's motivation, see Frances E. Williams, "To Hell with Bandanas," interview by Karen Anne Mason and Richard Cándida Smith, 1992–1993, transcript, pp. 71, 290, UCLA Oral History Program, Bancroft Library, University of California, Berkeley, accessed Oct. 21, 2015, https://archive.org/details /tohellwithbandan00will.

86. See discussion of Chen's background and influences in the *Daily Worker*, Jan. 28, 1938.

87. For sources that credit Frances Williams as appearing in *The Circus*, see, for example, Myrna Oliver, "F. E. Williams, Leader in L.A.'s Black Theater" (obituary), *L.A. Times*, Jan. 8, 1995; "Frances E. Williams" (obituary), *Variety*, Jan. 15, 1995.

88. Williams interview (1986). On the Ooma Percy name, see Williana Jones Burroughs FBI file, FOIA request #1149393.

89. Mary Christopher [Dorothy West], "A Room in Red Square," *Challenge* 1, no. 1 (1934), 15; Katrine Dalsgard, "Alive and Well and Living on the Island of Martha's Vineyard: An Interview With Dorothy West, Oct. 29, 1988," *Langston Hughes Review* 12, no. 2 (1993); West oral history, 66.

PART IV

1. Mikhail Bulgakov, *The Master and Margarita*, trans. Richard Pevear and Larissa Volkokhonsky (New York: Penguin, 2001), 387.

2. Anna Louise Strong, *Wild River* (Boston: Little, Brown, 1943), dust cover (first quotation), foreword [n.p.] (second quotation).

3. There's an argument to be made that this discourse revived in the 1960s, but that's beyond the scope of this study.

4. Kenneth Burke, "Revolutionary Symbolism in America," in *American Writers' Congress*, ed. Henry Hart (New York: International Publishers, 1935), 87–94.

5. On *Working Woman*, *Woman Today*, and the *Daily Worker*, see Van Gosse, "To Organize in Every Neighborhood, in Every Home: The Gender Politics of American Communists between the Wars," *Radical History Review* 50 (1991): 109–41; Elizabeth Faue, *Community of Suffering & Struggle: Women, Men, and the Labor Movement in Minneapolis, 1915–1945* (Chapel Hill: University of North Carolina Press, 1991). See also "Soviet Women Return to Homemaking," *Christian Science Monitor*, Jan. 26, 1938, 13; "Beauty in Russia: Women Turn to Cosmetics and a Vast New Industry Arises," *Literary Digest* 122 (Dec. 19, 1936): 44; Margaret I. Lamont, "What of the Soviet Family?," *Soviet Russia Today*, Nov. 1938, 41; William Schmidt, MD, "Land of Healthy Childhood," *Soviet Russia Today*, Nov. 1938, 48, 49, 62; Margaret I. Lamont, "Servicing Mother and Child," *Soviet Russia Today*, Jan. 1939, 20–21, 32. On working mothers, see Mildred Fairchild, "The Russian Family Today" (an address before the National Council of Parent Education, Chicago, 1936), *Journal of the American Association of University Women* 30, no. 3 (Apr. 1937): 142–48.

6. Anna Louise Strong, "Free Women," *Asia* (May 1936): 327–32.

7. Wendy Goldman, *Women, the State, and Revolution* (New York: Cambridge University Press, 1993), 291.

8. Barbara Alpern Engel, *Women in Russia, 1700–2000* (New York: Cambridge University Press, 2004), 181, 182.

9. Milly Bennett, fictionalized autobiography, box 8, folder 8, Milly Bennett papers, Hoover Library.

10. Markoosha Fischer, *My Lives in Russia* (New York: Harper & Brothers, 1944), 136; Bennett, fictionalized autobiography.

11. Fischer, *My Lives in Russia*, 222–23.

12. Sylvia Margulies ends her book, *The Pilgrimage to Moscow*, in 1937, suggesting the end of an era. Files from Intourist show the number of visitors to the Soviet Union increasing steadily from 1933, the year the Soviet Union was recognized by the United States, peaking in 1936 at 24,448, and continuing to decrease until 1945, where, at 11,168, numbers were less than half the 1936 total. F. 9612, op. 2, d. 146, Intourist files, State Archive of the Russian Federation (GARF), Moscow. On negative visitors' accounts, see, for instance, Edmee Delafield, *I Visit the Soviets: The Provincial Lady Looks at Russia* (New York: Harper, 1937); Violet Conolly, *Soviet Tempo: A Journal of Travel in Russia* (New York: Sheed and Ward, 1937).

13. Robert Robinson and Jonathan Slevin, *Black on Red: My 44 Years inside the Soviet Union: An Autobiography* (Washington, DC: Acropolis Books, 1988), 13–14. The practice of essentially forcing Americans in the Soviet Union to take on Soviet citizenship actually began earlier, but became more pronounced in the late 1930s. See Tim Tzouliadis, *The Forsaken: An American Tragedy in Stalin's Russia* (New York: Penguin Press, 2008), 63, 64,

134. Some residents sought ways of getting around this. For instance, in June 1941 Williana Burroughs made efforts to get a Soviet passport without having to give up her American citizenship. Burroughs to Comrade Ross, June 10, 1941, f. 495, op. 261, d. 3497, l. 27, Russian State Archive of Social and Political History (RGASPI), Moscow, from scholar Romy Taylor's notes, e-mailed to author by Carola Burroughs, Jan. 14, 2015. On the fate of foreigners in the 1930s, see Robert Conquest, *The Great Terror: Stalin's Purge of the Thirties*, rev. ed. (New York: Macmillan, 1973), 574; Oleg Vitalevich Khlevniuk, *The History of the Gulag: From Collectivization to the Great Terror*, trans. Vadim Stakio, with a foreword by Robert Conquest (New Haven, CT: Yale University Press, 2004), 144; Robert Conquest, *The Great Terror: A Reassessment*, 40th anniv. ed. (Oxford: Oxford University Press, 2008), 399–418; and John Earl Haynes and Harvey Klehr, *In Denial: Historians, Communism & Espionage* (San Francisco: Encounter Books, 2003).

14. Between 1937 and 1938 alone, close to 681,692 of those arrested were executed for counterrevolutionary crimes. An additional 1,473,424 died of "disease, cold, hunger, or accidents" while imprisoned, in camps, or in exile. Between 1934 and 1937, 3,750,000 people passed through the Soviet Union's labor camps, arrested for both criminal and political offenses. Wendy Z. Goldman, *Terror and Democracy in the Age of Stalin: The Social Dynamics of Repression* (New York: Cambridge University Press, 2007), 1–2. Note that historians drawing on archival sources have revised the original figures that Robert Conquest provided in his foundational work *The Great Terror*. See, for instance, J. Arch Getty, Gabor T. Rittersporn, and Viktor N. Zemskov, "Victims of the Soviet Penal System in the Pre-war Years: A First Approach on the Basis of Archival Evidence," *American Historical Review* 98, no. 4 (Oct. 1993): 1017–49.

15. Fischer, *My Lives in Russia*, 200.

16. Bennett to Kennell, Feb. 23, 1934, Ruth Epperson Kennell (REK) papers, University of Oregon, Eugene. Here she notes that Rose is getting "the run around," but she seems to assume Rose will emerge triumphant, which she did not. In 1937 she was arrested and then executed. John Callaghan and Mark Phythian, "State Surveillance and Communist Lives: Rose Cohen and the Early Communist Milieu," *Journal of Intelligence History* 12, no. 2 (2013): 134–55. Kennell's good friend May O'Callaghan had been involved in a lesbian affair with Rose's sister Nellie. See letters from O'Callaghan to Kennell in REK papers, University of Oregon, Eugene.

17. Mary M. Leder and Laurie Bernstein, *My Life in Stalinist Russia: An American Woman Looks Back* (Bloomington: Indiana University Press, 2001), 140.

18. Markoosha Fischer, unpublished memoir chapters, series 8, box 40, folder 4, p. 12, Markoosha and Louis Fischer papers, Mudd Manuscript Library, Princeton University.

19. Fischer, *My Lives in Russia*, 163, 212.

20. Peggy Dennis, *The Autobiography of an American Communist: A Personal View of a Political Life, 1925–1975* (Westport, CT: L. Hill, 1977), 113, 115. Gene and Peggy Dennis had willingly left their son behind at the end of their last stay in the Soviet Union because Party authorities had determined it would look too suspicious for them to come

back to the United States with a child who knew only Russian; with Gene a visible figure in the American Communist Party, Party officials wanted nothing that would confirm right-wing suspicions that the American party was taking orders from Moscow, and so their entire four-year stay had to remain a secret. Peggy Dennis had reluctantly accepted this logic in 1935, but the atmosphere in Moscow two years later was still a shock to her.

21. Elinor Lipper, *Eleven Years in Soviet Prison Camps* (Chicago: Regnery, 1951), 17, 14–15. One of the stories Lipper heard was that of a young woman given a five-year prison sentence for refusing to denounce her younger brother, who at sixteen had been arrested for aiding an organization of children protesting the arrest of their parents. Ibid., 71–74.

22. Markoosha Fischer, unpublished memoir chapters, pp. 10, 15, series 8, box 40, folder 4, Markoosha and Louis Fischer papers, Mudd Manuscript Library, Princeton University.

23. Ibid., 17–22.

24. Tracy B. Strong and Helene Keyssar, *Right in Her Soul: The Life of Anna Louise Strong* (New York: Random House, 1983), 192–93, 182; Anna Louise Strong, *The Stalin Era* (Altadena, CA: Today's Press, 1956), 59–66, 68 ("unjust arrests and executions"); S. J. Taylor, *Stalin's Apologist: Walter Duranty, the New York Times's Man in Moscow* (New York: Oxford University Press, 1990), 266–67; Goldman, *Terror and Democracy in the Age of Stalin*, 77–78 (other quotations).

25. See, for example, Conquest, *The Great Terror: A Reassessment*, 401; Timothy Snyder, *Bloodlands: Europe between Hitler and Stalin* (New York: Basic Books, 2010); Haynes and Klehr, *In Denial*.

CHAPTER 7

1. *The North Star*, directed by Lewis Milestone (1943; United Kingdom: Reel Enterprises, 2006), DVD; Margaret Bourke-White, *Shooting the Russian War* (New York: Simon and Schuster, 1942), 259.

2. The papers of Margaret Bourke-White at Syracuse University's Rare Book and Manuscript Library and of Lillian Hellman at the Harry Ransom Humanities Center (HRC) give evidence of the tremendous amount of publicity both women generated simply through their lives, relationships, and travels, as well as through their work.

3. It's not clear whether Bourke-White and Hellman knew each other personally, but they knew of each other, and Hellman wrote Bourke-White several times to solicit her support for various political causes. Both women had been associated with the Popular Front journal, *PM*, and had friends in common. Box 22 of Bourke-White's papers contains a letter sent by Lillian Hellman inviting her to a film by the left-wing Frontier Films (Dec. 10, 1938) and asking her to contribute financially to Frontier Films, as well as a letter asking her to support veterans of the Abraham Lincoln Brigade, which had fought for the Loyalist government during the Spanish Civil War (July 14, 1941).

4. Vicki Goldberg, *Margaret Bourke-White: A Biography* (New York: Harper & Row, 1986), 155.

5. On Bourke-White's setting the visual terms, see Beth Holmgren, "Russia on Their Mind: How Hollywood Pictured the Soviet Front," in *Americans Experience Russia*, ed. Choi Chatterjee and Beth Holmgren (New York: Routledge, 2013), 148.

6. Lillian Hellman, *Pentimento* (1973; repr., Boston: Little, Brown, 2000), 101–47; Lillian Hellman, "An Unfinished Woman," in *Three* (Boston: Little, Brown, 1979), 91. For an example of Americans' favorable impressions of the theatre festival, see Sanora Babb to James Wong Howe, Sept. 5, 1936, box 46, folder 6, Sanora Babb papers, HRC. On relationships forged during Hellman's 1937 trip, see Carl E. Rollyson, *Lillian Hellman: Her Legend and Her Legacy* (New York: St. Martin's Press, 1988), 141.

7. Lillian Hellman, *An Unfinished Woman* (London: Macmillan, 1969), 103. On Roosevelt's message to Goldwyn, see Gabriel Miller, *William Wyler: The Life and Films of Hollywood's Most Celebrated Director* (Lexington: University Press of Kentucky, 2013), Kindle edition. Unless otherwise cited, background on Hellman comes from her memoirs, *Pentimento*, *An Unfinished Woman*, and *Scoundrel Time* (New York: Little, Brown, 1976).

8. Theodore Strauss, "The Author's Case: Post-Premiere Cogitations of Lillian Hellman on 'The North Star,'" *New York Times*, Dec. 19, 1943, X5; Lillian Hellman and Jackson R. Bryer, *Conversations with Lillian Hellman*, Literary Conversations Series (Jackson: University Press of Mississippi, 1986), 117; Robert P. Newman, *The Cold War Romance of Lillian Hellman and John Melby* (Chapel Hill: University of North Carolina Press, 1989), 14–16; Deborah Martinson, *Lillian Hellman: A Life with Foxes and Scoundrels* (New York: Counterpoint, 2005), 188–89.

9. Hellman, *Pentimento*, 99–147; Martinson, *Lillian Hellman*, 350–53.

10. Paula Rabinowitz, *They Must Be Represented: The Politics of Documentary* (New York: Verso, 1994), 68–69; Caleb Crain, "It Happened One Decade: What the Great Depression Did to Culture," *New Yorker*, Sept. 21, 2009, accessed Mar. 22, 2014, http://www.newyorker.com/arts/critics/books/2009/09/21/090921crbo_books_crain?currentPage=1; Mary McCarthy, "Mary McCarthy: Portrait of a Lady," *Paris Metro*, 1978, 16.

11. Clement Greenberg, "Avant-Garde and Kitsch," *Partisan Review* 6, no. 5 (1939): 34–49; Robert Warshow, *The Immediate Experience* (Garden City, NY: Doubleday, 1962) (quotation on p. 8); Dwight Macdonald, *Masscult and Midcult* (New York: Partisan Review, distributed by Random House, 1961).

12. Todd Bennett, "Culture, Power, and *Mission to Moscow*: Film and Soviet-American Relations during World War II," *Journal of American History* 88, no. 2 (2001): 493.

13. Fannina W. Halle, "Free Women of Russia," *Woman's Home Companion* 70 (Feb. 1943), 30–31; Irina Skariatina, "Fearless Women of Russia," *Colliers* 110 (Nov. 7, 1942), 157; Rose Maurer, "Those Russian Women," *Survey Graphic* 33 (1944): 108–9.

14. Holmgren, "Russia on Their Mind," 165; Harlow Robinson, *Russians in Hollywood, Hollywood's Russians: Biography of an Image* (Boston, MA: Northeastern University Press, 2007), 115–45.

15. Ella Winter, *I Saw the Russian People* (Boston: Little, Brown, 1945), 86; Adrienne M. Harris, "Memorializations of a Martyr and Her Mutilated Bodies: Public Monuments to Soviet War Hero Zoya Kosmodemyanskaya, 1942 to the Present," *War and Culture Studies Journal* 5, no. 1 (June 2012): 73–90; "Heroes: Kosmodemyanskaya." *Time*, Mar. 2, 1942, 23.

16. National Council of American Soviet Friendship, "Pictures and Stories of Soviet Women in the War" (scrapbook), box 15, folder 2, NCASF papers, Tamiment Library, New York University (hereafter cited as NCASF papers).

17. Roger D. Markwick and Euridice Charon Cardona, *Soviet Women on the Frontlines during the Second World War* (London: Palgrave Macmillan, 2012), 2; Anna Krylova, *Soviet Women in Combat: A History of Violence on the Eastern Front* (New York: Cambridge University Press, 2010), 10, 13–14 (quotations at 10 and 14).

18. Choi Chatterjee, *Celebrating Women: Gender, Festival Culture, and Bolshevik Ideology, 1910–1939* (Pittsburgh, PA: University of Pittsburgh Press, 2002); Krylova, *Soviet Women in Combat*, 37 (quotation). Also see Markwick and Cardona, *Soviet Women on the Frontlines*. Ironically, after the war women's role was essentially erased from Soviet memory. Krylova, *Soviet Women in Combat*, 1–14.

19. Joshua S. Goldstein, *War and Gender: How Gender Shapes the War System and Vice Versa* (New York: Cambridge University Press, 2001).

20. O'Callaghan to Kennell, Oct. 3, 1943, box 7, folder 4, Ruth Epperson Kennell (REK) papers, University of Oregon, Eugene.

21. Anna Louise Strong, *Wild River* (Boston: Little, Brown, 1943), 271, 282 (quotations). On pro-Soviet media in the United States, see Michael Todd Bennett, *One World, Big Screen: Hollywood, the Allies, and World War II* (Chapel Hill: University of North Carolina Press, 2012), 198.

22. [Henry] Gregor Felsen, *Struggle Is Our Brother*, ed. Woodi Ishmael (New York: E. P. Dutton, 1943); Ruth Epperson Kennell, *That Boy Nikolka, and Other Tales of Soviet Children* (New York: Russian War Relief Inc., 1945). In the years leading up to the war, Kennell had been unable to publish a Soviet-themed juvenile, even after the success of two books in 1931 and 1932. She was only able to publish Soviet stories in Methodist periodicals from 1932 to 1945. See box 1, folder 4, REK papers, University of Oregon, Eugene. During the war, at least a dozen pro-Soviet children's books were published in the United States.

23. Lee Kingman, *Ilenka* (Boston: Houghton Mifflin, 1945), n.p. On the backlash against day care centers in the United States, see William M. Tuttle, *Daddy's Gone to War: The Second World War in the Lives of America's Children* (New York: Oxford University Press, 1993), 69–90.

24. A range of other organizations, most of them at least loosely connected to the CPUSA, also operated to promote goodwill to the Soviet Union.

25. Bennett, "Culture, Power, and *Mission to Moscow*," 497. On the OWI and American Library Association's joint project, see Joseph E. Davies, "Destroying the Legacies of Suspicion," *ALA Bulletin* 38, no. 3 (1944), 99–101.

26. Gaynor Maddox, Ransom Elwood Noble, and Russian War Relief Inc., *Russian Cook Book for American Homes* (New York: Russian War Relief Inc., 1942); Francis Henry Taylor, *Soviet War Posters* ([New York]: Russian War Relief Inc., 1944); Jerrold Beim and Lorraine Beim, *Igor's Summer, a Story of Our Russian Friends* (New York: Russian War Relief Inc., 1943); Kennell, *That Boy Nikolka.*

27. Exhibits Committee report, 1945 (on the 1944 exhibits); "Report on the Committee of Women," Nov. 5, 1945 (on the Committee on Education's activities); "Report on Cultural Committees," Nov. 22, 1943 (on the activities of the dance, art, and theatre committees). All in box 5, NCASF papers.

28. This is true despite the fact that the Committee of Women did not form until 1944.

29. "Mrs. Bethune Hails U.S.S.R.," *People's Voice*, Nov. 25, 1944, NCASF Committee of Women scrapbook, box 11, NCASF papers; "Sponsors and Members of the Committee of Women" (partial list), in *Women United for One World* (pamphlet), box 5, NCASF papers.

30. "The Purpose and Program of the Committee of Women of the National Council of American Soviet Friendship, Inc."; minutes of meeting of the Committee of Women of the NCASF, Oct. 30, 1944. Both in box 5, NCASF papers.

31. Mary Wells Ridley, "Soviet Woman Looks to U.S. Counterpart," *World Telegram*, Jan. 19, 1945; "Part Time Jobs for Women Urged," *New York Times*, Nov. 19, 1944. Both are in the NCASF Committee of Women scrapbook, box 11, NCASF papers.

32. Hellman and Bryer, *Conversations with Lillian Hellman*, 193; American Council on Soviet Relations, *Soviet Women to the Women of the World: The Moscow Women's Anti-Nazi Meeting and American Women's Response* (New York: American Council on Soviet Relations, 1941). The bulk of the pamphlet is a collection of responses from dozens of prominent American women, a large proportion of whom later joined the NCASF's Committee of Women.

33. Hellman sent a letter to the NCASF in 1950 insisting that she'd never joined; someone from the organization attached a card from July 28, 1944, showing her paid dues. These letters and the program for the First Conference on American Soviet Cultural Cooperation (Nov. 18, 1945) are in box 5, NCASF. Russian War Relief Inc. and Margaret Bourke-White, *Meet Some of the Soviet People* (New York: Russian War Relief Inc., 1941). There are mailings from the NCASF in box 70, Margaret Bourke-White papers, Syracuse University.

34. Chris Vials, *Realism for the Masses: Aesthetics, Popular Front Pluralism, and U.S. Culture, 1935–1947* (Jackson: University Press of Mississippi, 2009), 150 (on *Life* magazine); Bourke-White, *Shooting the Russian War*, 125 ("most commercially successful"); Holmgren, "Russia on Their Mind," 107 (remaining quotations; "complete modern Russian village" and "Russian pieces" are Holmgren quoting from MGM pressbook for *The North Star*, Margaret Herrick Library, Academy of Motion Picture Arts and Sciences); Alice Kessler-Harris, *A Difficult Woman: The Challenging Life and Times of Lillian Hellman* (New York: Bloomsbury Press, 2012), Kindle edition. On news coverage of Hell-

man's visit, in the United States and Soviet Union, see the scrapbook in box 154, Lillian Hellman papers, HRC, University of Texas (hereafter cited as Hellman papers). Also see Lillian Hellman, "I Meet the Front-Line Russians," *Colliers*, 1945. She also gave a number of interviews that focused on the visit and later wrote about it in *An Unfinished Woman*.

35. Bourke-White, *Shooting the Russian War*, 104; Winter, *I Saw the Russian People*, 76. On the slippery meaning of the domestic within the labor of female photographers, see Laura Wexler, *Tender Violence: Domestic Visions in an Age of U.S. Imperialism* (Chapel Hill: University of North Carolina Press, 2000).

36. Margaret Bourke-White, "This Is Moscow" (CBS radio script), July 4 and 7, 1941, f. 631, op. 10, d. 39, Russian State Archive of Literature and Art (RGALI), Moscow; Krylova, *Soviet Women in Combat*, 9–10.

37. Bourke-White, *Shooting the Russian War*, 125.

38. Ibid., 129.

39. On Burroughs's citizenship, see f. 495, op. 261, d. 3497, l. 27, Russian State Archive of Social and Political History (RGASPI), Moscow, from scholar Romy Taylor's notes, e-mailed to author by Carola Burroughs, Jan. 14, 2015. On her job at Radio Moscow, see Williana Jones Burroughs FBI file, FOIA request #1149393, citing *Philadelphia Tribune* article from Apr. 14, 1945.

40. Bourke-White, *Shooting the Russian War*, 180, 60–63, 14–15, 64–65.

41. Ibid., 62–63; Jeffrey Brooks, *Thank You, Comrade Stalin! Soviet Public Culture from Revolution to Cold War* (Princeton, NJ: Princeton University Press, 2000).

42. Bourke-White, *Shooting the Russian War*, 259.

43. Lillian Hellman, *The North Star, a Motion Picture about Some Russian People* (New York: Viking Press, 1943). On Hellman's refusal to self-identify as a feminist, see Kessler-Harris, *A Difficult Woman*.

44. For Hellman's research files, see box 81, folder 2, Hellman papers. An editor at Simon and Schuster recommended that she read *Timur and His Gang*, and James Muvey sent her a list of children's titles. Sonia Bleeker to Hellman, July 9, 1942; Muvey to Hellman, Aug. 28, 1942. Both letters are in box 84, folder 9, Hellman papers. Hellman's files contain a clipping describing *That Boy Nikolka*. Box 86, folder 12, Hellman papers.

45. Hellman's original script for *The North Star* is in box 30, folder 3, Hellman papers, but it is also published; see Hellman, *The North Star, a Motion Picture*.

46. Dan Georgakas, "The Revisionist Releases of *North Star*," *Cineaste* 22 (1996): 46; Hellman quoted in Strauss, "The Author's Case," X5.

47. Holmgren, "Russia on Their Mind," 23.

48. Hellman to Goldwyn, Oct. 20, 1942, box 84, folder 9, Hellman papers. An article from *Chicago Daily News*, June 27, 1941, notes Polish children were being marched to Nazi military hospitals to have their blood "banked" for future transfers; a United Press International (UPI) Dispatch dated February 11, 1942, notes that Germans were seizing the blood of Soviet children for wounded Nazis. In research file for *The North Star*, box 81, folder 2, Hellman papers.

49. Mary McCarthy, "A Filmy Version of the War," *Town and Country*, Jan. 1944, 72. Alice Kessler-Harris's discussion of this literary rivalry is particularly insightful; see Kessler-Harris, *A Difficult Woman*. Nora Ephron's play *Imaginary Friends* (2002) is focused on this rivalry.

50. Adolph Menjou, testimony before the House Committee on Un-American Activities, Oct. 20–24, 27–30, 1947, accessed July 1, 2015, https://archive.org/stream /hearingsregardin1947aunit/hearingsregardin1947aunit_djvu.txt; Bennett, "Culture, Power, and *Mission to Moscow*," 501.

51. Holmgren, "Russia on Their Mind," 158.

52. "Ayn Rand's HUAC Testimony," last modified Aug. 31, 2009, accessed July 31, 2015, http://www.noblesoul.com/orc/texts/huac.html; Ayn Rand and James McGuinness, testimony before the House Committee on Un-American Activities, accessed July 31, 2015, https://archive.org/stream/hearingsregardin1947aunit/hearingsregardin1947 aunit_djvu.txt.

53. Hellman to Milestone, Feb. 19, 1943, box 84, folder 9, Hellman papers.

54. Ibid.

55. Hellman quoted in Strauss, "The Author's Case," X5; "North Star," *Life* 15 (Nov. 1, 1943): 118; "A Moving, Human Drama," *Washington Post*, Nov. 19, 1943, 15; "The North Star," *Variety* 152, no. 5 (Oct. 13, 1943): 10; Andrea Passafiume, "The North Star," TCM Film Article, accessed Aug. 10, 2015, http://www.tcm.com/this-month /article/276075%7C0/The-North-Star.html (on *New York Mirror*); Georgakas, "Revisionist Releases of *North Star*."

56. John Scott, review of *Shooting the Russian War*, *Russian Review* 2, no. 1 (1942): 108. On the causes of their breakup, see Caldwell to Bourke-White, n.d. [although the letter is undated, it is probably November 1942], box 2, Erskine Caldwell papers, Syracuse University Special Collections. Also see Bourke-White to Mr. Weiss, Nov. 19, 1942, box 2, Caldwell papers. Photograph of Bourke-White and Caldwell's holiday card in box 1, Caldwell papers. Publicity shot of same picture with Caldwell cropped out in box 58, Margaret Bourke-White papers, Syracuse University.

57. Bourke-White, *Shooting the Russian War*, 57–58 (first quotation), 89 (second quotation); Margaret Bourke-White, "I Saw the Moscow Blitz: The Only Non-Russian Photographer, Armed with Six Documents, Photographed, Took These Notes," *Vogue*, Feb. 1942, 62.

58. Winter, *I Saw the Russian People*, 80.

59. Bourke-White, *Shooting the Russian War*, 231.

60. Ibid., 230.

61. Ibid., 231.

62. Ibid., 267–69.

63. Lillian Hellman, Russia diary, box 103, folder 2, Hellman papers.

64. Hellman to Stalin, Jan. 17, 1945, scrapbook, box 154, Hellman papers.

65. Letters in box 86, folder 12, Hellman papers; and Hellman Russia diary.

66. Hellman, *An Unfinished Woman*, 111; "The Moscow Trials: A Statement by American Progressives," *New Masses* 27, no. 6 (May 3, 1938): 19.

67. Genevieve Taggard, *Falcon: Poems on Soviet Themes* (Harper & Brothers, 1942), 16–17; Markoosha Fischer, *My Lives in Russia* (New York: Harper & Brothers, 1944). She notes having Genevieve Taggard as a visitor in 1936 (ibid., 138).

68. Georgakas, "Revisionist Releases of *North Star*," 47; on Bourke-White's photographs, see fig. 7.2 for an example.

69. Hellman interview with Eric Sevareid, CBS radio, Feb. 3, 1945, transcript in scrapbook, box 154, Hellman papers.

70. Margaret Bourke-White, "How I Photographed Stalin and Hopkins Inside the Kremlin," *Life* 11, no. 10 (Sept. 8, 1941): 26–27.

71. Bourke-White, *Shooting the Russian War*, 177–79, 99–103 (on Tatiana).

72. Robert E. Snyder, "Margaret Bourke-White and the Communist Witch Hunt," *Journal of American Studies* 19, no. 1 (Apr. 1985): 25 (quotation), 20 (Bourke-White quotation); Kessler-Harris, *A Difficult Woman*.

73. Snyder, "Margaret Bourke-White and the Communist Witch Hunt," 22–23; Erskine Caldwell to Mikhael Appeltin, Apr. 25, 1939, f. 631, op. 10, d. 39, RGALI, Moscow.

74. On Bourke-White's Jewishness, see Goldberg, *Margaret Bourke-White*; on Hellman's fraught relationship to her Jewishness, see Bonnie Lyons, "Lillian Hellman: The First Jewish Nun on Prytania Street," in *From Hester Street to Hollywood: The Jewish-American Stage and Screen* (Bloomington: Indiana University Press), 106–22.

75. See Elaine Tyler May, *Homeward Bound: American Families in the Cold War Era* (New York: Basic Books, 1988).

76. Strong, *Wild River*, 327; B. D. Wolfe, *New York Times*, Nov. 21, 1943, 30. *Wild River* did get some good reviews. "This book is more than propaganda," began backhanded praise in *Book Week*. "It is a realistic portrayal of the heroic efforts of the Russians in war and peace. It helps the reader understand the miracle of Russian resistance." A writer for the *Springfield Republican* insisted, "This noble story is woven of the strands of living contemporary history and of the most vital social experiments of our day." This reviewer called its characters "real and simple with dignity of creative labor," and said that the book is one "you will not easily forget." But several other critics began by saying some variation on "[this is] not a great novel." *Book Week*, Nov. 21, 1943, 3; Sarah Schiff, *Springfield Republican*, Dec. 5, 1943, 7; *Library Journal* 68 (Nov. 1, 1943); *New Republic* 109 (Dec. 20, 1943), 892. Also see *Weekly Book Review*, Nov. 21, 1943, 23; *New Yorker* 19 (Nov. 13, 1943): 112.

77. John Chamberlain, "Books of the Times," *New York Times*, May 30, 1944, 19.

EPILOGUE

1. Elinor Langer, *Josephine Herbst* (Boston: Little, Brown, 1984), 249.

2. Josephine Herbst, "Yesterday's Road," in *The Starched Blue Sky of Spain and Other Memoirs* (Boston: Northeastern University Press, 1999), 102.

3. Landon R. Y. Storrs, *The Second Red Scare and the Unmaking of the New Deal Left* (Princeton, NJ: Princeton University Press 2013), Kindle edition (quotation); Elaine Tyler May, *Homeward Bound: American Families in the Cold War Era* (New York: Basic Books, 1988).

4. Herbst, "Yesterday's Road," 102.

5. Ibid., 107, 108.

6. Ibid., 109.

7. Stephen Koch, *Double Lives: Spies and Writers in the Secret Soviet War of Ideas against the West* (New York: Free Press, 1994), 234.

8. Ibid., 232; Ellen Schrecker and Maurice Isserman, "The Right's Cold War Revision," *Nation* 271, no. 4 (2000): 23.

9. Koch's portraits are so one-sided that they offer a number of good examples: his brief descriptions of Mildred Harnack, for instance, an American member of the anti-Nazi resistance in Germany and a Soviet spy, are in marked contrast to the portrait of her in Shareen Blair Brysac's *Reisisting Hitler*, in Martha Dodd's recollection of her close friend, or in Harnack's own letters to Dodd. See Shareen Blair Brysac, *Resisting Hitler: Mildred Harnack and the Red Orchestra* (New York: 2000); and box 12, folder 14, Martha Dodd Stern papers, Library of Congress. Rayna Prohme, practically deified in memoirs by Milly Bennett, Sylvia Chen, and Vincent Sheean, is similarly flattened by Koch. See Milly Bennett, *On Her Own: Journalistic Adventures from San Francisco to the Chinese Revolution* (Armonk, NY: M. E. Sharpe, 1993); Si-lan Chen Leyda, *Footnote to History* (New York: Dance Horizons, 1984); Vincent Sheean, *Personal History* (Garden City, NY: Doubleday, Doran, 1935).

10. Tony Hiss, *The View from Alger's Window: A Son's Memoir* (New York: Vintage Books, 2000).

11. Anna Louise Strong personal file, f. 495, op. 261, d. 13, l. 91–94, Russian State Archive of Social and Political History (RGASPI), Moscow. Translation assistance by Galina Belovkurova.

12. Myra Page personal file, f. 495, op. 261, d. 2043, l. 5–11, RGASPI, Moscow.

13. Sylvia Chen personal file, f. 495, op. 225, d. 1185, n.d., RGASPI, Moscow. Her past in Moscow, her connections to China, and her links to Communist and Communist "front" organizations didn't help either. If she joined at all, she does not appear to have been active in the Communist Party (unlike her father and brother Jack), but the FBI monitored her closely. FBI file and correspondence related to naturalization efforts, both in Sylvia Chen Leyda papers, Tamiment Library, New York University.

14. Mary M. Leder and Laurie Bernstein, *My Life in Stalinist Russia: An American Woman Looks Back* (Bloomington: Indiana University Press, 2001),132–37.

15. Ruth Epperson Kennell, *Theodore Dreiser and the Soviet Union, 1927–1945: A First-Hand Chronicle* (New York: International Publishers, 1969), 7.

16. Kennell and Smith had met when they were both in Russia; Kennell had visited Smith at Russian Reconstruction Farms, which Smith started with her husband at the time, Hal Ware, and even considered working there herself.

17. The FBI informant cited in Kennell's file implies that she tried to blackmail him

(apparently Wood died penniless, and, without any evidence to support these assertions, the informant suggests that Kennell was siphoning money from him). Ruth Epperson Kennell FBI file, FOIA request #1149384.

18. Both Abt and Smith provided various kinds of information to Soviet authorities, according to Alexander Vassiliev's notebooks, the key source for Allen Weinstein's exposé *The Haunted Wood*. See, for example, Vassiliev, Black Notebook, translated from Cipher telegram dated 25.12.48, p. 477, accessed Dec.20, 2015, http://digitalarchive .wilsoncenter.org/collection/86/Vassiliev-Notebooks: "From materials received from Jessica Smith . . . the station learned that there are new trials in store." Allen Weinstein and Alexander Vassiliev, *The Haunted Wood: Soviet Espionage in America—the Stalin Era* (New York: Random House, 1999). Elizabeth Bentley, in testimony, would claim that there were important meetings with her operatives in the Abts' apartment. Kathryn S. Olmsted, *Red Spy Queen: A Biography of Elizabeth Bentley* (Chapel Hill: University of North Carolina Press, 2002), 65.

19. *Scope of Soviet Activity in the United States: Hearing before the Committee to Investigate the Administration of the Internal Security Act and Other Internal Security Laws of the Committee on the Judiciary, United States Senate* 84th Cong. 1143 (1956).

20. Louise Thompson Patterson FBI file, FOIA request #0923275.

21. Elizabeth Bentley, apparently, craved acceptance and power. Lauren Kessler, *Clever Girl: Elizabeth Bentley, the Spy Who Ushered in the McCarthy Era* (New York: HarperCollins, 2003). Agnes Smedley spied for the Soviets in China, hoping to help the Chinese Communists—and by way of that, to help Indian revolutionaries, who were her real passion. Ruth Price, *The Lives of Agnes Smedley* (New York: Oxford, 2005).

22. Like many other women, Dodd noted the decline in prostitution under the Bolsheviks, which could be explained by the fact that "economic change entitled everyone, including women, to hold jobs; easy marriage and divorce laws; the lack of a rich and corrupt class who could afford prostitutes. Most men who themselves had jobs were married, not 'chained,' to women they wanted, women who could also have jobs or careers if they wanted them." She was impressed, too, by the "hospitals, nurseries, kitchens, and recreation centers provided for the workers"; the short working day; the fact that "former palaces and mansions, and their parks, are turned into homes of culture and rest, playgrounds, medical centers, children's schools or vacation places"; and the fact that "all of this was done for workers by other workers who are the head of the state, as a beginning toward giving them the privileges and opportunities they deserve as the creators of the nation's wealth—and not as a means to pacify and keep them in hand, not as a sop to prevent other demands, rising self-respect, or a feeling of power." Martha Dodd, *Through Embassy Eyes* (New York: Harcourt, 1939), 178, 173. On Dodd, see Brysac, *Resisting Hitler*; John F. Fox Jr., "The Pilgrimage of an American Radical, Martha Dodd Stern and Family, 1933–1990" (PhD diss., University of New Hampshire, 2001); and Weinstein and Vassiliev, *The Haunted Wood*. Also see Erik Larson, *In the Garden of Beasts: Love, Terror, and an American Family in Hitler's Berlin* (New York: Crown, 2011).

23. Tracy B. Strong and Helene Keyssar, *Right in Her Soul: The Life of Anna Louise*

Strong (New York: Random House, 1983), 246. Strong's FBI file does raise some red flags: a report in the file dated July 11, 1946, notes that in July 1944 Strong "was reported as planning a trip to the Soviet Union as a correspondent for the 'Atlantic Monthly' magazine" and was reportedly in contact with Kheifets (the San Francisco KGB chief), supposedly to get his help arranging transportation. "Confidential sources" also reported that she had plans to take with her to the Soviet Union "certain 'cultural equipment'" that had been supplied to her by Louise Bransten, an accused spy. Anna Louise Strong FBI file, FOIA request #1149391-000.

24. Anna Louise Strong, *The Stalin Era* (Altadena, CA: Today's Press, 1956), 65.

25. Ibid., 65 (quotation), 70.

26. Ibid., 64–71. On Strong's bitterness toward the American Communists, see Anna Louise Strong to Harvey and Jessie O'Connor, Oct. 16, 1951, box 61, folder 24, Jessie Lloyd O'Connor papers, Smith College; on her correspondence with Students for a Democratic Society and interest in the Panthers, see letters from the late 1960s, Anna Louise Strong papers, accession no. 1309-019, University of Washington. "Ubiquitous Stalinist hack" is Koch's phrase, but it seems to be a general consensus. Koch, *Double Lives*, 218–19.

27. Hellman, *Three*, 205–7. See discussion in chapter 7.

28. Herbst, "Yesterday's Road"; Herbst, "Literature in the U.S.S.R.," *New Republic*, Apr. 29, 1931, 305–6.

29. Herbst, "Yesterday's Road," 126–27.

30. Back in the early 1960s, Lewis Feuer referred to a "Russian chapter" in American liberalism. Lewis S. Feuer, "American Travelers to the Soviet Union, 1917–1932: The Formation of a Component of New Deal Ideology" *American Quarterly* 24 (Summer 1962): 119–49.

Abbott, Grace, 63–64

Abraham Lincoln Brigade, 401n3

Abt, John, 330

A-Club, 58–59

Actors Studio, 203

Addams, Jane, 50, 356n25, 360n2

Africa, 253, 258

African Americans, 14, 50–51, 197, 241, 243; African American women, 246, 256; Communist Party, recruiting of, 257; double consciousness of, 272–73; as hypervisible, 246; Russian freedom, support of, 356–57n27; self-determination, right to, 255; in Soviet Union, 10, 20, 247–50, 252–55, 259–60, 263, 329, 352n66; in US popular culture, 247. *See also* Blackness

Aftermath (Burrill), 249

Agee, James, 294, 370n10

Alberga, Lawrence, 268

Aldridge, Ira, 247

Alexander, Raymond Pace, 259

Alexander, Sadie Tanner Mossell, 259

Alexander II, 46–47

Alexandrov, Gregorii, 314, 318

Alexievka, 111–12

Alien Act, 67

All American Commission for Russian Famine Relief, 94

Allan, Seema Rynin, 125–26, 195, 199

All-Union Central Council of Trade Unions, 256

All-Union Society for Cultural Relations with Foreign Countries (VOKS), 13

American Communist Party (CPUSA), 5, 21–22, 131, 282

American Council on Soviet Relations (ACSR), 303

American Friends Service Committee (AFSC), 73–75, 80–81, 83–86, 90–91, 93–94, 98–99, 104, 106, 118, 167, 362n12

American League Against War and Fascism, 331

American Library Association (ALA), 300–301

American Mercury (magazine), 121, 123–24, 175, 189–90, 330, 381n78

American Negro Labor Congress (ANLC), 256

American Red Cross (ARC), 80–81, 87–88

American Relief Administration (ARA), 73, 80–82, 90–91, 94, 97, 218

American Women's Emergency Committee (AWEC), 73–75, 85–86, 98

Amtorg (trading agency), 12, 125

Andreyeva, Madame, 58

anti-Semitism, 19, 188, 227, 276

Appletin, Michael, 322

Arle-Tietz, Corretti (Coretta Alfred), 244, 248–49

Armand, Inessa, 9, 59

Artef Dance Group, 224

Ashmun, Margaret, 376n8

Asia, 258, 270–74, 283, 295, 321

Axelrod, Tovi L., 173, 186

Baba, Haji, 357n29

Babb, Sanora, 16, 402n6

Baker, Josephine, 250

Bakunin, Mikhail, 56, 59

Balabaeva, Rosa, 271

Baldwin, Roger, 92, 359n52

Ballet Russes, 203, 208, 227

Barber, Margaret, 75, 77

Barker, Elsa, 60–61

Barker, Tom, "Hell in Siberia," 145

Barrow, Florence, 93–94

Barrows, Isabel, 51, 60, 62, 357n29

Barrows, Samuel J., 51

Barrymore, Ethel, 261

Bashkir Republic, 103

Bassow, Whitman, 165

Bates, Ruby, 258–59

Battleship Potemkin (film), 203

Bauer, Catherine, 14

Baxter, Anne, 309

Beatty, Bessie, 165–66, 363n21, 376n8

Beneath the Czar (film), 40

Benjamin, Walter, 163, 199

Bennett, Milly, 3, 21, 27, 121, 123–24, 125–27, 167–68, 173–77, 179–86, 187–90, 193–97, 199, 276, 284–86, 377n16, 378n33, 381n78, 382n91; Moscow, communication with, 328; *On Her Own*, 378n31; writing style of, 178

Bennett, Todd, 301

Beria, Lavrenti, 288

Berkman, Alexander, 21

Berlin (Germany), 27, 260, 327

Bethune, Mary McLeod, 302

Beyer, Jack, 137

Bialek, Bertha, 273

biomechanics, 204, 223

Birobidjian, 19–20, 367n84

Birth Control League, 86

Black and White (film), 243–44, 246–47, 255, 261–62, 265, 273, 278–79; cancellation of, 269–70; filming, postponement of, 267–68; publicity of, 260; script of, 263–64, 268–69; women, depiction of, 269

blackface, 247, 249, 254

Blackness, 19; performance of, 246, 250–54; as tragic condition, 247. *See also* African Americans

Black Panthers, 333

Blackwell, F., 14

Blackwell, Henry, 45, 52

Blake, Eubie, 250

Blatch, Harriot Stanton, 73, 75, 362n12

Blitzstein, Marc, 224

Bloody Sunday, 54–55, 211–12

Bloor, Ella Reeve, 104

Bolshevik revolution, 3–4, 10–11, 18, 37, 68, 79–80, 87, 212, 224–25

Bolsheviks, 15, 21, 29, 36, 64–66, 72–73, 75, 77, 80, 83–84, 87, 89–90, 93–94, 99, 103, 122, 124, 136, 138, 163, 166, 203, 255, 326, 330; and feminism, 6–7, 9, 63, 82, 154–55, 183, 334; foreign workers, recruiting of, 12; new morality of, 22–27, 123, 156; opposition, suppression of, 67–68; prostitution, decline under, 409n22; as puritanical, 23; sex, attitude toward, 22–23; show trials of, 30, 286; tourism, encouraging of, 12; veil, campaign against, 273; workplace discrimination, punishing of, 13

Bolshoi Ballet, 265

Bolshoi Theatre, 217–18

Borodin, Mikhail, 168–69, 190, 192–93, 196, 275, 333, 377n16

Bourke-White, Margaret, 4, 27–28, 32, 126, 204, 270, 275, 292, 309, 324, 370n10, 401n3; animosity toward, 322; criticism of, 294; FBI surveillance on, 293, 322; *Meet Some of the Russian People*, 304; Nazis, hatred of, 322; norms of femininity, resistance to, 323; *Shooting the Russian War*, 291, 294, 304, 306–7, 309, 315, 320–21; Stalin, meeting with, 320–21; war effort, women's role in, 305–7; in war zone, attitude toward, 314–18; women's perspectives, as vehicle for, 305; *You Have Seen Their Faces* (with Caldwell), 294

Bovington, John, 267

Bowman, Laura, 248

Branham, Lucy Gwynne, 73–74, 362n12, 376n8

Bransten, Louise, 410n23

Breshko-Breshkovskaya, Ekaterina. *See* Breshkovsky, Catherine

Breshkovsky, Catherine, 42, 55–56, 59, 61, 63–68, 356n25, 357n29; background of, 43; hard labor, 43; imprisonment of, 43; Siberia, exile in, 43, 60, 62; tour of, 42, 45–46, 48–54, 357n31; trial of, 60

Brik, Osip, 161

Britain, 66, 299, 347–48n19. *See also* England

British Empire, 258

British Friends War Victims Relief Committee (BFWVRC), 83–84, 87–88. *See also* Quakers

Browder, Earl, 198

Bryant, Louise, 66, 69, 71, 73–74, 77, 83, 85, 88, 92, 165, 201; *Six Red Months in Russia*, 70, 79, 166

Bulgakov, Mikhail, *The Master and Margarita*, 281

Bullard, Arthur, 49

Bunche, Ralph, 244

Burgoyne, Olga, 248

Burrill, Mary, *Aftermath*, 249

Burroughs, Williana, 256, 279, 306, 394n30, 399–400n13

Bushell, Garvin, 250, 252

Buzuluk, 83, 94, 96, 99–100

Cahan, Abraham, 52

Caldwell, Erskine, 292, 304, 306, 315, 322; *You Have Seen Their Faces* (with Bourke-White), 294

California Friends of Russian Freedom, 56

Calvert, Herbert Stanley, 131–33

Calverton, V. F., *Sex and Civilization*, 25

Canada, 122, 166

Cannon, Cornelia, 14, 30

capitalism, 3, 31, 124, 183, 333

Carpenter, Edward, 152–53, 359–60n60

Carr, J. (L. E. Katterfield), 95

Carter, Huntley, 201–2

Carver, George Washington, 273–74

Casino, Angel, 227

Catherine the Great, 318

Catt, Carrie Chapman, 7, 302

Central Children's Theatre, 393n23

Chambers, Whittaker, 260

Chaplin, Charlie, 301

Cheftel, Marc, 118

Chen, Eugene, 275

Chen, Jack, 167–68, 171, 408n13

Chen, Sylvia, 246, 267, 275–79, 329, 377n16; FBI surveillance on, 408n13

Chernyshevsky, Nikolai, *What Is to Be Done?*, 7, 47, 59, 158

Chicago (Illinois), 54, 355n25

Chicago Daily News (newspaper), 161, 176, 188

Children's Bureau, 64, 84–85, 302
Children's Colony on the Volga, A (Strong), 108–10
Children's Commission of the All-Russian Central Executive Committee (VTsIK), 113; Soviet Children's Commission, 107
Child Study Association, 302
child welfare movement, 64
China, 9, 167, 169, 174, 275–76, 289, 332
Chinese Revolution, 167
Chocolate Dandies (Blake and Sissle), 250
Chocolate Kiddies, 249–53
Christianity, 37. *See also* Social Gospel
Chung Mei news service, 174
Circus, The (film), 279, 314
Civil Rights Congress, 331
Cleyre, Voltairine de, 53
Cohen, Rose, 197, 286, 400n16
Cold War, 3, 5, 31, 282, 323, 326, 328, 332, 334
collectivization, 30, 193–94, 225–26, 264, 272, 283, 380n65; and collective farms, 293, 320
colonialism, 250
Comintern, 122, 132, 156–58, 161, 168–69, 197–98, 268–69, 327–29; on Black equality, 259; Fourth Comintern Congress, 18, 249; on Negro Question, 257; Sixth Comintern Congress, 255–56; Seventh Comintern Congress, 282
Communism, 5, 19, 37, 181–82, 282; as taboo subject, 334
Communist Party of the Soviet Union (CPSU), 9, 29–31, 113, 142, 145, 164, 196, 198, 217, 286
Communist Party of the United States (CPUSA), 13, 122, 142, 145, 164, 196, 198, 217, 258–59, 329, 332–33, 358n46, 366n68; African Americans, recruiting of, 257. *See also* Workers Party
Communist University of the Toilers of the East (KUTV), 22, 253, 256, 273, 277
Congregational Education Society, 260–61

Cooper, Hugh, 268, 301
Copland, Aaron, 301, 310
Corwin, Norman, 301
Council on African Affairs, 331
Counts, George, 260
Cowley, Malcolm, 260
Crain, Caleb, 294
Crisis (journal), 255
cruel optimism, 32
Crusader News Agency, 269–70
Cuba, 135, 226, 332
Czechoslovakia, 65, 250, 332

Daily Worker (newspaper), 282
Dalcroze, Émile Jacques, 202–3, 227
dance: ballet, 203, 207–8, 212–13, 216, 224, 227, 229–30; and kinesthesia, 208; mass dances, 235; and metakinesis, 208; "new Soviet dance," 236, 241; physical culture, 235; plastic dance, 236; self-expression, as form of, 202, 208, 212; in Soviet Union, 207–9, 213, 224–25, 229–30, 234, 236; in US, 208, 222–24, 235; and women, 208, 235. *See also* modern dance; radical dance movement; *and individual dance groups and dancers*
Darkest Russia (Donnelly), 346n8
Davis, Jerome, 77
Days of Glory (film), 296
Dell, Floyd, 209, 260; *Were You Ever a Child?*, 71
Delsarte, François, 202, 208
Demchenko, Marie, 283
De Mille, Agnes, 302
Denison House, 50, 357n31
Dennis, Eugene, 287, 400–401n20
Dennis, Peggy, 287, 400–401n20
Denny, Dorothy. *See* Detzer, Dorothy
Detroit (Michigan), 12
Detzer, Dorothy, 367n81
Diaghilev, Sergei, 203, 208, 212–13
Dinamov, Sergey, 322, 330
Dodd, Martha, 332, 409n22
Dorr, Rheta Childe, 165–66

Doty, Madeleine Z., 9–11, 165–66, 359n52

Double Lives (Koch), 327

Doyle, Ruth, 144–46

Doyle, Thomas, 144–46

Dreier, Mary, 73

Dreiser, Theodore, 162, 170, 175, 330, 370n1; "Ernita," 134, 161, 375n89

Du Bois, W. E. B., double consciousness, idea of, 247, 273

Dudley, Helena, 50, 54, 62

Duncan, Anna, 226

Duncan, Irma, 214, 216–18, 220–21, 223, 226

Duncan, Isadora, 4, 18, 32, 55, 72, 82–83, 101, 202, 207, 228–30, 233–34, 241, 248, 377n16; children, effect on, 213–18, 221–23; criticism of, 220–21; dancer of the future, 208–9, 211; death of, 223; idealism of, 215–16; on marriage, 219; new art, as symbol of, 209; as pioneer, 211; plastic dance, 236; revolutionary dance movement, influence on, 224–27; school of, 214–19, 223, 226; spirit of rebellion, embodying of, 211–12; utopian Dionysian ecstasy, representing of, 209

Duncanism, 223

Dunham, Katherine, 302

Dunn, Robert, 98–100, 366n67, 367n80

Duranty, Walter, 166, 170–71, 175, 376n8

Durland, Kellogg, 49

Eastman, Crystal, 4

Edelstadt, Vera, *Young Fighters of the Soviets*, 300

Edwards, Thyra, 254

Eisenstein, Sergei, 203, 231, 265–66, 278, 314, 318

Ellington, Duke, 250

Ellis, Havelock, 156, 208

Emmett, Pauline, 1

Engel, Barbara, 284

England, 40, 61, 211. *See also* Britain

Epperson, Ella, 130

"Ernita" (Dreiser), 134, 161, 375n89

Esenin, Sergei, 219–20, 387nn33–34

espionage, 287, 327–30, 350n42; and homosexuality, 380n67

eurhythmics, 202–3, 227

Europe, 16, 49, 63, 90, 208, 248, 253, 255, 258–59

Everyweek (magazine), 184

Eyes on Russia (Bourke-White), 292, 294

Falcon (Taggard), 319

famine: and child savers, 78, 80, 82–83, 91, 97, 100–101, 103, 107–9, 136, 215, 281; famine of 1921, 77; famine of 1932, 171; famine relief, 72–73, 81–84, 90–91, 94, 97, 260; in Poland, 93; in Russia, 11, 29, 37–38, 68, 71–72, 77–78, 90, 94–97, 99, 104, 135–36, 193–94, 201, 216, 264–65; in Ukraine, 30, 264

fascism, 282, 303

February Revolution, 7

Federal Bureau of Investigation (FBI), 293, 322, 408n13, 410n23, 331–33

Federal Theatre Project, 16, 204

Federated Press, 167, 175

Felsen, Henry Gregor, *Struggle Is Our Brother*, 300

feminism, 4–6, 9, 28, 63, 154–55, 183; left feminism, 334; tension within, 82

Feuer, Lewis, 410n30

Fight the Famine Council, 364n40. *See also* Save the Children Fund

Figner, Vera, 48, 56

Finland, 135, 282, 295, 320

First Five-Year Plan, 12–13, 29, 121, 125. *See also* Five-Year Plan

Fischer, Louis, 166, 170, 285

Fischer, Markoosha, 285–89, 319, 324

Fischer, Ruth, 107

Fisk Jubilee Singers, 248

Fitzpatrick, Sheila, 22

Five-Year Plan, 27, 119, 173, 188, 257. *See also* First Five-Year Plan

Flame of Paris, The (ballet), 229

Flanagan, Hallie, 16–17, 28, 204

Flomenbaum, Ada, 114–15
Fokine, Michel, 203, 212, 227–28, 230
Ford, James, 260–61
Foregger, Nikolai, 207–8, 236
Forsyne, Ida, 248
Fortune (magazine), 294
Fort-Whiteman, Lovett, 244, 260, 263–64
Foucault, Michel, 349n32
Foulke, William Dudley, 48, 52
France, 66, 211, 223, 250
free love, 3–4, 22, 25–26, 47, 51, 59, 62,
    123, 144–45
French Revolution, 66
Friedan, Betty, and feminine mystique, 32
Friends Council for International Service,
    108
Friends of Soviet Russia (FSR), 78, 104
Friends of the Soviet Union, 261
Frontier Films, 401n3

Gaidar, Arkady, *Timur and His Gang*, 309
Gamaleyevka, 99, 102
Gannett, Lewis, 170
Gapon, Georgy, 54
Garland, Mary "Mignon." *See* Garlin, Mary
    "Mignon"
Garlin, Mary "Mignon," 225–26, 350n42
Garner, Sylvia, 261, 264, 267, 270
Gee, Lottie, 250
Georgakas, Dan, 310
Germany, 11, 93, 135, 184, 211, 235, 250,
    294, 300, 305; German *Ausdruckstanz*,
    236
Gershuni, Gregori, 46, 59
Gershwin, Ira, 310
Gillis, Fay, 1
Gilman, Charlotte Perkins, 50–51
Gilmore, Glenda, 258
Glaspell, Susan, *Suppressed Desires*, 141
Goines, Baby, 250, 252
Goines, Bobby, 250
Gold, Mike, 131–33
Golden, Oliver, 273–74
Goldman, Emma, 4, 21, 46–49, 52, 54–56,
    59, 67–68, 203

Goldman, Wendy, 9, 26
Goldwyn, Samuel, 293, 304, 310–11
Goleizovsky, Kasian, 275–76
Goncharov, Andrei, 233
Gorky, Maxim, 58–59, 90, 220
Gornick, Vivian, 5
Gorow, Boris, 356n27
Granger, Farley, 309
Graves, Anna, 111–14
Great Depression, 12, 121, 195
Great Terror, 30, 162, 198–99, 228, 282,
    287, 289–90, 295, 324. *See also* Stalin,
    Joseph
Grebner, Georgii, 260, 268
Greece, 211
Greenwich Village, 7, 59
Group Theatre, 203
Gruber, Ruth, 16
Gruenberg, Sidonie, 302
Guliamova, Bakhri, 271
Gusev, Sergei Ivanovich, 191–92

Hahn, Simon, 139, 142, 159
Haines, Anna J., 73, 78, 83–85, 87–88,
    89–91, 365n46; *Health Work in Soviet
    Russia*, 118
Hall Johnson Negro Choir, 261
Hamilton, Alexander, 74
Hamilton, Alice, 106, 302, 367n81
Hammer, Armand, 362n12
Hammond, John, 260
Harding, Ann, 310
Harlem, 250
Harlem Liberator (magazine), 331
Harlem Renaissance, 10, 243, 249, 261–62
Harlem Workers' School, 256
Harnack, Mildred, 332
Harris, Emma, 244, 248, 262–65, 392n12
Hawaii, 174
Hawes, Elizabeth, 14, 302
Hayes, Ellen, 108, 114–15
Haynes, John Earl, 329
Haywood, William D. ("Big Bill"), 58, 129,
    132–33, 137–38
Helfman, Jessie, 48

Hellbeck, Jochen, 18, 349n32
Hellman, Lillian, 291–92, 303–4, 307, 309–11, 334, 401n3, 404n33; animosity toward, 322; blacklisting of, 321; criticism of, 294, 320; FBI surveillance on, 293, 322; Jewishness of, 322; Nazis, hatred toward, 322; norms of femininity, resistance to, 323; *North Star*, criticism of, 293, 312–14; Russian people, warmth toward, 318–19; Soviet Union, supporter of, 301; Stalinism, charges of, 319; in war zone, attitude toward, 317; women's perspectives, as vehicle for, 305
Henry Street Settlement House, 4, 49, 63, 224
Heptachor (dance commune), 213–14, 220
Herbst, Josephine, 325–28, 330, 334
Herrman, John, 330
Herzen, Alexander, 40
Higginson, Thomas Wentworth, 45
Hill, Leonard, 262
Hilliard, Mary, 62
Hindus, Maurice, 25, 27
Hiss, Alger, 328
Hiss, Tony, 328
Hitler, Adolf, 282, 295
Holmes, John Haynes, 108
Holmgren, Beth, 304
homosexuality, 19, 27, 62, 185, 196, 267; espionage threats, 380n67
Hoover, Herbert, 81–83, 90–91, 94, 96
Hoover, J. Edgar, 331
House Committee on Un-American Activities (HUAC), 311–12, 321–23, 330
Howe, Julia Ward, 45, 52
Howells, William Dean, 45, 58–59
Hughes, Langston, 243–44, 248, 254, 261–64, 267–69, 273–76, 278, 396n48
Huiswood, Otto, 249
Hull House, 54, 63
humanitarianism, 11, 37, 71, 90, 94; discourse of, 78, 79–80, 85, 100
Humphrey, Doris, 302
Hurley, Beulah, 97

Hurston, Zora Neale, 261
Hutchins, Grace, 16, 19

I Change Worlds (Strong), 117, 164, 196–98
Igor's Summer (Beim and Beim), 301
Ilenka (Kingman), 300
Ilin, M., *New Russia's Primer*, 119
immigration, 48–49; American immigration, waves of, 123–24; open policy toward, 122; restrictions on, 11, 21, 122; by skilled workers, 122
Industrial Workers of the World (IWW), 58, 130–31, 137, 142–43, 145
Institute for Research on Women's Styles, 126
Institute for the Protection of Mothers and Children, 15
Intercollegiate Socialist Society, 86, 98
International Association of Revolutionary Writers (MORP), 322
internationalism, 35–37, 86; Christian, 353n4; Communist, 228; new American, 80; progressive, 35, 353n1
International Labor Defense (ILD), 258–59, 331
International News Service, 196
International Women's Day, 154
Intourist, 347–48n19, 399n12
Isadora Duncan Museum, 214
Isserman, Maurice, 327–28
Italy, 250
Ito, Michio, 227
Iving, Victor, 221

jazz, 249–50, 252–53, 275
Jenkins, Katherine, 262
Jewish Enlightenment (Haskalah), 37
Jewish Joint Distribution Committee (JDC), 80–81
Jews: Jewish tradition, and messianic thought, 37; Jewish women, and socialism, 7; pogroms against, 55; in Soviet Union, 19–20, 37, 50–51, 81
Jim Crow, 247

John Reed Colony (JRC), 91, 107–17, 167, 281
Johnson, Helene, 28
Jones, Mildred, 262–63, 267–68, 273–74
Junghans, Karl, 260, 267–69

Kagonovich, Lazar, 191–92
Katz, Maude White, 256
Katz, Otto, 327
Kazakova, Halima, 271
Keller, Helen, 72–73, 301
Kemerovo (Siberia), 129, 134, 138, 140, 146, 152, 156–60, 188, 375n92
Kennan, George, 43, 45–46; *Siberia and the Exile System*, 44, 355n15
Kennell, Frank, 129–31, 133, 135, 138–39, 141–44, 147–49, 151–52, 155–59, 161, 175–76, 375n89
Kennell, Jimmie, 131, 133–34, 147–48, 151–52, 155–56, 158–59
Kennell, Ruth Epperson, 11–12, 26, 32, 121–27, 129–31, 134–36, 138–44, 146–53, 156–60, 174–76, 179, 181–82, 186, 189–90, 194–95, 197, 199, 249, 252, 286, 299, 330, 333, 370n1, 376n8, 381n78, 403n22, 408n16, 409n17; feminism, attitude toward, 154–55; as feminist icon, 161; firing of, 188; freedom, yearning for, 133, 154–56, 162; "Kuzbas: A Romantic Chronicle," 375n89; "The New Innocents Abroad," 121–22; professional aspirations of, 154; "Soviets Run Factory Kitchens to Relieve Women of Drudgery," 183–84; *That Boy Nikolka and Other Stories of Soviet Children*, 300–301, 309; *Theodore Dreiser and the Soviet Union, 1927–1945*, 329; "Where Women Are Really Equal," 185
Kerensky, Alexander, 36
Kharkov Writers' Congress, 327, 334
Khrushchev, Nikita, 333, 352n66
Khvalinsk, 107
kinesthesia, 208

kinetic movements, 12
Kirov, Sergei, 199, 228, 286, 316
Kishinev pogrom, 40, 45
Koch, Stephen, 328; *Double Lives*, 327
Kollontai, Alexandra, 9, 23, 63–64, 168, 351n51, 360n64; "winged eros," 24
Komsomol (Young Communist League), 286
Koner, Pauline, 4, 18, 225, 228–33, 275, 302; Jewishness of, 227, 349–50n37; Lesgaft Institute, involvement with, 234–36, 239; "new Soviet dance," 236, 241; physical culture parade, 239–40
Konstantinov, Evgeni, 185, 189, 382n91
Koreneva, Claudia, 254
Kornblitt, Bronca, 137, 159
Kosmodemyanskaya, Zoya, 296
Kostrikova, Eugenie, 316
Kravchinsky, Sergei (Stepniak), 44; *Underground Russia*, 45
Kropotin, Peter, 43, 49, 56, 61; *Memoirs of a Revolutionist*, 50
Krupskaya, Nadezhda, 59
KUTV. *See* Communist University of the Toilers of the East
Kuzbas (Autonomous Industrial Colony of Kuzbas) (AIK), 121–23, 131, 148–51, 155, 158–59, 161, 168, 176, 249, 370n1, 371n7; American control of, 142–43; American style of, 132; bourgeois morality, freedom from, 133; communal living in, 140–41, 143–45, 153–54; conflict in, 137–39, 142–46, 153; cooperative commissary, 153–54; end of, 160; free love, 144, 146; iconic status of, 188; international solidarity of, 133; mismanagement in, 160; as "new Pennsylvania," 129, 146, 160; pioneers, treatment of, 135–36; sanitation in, 138; as utopian experiment, 162; as utopian folly, 146; women of, as afterthought, 133; Workers Pledge, 133–34
Kuzbas Bulletin (publication), 122, 137, 149

Ladies Home Journal (magazine), 166

Laqueur, Thomas, 79

Lathrop, Julia, 64

Lazarev, George, 51–52, 357n29

Leder, Mary, 20, 286, 288, 329

Left, 6, 30, 68, 71; American Left, 333; New Left, 31, 330, 352n66; Old Left, 31, 330, 352n66

Lenin, Vladimir, 7, 9, 36, 59, 63, 67, 122, 129, 132–33, 137, 152, 171, 217, 219, 224–25, 261, 371n7, 375n88; glass of water theory, 23–24

Leningrad (Russia), 228–29, 235–36, 241, 262. *See also* Petrograd; Saint Petersburg

Lenin School, 22, 253, 394n30

Lerner, Noah, 144

Lesgaft, Pyotr, 234

Lesgaft Physical Culture Institute, 234–35, 239–40

Lewis, Juanita, 261

Lewis, Mollie, 244

Lewis, Sinclair, 170

Lewisohn, Alice, 73, 224

Lewisohn, Irene, 224

Leyda, Jay, 278

liberalism: American liberalism, 410n30; liberal narrative, 346n7; New Deal liberalism, 30, 282, 328

Liberator (newspaper), 71, 131, 249

Life (magazine), 292, 294, 304, 314, 322, 324

Lindley, Helen, 154–55, 158–59

Lipper, Eleanor, 287–88, 401n21

Lithuania, 135

Littledale, Clara Savage, 302

Little Review, The (magazine), 327

Litvinov, Ivy, 217

Litvinov, Maxim, 90, 217–18

Lloyd, Henry Demarest, 175

Lloyd, Jessie. *See* O'Connor, Jessie Lloyd

Lluang Ping, 331

Locke, Alain, 244, 261

London, Jack, 56

Louisiana Amazons, 248

Luben, Sonia, 21–22

Luce, Henry, 322

Luhan, Mabel Dodge, 108

Lunacharskaya, Anna, 253

Lunacharsky, A. V., 207, 217

Luscombe, Florence, 10–11

Lyons, Eugene, 5, 126–27, 166, 170, 379n57

"Mammy of Moscow," 392n12. *See also* Harris, Emma

Marinsky Ballet School, 230

Marling, Jeanya, 1

Martin, John, 208, 302

Marx, Karl, 37, 56, 261; *Capital*, 131

Maslow, Sophie: *Themes from a Slavic People*, 224; *Two Songs about Lenin*, 224

Mason, Charlotte Osgood, 261

Masses, The (newspaper), 327

Massing, Hede, 350n42

Master and Margarita, The (Bulgakov), 281

Maurer, Rose, 295; *Soviet Children and Their Care*, 303; *Soviet Women*, 303

Maya, Vera, 275

McCarthy, Mary, 294, 311

McCarthyism, 282, 328, 333

McClendon, Rose, 260

McCormick, Anne O'Hare, 26, 29

McGuinness, James, 312

McKay, Claude, 249, 349n37; "Soviet Russia and the Negro," 255

McKenzie, Allen, 262

McNairy Lewis, Thurston, 261–62, 268

Meadman, Dhimah, 225

Mehlman, Elsa, 149–51, 161

Mellett, Lowell, 301, 314

Memoirs of a Revolutionist (Kropotkin), 50

Mencken, H. L., 121, 378n37

Meshlauk, Valery, 169–70, 378n33

metakinesis, and kinesthesia, 208

Metropolitan Museum of Art, 301

Mexico, 168, 332

Meyerhold, Vsevolod, 204, 212, 223, 228

Mezhrobpom Studio, 260, 267–68, 274–75

Micheaux, Oscar, 247

Middle East, 253, 258

Milestone, Lewis, 293, 309, 312–14

Miller, Loren, 244, 268

minstrelsy, 247, 252

Mission to Moscow (film), 296, 311, 319

Mitchell, Elsie Reed, 149–50, 153, 161–62

Mitchell, Lucy Sprague, 301

Mitchell, Mike, 174

modern dance, 207, 225, 229, 231, 234, 240–41, 276; and biomechanics, 223; expressive movement of, 202, 208, 212; as gateway to soul, 209; kinesthesia, and empathy, 208; mass dances, 235; and metakinesis, 208; and physical culture, 235; and women, 208, 235. *See also* dance; radical dance movement; *and individual dance groups and dancers*

modernity, 31

Moon, Henry Lee, 255, 262, 268, 270

morality, 4; bourgeois morality, 133; new morality, 22–27, 123, 156

Moscow (Russia), 3–5, 10, 22, 72, 74, 77, 87–88, 96, 104, 107, 157, 167, 169, 171, 175–77, 189, 195, 199, 207, 212, 225–26, 228–29, 241, 243, 246, 248–49, 258–60, 262, 279; American women in, 126; fear and suspicion in, 289; as miracle city, 18; show trials in, 30, 240, 294, 319; theatre in, 28

Moscow Art Theatre, 203, 213

Moscow Daily News (newspaper), 192, 198

"Moscow Metro" (Blitzstein), 224

Moscow News (newspaper), 3, 123, 163, 166, 168, 170–71, 174–75, 177–79, 183–90, 192, 195–97, 199, 269, 274, 276, 286, 309; American community, as center of, 125–26; as hybrid, 164; staff, arrest of, 289, 333; women's issues, attention to, 173

Moscow State Yiddish Theatre, 349–50n37

Moscow Theatre Festival, 16, 224–25, 293, 319

Moscow Theatre for Children, 253–54, 393n23

Moscow Trials, 30, 240, 282, 294, 311, 319

Moscow Yankee (Page), 25, 257

Motion-Picture Alliance for the Preservation of American Ideals, 312

Museum of Modern Art, 302

Mussey, June Barrows, 357n29

Mussey, Mabel Barrows, 63, 357n29

Müzenberg, Willi, 260, 327

My Eleven Years in a Soviet Prison (Lipper), 287

My Lives in Russia (Fischer), 324

Nation (magazine), 74, 104, 129, 145–46, 154, 160, 166

National American Woman's Suffrage Association, 86

National Association for the Advancement of Colored People (NAACP), 255, 258, 356–57n27

National Committee for the Defense of Political Prisoners, 261

National Council of American Soviet Friendship (NCASF), 296, 300–301, 304, 324, 404n33; Committee of Women, 302–3; Committee on Education, 302

National Council of Negro Women, 302

National Federation of Women's Clubs, 302

National Negro Congress, 331

National Woman's Party, 54, 73, 85–86, 106

Nazimova, Alla, 55, 203

Nazism, 281, 289, 310–11, 313, 320, 322–23

Negro Boy and the Monkey, The (Sats and Rozanov), 393n23; race and gender-bending performances in, 253–54

Negro Question, 249, 255–59

Neighborhood Playhouse, 224

New Deal: male breadwinner, ethic of, 28; New Deal liberalism, 30, 282, 328

New Duncan Dancers, 226–27

New Economic Policy (NEP), 12, 29, 142, 347n17, 372n36

New Masses (newspaper), 319

new person, 204. *See also* new Soviet woman; new woman

new Soviet woman, 3–4, 27–28, 209, 235, 255–56; in American popular culture, 282, 290, 295, 298–99, 324; American women, as role model for, 294–95; as attractive, 296; bravery of, 31; challenge to, 284; cult of the heroine, 236; demise of, 282; family law, and women's rights, 284; feminine beauty, emphasis on, 282–84; in films, portrayal of, 295–96; Germans, resistance to, 296; natural beauty of, 27; "new spirit" of, 12; progress, as representative of, 236; promise of, 209; as role model, for American women, 294–95; as soldiers, 298, 305, 309; transformation of, 270–72; women's place, redefining of, 298. *See also* women; women's suffrage

Newspaper Enterprise Association, 176

New Theatre (publication), 225, 240

new woman, 5, 9, 27, 36, 39, 183, 281–82, 335; as familiar figure, 4; freedom, asserting of, 37; mocking of, 126; in popular culture, 4; progressive internationalism, proponents of, 35; revolutionary Russia, identification with, 45; Soviet experiment, interest in, 3, 14, 129–30. *See also* women; women's suffrage

New World Review (publication), 98, 331. See also *Soviet Russia Today*

New York American (newspaper), 166

New York City, 4, 58, 224, 226–27, 240, 256

New York Times (newspaper), 146, 166, 171, 184

New York World (publication), 104, 146

Nietzsche, Friedrich, 212

nihilism, 47

Nikitenko, Maria, 295

Nimura, Yeichi, 232

Ninotchka (film), 295–96

North Star, The (film), 291–93, 296, 304–5, 309–10, 324; criticism of, 311–12, 314, 320; Hollywood, Communist infiltration of, 311–12; praise of, 314

Nuorteva, Santeri, 88

Nuremberg, Thelma, 303

Obidova, Jahah, 271–72

Obolensky, Leonid, *Merchants of Glory*, 275

O'Callaghan, May, 161, 299, 375n88, 400n16

Ocko, Edna, 13, 225

O'Connor, Harvey, 175

O'Connor, Jessie Lloyd, 20, 175, 187, 195, 199, 376n8; "A Flapper in Russia," 27

October Revolution, 92

Office of War Information (OWI), 300–301

One Sixth of the World (film), 250

Orlenev, Paul, 55, 203

Orlova, Lyubov, 277, 279

Ortt, Kevah "Kitty," 149–50

Oumansky, Constantine, 275

Page, Myra, 25, 197, 257–58, 329

Palace of Motherhood, 15

Palestine, 19–20, 227, 349–50n37

Pankhurst, Sylvia, 345n3, 375n88

Paris (France), 3, 57, 126, 131, 223, 250

Parnakh, Valentin, 249

Patterson, Lloyd, 262, 279, 306

Patterson, Louise Thompson, 10, 20, 243–44, 260–61, 263–66, 268–74, 283, 331, 350n42; as security risk, 332

Patterson, William, 331

Pavlova, Anna, 203, 213, 230

Pearson, Alfred, 138–39, 141–42

Pennsylvania, 129, 135, 146

Pentecoast, Hugh M., 53

People's Institute, 131

People's Will, 46–47

Pepper, Claude, 301

Percy, Ooma, 279, 306. *See also* Burroughs, Williana

performance, 201; and biomechanics, 204, 223; concept of, 202; gender, and stylized repetition of acts, 202; and "new person," 204

Perovksaya, Sophia, 48, 56

Petrograd (Russia), 10, 74, 81, 135–36. *See also* Leningrad; Saint Petersburg

photojournalism, 80

physical culture (*fizkul'tura*), 236, 239–40; and dance, 235; gymnastics, emphasis on, 234; movement, cultural dimensions of, 234; and synchronization, 234; women's empowerment, 234–35

Pilnyak, Boris, 275

playgrounds movement, 368n101

Plyakova, Julia, 295

PM (journal), 401n3

Podvoysky, Nikolai, 216

Poland, 83, 93–94, 106, 135, 167

Polovinkin, Leonid, 253

Poole, Ernest, 58

Popova, Maria, 295

Popp, Walter, 150–51, 159, 161

Popular Front, 30, 282, 294, 301, 319, 326

Porter, Katherine Anne, 302

Poston, Ted, 262, 268

Price, James, 131

Price, Victoria, 258

Priekshas, Anna, 374n69

Prohme, William, 167–68

Provisional Government, 6, 65–66

Pudovkin, Vsevolod, 228, 230–34, 236, 239–40, 314, 318

Puritanism, 23, 131, 145, 256

Quakers, 71–73, 75, 77–78, 81, 83–84, 87–90, 92–98, 100, 103, 106, 108, 118. *See also* American Friends Service Committee; British Friends War Victims Relief Committee

race, 252, 255, 259–61, 279; racial hatred, 262; racial injustice, victims of, 258; racism, 20, 306

Radek, Karl, 111

radical dance movement, 224, 226–27, 235, 278–79. *See also* dance; modern dance; *and individual dance groups and dancers*

Radio Moscow, 264, 269, 304–6

Rand, Ayn, 312, 323

Rathbone, Nellie Cohen, 375n88, 400n16

Reagan, Ronald, "evil empire," 346n7

Red Army, 77, 265, 298–99, 309, 317–18, 330

Red Dancers, 224

Reed, John, 71, 83, 108

Resurrection (Tolstoy), 45

"Revolutionary Lives" (Strunsky), 68

Revolutionary News Bureau, 56, 60

Reyher, Rebecca, 15

Road to Life (film), 262

Robeson, Eslanda, 254, 256

Robeson, Paul, 254, 256

Robinson, Robert, 244, 285–86, 347n18

Rochester, Anna, 16, 19

Roosevelt, Eleanor, 288

Roosevelt, Franklin D., 293, 318, 330

Root, Elihu, 60

Rosie the Riveter, 298

Roslavleva, Natalia, 220

Rozanov, Sergei, 253

Rudd, Wayland, 261, 278

Rudneva, Stefanida, 213–14, 221

Rukeyser, Muriel, 302

Runnymede (utopian colony), 130

Russia, 16, 21, 33, 35, 39–40, 43–45, 48, 54, 56, 58, 60–61, 65, 67–72, 83–86, 92, 93–94, 111, 126, 129, 131–32, 134–35, 161–62, 165, 166–67, 175, 182, 189, 195, 199, 202, 214, 216, 223, 228, 231, 233, 241, 244, 262, 274, 290, 292–94, 314, 322, 334; African Americans in, 10, 247–48, 252; Alice in Wonderland reference, 379n57; Allied blockade of, 73, 77, 82, 87, 122; American feminists, attraction to, 32; American new woman, 5, 9; American women, appeal of, to, 130, 163, 205; American women, visible presence of, in, 12; appeal of, 32;

ballet in, 203, 208; Black performances in, 246; children of, 37–38; as classless society, 5; collectivization in, 30, 193, 194; communal living in, 59; cruel optimism, 32; dance in, 207–9, 213, 224, 229, 234; family codes in, 7, 9, 26; famine in, 11, 29, 37–38, 72, 77–78, 80, 90, 95–96, 136, 193, 194, 365n46; famine relief efforts, 81–82, 90–91, 97, 103; farming collectives of, 258; female equality in, 36; female role models, 4–5; film in, 203–4; foreign workers in, 125; free love in, 27; housework, socialization of, 7; immigration to, 123; industrial collectives in, 122; jazz in, 249; Jews in, 37, 50–51, 81; Jews, pogroms against, 55; new morality in, 156; new social order, 145; new woman in, 3–4, 27–28; passports, denial of, 98; *plyaska* (movement), attraction to, 212; romance with, 5–6; sex, attitude toward, 24–27; Silver Age of, 211–12, 248; theatre in, 12, 201, 203, 278; as utopia, 230; White Russia, 11, 82; women, emancipation of, in, 7, 9, 25–26. *See also* Soviet Union
Russian American Telegraph Company, 43
Russian children, 87–88, 95–96; famine deaths of, 78, 101–2; famine orphans, 107–8; famine relief, 73–75, 77, 79, 82–83, 100, 103, 107; saving of, 69–71; suffering of, 72
Russian Civil War, 11, 122, 247
Russian Cook Book for American Homes (Russian War Relief), 301
Russian Philharmonic Society, 250
Russian Reconstruction Farms, 106, 108, 118, 158, 408n16
Russian Revolution, 7, 9, 31, 36, 53, 55, 57–58, 60, 62, 64–65, 68, 71, 131, 165, 203, 211, 224, 228, 330; class-conscious woman, as symbol of, 28; women's citizenship, new models of, 54
Russian State Archive of Socio-Political History (RGASPI), 329

Russian War Relief, 300–301, 304
Russia's Message (Walling), 58
Rutgers, S. J., 132–33, 137–38, 142, 144, 153, 156, 159–60, 168

Saint Petersburg (Russia), 56, 211–12, 214; Black performers in, as center of, 248
Sample, George, 262
Sats, Natalia, 253
Savage, Augusta, 261
Save the Children Fund, 80–81, 89, 364n40. *See also* Fight the Famine Council
Schaub, Thomas, 346n7
Schecter, Amy, 144
Schrecker, Ellen, 327–28
Scott, John, 315
Scott, Leroy, 42, 49, 57–58, 358n46
Scott, Miriam Finn, 58, 358n46
Scottsboro Boys, 258–59, 261–63, 268, 331
Seattle Daily Call (newspaper), 92
Seattle Union Record (newspaper), 166
Segal, Edith, 224–27
serfdom, 249
settlement houses, 4, 36, 40, 48–50, 52, 84, 356n22
Sevareid, Eric, 320
sex: espionage threats, 380n67; and homosexuality, 19, 27, 62, 185, 196, 267, 380n67; and morality, 4, 22–27, 123, 133, 156; Soviet attitude toward, 22–27, 173, 185, 266
Sex and Civilization (Calverton), 25
Shapero, Lillian, 225; *One Sixth of the Earth*, 224
Sharp, Evelyn, 72, 97
Shaw, George Bernard, 80
Shchetinina, Anna, 295
Shipman, Sam, 141–43, 146–49, 151, 156–60
Shubin, Joel, 187, 190, 193, 289
Shuffle Along (musical), 250
Siberia, 9, 43–44, 60, 81, 87, 102, 122–23, 129–30, 132, 135–36, 155, 157, 161, 176, 196, 232, 286
Siberia and the Exile System (Kennan), 44, 355n15

Simkovitch, Mary K., 302

Simms, Margaret, 250

Sinclair, Upton, 170

Sissle, Noble, 250

Six Red Months in Russia (Bryant), 70, 79, 166

slavery, 247, 249

Smedley, Agnes, 168

Smith, Homer, 262

Smith, Jessica Granville, 11, 23, 73–75, 78, 80, 86–87, 100–103, 105–6, 108, 158, 303, 330, 350n42, 367n81, 408n16; and AFSC, 98–99, 104; Communism, conversion to, 98; loyalty of, 331; *Woman in Soviet Russia*, 118

Soblazhennye Stranoi Sovetov (Seduced by the land of the Soviets) (documentary series), 370n1

social Darwinism, 49

Social Gospel, 81; and socialism, 37. *See also* Christianity

socialism, 7, 18, 24, 37, 117, 122, 133, 178, 183, 207, 301, 333

Socialist Party, 92, 130–31

Socialist Revolutionary (Party) (SR, PSR) 40, 45–46, 48, 53, 60, 63–65

Society for Technical Aid to Russia, 111

Society for Technical Aid to Soviet Russia (STASR), 11, 122, 131, 133

Society of American Friends of Russian Freedom (SAFRF), 45–46, 48, 50, 52, 356n27

Society of Friends, 109. *See also* Quakers

Society of Young Duncanists, 220

Sojourners for Truth and Justice, 331

Sokolow, Anna, 225–27

Song of Russia (film), 296, 311–12, 324

Sontag, Susan, 80

Sorochinskoye, 99

Soviet Russia, 4, 9, 37, 67–68, 71, 73–75, 77, 82, 84, 88, 98, 106, 108, 118–19, 121, 123, 132, 134, 156–57, 162, 165, 177, 179–80, 199, 200, 211, 214, 230, 241, 255, 281, 324; African Americans in, 253; Allied blockade, 361n7;

Americans flocking to, 122; and racial groups, 392n12

Soviet Russia Pictorial (publication), 108

Soviet Russia Today (publication), 98, 283, 309. See also *New World Review*

Soviet Union, 3, 10–12, 33, 39–40, 68, 98, 107, 118, 125, 137, 150–52, 175, 182–83, 186–87, 192–93, 196–99, 219, 221, 223–24, 228, 241, 257, 261, 265, 268, 270, 276, 278, 290, 292–93, 295, 299, 301–2, 305–6, 309, 311–12, 316, 318, 321–23, 325, 327, 329–30, 332–33, 350n42, 410n23; abortion, outlawing of, 284–85; African Americans in, 20, 249–50, 252–55, 259–60, 263, 352n66; African American women in, 246, 256; American immigrants to, 124–25; "American Negro," notion of, in, 263; American women, drawn to, 31; anti-foreigner sentiment in, 240; anti-Semitism, outlawing of, 19, 227; attraction to, 22; Black jazz in, 249; Black performances in, 246; collectivization in, 226, 264; conservative gender politics, shift to, 285; cosmetics, boom in, 282–83; cotton industry in, 273–74; dance in, 208–9, 225, 229–30, 236; disenchantment with, 21, 31; as earthly paradise, 18; as evil empire, 5, 346n7; famine in, 264; foreign workers in, 121; idealization of, 20; Jews in, 19–20; journalism in, 164–65, 171; labor camp population, 400n14; Left, legacy of, in, 334; as living theatre, 202; lure of, as existential, 164; magic pilgrimage, 19, 349n37; mass spectacles in, 235; moral codes, in flux, 23; Negro Question in, 255, 257; New Economic Plan, 142; as new way of seeing, 163; nursery schools, as beneficial, 300; physical culture in, 234, 236; positive images of, 300; praise of, in American popular culture, 324; as promised land, 20; and race, 279; and racism, 262; Recognition Rally, 226; repres-

sive government, shift to, 285–89;
Scottsboro Boys, protests on behalf
of, 258–59; self-determination, policy
of, in, 254; sex, attitude toward, in,
24–26, 173, 185, 266; as taboo subject,
334; theatre in, 201, 204; tourists in,
13–17, 22; as transformative experience, 246; as utopian experiment, 132,
324; visitors to, 285, 399n12; "woman
question," 36; women in, as domestic
slaves, 133, 184–85; women in, as
new society, 202; women reporters in,
376n8; women's emancipation in, 31;
"wrecker" trials, 377n28, 379n57. See
also Russia; Soviet Russia
Spain, 196, 199, 241, 250, 289, 327, 328,
382n91
Spanish Civil War, 401n3
Spiridonova, Maria, 40, 42
Stalin, Joseph, 228, 230–31, 234–35, 241,
262, 299, 301, 307, 318, 321, 323–24,
333–34; purges of, 197, 240, 289–90,
294, 319–20; scorched earth policy,
310; and Strong, Anna Louise, 190–
91, 193–94, 196, 198
Stalinism, 5, 30–31, 319–20; and women's
identities, 235, 298
Stanislavsky, Konstantin, 203, 212–13, 225,
253
Stansell, Christine, 7
Stanton, Elizabeth Cady, 75
Starr, Ellen Gates, 50, 54, 62
Steffens, Lincoln, 92, 167
Stokes, Graham Phelps, 49, 57, 358n46
Stokes, Rose Pastor, 18, 249, 358n46
Stone Blackwell, Anna, 4, 45, 48, 51–52, 54,
62, 65–66, 302, 356–57n27; The Little
Grandmother of the Russian Revolution, 64
Strong, Anna Louise, 3, 11, 32, 73, 93–98,
104, 118, 123, 126, 174, 177–80, 182,
186, 187–88, 189, 275–76, 279, 283–84,
302, 312, 321, 328, 365n46, 377n16,
378n33; arrest of, 332; background
of, 91–92; Communist Party, attempt

to join, 197–98; FBI surveillance of,
410n23; I Change Worlds, 117, 164,
196–98; John Reed Colony (JRC),
107–17; loyalty of, 333; and Moscow
News, 163–65, 168–71, 173, 175;
reputation, as tarnished, 333; resignation of, 199; Soviet life, as chronicler
of, 165–67, 183; The Soviets Conquer
Wheat, 194; The Soviets Expected It,
309; Stalin, loyalty to, 323; Stalin,
meeting with, 190–95; The Stalin Era,
333; Stalinist hack, charges of, 333;
Trotsky interview, 106–7; Volga commune, 107; Wild River, 115, 281, 289,
299–300, 323–24, 407n76
Strunsky (Lorwin), Rose, 56, 60–62
Strunsky (Walling), Anna, 36, 39, 47,
56–60, 67
Students for a Democratic Society (SDS),
333
Sukloff, Marie, 63
Sun Yat Sen, 167, 275
Suppressed Desires (Glaspell), 141
Sussman, Harry, 144, 146, 154
Sweet, Barbara, 13

Taggard, Genevieve, 302, 319–20
Tamiris, Helen, 302
Tchaikovsky, Nicholas, 60–61, 359n56
terrorism, 46, 51
Theatre of Working Youth (TRAM), 276
"They All Come to Moscow" (Kennell and
Bennett), 123, 125
They All Come to Moscow (Kennell and
Washburne), 185–86, 189, 380n68
Thomas, Norman, 104
Thomas, Wilbur, 93, 96–98, 103–4, 106,
366n67
Thompson, Dorothy, 25–26
Thompson, Louise. See Patterson, Louise
Thompson
Three Russian Girls (film), 296
Three Songs about Lenin (film), 224
Thurman, Wallace, 261
Tietz, Boris Borisovich, 249

Tillard, Violet, 72
Todd, Helen, 54, 73–74, 94
Tolstoy, Leo, 40, 45, 49–50
Toronto Star (newspaper), 166
Trotsky, Leon, 18, 71, 106
Trud (newspaper), 256
Truman, Harry, Point Four Program, 331
Tunney, Gene, 181
Turgenev, Ivan, 40; "On the Threshold,"
    353–54n1
Twain, Mark, 44–45, 58–59

Ukraine, 30, 264, 320
Underground Railroad, 309
Underground Russia (Stepniak), 45
UNESCO, 331–32
Union of Soviet Socialist Republics (USSR).
    See Soviet Union
United Mine Workers, 58
United States, 4, 9, 11–12, 19–21, 24–25,
    30–33, 36, 39–40, 42–44, 46–48, 50–
    51, 53–56, 58, 61, 63, 65–66, 68, 78,
    84, 90, 98, 106–8, 113, 116, 118–19,
    122–24, 130, 135, 137, 146–47, 161–
    62, 164, 167–68, 170–71, 173, 177,
    186, 189, 198, 202–4, 218–19, 226,
    240–41, 246–47, 253, 256, 258–60,
    263, 278, 282, 289–90, 295, 299–302,
    306, 309, 312, 320, 329, 331–33,
    347–48n19, 399n12; Allied blockade,
    361n7; birth control, illegal in, 26;
    dance in, 208, 222–24, 235; day care
    centers, as threatening, 300; feminist
    ideas in, 7; "free love" in, 22, 59; Free
    Russia movement in, 45; Jewish women,
    and socialism in, 7; muckrakers in, 165;
    Negro Question in, 255; popular cul-
    ture, pro-Soviet messages in, 292, 299;
    Russian woman, as mythic figure in, 6,
    209; Soviet alliance, as fragile, 322–24;
    utopian traditions in, 22; women's
    movement in, 28
University Settlement, 49, 56–57, 58,
    358n46
Urban League, 260

US Food Administration, 90
utopia, 5, 12, 19, 22, 84, 121–22, 129–30,
    132, 141, 146, 209, 230, 298, 324;
    definition of, 162

Vanguard Club, 261
Vascov, Victor, 187–91
Vasutin, B. S., 170, 173
Veblen, Thorstein, 108
veil, 283; African American double con-
    sciousness, 247, 273; and Muslim
    women, 270–72; and paranja, 272
Vertov, Dziga, 224, 250
Vinogradova, Dusya, 13
Volkhonsky, Felix, 53
Volkonsky, Sergei, 202–3
Voroshilov, Kliment, 191
Vorse, Mary Heaton, 58, 80, 355n15, 363n21

Wald, Lillian, 4, 17, 32, 36, 49–50, 61, 64,
    66, 108, 224, 356–57n27
Walling, William "English," 49, 56–57, 59–
    60, 67, 356–57n27, 358n46; *Russia's
    Message*, 58
War Communism, 11–12
Ware, Clarissa, 367n78
Ware, Harold "Hal," 104, 118, 158, 330,
    366n68, 408n16
Ware group, 330
Washburne, John, 185
Watts, Arthur, 75, 77, 84, 87–89, 91, 95–96,
    362n12
Were You Ever a Child? (Dell), 7
West, Dorothy, 10, 26, 28, 243–44, 261–63,
    268, 274, 279; and Hughes, Langston,
    245, 267, 273; and Jones, Mildred,
    277; as performer, 261, 265–66, 278
West, Miriam, 97, 99
West, Nathanael, 327
Westover School, 62, 65
What Is to Be Done? (Chernyshevsky), 7,
    47, 59, 158
White, Constance, 262, 267
Whitman, Walt, 211
Whitney, Anita, 115

Whittier, John Greenleaf, 45

Wild River (Strong), 115, 281, 289, 299–300, 323–24, 407n76

Wilkes, Mattie, 248

Williams, Albert Rhys, 71

Williams, Frances E., 4, 15, 278–79, 394n30

Williams, Patricia, 247

Wilson, Helen Calista, 149–50, 153, 161–62, 182

Wilson, Lucy L. W., 13, 108

Winsor, Mary, 36

Winter, Ella, 24–25, 305, 316

Wolfe, Bertram, 323

Woman Patriot (magazine), 351n51, 360n64

Woman's Journal (publication), 50–51

Woman Today (publication), 282. See also *Working Woman*

women, 334–35; changing position of, 271; homeland (*fernweh*), versus homeness (*heimweh*), 162; modern dance, as pioneered by, 208; property rights, 7; right to vote, 7; war effort, contributions to, 306–7; Women's Trade Union League, 57. See also new Soviet woman; new woman; women's suffrage

Women's International League for Peace and Freedom, 86

women's suffrage, 7, 9–11, 15, 28, 36, 50, 54, 73, 86, 115, 302

Wood, Junius B., 161, 176, 179, 330, 409n17

Wooding, Sam, 250

Workers' Dance League, Spartakiades contests, 225

Workers Dreadnought (newspaper), 375n88

Workers International Relief, 260

Workers' News (newspaper), 186, 192

Workers Party, 78, 104, 116, 224. *See also* Communist Party of the United States

Workers' School, 261

Workers Theatre (publication), 225

Working Woman (publication), 282, 331. See also *Woman Today*

World War I, 11, 36, 67, 69, 80–81, 130–31, 248, 281, 289, 294–95

World War II, 4, 31–32, 282, 292, 319, 324, 330, 334

Wright, Ada, 259

Wyler, William, 293

Young, Cornelia, 99

Young Pioneers, 256

Youth Replies I Can (Becker), 300

Zangwill, Israel, *The Melting Pot*, 40

Zarchi, Natan, 230

Zasulich, Vera, 48, 56, 353–54n1

Zemtsova, Anna Nikolaevna, 233–34

Zetkin, Clara, 24

Zhenotdel, 8, 13, 15, 271; women's concerns, advocate for, 9. *See also* Communist Party of the Soviet Union

Zinoviev, Gregory, 111